2/3/51   R.J.

WITHDRAW

2-5-51

THE JOURNAL
of
NEGRO HISTORY

CARTER G. WOODSON
Editor

VOLUME XX
1935

THE ASSOCIATION FOR THE STUDY OF NEGRO LIFE
AND HISTORY, INC.
WASHINGTON, D. C.
1935

CONTENTS OF VOLUME XX

VOL. XX, No. 1, JANUARY, 1935

PROCEEDINGS OF THE ANNUAL MEETING OF THE ASSOCIATION FOR THE STUDY OF NEGRO LIFE AND HISTORY, HELD IN HOUSTON, TEXAS, NOVEMBER 10-14, 1934_____ 1

L. V. WILLIAMS: *Teaching Negro Life and History in Texas High Schools* _____ 13

J. A. BAILEY: *Perspective in the Teaching of Negro History*__ 19

C. G. WOODSON: *Some Attitudes in English Literature*_____ 27

BOOK REVIEWS _____ 86

    Cook's *Le Noir;* Holmes's *The Evolution of the Negro College;* Barnes's *The Antislavery Impulse;* Radin's *Racial Myth.*

NOTES _____ 100

    American and Foreign Books and Articles bearing on the Negro. The Passing of Ezra Eziekel Smith, Simon G. Atkins, George C. Clement, Levi J. Rowan, Charles Victor Roman, Ulysses S. Wharton, and Maggie Lena Walker.

VOL. XX, No. 2, APRIL, 1935

NEGRO HISTORY WEEK, THE TENTH YEAR_____ 123

RAY H. ABRAMS: *The Copperhead Newspapers and the Negro* 131

BLAKE MCKELVEY: *Penal Slavery and Southern Reconstruction* _____ 153

HARRY E. DAVIS: *Alpha Lodge, No. 116, New Jersey: An Extract from "The Prince Hall Sodality"*_____ 180

C. G. WOODSON: *Attitudes of the Iberian Peninsula*_____ 190

BOOK REVIEWS _____ 244

    Kelly's *Pedro de Alvarado, Conquistador;* Bollo's *Los Negros en Africa y America;* Bishop's *The Odyssey of Cabeza de Vaca;* Hawk's *Economic History of the South;* Davis's *Land-Grant Colleges for Negroes;* Tatum's *Disloyalty in the Confederacy;* Christensen's *Discovery and Re-Discovery of America.*

NOTES _____ 256

    American and Foreign Books and Articles bearing on the Negro. Charles Sumner Wormley; Martha Bailey Briggs.

VOL. XX, No. 3, JULY, 1935

BRAINERD DYER: *The Treatment of Colored Union Troops by the Confederates, 1861-65*_____ 273

DOROTHY B. PORTER: *Sarah Parker Remond, Abolitionist and Physician* _____ 287

JOHN B. CADE: *Out of the Mouths of Ex-Slaves*_____ 294

RALPH AND MILDRED FLETCHER: *Some Data on Occupations among Negroes in St. Louis from 1866 to 1897*_____ 338

BOOK REVIEWS --- 342
    Posey's *The Negro Citizen of West Virginia;* Barnes and
    Dumond's *Letters of Theodore Dwight Weld, Angelina Grimké
    Weld, and Sarah Grimké, 1822-1844;* Wilbois's *Le Cameroun;*
    Larsen's *Crusader and Feminist, Letters of Jane Grey Swiss-
    helm;* Bond's *The Education of the Negro in the American
    Social Order.*

NOTES --- 356
    American and Foreign Books and Articles bearing on the
    Negro.

VOL. XX, No. 4, OCTOBER, 1935

ANNUAL REPORT OF THE DIRECTOR ------------------------------ 363

PROCEEDINGS OF THE ANNUAL MEETING OF THE ASSOCIATION
    FOR THE STUDY OF NEGRO LIFE AND HISTORY AND THE
    CELEBRATION OF ITS TWENTIETH ANNIVERSARY, HELD IN
    CHICAGO, ILLIONIS, SEPTEMBER 9-11, 1935 ---------------- 373

W. SHERMAN SAVAGE: *Twenty Years of the Association for
    the Study of Negro Life and History* ---------------------- 379

LUTHER P. JACKSON: *The Work of the Association and the
    People* --- 385

RAYFORD W. LOGAN: *An Evaluation of the First Twenty
    Volumes of THE JOURNAL OF NEGRO HISTORY* --- 397

MARY McLEOD BETHUNE: *The Association for the Study of
    Negro Life and History: Its Contribution to Our Mod-
    ern Life* -- 406

CHARLES H. WESLEY: *The Reconstruction of History* -------- 411

LUCY HARTH SMITH: *Negro Musicians and Their Music* ------ 428

ALBERT B. GEORGE: *The Negro and the Public Mind Today* --- 433

F. ERNEST WORK: *Italo-Ethiopian Relations* --------------- 438

E. DELORUS PRESTON, JR.: *William Syphax, a Pioneer in
    Negro Education in the District of Columbia* ------------ 448

BOOK REVIEWS -- 477
    Kirby's *The Musical Instrument of the Native Races of South
    Africa;* Sadler's *Arts of West Africa;* Woodson's *The Negro
    Professional Man and the Community;* Beal's *Porfirio Diaz,
    Dictator of Mexico;* Siegfried's *Impressions of South America;*
    Munro's *The United States and the Caribbean Area;* Hall's
    Negroes in the United States, 1920-1932; Eyre's *European
    Civilization, Its Origin and Development;* Work's *Ethiopia,
    a Pawn in European Diplomacy;* Shaw's *The Adventures
    of the Black Girl in Her Search for God.*

NOTES --- 494
    American and Foreign Books and Articles Bearing on the
    Negro. Alice Werner; James S. Russell.

THE JOURNAL

OF

NEGRO HISTORY

Vol. XX—January, 1935—No. 1

PROCEEDINGS OF THE ANNUAL MEETING OF THE ASSOCIATION
FOR THE STUDY OF NEGRO LIFE AND HISTORY HELD IN
HOUSTON, TEXAS, FROM NOVEMBER 10 TO 14, 1934.

With a new feature, a conference of high school principals on the teaching of the Negro on the secondary level,
the annual meeting of the Association opened in Houston,
Texas, in the Odd Fellows Temple, on the tenth of November at 10:30 A. M. Mr. L. V. Williams, principal of
the Booker T. Washington High School of Dallas, in taking charge as the presiding officer made an appropriate
address on this topic. His experience in dealing with
this problem in his own school had the ring of a report
on serious and unselfish efforts to know what to do and
how to do it. Following him appeared Mr. J. Leslie Patton, instructor in history in the same high school. He
further outlined the work now being done in that institution and the aims kept in mind in presenting the facts
of history bearing upon the Negro. The paper showed
thorough knowledge of the objectives of the course and
enlightened those who came to learn from the experiences
of teachers thus concerned. Mr. E. O. Smith, of the
Wheatley High School, of Houston, then followed with
an address on the teaching of the Negro in general. He
had no particular experience to relate in this connection
but endeavored to explain how the teaching of Negro life
and history can be connected with practically all branches
in the elementary, secondary, and higher institutions. His

1

discussion was chiefly valuable in showing how the Negro may be taught not only about himself but about other matters in relation to himself. Every teacher, then, is an instructor in Negro Life and History. Finally followed a profitable general discussion opened by Mr. L. M. Johnson of the Terrell High School, of Ft. Worth, where similar efforts to teach the Negro are now being made.

In the afternoon of the same day the session was devoted to a round table discussion of the topic presented that forenoon. Mr. McDonald, of Galveston, presided. For the benefit of the larger audience which attended in the afternoon the chairman had the speakers of the forenoon briefly summarize the thought of their papers delivered earlier in the day. Miss Gertrude Green, of the John W. Hoffman High School, of New Orleans, was then introduced to begin the discussion. With the observations which had been made respecting the teaching of Negro life and history elsewhere she connected the recent efforts in her city to work out a regular course of study of the Negro for all grades and reported also on what is actually being done in her own school to demonstrate the feasibility of such a program.

Practically all high school principals present participated in the general discussion; and it proved to be valuable. This particular session not only enabled the body to learn from teachers in various parts the exact status of this new effort but caused surprise in bringing out the fact that so much is being done to teach the life and history of the Negro in the Lower South where it has been often thought that such steps would not be approved. It was especially emphasized that in practically all cases in which superintendents and boards of education have been properly approached with the request to introduce such courses and projects in the schools they have been granted. There was a tendency, too, to criticize teachers and principals for their apathy and lethargy in not doing more to advance this particular phase of the work when there is every opportunity for doing it officially.

The next session of the Association was the Sunday afternoon meeting at three o'clock on November 11, devoted to a discussion of Negro history in its broad aspects. Mr. W. L. Davis, secretary of the Southwest Branch, presided. The first address was delivered by Miss Oralee Baranco, instructor in history in the Jones Normal School, New Orleans, Louisiana. The address covered the three significant aspects of the task, namely, the reasons for offering such a course, the method for conducting it, and the results therefrom to be expected. The address, too, was worked out from the pedagogic point of view of the teacher training institution. Thus prepared and delivered, the discourse made an impression.

Dr. J. S. Clark, of Southern University of Louisiana, was next presented for an address. He spoke without any particular preparation inasmuch as he had not been notified that he would be thus called upon to function. However, he forcefully set forth the status of the Negro in the United States today and the necessity for preparing him to deal with conditions as he now finds them. In that scheme of education necessary for this arduous task he believes that training the race to appreciate its own background is an essential. For this reason he highly commended the work which is now being done and spoke of it as a source of great inspiration to those who must grapple with the problems of tomorrow.

The session closed with an address by Dr. Carter G. Woodson. For a few minutes he summarized briefly the work of the Association for the Study of Negro Life and History but devoted most of the time to a discussion of the background of the Negro in Africa. Out of that interesting history he believes the Negro race will find sufficient encouragement to battle more successfully against the odds now confronting it and eventually come into the enjoyment of those blessings of democracy which are now denied for having not apparently measured up to the standards of others better circumstanced. The Negroes of today, then, should make use of their African traditions as a great inheritance.

Following this session, between five-thirty and eight, a circle of Houston ladies entertained the visitors at tea in the social rooms in the same building. In the receiving line stood Mr. W. L. Davis, Dr. Carter G. Woodson, President Joseph J. Rhoads, President John B. Watson, Mrs. J. B. Watson, President J. S. Clark, Mrs. Lucy Harth Smith, President D. R. Glass, and Professor Rayford W. Logan. During the hour a number of persons who were not in a position to attend the afternoon session, because of the large crowd on hand, had the opportunity to greet at close range visitors from within and without the state of Texas.

The next concern of the Association was a visit to the Prairie View State Normal School. Professor W. R. Banks, in charge, had made special arrangements for the entertainment and comfort of the visitors. Transportation was provided for them from Houston to Prairie View and return. Principals and teachers from schools near the institution had been especially invited to attend this particular session. It was, therefore, a great success. In the forenoon at 10:30 several addresses were delivered in the college chapel. While these discourses dealt with the general purposes of the Association and the importance of the background of the Negro, they were so worked out as to meet some special needs of the student body. President A. S. Wilson, of Shorter College, talked about the general need of the Negro to become better acquainted with himself. Professor L. V. Williams restated for the special benefit of these students the work now being done in the study of the Negro at the Booker T. Washington High School in Dallas. Professor Rayford

W. Logan, of Atlanta University, spoke especially of the outstanding events in the history of Haiti, and C. G. Woodson briefly recited the deeds of the outstanding heroes and heroines in Africa who nobly fought for their soil when they were being dispossessed of it by the Europeans. That afternoon the delegates, after having been entertained at an excellent luncheon, visited the various departments of the institution and returned to Houston about five o'clock.

At five-thirty began the Get-Acquainted Dinner in the dining room of the Odd Fellows Temple. About one hundred persons were present. These represented the delegates and certain professional and business men of Houston. Mr. James D. Ryan, of the Yates High School, served as toastmaster. On rising to welcome the guests the speaker emphasized the significance of the occasion of so many persons assembling in the Southwest part of the United States to carry forward a task so essential to the work which they must do in the future. Mr. John W. Rice of Houston further strengthened these remarks with additional words of welcome from the city. Most fitting responses to these addresses were delivered by Professor F. L. Rousseve, of Xavier University, New Orleans, Louisiana; and by Professor Lorenzo J. Greene, of Lincoln University of Missouri. Visitors were then called upon to state briefly who they were and what they represented that one might become acquainted with the other. Other visitors including the Director of the Association were also asked to make a few remarks. The Director had little to say except to avail himself of the opportunity to speak of what is being done by the delegates in the various cities and states. He emphasized especially the unique work of Mr. Herman Dreer in St. Louis.

The next session was "An Evening with Negro Musicians and their Music" in the Auditorium of Odd Fellows

Temple at eight-thirty. The program began with inform-
ing introductory remarks by Mr. C. F. Richardson,
the presiding officer, and with a remarkable address on
Negro music by Mrs. Lucy Harth Smith, of Lexington,
Kentucky. The program was arranged by Mrs. P. O.
Smith, who had the support of the Coleridge-Taylor
Choral Club, the Houston Glee Club, and musical organizations from the local public schools. Prominent among
these performers were Mrs. J. A. Atkins, Mr. J. W.
Jones, Dr. P. D. Foster, and Mrs. L. L. Love. Miss Helen
Hagan, the noted pianist, rendered in most pleasing fashion a number of selections which the audience loudly
applauded. As a demonstration of what the Negro has
achieved in this art this session was highly successful.

The next session of the Association was on Tuesday
morning at ten-thirty. The addresses tended to be a continuation of the discussion of Saturday. President M. W.
Dogan, of Wiley College, presided. He talked briefly of
his support of this effort and interest which he has long
manifested therein. He then introduced Professor J. A.
Bailey, of the Arkansas Agricultural, Mechanical, and Normal College. He discussed ''Perspective in the Teaching
of Negro History.'' He made it very clear from the
beginning that unless it is known beforehand exactly
what we are undertaking to do in teaching the background
of the Negro and how we expect to proceed there is
danger of fruitless effort being spent on ill-conceived
plans. Folowing him appeared Dr. W. L. Turner, of
Houston, with a discussion of African Culture. Having
engaged for a number of years in educational and religious work in Africa, he had firsthand information as to
the life of the people there from birth until death.
Charged with these facts, he proved to be an interesting
and instructive speaker.

Tuesday afternoon at three-thirty came the discussion
of the ''Neglected Aspects of Negro History.'' The first

speaker was Professor John B. Cade, of Prairie View State College. He discussed the topic "Out of the Mouth of Ex-Slaves." This paper was made up mainly of interesting and valuable testimonies collected from ex-slaves in the Southwest, especially in Louisiana. These facts therein presented covered almost every aspect of the life of the bondmen prior to the Civil War. Following this speaker came Professor C. A. Bacote, guest-professor at Wiley College, with a discussion of "Negro Suffrage in the United States from 1865 to 1868." Professor Bacote outlined the various objections to Negro suffrage and the disinclination of the Northern States to take action thereupon even while the Negro was being enfranchized in the South. Although noting the mistakes of both sides during the reconstruction, the speaker, nevertheless, contended that the granting of the ballot to the Negro was the only way to prevent his reenslavement. There followed a very interesting general discussion. Participating among others were President J. B. Watson, of the Agricultural, Mechanical, and Normal College of Arkansas, Professor L. D. Reddick, of the Kentucky State College, and the Director of the Association.

At the evening session on the same day President J. B. Watson presided. In taking the chair, he spoke on Negro history as a means by which the race may develop greater self-respect. He asserted that the only reason why so many are satisfied with segregation and accept its badges and incidents is that they are not inspired to self respect by knowledge from the background of the Negro. The first speaker for the evening was Professor R. O. Lanier of Houston College. He discussed the attitude of psychologists toward the Negro. He briefly reviewed the first efforts with cranial measurements, next with the mental tests, and finally with the anthropometric method of approach. He showed conclusively that these tests, used to establish the inferiority of the Negro, had fallen down; for, although we can measure what the individual has actually acquired, no one has yet been able to work out a device to determine how much mental capacity a person has. The closing address of this session was delivered by Professor Rayford W. Logan of Atlanta University. He spoke on the Negro in Latin America. In this he explained the distinctions made in the social order with respect to the various shades of color and showed how utterly impossible it was to draw such sharp lines thus undertaken. The speaker finally contrasted the Latin attitude with that of the Teuton. While he did not find the Latin perfect, he was not so lacking in humanity as the Teutonic element which often manifested itself altogether to the contrary.

At the session on Wednesday morning at ten-thirty Mr. John W. Rice, of Houston, presided. Speaking as a member of the Southwest Branch, which is now trying to bring the thought of the Negro nearer home, he found himself in hearty accord with what is being done to enlighten further not only that region but all persons who do not yet appreciate what the Negro has thought and felt and attempted and accomplished. The first speaker was Mr. J. Mason Brewer, of the Booker T. Washington High School. He discussed the Negro in Texas from the regional point of view. He tried to show some advantage in thus approaching racial history inasmuch as environment counts as a great factor. The thought on this topic advanced by advocates of the regional approach in the study of history was briefly reviewed. There arose, however, a question as to whether or not too much regional history may become decidedly sectional and thus do more harm than good.

Professor D. J. Jackson, of Xavier University, was next introduced to discuss "The Negro in New Orleans." He delved for a few moments into the Latin background of that city and then briefly rehearsed all but charming stories of heroes and heroines of the people of color during the early days. He dwelt in extenso on the careers of the teacher and patriot, Armand Lanusse; of the philanthropist, Thomy Lafon; of the editor, I. Roudanez; of the artist, Eugene Warbourg; of the inventor, Norbert Rillieux; of the benefactress, Madame Bernard Couvent; of the musician, Edmund Dede; and of the poet, Victoria Lecesne. He spoke also of the more favorable attitude of the Latins toward the Negro and especially that of the Catholic Church. In the discussion of this address, which followed immediately, Professor Rayford W. Logan raised the question as to what the Catholic Church did to abolish the institution of slavery. He conceded that they were more kindly disposed toward the slaves than the Protestant and did more than other sects to ameliorate the condition of the slaves. He wanted to emphasize, however, the point that the Catholic Church as an institution did not actually try to destroy slavery.

In the afternoon followed the business session of the Association. The reports of the officers of the Association, already published in the July issue of this magazine, were read, discussed, and approved. The officers were commended for their fine work during the trying times. The following officers were then elected for the ensuing year. John Hope, as President, Louis R. Mehlinger as Secretary-Treasurer, and Carter G. Woodson as Director and Editor; and as members of the Executive Council the foregoing officers together with the following: James H. Dillard, Charlottesville, Virginia; John M. Gandy, Virginia State College; Lucy Harth Smith, Lexington, Kentucky; Mary McLeod Bethune, Daytona, Florida; Evarts B. Greene, New York City; H. Councill Trenholm, Alabama State College; Edwin R. Embree, Chicago, Illinois; Joseph J. Rhoads, Marshall, Texas; W. R. Banks, Prairie View State College; Alexander L. Jackson, Chicago, Illinois; A. M. Schlesinger, Harvard University; Bishop R.

A. Carter, Chicago, Illinois; Harry E. Davis, Cleveland, Ohio; and T. Wingate Todd, Western Reserve University.

This session took up also the important matter of bringing from Europe to this country outstanding scholars who have made a scientific study of Africa. The Director spoke of his discussing lecture tours with several of them during his visits to Europe for the last three years. He mentioned the possibility of presenting Henri Labouret on such a mission in 1935, and pledges to the amount of $1,350 were immediately obtained. The meeting took under consideration also the matter of celebrating appropriately in Chicago on September 9, 1935, the twentieth anniversary of the Association for the Study of Negro Life and History. This body was organized there on September 9, 1915. It was unanimously voted that this be done and that every effort be made to make the celebration impressive. The members of the Executive Council present together with such other persons as they may later associate with themselves were appointed as a committee with power to act in working out the preparation for this celebration. This committee with the additional members will be announced in the near future. A Committee on Findings for this particular session was also appointed with the power to act. This last mentioned committee consists of: Mrs. Lucy Harth Smith, of Lexington, Kentucky, Chairman; Mr. L. V. Williams, of Dallas; Dean R. O. Lanier, of Houston; Miss Gertrude Green, of New Orleans; Mr. Herman Dreer, of St. Louis; President Joseph J. Rhoads, of Bishop College; Professor Lorenzo J. Greene, of Lincoln University in Missouri; Professor Rayford W. Logan, of Atlanta University; Professor L. D. Reddick, of Kentucky State College; Mr. Ferdinand Rousseve, of Xavier University; Professor C. A. Bacote, of Wiley College; Mr. J. A. Atkins, of Houston; Mr. Joseph Bailey, of Arkansas State College; and Professor D. J. Jackson, of New Orleans. This meeting promptly adjourned to attend a dinner at the Houston Municipal College, directed by Dean R. O'Hara Lanier, who elaborately entertained the Association.

At the final session of the Association on Wednesday at eight o'clock Mrs. Lucy Harth Smith, a recently elected member of the Executive Council of the Association, presided. The first speaker was Professor L. D. Reddick, of the Kentucky State College. He delivered an address on "Why Study the Ex-Slave?" Having for some time devoted hmiself to this particular field, he presented social, economic and literary aspects of which we have heard very little. Professor Reddick seems to have well conceived the task at hand and how to perform it. The next speaker was President Joseph J. Rhoads, of Bishop College, who spoke in the same field but along a slightly different line. He discussed "The Ex-Slave Family." In this discourse he was concerned largely with the manners and customs which developed out of their slave life. He made a distinction between those customs which may have been survivals from Africa and others which probably resulted from the peculiar environment of the United States. The assertion that the African retained nothing that he brought from Africa except his temperament was questioned.

The history prizes were then presented. Irving Dilliard, the winner of the first prize for the best article, and Luther P. Jackson, the winner of the next prize for the second best article, could not be present. Although Professor V. B. Spratlin, of Howard University, who won the prize for the second best review, was absent also, Prof. L. D. Reddick, the winner of the first prize for the best review, received it in person amid great applause.

The report of the Committee on Findings:

1. That the study of Negro life and history should be made an integral part of the curricula of every school with accredited courses on par with other work, and with this

study of the Negro should be correlated the other courses in literature and history.

2. That the apparent laxity and inertia of principals and faculties in failing to request of school authorities permission to revise their curricula so as to include the study of Negro life and history must be viewed as an inexcusable dereliction of duty when they, the principals especially, should be the leaders in the construction of the much needed new program of education for teaching the Negro first about himself and then about other things in relation to himself.

3. That there should be developed a uniform outline for the study of Negro life and history which will embrace uniform objectives and at the same time will be sufficiently flexible to make use of valuable data collected in communities which have contributed to the making of Negro history.

4. That inasmuch as the training of pupils begins in the homes the life of the children should be impregnated with the study of their background by making available simple stories from the life and history of the Negro, adapted to the capacities of children of all ages from the kindergarten to the junior high school.

5. That the establishment of other branches of the Association like the Southwest Branch in order to stimulate the collecting of data of Negro life and history and the extension of the study of these aspects of our past and present throughout such regions should be encouraged.

6. That there should be established through the Association a scholarship fund to defray the expenses of the research by writers of these regions who are interested in such task and have shown the capacity for original treatment and independent effort in these fields.

TEACHING NEGRO LIFE AND HISTORY IN TEXAS HIGH SCHOOLS*

Today in America we need citizens as we have always needed them, citizens who are able to see their greatest self-satisfaction in service to others, people who believe that the greatest development of the individual comes through the development of a sense of individual responsibility in a group, and the responsibility of a group among other groups.

We are beginning to see wherein society as a whole, made up of various racial groups, benefit so much more through a competitive plan than through group consciousness. It has been aptly pointed out in this connection that under the co-operative form of society, man is pitted against man, and society receives only their difference; whereas in a non-co-operative society, man works with his fellow-man and society is the beneficiary of their product. This was clearly recognized among the early advocates of education for Negroes comprising the group who desired to increase the economic efficiency of their labor supply, and who, in spite of the measures passed to prohibit the education of slaves, continued to teach them in defiance of this hostile legislation.

This briefly interprets one phase of citizenship as an objective which is listed as one of the cardinal principles of education. Whether the designers of this purpose of citizenship development included the idea of race co-operation may be questioned. But to be sure, secondary education should prepare people to live together, and leave to more specialized institutions the business of teaching how to make a living.

For the Negro high school student, very little has been done, for only here and there have efforts been put forth to teach him something of his own racial background.

*An address delivered at the annual meeting of the Association for the Study of Negro Life and History in Houston, Texas, November 10, 1934.

13

For the white high school student, no effort is made to teach him of these people of color with whom he moves and mingles daily. Some sympathetic and far-sighted Negro colleges embrace courses in Negro history and literature and other related courses, while a number of white colleges offer courses in race relations, ethnology and anthropology. It would be trite to state that courses in Negro life and history and race relations could better be offered during the high school period for both groups, since it is within this adolescent period that right attitudes and concepts toward other racial groups can best be developed.

In order to determine to what extent the Negro high school student in Texas is being instructed in courses in Negro life and history we used the questionnaire method. Though somewhat limited in the number of schools reached, it is believed that the data found, give a fair cross-section of what is actually happening in the matter of instruction in Negro life and history.

Fifty-five accredited high schools of the state were selected for the survey with returns coming from thirty-one of these institutions; or, roughly speaking, with responses from 56 per cent of these schools. The thirty-one schools replying, represented twenty-seven counties within the state that show a Negro population of 185,520. Of this Number 13,346 are enrolled in the various high schools represented in this survey.

TABLE I

Negro History	Number of Schools	Total Negro Population	Total High School Enrollment	Total No. of Pupils Taking Negro History	Total Pupils to Graduate This Year
Courses Offered	5	49,800	2,456	214	396
Part Time	*2	3,000	396	60	50
Courses Not Offered	24	132,720	10,194	0	946
Grand Total	31	185,520	13,346	274	1,392

*Washington County Training School, Chapel Hill, Texas; and the Kemp High School, Bryan, Texas.

It becomes evident as shown in Table I, that only five schools in the state are offering full and accredited courses in Negro history. Within the county district of these five schools, there is a total Negro population of 49,800 with 2,456 of these enrolled in the high schools. Two other schools offer the course as a part of the regular American history work, thereby giving no credit for the study of Negro History as such. In the five schools offering the accredited courses, the usual class period length ranging from 40 to 60 minutes is observed with recitations five times a week. The course is pursued for one semester and yields one-half unit of credit toward graduation. Twenty-four other schools, representing a Negro population of 132,720 with 10,194 enrolled in these high schools, do not offer any work in the study of the Negro; not even as a supplement to other history courses.

Further tabulations show that within the twenty-seven counties represented and among the thirty-one schools reporting, that of the 13,346 high school pupils enrolled, only 274 or 2 per cent, are engaged in the study of the Negro. Considering the statement of the replies that the course is offered to pupils of senior grade (those of the graduating classes), and that in this group there are 1392 pupils to graduate, we find that about 81 per cent of the pupils will graduate this year without having studied anything concerning their racial background.

TABLE II

School	Location	Year Course Was Begun	Length of Course	Length of Class Period	Credit Given
Booker T. Washington	Dallas	1930	one Sem.	45 Min.	½ Unit
Cameron High	Cameron	1925	one Sem.	60 Min.	½ Unit
Jarvis High	Hawkins	1928	one Sem.	45 Min.	½ Unit
Fred Douglas High	Jacksonville	1931	one Sem.	45 Min.	½ Unit
Liberty High	Liberty	1933	one Sem.	40 Min.	½ Unit

Among the materials listed as used, it was found that each school used as the text, *Negro Makers of History,* by Carter G. Woodson. Reference materials show the possession of 59 volumes of Negro books in the libraries of the seven schools that study the Negro. Forty-three of these volumes are to be found in one school. Eight periodicals are subscribed for regularly. These include the *Houston Informer,* the *Houston Defender,* the *Pittsburg Courier,* the *Dallas Express,* the *Dallas Gazette,* the *Journal of Negro History, Opportunity* and the *Crisis.* These same periodicals and fewer volumes on the Negro may be found distributed in 9 other schools replying to the questionnaire, while the remaining 15 schools report no materials at all, either for use as part of other courses or for the recreational reading of pupils.

Among the schools offering the courses, the matter of subject presentation seems to be about the same as the usual method and procedures in the teaching of other high school courses. Some further methods of Negro history presentation were described as offered through the various school activity programs. Six schools reported—two of these offering the accredited courses and four of the twenty-four schools that do not offer courses—that attention is directed to Negro life and progress through school clubs. Such mediums mentioned include history clubs, manners clubs, Dunbar clubs, Phillis Wheatley clubs, quill clubs, school assembly programs, literary societies, commencement programs, and music organizations. Practically all schools reported that special Negro celebrations were observed such as Negro History Week, Negro Health Week, Rosenwald Day, birthdays of famous Negroes, and the like, either sponsored by or participated in by the school.

Certain objectives are set up in the offering of any course, and results are always checked to note whether the desired goals are in any way being achieved. It is expected that pupils will develop certain attitudes and concepts from their study of Negro history; and it has been pointed out, by the schools that have the course, as having produced a feeling of race pride and confidence. One school reports the cultivation of business initiative and constructive thinking as necessary elements in racial progress and the necessity for collective efficiency as among the concepts of its Negro history students. In each school the student is found to have a deep gratitude for the discovery of the Negro's brilliant and imperishable contributions to the world's civilization.

In every instance where the study of Negro history is in progress, the members of boards of education and trustees have expressed willingness unhesitatingly for the beginning of these courses. In cases where the courses have not begun, replies to the questionnaire indicate unquestionably in ninety-five per cent of the counties that the only reason for this failure is that no request has been made for its inclusion in the curriculum. The attitude of the white superintendent in the city and county districts is favorable. The following quotation of a letter to the writer indicates the attitude of the State Department of Education as written by Mr. D. B. Taylor, Supervisor of Division of Negro Education:

"May I say that I am heartily in accord with the plan of having important phases of Negro life and history incorporated in the curriculum of Negro high schools. I think such material incorporated in the high school curriculum for Negro schools would help enrich the life of high school pupils, develop a healthy race pride, and help them to appreciate the Negro along with other races of the world. I think furthermore, that such material would be of great value in citizenship training in Negro high schools."

The matter of the institution and inclusion of the study of Negro life and history as an integral part of the school curriculum, ought to stand strategically first in importance among the responsibilities of the high school principals. A study of American education shows an incompleteness because it does not provide for the training of its adolescent youth in the heritage and growth of a people that make up one-tenth of its population. The Negro principal should therefore realize that his task is far from being done unless he places himself as an important cog in the wheel of education and presents himself as an interpreter of the Negro people. There has been much error on the part of our characteristic white friend in assuming that he is familiar with the whole range of Negro life and every type of Negro character. Some of the first-hand information gained by the white man, with regard to the Negro, should by no means serve as an authentic interpretation of the background and growth of this race. Rather should this interpretation come from the Negro himself. In both white and Negro high schools, then, here is the opportunity to develop a society where the code of human rights is written in the consciousness of the individual.

L. V. WILLIAMS

Booker T. Washington High School,
Dallas, Texas.

PERSPECTIVE IN THE TEACHING OF
NEGRO HISTORY*

In the few minutes that I shall appear before you, I wish
to raise two questions, and attempt to suggest tentative
answers to these two questions. The first question is:
What is the Negro? and the second is: What should be
the objective in the teaching of Negro history? I have
chosen the following subject around which to build this
discussion: "Perspective in the Teaching of Negro History."

This clarification of vision is necessary, for when a person starts on a journey he should know where he is going.
Consider with me, then, a concrete case. A young man is
seated at a desk. In his hand is a textbook on Negro History.
He has a college degree, and possibly an advanced degree.
Before him is a class of students—some enthusiastic, some
bored, others indifferent. The seats are arranged in such
manner that the light falls from the left, in order that
there be no unnecessary strain upon the eyes of the students. The color of the wall, and the design of the seats
have been scientifically determined. Educational psychologists have declared that the period should be a certain
number of minutes in length. At the given hour a bell
rings, and the class in Negro History is called to order.
Where is it going? What is the goal of such painstaking
effort? There may be several goals, but it is my purpose
to point out one goal that should always be the aim of
every class of students in the study of Negro History.

I agree with the writer who wrote these words, "The
most fundamental thing about a man is his outlook on
life." To emphasize the significance of this statement, I
shall cite several cases: A certain man believes that his
every act, word, or thought has been previously determined for him by some super-human power. What is the

*An address delivered at the annual meeting of the Association for the
Study of Negro Life and History in Houston, Texas, November 13, 1934.

result of such a belief? The man is not responsible for what he does, according to his way of thinking. Another man believes that God made the world for his personal benefit and profit. What is the result? He takes what he can from anybody that he can, regardless as to the method. A former president of a certain Negro college used to take delight in having his student body sing this spiritual as often as possible: "You may have all this world; give me Jesus." This president, by the way, owned about 1,000 acres of good land, and had a substantial bank account. The large majority of the students were uncomfortably poor. A family in one of our Southern States lived in the backwoods where existence was a constant struggle with nature. They read no papers, nor magazines, attended no theaters, ate simple coarse food, and wore the plainest of clothes. One day during the winter a visitor asked the father of the family of six why he burned the balustrade around the front porch instead of going to the nearby woods for fuel. The father's reply was, "Oh, we can make out with less."

These examples are sufficient to bear out the significance of the statement that the most fundamental thing about a man is his outlook upon life. What, may I ask, should be the outlook of the character that we call the "average" Negro?

Before attempting to suggest a tentative answer to this question, it is in order for us to scrutinize more closely the "average" Negro, that we may better understand how to guide him. Dr. E. B. Reuter, in his book *The American Race Problem,* (pp. 7-9), says, "The Negroes brought into the New World situation and presently reduced to a perpetual servitude became very rapidly accommodated to the environment and the status. The explanation of the comparative ease with which this was brought about doubtless lies in part in the peculiar racial traits of the Negro people themselves. They are strong and robust in physique and so everywhere sought after as laborers. In disposition they are cheerful, kindly, and sociable; in temperament they are characteristically extrovert, so readily obedient and easily contented. More than most other racial groups they are patiently tolerant under abuse and oppression and little inclined to struggle against difficulties . . .'' Referring especially to the mental attitude of the Negro, he says further, ''The Negro was thus not alone a slave in body; he was a slave in mind as well. Without such mental attitudes no people could be kept in such servitude as characterized the American Situation; no slave system can rest alone on the basis of physical force.'' Dr. Reuter should have added that this peculiar character is not racial and that it is that of the enslaved American Negro only, for Africans who have not had such an experience are of a decidedly different type.

Mr. Edwin R. Embree, president of the Julius Rosenwald Fund, gives in *Brown America* (p. 22) this slightly different description in saying that the ''Negro is expressive. He has an amazing capacity for meeting buffets with laughter—not with a smile but with hearty guffaws of Olympian laughter. He laughs at himself and his own embarrassments; he laughs at his persecutors; he laughs at the quaint habits and intricate ratiocinations of his Nordic neighbors.'' To set forth more clearly what he means by the foregoing, Mr. Embree shows that the, ''Negro sings at his work, and plays and dances as soon as his work is done, and his music and dance are no mere imitation of the practice about him. In folk art he has made creative contributions unequalled in the drab life of southern farms or northern industries . . . Into religion he has poured his soul with abandon and ecstasy'' . . . ''The Negro,'' Mr. Embree continues, ''has native dignity, grace, and good manners. He is free from self-consciousness and from being awkwardly ugly in trying situations. His manners to both white folks and his own fellows are quite astonishing in their consideration for the feelings of others and in their courtliness.''

To other writers the Negro is an oppressed tenth of the American population. Still others consider the Negro as a ''problem'' that is too difficult to be solved. Mr. Embree informs us that a new race is emerging in America—a brown race with characteristics different from the native African and the Nordic peoples.

Professor Alain Locke, who declares that a ''New Negro'' is growing up in America, has his own views on the matter. ''The Old Negro,'' he asserts, ''was a creature of moral debate and historical controversy. His has been a stock figure perpetuated as an historical fiction partly in innocent sentimentalism, partly in deliberate reactionism . . . . The Negro has been more of a formula than a human being—a something to be argued about, condemned or defended, to be ''kept down,'' or ''in his place,'' or ''helped up,'' to be worried with or worried over, harassed or patronized, a social bogey or a social burden. The New Negro is ''vibrant with a new psychology,'' and a new spirit. He is marching forward with new self-respect.

Let us examine the ''average Negro'' in terms of race. Dr. Reuter states, ''Applied to human beings, the term race implies a blood related group with characteristic and common hereditary traits.'' If this is true the American Negro is certainly not a race. Dr. Woodson, Professor Brawley, and others inform us that the African people in this country had a varied ancestry. They were neither of the same race stock nor did they speak a common language. On the same plantation a variety of customs could be noticed. Religious practices varied from voodooism to Mohammedanism. Facial features were not the same; texture of the hair and color of the skin were not uniform. Habits of thought were not the same, nor ideals. Obviously, then, the American Negro is not a race from a biological point of view. The term has been constantly redefined to meet certain needs.

Many families trace their ancestry back to some illustrious person, but they take care, less they make mention of the skeletons in the closet. And so it is with nations. We are informed that there are no pure races in the world. The term "Negro," therefore, is a political and sociological concept subject to new definitions. Such an attitude should keep the teacher from becoming discouraged over the difficulty of getting unified action on the part of Colored America. He will not give up in despair when all Negroes fail to carry out a cut-and-dried program. In my present way of thinking, there is but one fundamental attitude that the teacher of Negro History should have, namely, Negroes cannot be reduced to the definiteness of mathematical law; they are just ordinary beings like other people with strong and weak points, good points and bad points; they can be improved by means of proper training, or degenerate through the absence of it.

In the face of these facts it appears that the term "average Negro" is very elusive, and that the strongest bond holding Negroes together is oppression. This brings us, then, to a consideration of the second question raised at the outset. What should be the objective here? With respect to teaching history Professor Henry Johnson says: "The *aims* of instruction determine for any subject the materials to be selected and the manner of dealing with them. The *value* of instruction is measured by the results of instruction." (*Teaching of History*, p. 55). This, however, opens the way for history made to order. A certain writer of history textbooks, I am told, once wrote one book to please the South, and another on the same subject to please the North. The same facts were treated in both books, but the interpretation was different. This case brings out the importance of well selected aims in the teaching of Negro History, since the aims determine the materials and the interpretation.

The teacher of Negro History might unknowingly develop into a propagandist, who, like certain radical groups, starts out with a biased point of view. Commonwealth College at Mena, Arkansas, for example, thus states its main purpose: "Commonwealth College is a non-factional labor school which has as its function the training of young men and women for active service in some militant organization in the labor movement. Its courses, which include economics, history, labor problems, proletarian culture, creative writing, public speaking, journalism, psychology, etc., are taught from a point of view partisan to the working class." This college frankly admits that it is biased.

Should the teacher of Negro History take a similar biased attitude towards his subject? If so, he will then dwell on the horrors of the slave factories, the filthy middle passage across the ocean from Africa to America, the whipping and branding of slaves, the sexual exploitation of Negro womanhood, the separation of husband and wife or mother and child. He will extol the virtues of the Negro, showing him to be faithful under harsh treatment, a hard worker under the scorching rays of the southern sun beaming down on white fields of cotton, a protector of the master's household when the master was fighting to keep him a slave. He will dwell on the horrors of the Ku Klux Klan, the injustices of the grandfather clauses, the political disfranchisement of the Negro. He will call forth fire from heaven to consume body and soul the oppressors of a noble but downtrodden group. He will advocate taking the law into his own hands and settling all disputes with the bomb and rifle; nor will he attempt to soften the effects of such a dark picture. Obviously, then, such a position or bias has no place in the teaching of Negro History.

The teacher of Negro History might develop as an objective the stimulation of nationalistic desires among Negroes. Marcus Garvey has demonstrated that such feelings can be aroused among large numbers of Negroes. Mr. T. G. Standing, of the University of Iowa, wrote an article in the September, 1934, issue of the *American Jour-*

nal of Sociology, entitled "Nationalism in Negro Leadership." In this article he analyzes the trends in Negro leadership since the time of Frederick Douglass. After mentioning Booker T. Washington and Dr. DuBois he declares that the most thoroughgoing and consistent nationalistic leader the Negro has had was Marcus Garvey, although the "Garvey Movement" is at present generally discredited. Garvey advocated "the frank repudiation of white standards and the substitution, whenever possible, of black ones."

"I asked, where is the black man's government?" said Garvey. "Where is his president, his country, and his ambassadors, his army, his navy and his men of big affairs? I could not find them and then I decided, I will help make them. My young and ambitious mind led me into great flights of imagination. I saw before me then, even as I do now, a new world of black men, not peons, serfs, dogs, and slaves, but a nation of sturdy men making their impress upon civilization and causing a new light to dawn upon the human race."

Such an aim as this would also be partisan or biased, in view of the fact that we are American citizens by birth and by right of toil, and the realization of it would be extremely difficult since the desirable parts of the world are already appropriated to the uses of the world powers. Numerous writers refer to Africa as a white man's country. Where, then, will the Negroes thus led establish their empire?

A more academic minded teacher may set up such aims as these: To get historical information, recognize names, remember dates, and detailed facts, most of which will be forgotten shortly after the final examination. Another aim may be to develop the mind in the weighing of historical evidence so that one may be able to put historical material under the microscope and examine it minutely to determine whether or not it contains any impure or foreign matter. A further aim may be that of furnishing high class entertainment through selected readings about the Negro, so that one may have interesting literature to gladden his leisure moments. A popular aim in the teaching of history has been that of stimulating patriotism and loyalty to one's country under all conditions. "My country, right or wrong, My country!"

Regardless as to the merits or demerits of the aims mentioned thus far, it is my opinion, along with others, that the teacher of Negro History should take as his aim the dissemination of the truth. He should examine the past carefully with the idea of opening the minds of the class to the possibilities of the future. The study of the past should reveal the achievements as well as the mistakes and shortcomings of the Negro. He should then use his mistakes as stepping stones, and his achievements as inspiration. Professor John W. Wayland believes:

"History teaches a man how small he is by showing him so many greater. It teaches him how great he may be by showing him what less favored men have done. It purges him of conceit by revealing his fancied originality as a commonplace of centuries gone. It overthrows his dogmatism by proving to him that other men no less honest than he, and much wiser, have been mistaken in their judgments. It convinces him that he did not begin with himself, and that he cannot end with himself—that the most he has others have given him; that the most he knows others have taught him; and that all he can do he owes to others. History helps him to see himself as one among countless millions, yet it brings him to know himself as a man, in whom is potentially every power, feeling, thought and achievement that any man has had, felt, known, or done" (*How to Teach American History,* p. 3-4).

Professor Alain Locke is of this opinion:

"The intelligent Negro of today is resolved not to make discrimination an extenuation for his shortcomings in performance, individual or collective; he is trying to hold himself at par, neither inflated by sentimental allowances nor depreciated by current social discounts. For this he must know himself and be known for precisely what he is, and for that reason he welcomes the new scientific rather than the old sentimental interest."

JOSEPH A. BAILEY

Arkansas State College.

SOME ATTITUDES IN ENGLISH LITERATURE

According to an ancient tradition there were no domestic slaves in Greece, but we find them mentioned in the Homeric poems—usually prisoners taken in war, also victims kidnapped and bought and sold. Slaves at that time, however, were mostly confined to the homes of the wealthy. No disgrace was attached to the condition of slavery during those days, for the fortune of war levelled all distinctions. The position of slaves in classical times was so very different from that centuries later in the days of the rise and fall of the slave trade that, apart from devoting an article on the subject, no purpose can be served in going into details. The number of "blacks" compared to that of "the barbarians" captured in warfare, moreover, was comparatively small. In many cases slaves occupied honoured posts in Greek and Roman households; they might be bakers, cooks, tailors. In Rome they were largely personal attendants; some Romans possessed 10,000 or 20,000 slaves. The inferior slaves worked in mines where they operated in chains. Others served as mechanics, clerks, actors, teachers, surgeons, physicians, and the like. The games of the amphitheatre required an immense number of slaves trained for the purpose. Like the slaves in Sicily, the *gladiatores* in Italy rose in B. C. 72 against their oppressors; and under the generalship of Spartacus were not subdued till B. C. 71, when, according to Livy, 60,000 had fallen in battle. The spread of Christianity tended to improve the condition of slaves until the unprecedented traffic started in the fifteenth century and prostituted Christianity to its nefarious purpose.

The closing centuries of the Roman Republic saw a new development in slavery. Rome engaged in the plunder of the East; the marvelous discoveries of fifteenth century Spain, Portugal, Holland, France, and England led to as ruthless a plundering in distant lands. In both cases this plunder led to a rapidly developing commerce in slaves and

27

changed what may be considered a domestic affair into an industry on a large scale. In the ancient world, 146 B. C., Delos became the center of unrivalled importance as slaves from conquered cities or devastated areas passed through the port to be sold to merchants and others. According to Strabo 10,000 slaves could be landed at Delos in the morning and sold before evening. Nothing to compare with this wholesale dealing in human beings occurred until the beginning of the West African trade, though Medieval Europe indulged to a certain extent in this traffic. Europe's first contact with the defenceless natives was exceptionally ruthless and cruel. Sir John Hawkins, in the sixteenth century, was a pioneer in the chase. In the eighteenth century Liverpool merchants financed ships which transported some 300,000 slaves from Africa to the West Indies in eleven years at a profit of £15,000,000.

It must be remembered that Chatham and Nelson looked upon this disgraceful traffic as necessary to England's expanding commerce which only became a problem of conscience towards the end of the eighteenth century; the passionate sense of Christian responsibility gradually ended British slavery.[1] The movement found its parliamentary leader in Wilberforce, though Thomas Clarkson did as much as any man to secure the triumph of the cause. In 1785 Clarkson won the Latin Essay Prize at Cambridge with an essay on "Is it right to make men slaves against their will?" and to him Wordsworth dedicated his poem when the trade was abolished. Nor must Granville Sharp's determined efforts in this connection be forgotten, for he it was who forced Lord Mansfield's emancipating judgment delivered in June, 1772. The task was completed by Zachary Macaulay, Lushington, and Buxton.

[1] R. Coupland, *The British Anti-Slavery Movements*, 1933—"Granville Sharp;" *Frampton Dialogue*, "Yroni and Steele," 1580, page 149; S. Sewall, *Diary*, June 22, 1716; M. G. Lewis, *Journal West Indies*, 1834, page 64.

The increasing number of Negroes in England itself brought the question nearer home. The appearance of colored attendants in the seventeenth and eighteenth century books became common. They were fashionable and gave an air of luxurious wellbeing, especially to the masters and mistresses upon whom they waited.[2] In the *Gentleman's Magazine* of October, 1764, it was said, "The practice of importing Negro servants is said to be already a grievance that requires a remedy, and yet it is every day encouraged; insomuch, that the number in this metropolis only is supposed to be near 20,000." Negroes had become an article of commerce in London.[3] Protests in both poetry and prose, then, began to enrich the literature of England. In these productions may be traced the attitudes of the best thinkers of that country.

To develop the thought of the Negro in English literature one must bear in mind the various words used in referring to the people of Africa. The Moors as a result of the sweep of Islam through North Africa into Europe had brought into Spain a larger number of black Africans than had reached the continent through the commercial intercourse of the City States of the Mediterranean during the Middle Age. These Mohammedanized Africans were first called Moors or Saracens, but to distinguish them by color from others the Spaniards began to use the word *Negro* and the English first *Blacke* and later the foreign term *Negro*.

One of the first to use the word was Richard Eden, a diligent interpreter of the work of others. His object was to make known to the English what the Portuguese and Spaniards had done in the way of navigation and discovery; and in 1551 he translated from Peter Martyr's *The Decades of the New Worlde or West Indies, conteyning*

[2] *Gentleman's Magazine*, October, 1764.

[3] From William Bragge's *Account-Book* (1621) contained in his "Petition to the Honble. Sir Thomas Smith and all the Company of the East India and Sommes Islands"—(N. & G. 3 S. II, 345 (1762).

*the Navigations and Conquests of the Spanyardes, with
particular description of the most ryche and large Landes
and Islandes lately found in the West Ocean.* So far as
is known the *Decades* contain the first mention of the word
Negro in the interesting passage, "They are not accustomed to eat such meats as do the Ethiopians or Negroes." This work was followed in 1577 by John Frampton's *Dialogue of Yron* in his translation from the Spanish of the *Joyful Newes out of the New Founde Worlde.*
When writing of the origin of money, he says, "And in all
Gínea the blacke people called Negroes dooe use for
money, for the same effect, certaine little snayles, which
they finde in the Sea, as also other nations doe use of
things lyke to this."

In Volume I of the Second Part, Eden says, "The
blacke people that hath gone from these parts to the Indias, hath taken the same maner and use of the Tobacco,
that the Indians hath, for when thei see themselves wearie,
thei take it at the nose and mouthe, and it dooeth happen
unto theim, as unto our Indians, lying as though thei were
dedde three or fower howers: . . . and the thyng is come
to so much effecte that their maisters doeth chasten theim
for it, and doe burne the Tobaco, because thei should not
use it, whereupon thei goe to the desartes and secrete
places to doe it, because they maie not bee permitted, to
drinke them selves drunke with wine, and therefore, thei
are gladde to make them selves drunken with the smoke
of Tobacco. . ."

In early miracle mystery plays introducing the Nativity,
the black man was conspicuous. In that of the "Magi,"
or "Three Kings of Cologne," Melchior, King of Nubia,
the shortest of the three, on hearing of the birth of Jesus
Christ, came to Bethlehem with gold offerings indicative
of royalty. Gaspar, King of Tarshish, an Ethiopian, the
tallest of these, offered myrrh, symbolic of death. European artists have preserved this tradition, as almost any

art gallery will attest, although the Negro does not figure conspicuously in the art of later periods in England.

In Legends

In the Arthurian legends as they gripped the people of Mediaeval England in their original form, the Negro, conceived as being a "Black Moor," "Blackamoor," or "Saracen," was a conspicuous factor. The black man as he was generally pictured at that time was considered necessary to make these scenes colorful. Along with other knights he, too, was portrayed as an all but perfect specimen of humanity in conformity to the ideals of chivalry. These knights were the representatives of the best of their day, men of honor, manifesting, above all things, loyalty, bravery, and sacrifice for a just cause. Into these legends as they changed in the conceptions of writers from period to period came the elements of romance and religion. Often the black element is presented as the pagan in conflict with the Christian.

King Arthur and his Twelve Knights, in imitation of the Twelve Paladins of Charlemagne, sat at the Round Table because it was symbolic of perfection which the Knights represented. Palamides, the black, next to the three great knights, Launcelot, Tristram and Lamorake, was the strongest and bravest of the Round Table Knights. Palamides, although unbaptized, was described as well-made, cleanly, tall and middle-aged. His manners were polite, and he was true to his word. The daring feats of the Knights delighted the world until Arthur himself breaks up the circle by defiling the Round Table with incest. But Arthur, like all the others of the circle, is whitewashed by later versions; and the whole story continues that of heroes of the earlier days drawn from various parts, among which, of course, was the land of the blacks.

Palamides, the Black Knight, mounted on a great black

steed and bearing a black shield and a harp, appears in becoming array at the palace of King Mark of Cornwall. He
refuses to play the harp until the king grants his desire,
which is the beautiful Queen Isolde. Moved by the en-
chanting tune, she goes with him; but Tristram, another
knight, appears upon the scene, and she is charmed by the
rote of this man whom she loves and who loves her as man
never before loved woman. Isolde induces Palamides to
bring her ashore. There ensues a combat between Palamides and his enemy and friend, Tristram. Seeing that it
must prove fatal, Isolde implores the black prince to cease.
Palamides cannot refuse the request of a woman; and he
thus leaves Tristram the victor.

In the quest of the Holy Grail the knights still had
among them, according to the earliest versions, the black
Saracen or Moor. The Holy Grail had departed from the
possessors inheriting the sacred vessel from those who
received it from Joseph of Arimathea. They had become
corrupt; and only the pure could approach the Holy Grail.
The knights of honor, among whom was one in black, went
in quest of the vessel; and Galahad secured it because his
heart was pure. Others have made Parsifal the hero.
Upon the legend Wagner based an opera; and Matthew
Arnold, Swinburne, and Tennyson some of their best
works. Said Tennyson in his *Idylls of the King*:

> And Arthur and his Knighthood for a space
> Were all one will, ...
> Fought, and in twelve great battles overcame
> The heathen hordes, and made a realm and reigned.

Richard Coeur de Lion, of the thirteenth century, the
geste of a great English Prince, contains the grim episode
of the cooking of the Saracen's head instead of a pig's jowl,
and tells of the king's banquet to the Paynim ambassadors
on the same food. According to Professor George Saints-
bury this is the first and best fighting poem in Middle
English:

"And swore by Jesu that made moon and star
Agenst the Saracens he should learn to war."

From the fourteenth century the Saracens are mentioned in romances. The black king, the Magi, appears in
the cycle of religious plays bringing from afar his offering to the babe Jesus. Saracens appear in *King Horn*,
(1225?), probably composed to be sung to popular audiences; and in the *King of Tars* (1325?) in which the
Saracen Sultan of Dammas sues for the hand of the
daughter of the King of Tarsus. Not being a Christian he
is rejected. He then invades the country and causes so
much havoc that the princess begs to be allowed to give
herself to the sultan. A child is born without face or
limbs; and, in reply to her husband's reproaches, the
mother tells him to see if his gods can make a perfect
child of the lump of flesh. As they do not succeed the
sultan destroys their image and declares he will forsake
Mahoun if God will do what his own gods have failed to
do. The mother asks a priest among the prisoners to
christen the child and instantly the lump of flesh is converted into a fully formed babe. The mother then says
the father can have nothing to do with either her or the
child unless he becomes a Christian. This he does after
some training from his wife. At his christening his appearance is changed from a forbidding aspect, and becomes
kindly and attractive. The people are all compelled to
Christianity. Those who remain pagan are slain, and
neighbouring kings who resist are executed.[4]

One of the most popular of medieval romances tells how
Guy of Warwick (C. 1330-40) becomes a pilgrim and fights
a Saracen giant, Amorant. Sir Beues (Bevis) of Ham-
toun (C. 1300) among his many adventures has a great
battle with Saracens on Christmas Day. Horn, of an early
romance, is the beautiful son of King Murray whose king-

[4]J. E. Wells' *Manual of Writings in Middle English*, 1050-1400 (1926),
2042.

dom is described as being "biweste." As Murray was riding by the seashore he met with fifteen shiploads of Saracens who said their intention was to slay the land-folk, and began with the king. Horn's beauty saves him from death, but he and his two companions are set adrift. After many adventures and the marriage of Horn to the daughter of the king of Westernesse, he meets the slayer of his father and "smote him through the heart."[5]

The Black Knight continued in the early English litera-ture. In *The Tragical Battle of Alcazar in Barbary, with the Death of Three Kings and Captain Stuckeley, an Eng-lishman,* this character is prominent.[6] Stuckeley, an overweening and adventurous Englishman, bound on an expedition to beat all the English out of Ireland, lands in Portugal just when Sebastian, the King, with two Moorish Kings are about to set off for Africa; and Stuckeley is persuaded to join them. In the Battle of Alcazar, August 4, 1578, they are disastrously defeated, and Stuckeley lost his life.

> "A fateful fight, where in one day was slain
> Three Kings that were, and one that would be fain."

The presenter at the beginning of Act I, says:

> Honour, the spur that pricks the princely mind
> To follow rule and climb the stately chair,
> With great desire inflamed the Portingal
> An honourable and courageous King,
> To undertake a dangerous dreadful war
> And aid with Christian arms the barbarous Moor.
> The Negro Muly Hamet, that withholds
> The kingdom from his uncle Abdemelec.

Muly Mahamet, the Moor, begins by murdering his two younger brothers and his uncle Abdelmunen, to make his own position quite safe. In scene i Amurath the Great sends picked soldiers to help Abdemelec:

[5]Wells, *op. cit.*, C. 1300 and C. 1330-40.
[6]Green and Peele *Dramatic and Poetical Works*, 1861.

Amurath hath sent scourges by his men,
To whip that tyrant traitor-king from hence,
That hath usurp'd from us, and maim'd you all.

Abdemelec continues and explains their descent from
Mahomet and the law made by his ancestor Muly Maha-
met-Xeque that "in his kingdom should successively his
sons succeed," a law now broken by Muly Mahamet, who
therefore must be punished for seizing the throne of
Barbary. In Act II, the presenter announces that Abdemelec has been installed in his royal seat by Amurath's
soldiers, and that Muly Mahamet "furiously implores Sebastian's aid, brave King of Portugal. In scene ii comes
the arrival of Irish Bishop and Englishmen including
Stuckeley. In scene iii, the Moor's wife describes how
Sebastian attracted by promise of the kingdom of Morocco
is coming over and that he will be got rid of as soon as
victory is obtained; in Act. V there comes the death of
Abdemelec after temporary defeat. The continuation gives
an account of the battle, the curses of Muly Mahamet on
every one, including his mother; he is terrified when he
finds that he is being beaten and tries to run away.

In the study of works based upon these legends one must
bear in mind that later writers have so changed these as to
eliminate the Negro element or to whitewash the blacks
therein participating. Inasmuch as the English-speaking
world during the modern stage of their literature was growing rich off the slave trade and slaveholding bias and prejudice required this change in attitude. Treatments of these
early efforts have conformed accordingly, even parts of the
Cambridge History of English Literature. This early literature has been remade according to the attitudes of
slave traders and slaveholders.

IN DRAMA

In early England, as in other European countries, before real slavery developed, the few Negroes taken to

those parts were favorites among aristocratic men and women. This was so common that it became a matter of dramatization. Shakespeare's writings reflected this beyond a doubt. For example, in

Two Gentlemen of Verona (C. 1590-92)—Act V and scene ii, Proteus says to Thurio:

> Black men are pearls in beauteous ladies' eyes.

In *Merry Wives of Windsor* (C. 1600) Act V, scene v) we hear of:

> Fairies, black, gray, green, and white (in Windsor Park).

In *Titus Andronicus* (before 1584-89) he refers to "Aaron, the Moor, beloved by the Queen of the Goths."

In *Othello* (1604), Act I, scene iii), the Duke of Branbantio says:

> If virtue no delighted beauty lack,
> Your son-in-law (Othello) is far more fair than black.

And in Act III, scene iii, Othello says, among other things:

> Haply, for I am black
> And have not those soft parts of conversation
> That Chamberers have.

Showing Shakespeare himself against the background of his times, a recent writer has given us a new portrait of the author. His friendship with the Earl of Southampton was severely strained (1594?) over the affairs of a black woman. Says, G. B. Harrison, "She was evidently a courtesan, notorious to fashionable young gentlemen who took their pleasures in Clerkenwell; and for a time Shakespeare became her lover. The adventure stirred him profoundly. By ordinary standards the woman was not beautiful, yet irresistibly fascinating; his will led him to her; his reason was resolved, as he expressed it in a sonnet:"

> The expense of spirit in a waste of shame
> Is lust in action, and till action, lust

> Is perjur'd, murderous, bloody, full of blame
>
> .   .   .   .
>
> All this the world well knows yet none knows well,
> To shun the heaven that leads men to this hell.

"Yet he was not blindly in love, for he could stand aside from himself and thus criticise both himself and her:"

> My mistress' eyes are nothing like the sun,
> Coral is far more red, than her lips' red,
> If snow be white, why then her breasts are dun
> If hairs be wires, black wires grow on her head,
> And yet by heaven I think my love as rare
> As any she belied with false compare.[7]

The woman, however, was not permanently attached to him, and when Southampton came her way "she readily deserted Shakespeare. It was a galling situation. He wanted his mistress again,[8] but not at the expense of friendship. To Southampton, then, he wrote:[9]"

> That thou hast her, it is not all my grief,
> And yet it may be said I lov'd her dearly;
> And here's the joy; my friend and I are one;
> Sweet flattery! then she loves but me alone.

To the woman:

> Two loves I have of comfort and despair,
> Which like two spirits do suggest me still:
> The better angel is a man right fair,
> The worser spirit a woman, colour'd ill
> To win me soon to hell, my female evil
> Tempeth my better angel from my side,
> I guess one angel in another's hell:
> Yet this shall I ne'er know, but live in doubt,
> Till my bad angel fire my good one out.

In the commentary Harrison says, "The tone of Shakespeare's Sonnets to her (the Dark Lady) suggests that she was not a person of any position, and there is scattered evidence that in the 1590's one of the well-

---

[7]*Shakespeare under Elizabeth*, by G. B. Harrison, London, 1930, page 64.
[8]*Ibid*, page 26.
[9]Harrison, *op. cit.*, p. 310.

known courtesans was notoriously dark. In the Gray's
Inn Revels, amongst those brought in to pay mock hom-
age to the Prince of Purpool "*Lucy Negro, Abbess de
Clerkenwell,* holdeth the Nunnery of *Clerkenwell,* with the
Lands and Priviledges thereunto belonging of the Prince
of *Purpoole* by Night-Service in *Cauda,* and to find a
Choir of Nuns, with burning Lamps, to chaunt *Placebo*
to the gentlemen of the Prince's Privy Chamber, on the
day of His Excellency's Coronation."[10] This 'Lucy Negro' I would very tentatively identify as the Dark Lady.

"In Weaver's *Epigrams,* 1599, Third Week, Epigram 12,
are these verses *In Byrrham:*"

> Is Byrrha browne? Who doth the question aske?
> Her face is pure as Ebonie ieat blacke,
> It's hard to know her face from her faire maske,
> Beautie in her seemes beautie still to lacke,
> Nay, she's snow-white, but for that russet skin,
> Which like a vaile doth keep her whiteness in.

To this Harrison would add this chat between Lorenzo
and Launcelot Gobbo (*Merchant of Venice, III, v.* 40) concerning the Moor, which he considers to be typical:

LOR.: I shall answer that better to the commonwealth than you
can the getting up of the negro's belly: the Moor is with child by
you Launcelot.
LAUN.: It is much that the Moor should be more than reason:
but if she be less than an honest woman, she is indeed more
than I took her for.

"That there were such coloured women," continues Harrison, "is apparent from a letter dated 1602 from one Den-
nis Edwards, addressed to Thomas Lankford, Secretary to
the Earl of Hertford or Mr. Cross, Clark of the Kitchen.
He writes, 'Pray Enquire after and secure my negress; she
is certainly at the Swan, a Dane's beer-shop, Turnbull
Street, Clerkenwell.'"

Shakespeare's attitude is further shown in his delinea-
tion of the character of *Othello.* He is the noble, brave, and

[10]Malone, *Soc. Reprint,* p. 12.

trustful black man, transported into a world not his own, and loved by Desdemona. In unfamiliar surroundings he became suspicious and only too easily persuaded of his wife's guilt. The marriage is treated by Shakespeare as not in any way unnatural and above reproach. Othello speaks but once of his blackness as the cause of Desdemona's unfaithfulness.[11]

Othello, according to Rose, "has a strong and healthy mind and a vivid imagination but they deal entirely with first impressions, with obvious facts." Miss Lillian Winstanley thinks that *Othello* is a symbolical allegory, at once of the domination of Italy by Spain, of the relations of Philip II (Othello) with his wife and minister Amborio Perez (Iago). If such an intention had been intelligible, the censor would not have passed it.[12] The best recent critics, however, have made it clear that he was a Negro; one of them, Bradley, emphasizing especially the following:

> Her name that was as fair as Dian's visage,
> Is now begrim'd and black as mine own face.

To Othello Coleridge pays high tribute. In his *Notes* (p. 267), the writer says, "Finally, let me repeat that Othello does not kill Desdemona in jealousy, but in a conviction forced upon him by the almost super-human art of Iago, such a conviction as any man would and must have entertained who had believed Iago's honesty as Othello did . . . . We shall feel the fundamental difference between the solemn agony of the noble Moor, and the wretched fishing jealousies of Leontes, and the morbid suspiciousness of Leonatus, who is, in other respects, a fine character. Othello had no life but in Desdemona: the belief that she, his angel, had fallen from the heaven of her native inno-

---

[11]"Haply, for I am black and have not those soft parts of conversation that chamberers have."

[12]Edward Rose, *New Shakespeare* (Soc. Trans., 1880-2); and E. K. Chamber's *William Shakespeare*, Vol. I, page 462.

cence, wrought a civil war in his heart. She is his counterpart; and, like him, is almost sanctified in our eyes by her absolute unsuspiciousness, and holy entireness of love. As the curtain drops, which do we pity the most?''[13]

Shakespeare in thus projecting a man in black upon the screen showed that he believed in equality not only of the blacks, but of all men, for they as slaves in Europe were exceptions to the rule in that day. The large majority of bondmen of that time were the unfortunate Europeans reduced to servitude or captives taken in wars. Slavery did not become a status peculiar to the Negro until near the beginning of the eighteenth century. Elsewhere, moreover, Shakespeare gave evidence of his interest in universal freedom. Referring to the rise of workers, Shakespeare once wrote:

> Mechanic slaves
> With greasy aprons, rules, and hammers, shall
> Uplift us to the view.[14]

The status of the slave, too, has never been more aptly described than in Shakespeare's well chosen words in the two following quotations:

> Thou art a slave, whom fortune's tender arm
> With favour never clasp'd; but bred a dog.

> You have among you many a purchas'd slave,
> Which, like your asses, and your dogs, and mules
> You use in abject and in slavish parts
> Because you bought them.

And it sounds a little revolutionary for Shakespeare to use the drama to say that ''every bondman in his own hand bears the power to cancel his captivity.''[15] He realized as did Seneca ''how great would be our peril, if our slaves began to number us.''

[13]*The Literary Remains of Samuel Taylor Coleridge*, London, 1836, Vol. II, page 266.

[14]Charles N. Douglass, *Forty Thousand Quotations*, New York, 1917, page 1612.

[15]Douglass, *op. cit.*, 1612.

The next period in the development of the Negro on the stage was the result of the seventeenth century realism ushered in by Aphra Behn. She was the daughter of John Johnson, but she accompanied as "daughter" the appointee as Governor of Surinam to Dutch Guiana, which once belonged to England. Either in that tropical country or after her return home she married one Mr. Behn. From the impressions of the beauty of the land and the natives there enslaved she produced, in 1678, a realistic novel, *The History of Oroonoko* or *The Royal Slave*. The author says she "was an eye-witness to a great part of what you will find here set down; and what I could not be witness of, I received from the mouth of the chief actor in this history." ... She writes of the friendly relations of the English traders with the natives in their own homes; (we) "caress 'em with all the brotherly and friendly affection in the world."[16] Prince Oroonoko, grandson of the King of Coramanbien, who suceeded his grandfather at the age of seventeen, is described as humane, honourable, generous, with true greatness of soul. He spoke French and English. Imoinda, the girl he loved, is coveted and taken by the successor to the throne (Oroonoko's father) in spite of her protests; the father, furiously jealous of his son, finally in his rage sells Imoinda as a slave. The book, too well-known to require detailed description, tells the adventures of the hero, who is seized as a slave, until his death by violence.

Philip Henderson, in an introduction to the 1930 edition, says that Mrs. Behn in *Oroonoko* foreshadows Rousseau; she "so bitingly contrasts the natural honour of the African Oroonoko with the faithlessness of white men and their "Christianity." Jusserand says, "She carries us at once beyond the times of Defoe, Richardson, and Fielding, and takes us among the precursors of the French Revolution. In Scott and Saintebury's *Dryden* (Vol. XVIII,

[16]Aphra Behn, *Oroonoko*, page 4.

page 179) it is said, "The hero of Mrs. Behn's novel and
Southerne's tragedy, the noble Oroonoko is . . . the original ancestor of a long line of descendants with whom English fiction both on and off the stage has since become
sufficiently familiarized. He is a Pagan full of all the
Christian virtues who, after being dragged from his native kingdom into slavery on a West Indian Island, is
there, after an unsuccessful attempt at revolt, cruelly put
to death. The line "Pitys akin to love," has passed into
a proverb.[17]

Like *Uncle Tom's Cabin,* which later so stirred the
United States and Europe as to be dramatized, *Oroonoko*
was adapted to the stage. The influence of *Oroonoko* on
Defoe, Richardson, St. Pierre, Chateaubriand, Fielding,
and others, has been recognized. *Oroonoko,* Thomas
Southerne's tragedy (1696), a conspicuous triumph,
founded on Aphra Behn's tale of the virtues of this Negro
slave, enjoyed considerable popularity owing to the novelty of its theme, and its choice of hero.[18] The play was
staged also in Germany, and was translated into French
in order to be likewise presented.

The Negro figured also in the opera. The character ap-
pears in *The Padlock* by Isaac Bickerstaffe, a comic opera
written in 1768, set to music by Dibdin, and acted at
Drury Lane that same year. The opera is founded upon *The
Jealous Husband* by the author of Don Quixote. The chief
addition to the fable is the circumstance of the padlock.
Don Diego, the jealous husband, has a Negro slave, Mungo.
In *The Blackamoor Wash'd White,* a comic opera by Henry
Bate, acted at Drury Lane in 1776, another such effort was
made. Of this we have only the music. The songs only
were printed. From the first performance this play was
disapproved of, and on the third night took place a free
fight in which the actors participated. On the fourth it

[17]Dates for publication taken from British Museum catalogue.
[18]A. W. Ward, *A History of Eng. Dram. Lit.,* Vol. III, page 422.

was decided to give up all hope of presenting the play. The audience was pacified only by the assurance that the piece would be withdrawn.

The reaction of this infuriated crowd, however, cannot be easily determined, for we have neither the words nor the music of this opera. We know that *The West Indian*, a comedy, by Richard Cumberland, staged at Drury Lane two years earlier, was performed with great success. The latter was the story of one Belcour, the unacknowledged son (though born in wedlock) of Stockwell, a wealthy merchant, who arrived in London, accompanied by several black servants. Belcour Senior's daughter, the mother of the young man, had laid him as a foundling at her father's door; he was adopted by his grandfather, who left him his estate when he died. The curious and undisciplined behavior of the young West Indian causes considerable trouble all round, but after many adventures he settles down and marries Louisa Dudley, with whom he had fallen in love at first sight.[19]

With the exception of the usual presentation of *Othello* with varying interpretations as to the parts the Blackamoor played no other dramatization based upon the life of the Negro deeply moved the English public until we come to *Uncle Tom's Cabin*. This production both as a novel and as a play stirred all the leading nations of Europe. In England the adaptation to the stage was worked out in three acts by Mark Lemon and Thomas Taylor. The play was first performed at the Theatre Royal, Adelphi, November 29, 1852. It did not profess to be a mere stage version of the tale by Harriet Beecher Stowe but a play in which free use had been made of many of her chief characters and most striking incidents. For dramatic effect the threads of the fortunes of Eliza and George, of Uncle Tom and Eva, of Emmeline and

[19] R. Cumberland, *The West Indian*, 1774.

Cassy were interwoven. An effort was made to preserve the spirit that breathes through the pathetic pages of Mrs. Stowe, although the relations of characters and sequence of incidents were altered. Madame Celeste, the producer, visited the localities in which the action was supposed to take place. She took the part of Cassy, and Mrs. Keeley the part of Topsy, while Uncle Tom was played by G. Smith.[20]

IN POETRY

English poets, without visioning the Negroes in particular but thinking of them among others as deserving freedom, dared to dwell occasionally upon the theme of liberty at the very time that absolutism was being developed in Europe. This, to be sure, did much to establish the right of freedom of speech which in later years was used to great effect by British reformers. Assisted by poets and novelists, these thinkers championed the cause of the Negro.

That he might speak out as becomes a man inspired to plead the cause of the oppressed Milton said:

Give me the liberty to know, to think, to believe, and to utter freely according to conscience, above all other liberties.

Indicating the tendencies of that time, he referred to this situation:

In nations grown corrupt, and by their vices brought to servitude to love bondage more than liberty; bondage with ease than strenuous liberty.

Taking up the serfdom of his day, which scarcely resembled the bondage of later centuries, he was so displeased with the questionable custom as to say in "Paradise Lost:"

O execrable son! so to aspire
Above his brethren; to himself assuming
Authority usurp'd, from God not given:

[20] The play is No. 191 of Webster's *Acting National Drama* (1885).

He gave us only over beast, fish, fowl,
Dominion absolute; that right we hold
By his donation; but man over men
He made not lord; such title to himself
Reserving, human left from human free.

Dryden once dared to say that "the love of liberty with life is given." Addison believed that "a day, an hour of virtuous liberty is worth a whole eternity of bondage." Writing further of liberty, he said still more beautifully than ever:

O Liberty, thou goddess, heavenly bright,
Profuse of bliss, and pregnant with delight!
Eternal pleasures in thy presence reign,
And smiling plenty leads thy wanton train;
Eas'd of her load, subjected grows more light
And poverty looks cheerful in thy sight;
Thou mak'st the gloomy face of nature gay,
Giv'st beauty to the sun, and pleasure to the day.

Alexander Pope, of the Eighteenth Century, a writer who two generations later influenced the style of Phillis Wheatley,[21] wrote in 1736 all but in the spirit of an abolitionist:[22]

Oh stretch thy reign, fair Peace! from shore to shore
'Till conquest cease, and slav'ry be no more;
'Til the freed Indians in their native groves
Reap their own fruits, and woo their sable loves.

James Thomson in "The Seasons: Summer" published in the eighteenth century, inquires:[23]

[21]Phillis Wheatley, the Negro woman poet, was taken to England in 1773, and introduced to Lady Huntington, Lord Dartmouth, and others. She had been captured on the West African Coast and taken to Boston, Massachusetts, when about seven years old. She had been purchased by John Wheatley in whose household she was the personal attendant on Mrs. Wheatley. She soon began to study Latin and to write poetry. On her return from England she married a Negro named Peters. Her poems were printed in 1787 by Joseph James, in Philadelphia.

[22]*Complete Works of Alexander Pope*, Vol. I, page 408.

[23]James Thomson's *Poetical Works*, Vol. I (1866), p. 70.

But what avails
Her (Africa's) odorous woods, and shining ivory shores?
Ill-fated race! the softening arts of peace,
Whate'er the humanizing Muses teach.
The godlike wisdom of the tempered breast;
Progressive truth, the patent force of thought;
Investigation calm, whose silent powers
Command the world; the light that leads to Heaven;
Kind equal rule, the government of laws,
And all-protecting freedom, which alone
Sustains the name and dignity of man:
These are not theirs. The parent sun himself
Seems o'er this world of slaves to tyrannize; . . .

William Cowper, a man of a decidedly religious bent, could not like slavery. In many of his writings, then, he made some reference to freedom, liberty, or the right of all men to enjoy this natural boon. On one occasion he wrote:[24]

'Tis liberty alone that gives the flower
Of fleeting life its luster and perfume;
And we are weeds without it.

Thinking at the same time of the large masses of people then being transported from their own land to be denied life, liberty, and the pursuit of happiness, and to be brutalized thereby, Cowper said:[25]

No, Freedom has a thousand charms to show,
That slaves, how'er contented, never know.[26]

To grasp the real spirit of Cowper one should read his poems in their entirety. Cowper did not think of the plight of the Negro merely occasionally as did some others herein mentioned.[27] In the poem, "The Time-Piece," we find him taking the same high stand for freedom in saying:[28]

[24] "The Winter Morning Walk," 446.
[25] Table Talk, 260.
[26] He was in sympathy with the slave. Without connecting this thought with the rest of the poem the author may not be understood.
[27] See "The Time-Piece."
[28] The Task: Book II, "The Time-Piece."

My soul is sick with every day's report
Of wrong and outrage with which earth is filled.
There is no flesh in man's obdurate heart,
It does not feel for man; the natural bond
Of brotherhood is severed as the flax
That falls asunder at the touch of fire.
He finds his fellow guilty of a skin
Not coloured like his own and, having power
To enforce the wrong, for such a worthy cause
Dooms and devotes him as his lawful prey

. . . .

I would not have a slave to till the ground,
To carry me, to fan me while I sleep.
And tremble when I wake, for all the wealth
That sinews bought and sold have ever earned.

. . . .

We have no slaves at home—then why abroad?

Cowper exults exceedingly, too, over the significant decision of Lord Mansfield in an opinion respecting the petition filed by Granville Sharp in behalf of the slave Somerset.[29]

Slaves cannot breathe in England; if their lungs
Receive our air, that moment they are free:
They touch our country and their shackles fall.

In "Charity" Cowper writes further of the loathsome traffic:[30]

The sable warrior, frantic with regret
Of her he loves and never can forget
Loses in tears the far receding shore,
But not the thought that they must meet no more;
Yes to deep sadness sullenly resigned,
He feels his body's bondage in his mind;
Puts off his generous nature; and, to suit
His manners with his fate, puts on the brute

. . . .

Oh, 'tis a godlike privilege to save,
And he that scorns it is himself a slave.

[29] "The Time-Piece, 40.

[30] J. C. Bailey, *Poems of William Cowper*, 1906.

Believing with Shakespeare that the slaves themselves had a weapon with which to right their wrongs, Cowper said:[31]

> But slaves that once conceive the glowing thought
> Of freedom, in that hope itself possess
> All that the contest calls for; spirit, strength,
> The scorn of danger, and united hearts,
> The surest presage of the good they seek.

Significant among these expressions of thought respecting slavery was Shelley's excellent tribute to freedom in his "Mask of Anarchy:"

> What art thou Freedom? Oh! could slaves
> Answer from their living graves
> This demand—tyrants would flee
> Like a dream's dim imagery:
>
> Thou art Justice—ne'er for gold
> May thy righteous laws be sold,
> As laws are in England—thou
> Shield'st alike high and low.
>
> Thou art Peace—never by thee
> Would blood and treasure wasted be
> As tyrants wasted them, when all
> Leagued to quench thy flame in Gaul!
>
> Thou art love—the rich have kist
> Thy feet, and like him following Christ
> Gave their substance to be free
> And through the rough world followed thee.

Notice must be taken, too, of what Shelley said on this wise in the following lines from his poem entitled "Laon and Cythna," expressing his impatience with "all the oppressions which are done under the sun:"

> Thus, Cythna mourned, with me the servitude
> In which the half of human kind were mewed
> Victims of lust and hate, the slaves of slaves,
> She mourned that grace and power were thrown as food
> To thy hyaena lust, who, among graves,
> Over his loathed meal, laughing in agony, raves.

[31]Winter Morning Walk, 374.

In the treatment of many of the poets giving thought to the Negro during the eighteenth and nineteenth centuries it is evident from the very tone of their productions that they are more deeply concerned than those of former years. The number of such writers during these years so greatly increased as to give rise to what is known as abolition literature. These writers, however, were distinguished in England as abolitionists who believed in the prohibition of the slave trade and emancipationists who were endeavoring to liberate the slaves. Most of such writings had a social and political rather than a literary effect. Only those of some literary merit can be herein considered.

Among the reformers resorting to such writing should be mentioned the poets who figured in the circle of the anti-slavery workers in Liverpool which at one time bought and sold annually 27,000 slaves, five-eighths of the English slave trade, and three-sevenths of all that of Europe. The Liverpool writers inveighing against the traffic were Edward Rushton with his *West Indian Eclogues* (1787), William Roscoe with *Mount Pleasant* (1777), and *The Wrongs of Africa* (1787), and Dr. James Currie and W. Roscoe with *The African* (1788).[32] To this circle belong also the writers of verse cooperating with Clarkson, Wilberforce, Zachary Macaulay, Granville Sharp, Lushington, and Buxton, as already pointed out by such writers as Pittman, Klingberg, Mathieson, and Wesley. It should be noted, moreover, that in 1806 was published *Africa Delivered; or the Slave Trade Abolished,* by Grahame, occasioned by the legal prohibition of the traffic. There appeared in 1809 *Poems on the Abolition of the Slave Trade,* by James Montgomery, dedicated to His Royal Highness, the Duke of Gloucester, Patron, and to the Director and Governors of the So-

[32] *The Journal of Negro History,* Volume XIII, page 265-285.

ciety for Bettering the Condition of the Natives ot Africa.

What Byron had to say about freedom should not be minimized in any treatment of the development of the English toward democracy. In several of his best poems the frequent allusions thereto indicate this noble sentiment. While few oppressed Negroes were sufficiently enlightened at that time to appreciate this beautiful thought, the friends of their cause must have been heartened by his words on liberty.

> The wish—which ages have not yet subdued
> In man—to have no master save his mood.

Growing still more poetic, Byron thus clarified the picture of liberty:[33]

> Eternal Spirit of the chainless Mind!
>   Brightest in dungeons, Liberty! thou art,
>   For there thy habitation is the heart—
> The Heart which love of thee alone can bind;
> And when thy sons to fetters are consign'd—
>   To fetters, and the damp vault's dayless gloom,
>   Their country conquers with their martyrdom,
> And Freedom's fame finds wings on every wind.

Considering slavery a curse to the enslaver as well as to the enslaved, Byron prophesies the degradation of the oppressor in these words:[34]

> The hearts within thy valleys bred,
> The fiery souls that might have led
> Thy sons to deeds sublime,
> Now crawl from cradle to the grave,
> Slaves—nay, the bondsmen of a slave,
> And callous, save to crime.

The horrors of the system and its debasing effects have never been more succinctly set forth than in these few lines from Canto V of Byron's *Don Juan*:

[33]In the "Sonnet on Chillon."
[34]From the "Giaour."

> A crowd of shivering slaves of every nation,
> And age, and sex, were in the market rang'd;
> Each bevy with the merchant in his station:
> Poor creatures! their good looks were sadly chang'd:
> All save the blacks seem'd jaded with vexation,
> From friends, and home, and freedom far estrang'd;
> The Negroes more philosophy displayed,—
> Used to it, no doubt, as eels are to be flayed.

Byron, like most opponents of the slave system, looked to the bondmen themselves for some means of deliverance, or he believed that the disastrous effects of the institution on society would defeat its own purpose and work its own abolition.[35] He said:

> They never fail who die
> In a great cause: the block may soak their gore,
> Their heads may sodden in the sun; their limbs
> Be strung to city gates and castle walls;—
> But still their spirit walks abroad. Though years
> Elapse, and others share as dark a doom,
> They but augment the deep and sweeping thoughts
> Which overpower all others, and conduct
> The world at last to freedom.

Expanding the thought further in most familiar lines which have become popular throughout the English-speaking world, he says:

> For Freedom's battle once begun,
> Bequeath'd by bleeding sire to son,
> Though baffled oft is ever won.[36]

In cryptic fashion this thought of Thomas Hood, likewise concerned with humanity, is expressed in his "Black Job:"[37]

We've scrubbed the Negroes till we've nearly killed 'em,
And finding that we cannot wash them white,
But still their nigritude offends the sight,
We mean to gild 'em.

[35]From "Marino Faliero," Act II, scene ii.

[36]From the "Giaour."

[37]This is the conclusion of the poem.

In a most sympathetic fashion Charles Lamb approached the thought of the plight of the Negro in these lines:

In the Negro countenance you will often meet with strong traits of benignity. I have felt yearnings of tenderness towards some of these faces, or rather masks, that have looked out kindly upon one in casual encounters in the streets and highways.

William Wordsworth's belief in justice and fair play impelled him to express himself in behalf of the Negro. Among his sonnets dedicated to liberty and order is the following to Toussaint Louverture:[38]

Toussaint, the most unhappy man of men!
Whether the whistling Rustic bend his plough
Within thy hearing, or thy head be now
Pillowed in some deep dungeon's earless den;—
O miserable Chieftain! where and when
Wilt thou find patience! Yet die not; do thou
Wear rather in thy bonds a cheerful brow:
Though fallen thyself, never to rise again,
Live, and take comfort. Thou hast left behind
Powers that will work for thee; air, earth, and skies;
There's not a breathing of the common wind
That will forget thee; thou has great allies;
Thy friends are exultations, agonies,
And love, and man's unconquerable mind.

"Among the capricious acts of tyranny that disgraced these times," he said a little later, "was the chasing of all Negroes from France by decree of the government; we had a fellow-passenger who was one of the expelled."

We had a female passenger who came
From Calais with us, brilliant in array—
A Negro Woman, like a lady gay,
Yet downscast as a Woman fearing blame;
Meek, destitute, as seemed, of hope or aim
She sate, from notice turning not away,
But on all proffered intercourse did lay
A weight of languid speech, or at the same
Was silent, motionless in eyes and face:
Meanwhile those eyes retained their tropic fire,
Which, burning independent of the mind,

[38]Woodsworth's *Works*, "Toussaint Louverture."

> Joined with the lustre of her rich attire
> To mock the outcast—O ye Heavens, be kind!
> And feel, thou Earth, for this afflicted Race!

In 1843 Miss Barrett (Elizabeth Barrett Browning, 1806-61) took up the theme of humanity in the "Cry of the Children," suggested by the report of the commission appointed to investigate the subject of the employment of young children. "Do ye Hear the Children Weeping, O My Brothers" was first printed in *Blackwood's Magazine,* August, 1843. She was profoundly moved by the agitation for freedom.

In her letter to H. S. Boyd, December 21, 1846, she says, "I have just finished my anti-slavery poem for America, too ferocious, perhaps for the Americans to publish." To Miss Milford, February 8, she wrote, "I have just finished my anti-slavery ballad and sent it off to America, where nobody will print it, I am certain, because I could not help making it bitter."[39] In a collection in 1850 she published "The Runaway Slave at Pilgrim's Point."[40]

In "The Inn Album" by Robert Browning, Mrs. Browning's husband, there is a reference to the status of the Negro.

> Every lover knows
> Love may use hate but—turn to hate, itself—
> Turn even to indifference—no, indeed!
> Well, I have been spell-bound, deluded like
> The witless Negro by the Obeah-man
> Who bids him wither: So, his eye grows dim,
> His arm slack, arrow misses aim and spear
> Goes wondering wide,—and all the woe because
> He proved untrue to Fetish, who, he finds,
> Was just a feather phantom!

In "Luria," a poem tragedy, published in 1846, Browning shows further his interest in the lowly. Luria, an

[39]For a further discussion of the attitude of Elizabeth Barrett Browning consult Benjamin Brawley's "Elizabeth Barrett Browning and the Negro" in the *Journal of Negro History,* Vol. III, pages 22-28.

[40]Poems by Elizabeth Barrett Browning, 2nd edition, 1850, Vol. II.

heroic Moor, hired commander of the Florentine forces, is trusted by his troops, but feared by the Signory for his popularity who in their arrogance, plot to overthrow him when he shall have achieved victory. The Pisan commander, Tiburzio, brings Luria an intercepted letter to the Signory from Braccio, who has been set to spy upon Luria. Luria, the soul of loyalty, refuses to read it. He is overcome with indignation when he learns of the plot against him in his hour of victory; and he is deeply wounded at the behaviour of Domizia, a noble Florentine Lady, who has also been acting as a spy. Although he has Florence and Pisa at his mercy, he refuses to take advantage of his strong position and feels that only his disappearance can save the situation; he, therefore, takes poison and dies.

In Act I while he (Luria) speaks of Florence, he turns to it (a Moorish sketch he had made for the front of the unfinished Duomo) as the Magi Negro King to Christ, the babe.

In a discussion as to what action Luria will take when he discovers the treachery, between Florence's old commander, Puccio, appointed to be Luria's Chief Officer, and Jacopo, Braccio's Secretary, Puccio says:

> But Mankind are not pieces—there's your fault!
> You cannot push them, and, the first move made,
> Lean back and study what the next should be.
> In confidence that when 'tis fixed upon,
> You find just where you left them, blacks and whites:
> Men go on moving when your hand's away.

Luria thus reproaches his enemies (Act III; present Piccio, Jacopo, Braccio, and Domizia discussing Luria's trial and what his sentence will be)

>   Now, Florence,
> Is it to be?—You will know all the strength,
> O' the savage—to your neck the proof must go?
> You will prove the brute nature? Ah, I see!
> The savage plainly is impassible—

He keeps his calm way thro insulting words,
Sarcastic looks, sharp gestures—one of which
Would stop you, fatal to your finer sense:
But if he steadily advanced, march mute
Without a mark upon his callous hide,
Thro' the mere brushwood you grow angry with
And leave the tatters of your flesh upon,
—You have to learn that when the true bar comes,
The murk mid-forest, the grand obstacle,
Which when you reach, you give the labour up,
Nor dash on, but lie down composed before,
—He goes against it, like the brute he is!
It falls before him, or he dies in his course!
I kept my course thro' past ingratitude—
I saw—it does seem, now, as if I saw,
Could not but see, those insults as they fell,

.   .   .   .

       While you so despised
The Moor's dull mute inapprehensive mood,
Was saving you; . . . .

(To Domizia) You Lady,—You have black Italian Eyes!
I would be generous if—I might: Oh, yes —
For I remember how so oft you seemed
Inclined at heart to break the barrier down
Which Florence makes God build between us both

.   .   .   .

(Luria alone) . . . Ah, we Moors get blind
Out of our proper world where we can see!
The sun that guides is closer to us! There—
There, my own orb! He sinks from out the sky.
Why, there! a whole day has he blessed the land,
My land, our Florence all about the hills,
The fields and gardens, vineyards, olive-grounds,
All have been blest —

       - - -

(Luria takes a phial from his breast)

Strange! This is all I brought from my own Land
To help me: Europe would supply the rest,
All needs beside, all other helps save one!

.   .   .   .

              Florence
Is saved: I drink this, and ere night,—die! Strange!

In Act V Luria interviews separately—first those who have
been his friends, then Domizia, all of whom not knowing he has

taken poison come to acknowledge his great merits, some to beg
him to escape from his sentence, others to implore him to continue
his leadership in spite of the Signory.

Luria says to Domizia who has been blaming herself for her
mean behaviour:

> Speak not against your nature: best, each keep
> His own—you, yours—most, now, that I keep mine,
> —At least, fall by it, having too weakly stood.
> God's finger marks distinctions, all so fine,
> We would confound: the Lesser has its use,
> Which, when it apes the greater, is foregone.
> I, born a Moor, lived half a Florentine;
> But, punished properly, can end a Moor.[41]

In the poem, "The Ring and Book," the Negro appears
again in stating the case against Pompilia and taking
into account the excuses that would be made by her
friends[42]

> —Because fools are sure
> —Oh, not of my wife nor your daughter! No!
> But of their own: the case is altered quite,
> Look now,—last week, the lady we all love,—
> Daughter o' the couple we all venerate,
> Wife of the husband we all cap before,
> Mother o' the babes we all breathe blessings on,—
> Was caught in converse with a Negro page
> Hell thawed that icicle, . . .

This murder story of Rome in 1698 is told ten times
over. Count Guido Franceschini, impoverished nobleman
of Arezzo marries Pompilia Comparini whom he im-
agines to be very wealthy. When he discovers that she
is not even the daughter of Violante Comparini but adopted so as to defraud Comparini's rightful heirs he accuses
her of infidelity and persecutes her until she persuades
the man suspected of being her lover (the priest Capon-
sacchi) to take her away to her old home. Guido follows
in pursuit and has them arrested. Pompilia when tried
declares her innocence and is sent to a convent which she

[41]Robert Browning's *Works*, Vol. III, 1912.
[42]Robert Browning, "The Ring and the Book," a poem published in 1869
"Was caught in converse with a Negro" (717-34; 4, 870).

leaves for home when about to become a mother. Guido and four ruffians murder her and her supposed parents one night. Guido is arrested, tried, and executed on the Pope's final decision. Book IV gives the gossip of the aristocracy about the case, with its excuses for and condemnation of both parties.

In Prose

The African and his continent as a result of the role that his land had begun to play became an object of treatment in nineteenth century prose as well as of poetry. Not much actual literary material in prose appeared during the seventeenth or eighteenth centuries. The most striking productions of the earlier period have already been mentioned above in connection with the legends, dramas, and poems. The discussion of the styleless propaganda productions has been given attention by other writers as noted above; and such an effort does not come within the compass of the task herein undertaken.

One significant fact not yet herein noted is that in 1720 Daniel Defoe (C. 1659-1731) wrote in plain, straightforward narrative the *Life and Adventures and Piracies of the Famous Captain Singleton*. The hero kidnapped and sold to gypsies, heads a band of mutineers, crosses Africa from Madagascar and becomes a successful pirate. The descriptive part is based upon authentic tales of travellers. The book aroused much interest in Africa rather than in the natives. Two years later Defoe published *Colonial Jack,* one character of which was a devoted slave. In this work the author advocated a better treatment of Negroes just as fearlessly as he had attacked the slave trade in *The Reformation of Manners.*

Still more significant were the *Letters of Horace Walpole,* which showed that few prominent English dared to brave the stigma of advocating the unpopular cause. In a letter to Horace Mann, February 25, 1750, he said, "We have been sitting this fortnight on the African Company: we, the British Senate, that temple of liberty and bulwark of Protestant Christianity, have this fortnight been pondering methods to make more effectual that horrid traffic of selling Negroes. It has appeared to us that six and forty thousand of these wretches are sold every year to our plantations alone!—it chills one's blood. I would not have to say that I voted in it for the continent of America! The destruction of the miserable inhabitants by the Spaniards was but a momentary misfortune, that flowed from the discovery of the New World, compared to this lasting havoc which it brought upon Africa. We reproach Spain, and yet do not even pretend the nonsense of butchering these poor creatures for the good of their souls!"[43]

To Richard Bentley, July 9, 1754, Walpole said further, "I was reading t'other day the Life of Colonel Codrington (Colonel Christopher Codrington, 1668-1710), who founded the library at All Souls: he left a large estate for the propagation of the Gospel, and ordered that three hundred Negroes should constantly be employed upon it. Did one ever hear a more truly Christian charity, than keeping up a perpetuity of three hundred slaves to look after the Gospel's estate? How could one intend a religious legacy, and miss the disposition of that estate for delivering three hundred Negroes from the most shocking slavery imaginable? Must devotion be twisted into the unfeeling interests of trade?"

Writing Sir Horace Mann, December 22, 1772, Walpole said, "Would you believe, I read that epithet (disaffected) the other day in a Portuguese relation of a mutiny among their Negroes in the Brazils. Hacked, hewed, maimed, tortured, worked to death, poor Africans do not *love*

[43]*The Letters of Horace Walpole, Fourth Earl of Oxford, 1903,* Volume II, 1743, pages 432-433.

their masters! Oh, Tyranny, thy name should henceforth be Impudence! . . . .''

To the Reverend William Mason, February 14, 1774, after mention of the rupture with America, he said, ''If all the black slaves were in rebellion, I should have no doubt in choosing my side, but I scarce wish perfect freedom to merchants who are the bloodiest of all tyrants.[44] I should think the souls of the Africans would sit heavy on the swords of the Americans.[45] . . . .''

To Miss Hannah More, in September, 1789, he added, ''I can administer some comfort to you about your poor Negroes. I do not imagine that they will be emancipated at once; but their fate will be much alleviated, as the attempt will have alarmed their butchers enough to make them gentler, like the European monarchs, for fear of provoking the disinterested, *who have no sugar plantations,* to abolish the horrid traffic.''[46]

Addressing her again, November 4, 1789, he said, ''You rejoice *me,* not my vanity, by telling me my idea of a mechanic succedaneum to the labour of Negroes is not visionary, but thought practicable [in his former letter H. W. wished that some system of machinery could be introduced whereby the heavy labour of the Negroes might be lightened]. Oh, how I wish I understood sugar and ploughs, and could marry them! Alas! I understand nothing useful. My head is as un-mechanic, as it is un-arithmetic, un-geometric, un-metaphysic, un-commercial: but will not some one of those superior heads to whom you have talked on my indigested hint reduce it to practicability? How a feasible scheme would stun those who call humanity romantic, and show, from the books of the Custom House, that murder is a great improvement of the revenue! Even the present situation of France is

[44]*The Letters of Horace Walpole,* Volume III, page 249.
[45]*Ibid.,* Volume III, page 423.
[46]*Ibid.,* Volume VIII, page 209.

favourable. Could not Mr. Wilberforce obtain to have
the enfranchisement of the Negroes started there? The
Jews are claiming their natural rights there; and blacks
are certainly not so great defaulters as the Hebrews,
though they too have undergone ample persecutions.''[47]

Writing to Miss Mary Berry, April 23, 1791, he observed, ''The abolition of the slave trade has been rejected by the House of Commons, though Mr. Pitt and
Mr. Fox united earnestly to carry it; but commerce
chinked its purse, and that sound is generally prevalent
with the majority; and humanity's tears and eloquence's
figures and arguments had no more effect than on those
patrons of liberty, the National Assembly in France;
who while they proclaim the rights of men did not choose
to admit the sable society of mankind to a participation
of those benefits.''[48]

Refusing to read Deborah Barbauld's verses, Walpole
wrote Hannah More, September 29, 1791, ''No, my good
friend: Deborah may cant rhymes of compassion, but she
is a hypocrite; and you shall not make me read her, nor
with all your sympathy and candour, can you esteem her.
Your compassion for the poor blacks is genuine, sincere
from your soul, most amiable; hers a measure of fashion.
Her party supported the abolition, and regretted the disappointment as a blow to the good cause. I know this. Do
not let your piety lead you into the weakness of respecting
the bad, only because they hoist the flag of religion, while
they carry a stiletto in the flag-staff.''[49]

George Cumberland attracted thus some attention in
publishing in 1798 *The Captive of the Castle of Sennaar*,
an African tale containing various anecdotes of the So-
phians hitherto unknown to mankind. An African Negro,
a Caafra, accompanies Lycas and the Jew, who had

[47] *The Letters of Horace Walpole*, Volume VIII, page 229.
[48] *Ibid.*, Volume VIII, page 418.
[49] *The Letters of Horace Walpole*, Volume XV, page 72.

adopted him, to the island of Sophis in the upper end of the Lake of Zamtree, the Jew dying on the way. Sophis was described as a wonderful place where the inhabitants are "the very happiest, the most beautiful, and the best people on earth." Wearing the scantiest clothing they are without gold, without commerce, and without war. They reach the delightful spot and, after some misunderstandings, are finally admitted as residents, and Lycas marries Mica, a most attractive girl of Sophis. After many happy years Mica and the two boys were drowned; and Lycas, inconsolable, left Sophis and returned to Sennaar, where he showed his zeal for preaching and teaching the people the love of our fellow creatures whether men or beasts. On his way to Sennaar tribes of wandering black people entertained him with kindness and hospitality, but at Sennaar he excited the jealousy of the cruel rulers; and Lycas, who persisted in carrying on his good work, was imprisoned in an isolated tower of a fortress for the rest of his days. Lycas tells the story of his life to another prisoner whom he seeks to console.

In 1826 appeared *The Negro Servant* in *The Annals of the Poor,* by the Rev. Legh Richmond, Chaplain to His Royal Highness the Duchess of Kent. This very popular story of the beginning of the nineteenth century, the first issue of which appeared in 1805, was translated into many languages including Dutch and Russian. Written before the abolition of the slave trade, it tells of the conversion to Christianity of a young African who had been kidnapped as a child and sold to a planter in Jamaica. After four years he entered the service of a Captain in the Navy who gave him his liberty. He travelled with the Captain and his family to America where he became a Christian, and afterwards came to England where he was baptized.

The author of *The Negro Servant* did not make a deep impression with the narrative of a young Negro in 1820; nor did W. Naish in 1830 with *The Negro Slave,* a tale addressed to the women of Great Britain. Doubtless those who might have been moved by the story were too far removed from contact with large numbers of Negroes; and those who personally profited by such connections beyond the shores of England paid little attention to this work. Yet England abolished slavery in 1833.

Harriet Martineau became the chief actor in this sphere in 1840 in publishing *The Hour and the Man,* an historical romance which may be compared with *Uncle Tom's Cabin.* The hero is Toussaint Louverture and the time and place the revolution (1791-1803) which he headed in Hayti, then known as St. Domingo. The sympathies of the author were deeply aroused by the struggle for freedom of the unfortunate mulattoes. Negroes, hearing much of the liberty brought in by the French Revolution, expected a share in the new civil rights; and her indignation at Napoleon's duplicity can easily be imagined. A Negro who could attempt a system of social and political government which she considered the ideal one could not fail to command her whole-hearted admiration. The tragedy of the book resides in the fact that Louverture loves and reveres the whites as if they were his friends; and this causes many of the blacks to turn against him though they believe and trust in their leader. The great betrayal is that of Napoleon who expresses a real and earnest friendship for the natives of St. Domingo.

The second volume of Martineau's *Society in America* (1837) is devoted to the Negro slave in the United States, the institution of slavery and the efforts genuine and otherwise to alter the state of things. She describes the objects of the Colonization Society founded to establish "free persons of colour" on the shores of Africa but points out that no leading member of the society had freed any of his slaves, and that its advocate in the South objected to abolition. The author observed, too, that the prohibition of books containing anything against slavery had proceeded to a great length. Mrs. Barbauld's works were sent back into the North by the Southern book-sellers, because the *Evenings at Home* contained a "Dialogue between Master and Slave." Miss Sedgwick's last novel, *The Linwoods,* was treated in the same way, on account of a single sentence about slavery. The *Tales from Woods and Fields,* and other English books, had shared the same fate.[50]

The reading public of Great Britain apparently paid little attention to some other minor works of this period. Edwin Selwyn's *Negro Boy,* published in 1826, did not find a large audience. We hear very little of Edwin L. Sabin's *Rio Bravo,* a romance of the Texas dealing with the slavery question in connection with the Mexican War. Such evidently was the reception given Mrs. William Noy's *The Slave Son,* which appeared in 1854. The people of that country had to be thus moved by those who were nearer to the scenes of plantations and colonial mansions. The English public had changed considerably in this respect since the emancipation in the West Indies had been finally carried out. The problem to some of the people had become a foreign question.

The Negro is projected also on the screen in *Vanity Fair,* by W. M. Thackeray. This novel without a hero is too well-known to require any thing approaching a detailed resumée. We are only concerned with the appearance of the wealthy West Indian heiress, a mulatto, so enthusiastically received by the Misses Osborne who were anxious to see their brother married to Miss Swartz. Old Osborne too went out of his way to be amiable to the heiress though he treated with arrogance Amelia Sedley, the daughter of his old friend, John Sedley, who had recently lost all his money. A heated interview on the subject of the marriage ends in George Osborne's being

[50]Harriet Martineau, *Society in America,* Vol. II, pages 109, 111 and 137.

turned out of his home, and shortly afterwards marrying the gentle, well-loved Amelia. Miss Swartz's appearance is a brief one. She is a friendly, naive, undeveloped character.

In "Shooting Niagara" and "After 1867," (*Critical and Miscellaneous Essays,* Volume V, 1899) Carlyle holds forth against democracy in general, the Negro Emancipation in particular, and the hypocrisy of the times; in "The Nigger Question"[51] Carlyle compares the conditions under which the West-Indian Negroes live with that of the British whites. He questions the policy of introducing more blacks as a remedy for the labour shortage; and, in general, he finds fault with the poor attempts at righting the wrongs from which both blacks and whites are suffering, adding that the man who will not work according to his ability has no right either to food or land. Carlyle asks "Do I, then, hate the Negro? No, except when the soul is killed out of him. I decidedly like poor Quashee; and find him a pretty kind of man. . . I understand well your rage against the poor Negro's slavery; what said rage proceeds from; and have a perfect sympathy with it, and even know it by experience." He also is capable "of flying out into fiery wrath against oppression"; but Carlyle points out that hardship, oppression, and injustice are not unknown in the world, that we all suffer. "It is said, man of whatever colour, is born to such, even as the sparks fly upward. . ." "My friends, I have come to the sad conclusion that *Slavery,* whether established by law, or by law abrogated, exists very extensively in this world, in and out of the West Indies; and, in fact, that you cannot abolish slavery by act of parliament, but can only abolish the *name* of it, which is very little."[52]

[51]Precursor to *Latter-Day Pamphlets,* 1849, Crit. and Misc. Essays, Vol. IV, 1899. First printed in *Fraser's Magazine,* December, 1849.

[52]Carlyle, *Works,* pp. 357, 358, 359.

In the later pages Carlyle tries to find remedies, such as a fixed legal sum in every state, on paying which, any black man may be entitled to demand his freedom. Settle a fair sum; and let it stand fixed by law.[53] If the poor black can, by forethought, industry, self-denial, accumulate this sum, has he not proved the actual *freedom* of his soul, to a fair extent: in God's name, why will you keep his body captive?" "This new question has arisen, milion-voiced: What *are* the wages of black servant, hired by life by white men? This question must be answered, in some not insupportably erroneous way—gods and men are warning you that you must answer it. . . ."

"It often happens," says Carlyle elsewhere, "that the slave himself has neither the power nor the wish to be free. He is then brutified; but this apathy is the dire effect of slavery, and so far from being a justifying clause, that it contains the grounds of its bitterest condemnation. The Carlovingian race bred up the Merovingi as beasts; and then assigned their unworthiness as the satisfactory reason for their dethronement. Alas! the human being is more easily weaned from the habit of commanding than from that of abject obedience . . . As we, . . . or

[53] There has been considerable correspondence recently about Carlyle's approval of the policy of Governor Eyre, probably due to Sidney Ollivier's book on the subject. Ollivier is definitely critical of Eyre's method of handling the Negroes. The behaviour of the Governor of Jamaica, Edward John Eyre, during the native rising at St. Thomas comes in for a scathing indictment. The author, a distinguished public servant, has gone thoroughly into the subject, dealing with errors in a recent official Jamaican publication wherein the local uprising is described as a serious insurrection of the peasantry; he claims that George William Gordon, the leader, the illegitimate half-caste son of a Government official, was a good man and a saint upon earth, a loyal subject of the Queen, and a true friend to his humble brethren.

The account of this hideous page in our colonial history shows to what lengths man will go under the influence of panic fear, for Eyre had been successful as an explorer in the Australian wilds, and "his exceptional kindness, combined with firmness, towards the aborigines," was generally acknowledged. See *The Myth of Governor Eyre*, by Lord Ollivier, 1933.

our ancestors must have inoculated our fellow-creature with this wasting disease of the soul, it becomes our duty to cure him. . ."[54]

The discussion is renewed in *Black Ivory, a Tale of Adventure Among the Slaves of East Africa,* by R. M. Ballantyne, 1873. This work gives a picture of the slave-trade on the East Coast of Africa based on trustworthy sources, including Parliamentary Blue Books. It is an effort to interest the young in the total abolition of the African Slave Trade. The hero of the story is the young son of a London merchant who sails as supercargo in a brig chartered by his father to carry beads, cotton, cloth, and brass wire to Zanzibar. With the man-at-the-wheel he escapes from the wreck off the east coast of Africa where they meet with an African slave trader, Yoosoof, who decides to take the two Englishmen with him so as to prevent the possibility of their falling in with any of the crew of a British cruiser searching for slave-raiders. After hair-breadth escapes, cruelty on the part of Yoosoof, and Marizano, the villian, Harold, the hero, Disco, the man at the wheel, and Lieutenant Lindsay, of the cruiser, found a colony at the Cape where certain slaves they have freed settle down with them as domestic servants. According to Disco there's only one way to cure the trade, namely, by bringing "the Portuguese and Arabs to their marrow-bones; put the fleet on the East Coast in better working order; have consuls everywhere; start two or three British settlements—ports o'refuge—on the mainland; . . ."

For a short while public attention was directed to *The Reverend John Creedy,* by Grant Allen. This work first appeared in the *Cornhill Magazine* (Vol. 48, in 1884), published in a collection of "Strange Stories" in 1889 included in "Twelve Tales." In the preface to "Strange Stories" Grant Allen states that *The Reverend John*

[54]Carlyle, *op. cit.,* "Omniana"—"The Vices of Slavery," *Essays.*

Creedy is a study from within of a singular persistence of hereditary character, well-known to all students of modern anthropological papers and reports. Members of barbarous or savage races, trained for a time in civilized habits, are liable at any moment to revert naturally to their primitive condition, especially under the contagious influence of companionship with persons of their own blood, and close subjection to the ancestral circumstances. The tale which I have based upon several historical instances in real life endeavours briefly to hint at the modes of feeling likely to accompany such a relapse into barbarism in an essentially fine and sensitive savage nature . . . those who know intimately the whole gamut of the intensely impressionable African mind will be able to treat its temptations and its tendencies . . . sympathetically.''

A review of the collection in the *Athenaeum,* December, 1884, does not approve; it says, ''The author might be thought to be doing the utmost violence to Exeter Hall by representing a converted Negro turned missionary as a ridiculous manufacture; but when in the midst of his ministration he suddenly breaks out into all the savagery of race, he is only ''a study from within of a singular persistence.''

John Creedy, educated at Oxford before going out to Africa as a missionary, stays for two months at the vicarage of Walton Magna where he falls in love with a charming, simple English girl whom he marries. After about a year's happiness at the little mission bungalow at Butabué John Creedy began to feel—at first dimly—the call of his earliest recollections which suddenly dominated him at the sound of the tom-toms at the harvest battle-feast. This was only a temporary moment of excitement; he was recalled to his present ideas and views by his wife. He begged for forgiveness which was readily granted, but later on she came home one evening from

her girls' school to find John absent and his black coat
and European clothing torn to shreds in the bedroom.
Staggering down the street, she heard the noise of shouts
and laughter and a group of natives dancing round a Negro in native dress, shaking a tom-tom and singing a
Fantee song. This person she discovered to be her husband. As soon as John Creedy saw his wife—to whom
he was devoted—standing on the fringe of the gathering,
like a marble figure, he came to himself, picked her up
and carried her home, saying, "She has the fever." "Sit
by her," to the wife of the catechist; and he then started
off 30 miles through the jungle to the nearest mission station at Effuenta. Arrived there, he said that Missionary
John Creedy wanted European clothes as the Butabué
people had stolen his. With his bundle he returned to
Butabué, stopping outside the village to dress himself in
English clerical dress. A short time after his return,
Ethel, seriously ill with yellow fever, regained consciousness. Her first question was where had the clothes come
from, and he reminded her that they had come from
Oxford at which "she gave a great cry of joy. Then it
was a dream, a horrid dream, John, or a terrible mistake?" To which John replied he did not know what she
meant. Satisfied, Ethel said, "It is all well. I don't mind
if I die now." And the catechist's wife warns him that
he will have to answer for the lie to a dying woman with
his soul. Ethel lingered on for five days and just before
her death John again swears that the whole terrible incident was only her delirium. The next morning, after
digging a grave and fashioning a rough coffin without
any help—for no one was to touch his well-loved wife but
himself—he read for the first and last time the Anglican
Burial Service, after which he returned to his desolate
hut and in a despairing voice said, "The one thing that
bound me to civilization is gone. Henceforth I shall never
speak another word of English. I go to my own people."

Then, once again, tearing up his European clothes and, arraying himself in native fashion, he fasted and wailed piteously, like a broken-hearted child.

This work is referred to as a tragic study of the racial question, according to Baker's *Guide to the Best Fiction*. This is an extremely painful example of the subject though not more so than *In the Shadow*. Evidently it served as a blow to the evangelization of the natives and at the same time as propaganda against race admixture. The increasing race prejudice in England may be partly accounted for by such productions.

John Buchan, the heir of the romantic school which derives from Walter Scott and Robert Louis Stevenson, moved the world in 1910 with *Prester John*. This is one of the most stirring books written about a rising of the blacks in South Africa. It is told with a comprehension of their yearnings for mastership in what is their own country and an attempt (doomed to failure) to revive their old empire under the leadership of one John Laputa who announces that he is the Umkulunkulu, the incarnated spirit of the mysterious "Prester John." His motto was "Africa for Africans." The scenery is admirably described, and the escapes and adventures among the mountains and caves of the Berg are compact of terror. Laputa is a somewhat sinister figure in his combination of Christian missionary warring with his natural instinct; but as Arcoll, one of the whites, says, "If he had been white he might have been a second Napoleon. He is a born leader of men, and as brave as a lion. There is no villainy he would not do if necessary; and yet I should hesitate to call him a blackguard. There's fineness and nobility in him. He would be a terrible enemy, but a just one. He has the heart of a poet and a king, and it is God's curse that he has been born among the children of Ham. I hope to shoot him like a dog in a day or two, but I am glad to bear testimony to his greatness."

Laputa has been described as a real Rider Haggard figure. The villain of the piece is a Portuguese, one Hen-
riques, the chief agent for the conversion of diamonds
(stolen from the mines) into coin with which the blacks
bought guns and ammunition.   There is no feminine interest, "for what have women to do with this 'man's
life'." This book has been translated into French to supply the popular demand.

Black Mary, by Allan MacAulay, (pseudonym of Charlotte Stewart), published in 1901, is the next interesting
production with this theme. It is the story of Perthshire
folk and the half-caste daughter of a ne'er-do-well emigrant to Jamaica. Her life of hardship, danger, and disappointment is nobly borne. She is first introduced into
the Ardwinnoch household at the age of eight, overawed
at the cool reception she meets with from the Laird of
Ardwinnoch, James Hepburn, and his sister Barbara. Her
unexpected appearance and the letters she brings from his
rolling-stone of a brother, Anthony—the spoilt darling and
the trial of the family—and from his friend, the latter an-
nouncing Anthony's death while the former announced
the arrival of his natural daughter, Mary, whom he wished
to be brought up on plain lines as befitted a girl who
would have to work for her living, caused considerable
distress in the quiet country household. James Hepburn,
hard but just, insists on the child being kept under the
roof in spite of his sister's protests. No one, not even
Rachel, the servant, showed the poor orphan the slightest
sign of affection. She heard no words of kindness and
was never indulged in any way. As Rachel refused to
have her in the kitchen, she took her place with—and yet
apart from—her uncle and aunt. The arrival of Robert,
a nephew, aged twelve, brings a complete change to Mary,
for he is a light-hearted, jolly, good-natured boy and takes
Mary fishing. Gradually as the health of Uncle James becomes weaker he leans more and more upon his niece

whom he loves tenderly. Aunt Barbara, although she makes no demonstration, learns to appreciate the gentle, retiring inmate of the household; and even Rachel refrains from her gibes, so that when Anthony's friend from Jamaica suddenly turns up to claim his daughter there is despair in the home; but Caleb Dickinson proves that his claim is correct, and once again Mary sets out on a new and untried life, after a pathetic parting from Uncle James, unwonted kindness from Aunt Barbara, and a basket of food thrust on to Mary's lap by Rachel as the carriage left Ardwinnoch.

After some years in Jamaica, where Mary's presence has a humanising influence on her reckless, drunken father, he dies suddenly on the eve of a Negro rising for which he was largely responsible. Mary is rescued by a young Englishman, Monteith, who decides to send her to England as his affianced bride. He genuinely respects the girl whose large fortune is not without its attraction, and whose father had suggested the match to Monteith an hour or so before his death. Mary finds herself in England in the household of the Duke at Oldenham, where she is made welcome by the Duchess and her six unmarried daughters. Then Mary discovers that long ago the Duke and his son had spent a day at Ardwinnoch, and so understands why Monteith had always seemed in some vague way familiar to her. She hears of the death of both James and Barbara at Ardwinnoch, and that Robert, the present Laird, is obliged to let the property go in spite of every effort on his part to keep it. After hearing this, Mary decides she must go to Ardwinnoch to see if there is still time to save the property for the old friend to whom she has always been devoted—Robert; she explains to these people who have treated her with so much kindness that her place is not amongst them highly as she appreciates all that they have done for her. The Duchess when leaving said, ''You might have been the mother of my grandsons—the mother

of great men!'' And Mary replies that she is not fitted
for that destiny, that there is a taint in her blood deeper
than the mere taint of race and prays that, therefore, she
may never be the mother of children. After much trouble
she finds Robert dying in dingy lodgings in Southampton,
for he had been sent home very ill some time previous and
got no farther than the port. As she had been told by
the Ardwinnoch agent, the wife he had adored had squan-
dered his money and then left him for some one else; and
he had ruined himself so that she might have the divorce
she wished for. Poor Robert (only thirty-two) was not
to see his home again, now his through Mary's generosity,
but there was still work for her to do. Robert's only son
ran straight into her arms when he arrived at Southampton, and there are still Hepburns at Ardwinnoch.

In *No Other Way,* published in 1902 (period 1750-3) the
Negro is presented from a new point of view. This story
may have its origin in the economic hardships of an impoverished people. A Negro is introduced to bear the burden of his wife's debts. She, a woman of fashion, marries
him so as to transfer her liabilities. As he is sentenced
to death she attains her end with the minimum of discomfort. Here the plot is made much more direct than in our
own Willis Richardson's ''House of Sham.''

The novel has served during these years, too, as the
delineator of pioneer work in the wildest parts of Africa.
Harold Bindless introduces the Black Man into several of
his novels—as traders in gum and the like in *Concession
Hunters,* 1902; with its ju-ju sacrifice, *Anslie's Ju Ju,* a
romance of the hinterland, published in 1900. *Beneath
Her Station,* 1906, is a story of the victory of early
associations over a veneer of a civilization alien from
tradition; *The Liberationist,* 1908, deals with the release
of kidnapped slaves. Most of the author's stories are full
of exciting adventure. The hero in *Ainslie's Ju Ju* owes
his escape from serious peril in the hinterland of Lagos,

Nigeria, to the possession of a mystic ju-ju or talisman, which on his return to a farm in Cumberland he flung into a tarn—the charm was over.

In the Shadow, by Henry Cottrell Rowland, in 1906, is another story to attract attention. The first part of this book is placed in England, the scene a pleasant country-house of the Maltbys in which Manning Moultrie, a rice-planter in Carolina, and his sister, Virginia, are guests. Giles Maltby, the son of the house, has a chum at Oxford, a Haytian, whom he much admires to the great disgust of Manning who fails to understand Giles' attitude when he explains that "Dessalines is a gentleman—a much better sort than a good many one meets; besides, he's well-born in his own country. He's a count." Sir Henry Maltby, deeply in sympathy with what is being done for the advancement of the Negro, tries to engage Manning in conversation on the subject; but he, finding the topic distasteful, avoided it. It happens, however, that Dessalines who is staying in the neighbourhood saves Giles and Virginia from drowning when they are caught in the weir. His amazing strength succeeded in tearing away the beam by which they were held. Then he shares the honours with Giles when the two win a hotly contested local cricket match. Virginia, torn between her gratitude to the man who has saved her life and that of her fiancé and the remnants of an hereditary objection to Negroes, asks Dessalines to call on her at his convenience. At tea the following day Dessalines describes Hayti as "a country which promises no safety to life or property, because it is a Negro Republic, and the Negro has not yet learned to govern himself or others." There is much discussion of the Negro mind and an analysis of the Negro character in this book.

The second part takes place in Hayti where Dessalines is expected to head a revolution with the object of being proclaimed Emperor; but when he should have been preparing for action he, in spite of a terrific struggle against native emotional tendencies, is persuaded by the mulatto wife of Dr. Fouchère, a seductress, to assist at the bamboula, an orgy lasting three days. "He is absent when a message comes saying he must strike at once or all is lost."

The third part takes place in Carolina at the Moultrie rice-plantations, where Giles and Virginia are on a short visit to Manning, before their wedding. There is a distressing scene of a Negro hunt, the Negro being Dessalines. Now he reaches Manning's home and is cared for until the hunters arrive, and in spite of all that Giles and Virginia can do, Dessalines is killed, dying in Giles' arms. This is a harrowing tale except for the sanity and freshness introduced in the persons of Virginia, Giles, and Dr. Layden. It seems to have the purpose of so many books of the time, written to discourage even the Negro who has had all the advantages of modern civilization. *Emperor Jones* is an adaptation possible from more than one work.

Interesting, too, is *Multitude and Solitude,* by John Masefield, 1909. The hero, Roger Naldrett, is a dramatist who after the failure of his play and the sudden death by drowning of the woman he loves, decides, in order to justify his existence and show himself worthy of his love, to go with a friend to Africa to fight sleeping-sickness and, if possible, find a cure. His friend has been engaged in medical research and has been out in Uganda in order to study the disease. He says, "I want to get to the bottom of the teypanosome. We don't even know what it is in him which causes the disease; and we don't know very much really about the tsetse, nor what part the tsetse plays in the organism's life. He then describes his experience in a little place called Ikupu, alone with a "sleeping village in all stages of the disease."

These adventurers, as the story goes, experienced terrible mental and physical suffering. His friend, Lionel Heseltine, was on the verge of dissolution, and the natives they have been trying to save by the use of a toxyl were dying like flies, and he himself was showing symptoms of the disease. In desperation, using on both themselves and friends a special animal serum which had not succeeded with the natives they then had under observation, they both recovered sufficiently to leave their deadly quarters. They knew they had discovered a cure for some cases, and cleared some three miles of fly belt, surveyed the whole and excavated a part of the Zimbabwe, and saved the lives of at least four natives; probably more, but the others had decamped as soon as they had sufficient strength. The part dealing with the development of the disease and the natives is remarkably good, and easy reading. On their journey home they meet a German scientist who tells them of the sure remedy discovered by Muhlbauer. The African part of the book contains picturesque descriptions, and the characterization is fine.

Love in Black, by Sir H. Hesketh Bell, attracted some attention about a generation ago. This is a collection of stories mostly written during the author's days of service on the Gold Coast. *Love in Black* itself was suggested to the author by the opening lines of a hymn:

> I thank Thee too . . . .
> That in the darkest spot on earth
> Some love is found.

These were sketches of Negro plot and passion, some of which first appeared in *Macmillan's Magazine, The Idler,* and *The Argosy.*

The tale which gives the title to the book concerns the love of Kwamin Fori, a fine type of West African, for Kusa and her love for George Warren, the young Methodist missionary stationed at a village perched on a spur of the Akwapim Hills. Kusa gets very impatient when Warren tells her of the wife and child he hopes soon to rejoin. The scene changes to the ju-ju house at the edge of the

jungle where the priests decided that the man who has substituted the great fetish of the white men, and influenced
the young men of the town to pass by their own fetish
with contempt on their faces, must die "ere that moon
shall show her horns." Some fever-causing poison must
be administered similar to that given to his Christian
brothers. Shortly after the priests had retired the drum
which served as a gong for entrance to the temple sounded
and Kusa implored to be given a love potion "to make the
white man love me." The old guardian-priest, though exceedingly angry at being disturbed by a mere child,
changed when he found this instrument ready to his hand
to wreak vengeance on the missionary. The following
day Warren receives a letter from England recalling him
at once on urgent business, and again he tells Kusa of his
joy at rejoining his wife and child. She, unfortunate being, is consumed with jealousy and drops the poison powder into his lemonade; but as she does so she gazes out
into the moonlight and sees the three priests dancing the
dance of death and understands at once what is going to
happen. She rushes into the room, snatches the glass
from the missionary, and drinks the contents. Her grandmother obtained the antidote to the poison, and saved the
girl's life. She married the man who loved her, Kwamin
Fori.

A little stir was experienced in 1911, when appeared
*The Garden of Resurrection—Being the Love Story of an
Ugly Man,* by E. Temple Thurston. From the Englishman's point of view the "tale is told with charm and a
certain firmness of touch." The hero, greatly disfigured
by smallpox, feels that no one can bear to be in his presence and lavished all his affection on an attractive dog,
Dandy. Dining at a restaurant one evening, he overhears
a conversation between a (distinctly objectionable) young
man and a woman of twenty-eight about a girl of Negro
ancestry, whom he intended to marry on account of her

wealth. With that object she had been brought to England and was in the care of his two elderly narrow-minded spinster aunts. She was kept a prisoner in the remote somewhat dismal home in Ireland, at Ballysheen, and never allowed to see any one and only taken out after dark with a veil over her face. The story as overheard fired the imagination of the lonely man, Bellairs, who realized what the girl must be suffering, thus shut in away from all friendliness and bereft of the sunshine of her native land, Dominica. She had never been allowed any freedom for fear some of the neighbors might discover that she was not a pure white. "In Ireland, you know, a drop of black blood is the greatest curse you can have," says the young man.

Clarissa, the girl, who was not allowed to wear her canary-coloured satin dress, becomes an obsession. The hero receives a letter from an old friend inviting him to some fishing and notices the address is Ballysheen; he goes to stay with Cruikshank and his understanding wife, Bellwhatele, and after some manoeuvering manages to meet Clarissa and tries to warn her against the young man—the man she loves. Obviously she will not believe what she is told to be the truth, and is full of indignation against Bellairs, who is trying to save her from an unhappy future. Some time later, after Clarissa has left Ireland with young Fennell to be married in London from the house of an aunt, Bellairs sees Clarissa, Fennell, a man, and the woman of the earlier meeting together at a restaurant. Fennell leaves before Bellairs can speak to him, and Clarissa in reply to a note delivered by the head-waiter disclaims any acquaintanceship; whereupon Bellairs, having completely failed to help the woman he feels convinced is being badly treated, decides to go abroad. Having made all his arrangements he is ready to start when suddenly Clarissa arrives at his flat, ill, hungry. The young man has spent all her money and deserted her. She is so ill that she is obliged to remain on in the flat, and Bellairs to save trouble and gossip insists upon the nurse and his servants addressing her as Mrs. Bellairs. The child is born dead, and Clarissa's recovery is slow, the intervening time being occupied by Bellairs in building a cottage for her in the country; but Clarissa, thoroughly humbled by events, says she must return to Dominica. Bellairs sees a broken-hearted woman off at the station. He, so secure in the conviction that his ugliness must prevent any woman from loving him, lets her go. Two days later he receives a telegram from his understanding friend, Bellwhatele, telling him to come over at once; and on arrival is told it is about the old stone cottage on the cliff which the Cruikshanks had given him. On the road to it Bellwhatele asks him why he let Clarissa go and dares to say that Clarissa loves him but thought she was unworthy, and he had said nothing. Then Bellwhatele tells him to go up to the cottage alone as she is tired. Full of hopes for the future, he opens the door; and there quite unexpectedly finds Clarissa in her canary-coloured gown.

In *God's Step-Children*, by Sarah Gertrude Millin (1924) there is a striking story of race admixture and the ghost which eternally haunts the Nordics. The Rev. Andrew Flood "had recently heard a tremendous sermon preached about the essential equality of all human beings, whatever their colour, in the eyes of their Creator. It was, throughout Britain, the creed of the moment." As a result he went to the Cape in 1821; within a month of being ordained he offered himself to a mission society to spread the Word in Africa.

Benumbed with the strangeness of his surroundings and suffering from the long journey over rough tracks in sweltering heat, the awkward-looking, silent man arrives at Canaan (one hundred miles from any white settlement) a circle of thirty reed huts inhabited by a tribe called the Korannas. The first interview with his flock was disconcerting. He felt an underground of mockery in spite of his efforts; and their questions were such as he was not prepared for, although they were, in the main, stupid and indolent. Moreover, they were firm believers in witchcraft.

His first serious brush with his flock was when they danced in the new moon. Although Titus, his interpreter, explained to him that because they believed the stars to be the eyes of the dead, and the moon to be God, they sang and danced in prayer, the Rev. Mr. Flood insisted on calling them from their sleep; and when, worn out, they all refused to come to him, he went to them; they listened with indifference and danced again when night came. After a spell of depression and an attack of hysteria, the Rev. Mr. Flood asks his cook, Cachas, and her daughter, Silla, what it is that stands between him and the people and finds that they are convinced that God does not feel for a brown man as he does for a white man, to which he replies, "We are all God's children;" and as the Rev. Mr. Flood hesitates for a reply to the question "But is God Himself not White?" Cachas makes the significant comment, "Perhaps we brown people are only His Step-Children."

In his desperate anxiety to bring these "children into the fold and prove that there is no difference between brown and white, Flood decides to marry the young Silla in spite of the remonstrances of the Rev. Thomas Burtwell of the next mission station, whither he travelled with Cachas, Silla, and her cousin so that the marriage ceremony might be duly performed. By the time the third child has arrived the Rev. Mr. Flood realized that he had in no way advanced the cause by his marriage and that the members of his flock regarded him as a fool. Though one or two had genuine religious instincts and really liked the idea of a God and Saviour, of Heaven and Hell, not until the serious illness of his baby and the magic rites he observed did he feel the completeness of his fail-

ure. The baby died, and the father was blamed for his
interruption at the moment the bad spirits were about to
he exorcised; the mother returned to her own home, leaving the two children behind.

Some time later the Rev. Thomas Burtwell came to
Canaan on his annual visitation and, finding the Rev. Mr.
Flood growing more and more despondent, more and
more ungainly and dirty, decided to take Deborah, the
daughter of twelve years of age, back with him to train
as a school-assistant or, as her father suggested, to help
Mrs. Burtwell in the house. Mrs. Burtwell was furious
with her husband, saying trouble is sure to follow; and it
did when Deborah was sixteen, for she fell in love first
with a full-blooded young Hottentot, and when Mr. and
Mrs. Burtwell put a stop to their meetings her next venture was with an emigrant farmer who had come northward to settle. In reply to Mr. Burtwell's question Hans
Kleinhans said he would not think of marrying a brown
girl, but Deborah when told of this replied, "It is no use
talking any more. There is going to be a child!" And
the Burtwells arranged for her to return to her father.
It must be realized that Deborah was not unhappy in the
Burtwell household; they were all kind to her. But their
ways were not her ways, and she was lonely.

Not long after the Rev. Mr. Flood died; his reason
had fled, and another missionary had been sent out to take
up the work for which the Canaan Pastor had been so unfitted. The new man was of very different stuff, and his
people did not laugh at him long.

Deborah, her son Kleinhans, and her grandmother
Cachas left Canaan and joined the community of Hottentots and Bastaards who dwelt in Griqualand East, ruled
over by Adam Kok, the fifth of his line. This was in 1860.
Kleinhans, now eighteen, was a husbandman by nature;
he vigorously farmed his land, worked in wood and iron,
was sober, frugal, religious, but full of bitterness that bred

against his mother and the people with whom he lived; and he was proud of his white ancestry. When he was twenty-nine he left Kokstad and trekked to the diamond fields, eager to be rid of his mother and companions in order to live among white men and marry a woman of their race.

Kleinhans' first day in a small town was full of disappointment and suffering. In spite of a certain likeness to the Boers his mixed blood was betrayed in his speech; he found himself ostracized, turned out of an inn, objected to by the agent for the diamond diggings, and almost beaten to death by the father of a little girl who had lost one of her goats which Kleinhans kindly offered to help her find. He was picked up more dead than alive by an Englishman returning from the diamond fields, who with his wife and two daughters and a young Cape girl as assistant in the house had settled on a farm in Africa in search of health. Mr. Lindsell, who wanted a competent man on the farm, kept him there. Kleinhans helped the Englishman with his own stock and received a small share of the profits.

Within a year he had married Lena Smith, the girl from the Cape, whose father was a German, her mother, a coloured woman with a little Malay blood and a little St. Helena infusion mixed with that of the white. When their first child, Elmira, was born in 1872, Deborah, who had come over from Kokstad for the event, was amazed at the beauty of her grandchild. When Lindsell's two daughters returned from boarding school their mother thought they would have more chance of settling down if they went to England. So the three left for home and Lindsell, to his surprise, missed the presence of his nagging, ill-tempered wife, and sought companionship at the Kleinhans' house. Lindsell thinks that Elmira, a lovely child, with no trace of colour, should be sent to a good school and offers to take her to a convent, knowing that she would not be accepted if the sisters saw her.

So for several years the child lives a life of pretence among her school friends and a life of antagonism with her brothers and sisters when at home until an epidemic of serious scarlet-fever makes the Nuns send for the Kleinhanses . The Mother Superior greeted them kindly, but Elmira, now on the way to recovery, resented their presence; and as soon as her restoration to health was complete she returned to the farm and was sent far away to Cape Town to the same school which the Lindsell girls had attended. There the brother of a school-friend fell in love with her. The father of the young man wrote to Lindsell asking whether she was a suitable wife for his son and Lindsell told the truth about her origin in a far from kindly manner.

Apparently he was already contemplating taking her as his second wife, for his wife had died in England. The girl was very attractive, pretty and modest; he cadaverous, with sparse hair and claw-like hands, was sixty-five to her eighteen. The marriage came about without any protest from Elmira, for her family's position depended upon her acquiescence. At first Lindsell lavished presents of all sorts upon his wife and was kind to her though very exacting. She never protested against anything and was always calm and indifferent to the admiration she met with in the town. Then one day after they had returned to the farm he, in a moment of ill-temper, referred to her complexion, saying, "You ought to pay more attention to your complexion than other women." This slight roused all the pent-up feeling. She told him she hated him and that he was an ugly old man.

For days she went about her duties as usual, and then one Sunday told her husband she was going home. He remonstrated with her; and this time she told him exactly and at some length what she thought of this man who "looks like a tortoise and is old enough to be my grandfather." She remained on at the farm until her son, Barry, was born, a small, weakly child, but "a proper white child," so her mother said. Lindsell was now overcome with happiness; he had never cared for his unattractive daughters. The younger one had married and the elder had run away when her father announced his intention of marrying again; but this child, the son of his old age, was a miracle, and the child loved and was happy with his father, his constant companion.

Elmira settled down to motherhood until the child was two and one-half years old, when she disappeared from the hotel where they were staying. Fortunately there was an efficient nurse, Mrs. Gadd. Lindsell then had an apoplectic fit and Mrs. Gadd had two charges to look after; his two daughters refused to go and see him, until news that he was worse came. May and her husband went to the farm; Edith with compressed lips refused to accompany them. They had never felt much affection for their father and since his second marriage had hated and abused him in spite of his generosity in the way of allowances. Finally Lindsell died; and the two families, the brown and the white, including proud Edith, met at the funeral. Lena, his brown grandmother, a kindly soul, put her arms around the rigid figure of the boy of seven, whose sole friend and companion for years had been an ailing father, saying, "Come to your granny, my little heart," when suddenly he broke from her, flung himself against Edith's gaunt, unyielding body, crying, "Don't let the brown people take me! Don't let them!" Weeping wildly for the first time in her lonely life, Edith felt that some one needed her; and she said, "I'm taking him."

Edith settled in Cape Town with the child, where they led an isolated life. Never comfortable with other children, he had "the contempt for black blood which is one of the nails in the cross that the black-blooded bear, and Barry always spoke passionately against black, brown, and yellow. At the age of forty-two Edith fell in love with a local minister, whose jovial kindly manner entirely misled her, and when the blow fell, and his engagement was announced to a young girl of eighteen, she indeed felt that God had failed her.

Barry, now thirteen, who had been a witness of all that was happening, was full of commiseration with his half-sister's disappointment and determined to devote his life to her, though he never mentioned this decision. He had curious resemblances to his great-great grandfather, the Rev. Andrew Flood, especially the desire for real self-sacrifice. After a harrowing scene in which Edith tells Barry he must never marry on account of the taint in his blood, Barry, for the first time in his life, tells her she is jealous because of her disappointment and says he had better leave her.

However, the following evening he feels how unjust he has probably been, begs forgiveness and decides to dedicate himself to Christ. He goes to Oxford at the age of twenty-one; after three years came the war, and he was to join as a chaplain to the forces. After two cases of shell-shock he remained in England, only returning to South Africa in 1920 with his wife. When a child is expected Edith again renews the attack and insists upon his telling his wife, Norah, of the risk. Norah, a pretty, impulsive, kind-hearted girl, refuses at first to worry, but gradually becomes a victim to dread of having a black child. Barry is called to the Kleinhans' where his mother is dying. He stays until her death and helps them generously, and on his return decides that Norah must return to England to have her child, and that he is going among his brown people to settle near Canaan, where the Rev. Andrew Flood had his mission. "For the first time in his life Barry showed strength—His people wanted him!"

The Adventures of the Black Girl in Her Search for God, published by George Bernard Shaw in 1932, has caused considerable comment. It is written in the nature of a parable showing the various conceptions of the Deity to be found in the world—God as He is described in the Old and New Testaments, the God of Mahomet, the God of Voltaire, and the God of Natural Science. The book is clever enough in a somewhat flippant way but contributes nothing new to the problem where God is to be found. In an "Afterword" the author attempts an evaluation of the Bible, according to which it is an interesting record of how the idea of God developed from childish idolatry to the sublime notion of a loving father. He points out that not one but many conceptions of God are to be found in the Bible, for instance, the God of Noah, of Job, of Micah, and of Jesus Christ.

Charles Herbert Maxwell wrote in 1933 a reply entitled *Adventures of the White Girl in Her Search for God*, in which he inserts a note, "Let not the reader think it strange that the White Girl should carry a 'niblick.' To anyone acquainted with things African, this is far less extraordinary than that a Bantu Girl should carry a 'knobkerry,' as happens in Mr. Bernard Shaw's *Adventures of the Black Girl in Her Search for God*."

In 1933 appeared also *The Adventures of Gabriel in His Search for Mr. Shaw*, by W. R. Matthews, a modest companion for Mr. Shaw's *Black Girl*. There is conversation between Peter and Gabriel showing the exceptional interest Mr. Shaw's activities have aroused in heaven. The result is that at Peter's suggestion the Archangel Gabriel agrees to spend a week-end on Earth, disguised as a private detective, to look into the Shaw mystery—to find out which is the real Shaw. The story gives the many "appearances" that Shaw presents to the world. He is so elusive that Gabriel does not find it easy to discover him again, each time he disappears. *The Black Girl* is not mentioned; only Shaw's omniscience is caricatured.

C. G. Woodson

BOOK REVIEWS

Le Noir. By W. Mercer Cook. Edited with Introduction, Exercises, and Vocabulary. (New York: American Book Company, 1934. Pp. X + 173.)

The teacher of French who desires to see an occasional black face among the Perrichons, Poiriers, and Colombas who invade his class-room will welcome the publication of *Le Noir.* Since propaganda in behalf of some ideal or other is becoming an important factor in education, the inclusion of race-consciousness among the objectives of language study is altogether consonant with the modern trend. Use of this book will prove an effectual aid in the correcting of an attitude of mind illustrated by the colored boy in a mixed class who stoutly refused to name the blacks when called on for a survey of the races of men. Dr. Georgiana Simpson's book on Toussaint Louverture was designed to meet this need; Mr. Cook's anthology on the black motif will likewise prove invaluable in the program of rehabilitation.

The author, who is Assistant Professor of French at Howard University, has made a searching study of the familiar as well as outlying fields of French literature in an endeavor to determine the attitude of French writers toward the Negro. In *Le Noir* he presents his findings in the case of twenty-nine Frenchmen of major importance. He has proceeded with the objectivity of a scholar and has not withheld evidence that indicates hostility. The majority of the pages of his book, however, attest so convincingly the understanding and sympathy that black people are wont to associate with the French, that the dissenting note of a Balzac, for example, need not prove disquieting. Of primary importance is the fact that men of the stature of Voltaire, Victor Hugo, and Anatole France have concerned themselves with the Negro.

The skillful editing of the morceaux that compose *Le Noir* gives it added attraction as a text. A short biographical sketch of each author precedes selections from his works; the notes are succinct and adequate; a questionnaire for oral interpretation of the text is included; the vocabulary has been prepared with care; and bibliographical data are presented for students who desire to read more extensively in this field. The book does not claim to be exhaustive; it serves rather to give promise of the satisfaction that an intimate acquaintance with French literature can bring to the reader who resents the distorted portrayal of the Negro that American writers pander to a willing public.

ı This text need not be used only in advanced courses; the French involved, though literary, will not prove beyond the comprehension of second year students. The passages are brief and varied enough to sustain the interest of the neophyte who might feel intimidated in the presence of literature that strikes a deeper note than is struck by the average elementary reading text.

The first selection is the familiar passage on Negro slavery from the *Esprit des Lois of Montesquieu*—a timely warning to the student to proceed thoughtfully, lest the subtleties of French dialectic confound him. While the anthology is not limited to literature of a controversial nature (exposition and description are represented by the modern authors), it is these passages inspired by the liberalism of the Revolution that the student will doubtless read with keenest interest.

Now that the physical emancipation of the black race is no longer an issue, it might be argued that such literature has an historical rather than aesthetic significance. The reviewer recalls a similar verdict passed on "Uncle Tom's Cabin" by a critic who maintained that Mrs. Stowe's novel was at best a counterfeit masterpiece, real to one generation, but unreal to the following. This appraisal is hardly final; indeed, at the present time when the old Tolstoyian idealism that found supreme art in a peasant's song and humanized all artistic expression is to be reckoned with as an important principle of literary criticism (even in parts that look askance at the hammer and sickle) such a summary dismissal is as unconvincing as dogmatic. Does not the recent revival of the dramatic version of the story of Tom and Eva prove that literature of humanitarian inspiration is perennially vital regardless of the transitory phenomena that give it being? George Sand sensed this; in her letter of appreciation to Mrs. Stowe, reproduced in *Le Noir*, she expresses the modern ideal so happily that we wonder if her muse was as archaic and tawdry as her detractors would have us believe.

The announcement accompanying *Le Noir* is to the effect that it was designed for use in Negro schools. Such a limitation is not necessary. Whereas the book will undoubtedly be widely read in Negro schools, it will not be without significance in all schools of liberal orientation. One of the hopeful signs on the Negro's horizon is the activity of white students of the vanguard in behalf of a sane and equitable revision of the status of black people. Such students will hardly be less interested than their darker fellows in what a Buffon, Maupassant, or Bourget has to say on the subject.

Literature, however occasional or particular its inspiration may be, surmounts the limitation of theme in proportion to the genius of the author. Under the pen of a Montesquieu or Voltaire a discussion of the Negro can become a treatise on human relations. No social phenomenon is isolated from the organism of society, and the analysis of it is bound to suggest important ramifications. When Montesquieu writes that the enemies of the Negro argue his inferiority because "he esteems a glace necklace more than gold, *which among the civilized nations is of greatest consequence*," he is probing western civilization much as we have seen Tagore probe it in our day. And the prophet-stoning Voltaire is strangely prophetic when, in his discussion of the possible disappearance of the Albino type, he writes "if we in Europe continue to depopulate the earth in order to determine who shall govern it, I do not give many more centuries of life to our poor species."

Even "Der Führer" might read *Le Noir* with profit. Concerned as he is with a renaissance of the old Germanic traditions, he might find the revelation on page 17 a helpful guide to orthodoxy in the matter of racial attitudes. Or would he make auto da fe of a page that impiously recalls the catholic viewpoint that was once the lodestar of the German universities? Obviously the tribute of "vir nobilissime et clarissime" paid to the black savant Antoine-Guillaume Amo by the rector of Wittenberg and the assurance of the non-existence of race prejudice at that university are heresies subversive to the dogma of racial exclusivism as propounded by the National Socialists.

A harassed world in general might find food for thought in this book. The enslaved Negro in France and her colonies constituted a problem; *Le Noir* shows how the French mind proceeded

to a solution. Passion and prejudice stand aside, and reason leads
the way. Conceptual obscurity is dispelled by the "clarté intel-
lectuelle" that is the Frenchman's heritage. Voltaire finds dif-
ferentiation among the apes and concludes that variation is desirable in the human species. In the selection from L'Abbé
Gregoire a statesman suggests that the whole question of slavery
be envisaged from the point of view of the blacks—a simple and
logical procedure generally tabooed by the judges in the court of
human relations.

Contemporary thought, of course, has made a museum-piece
of French rationalism. Sensibility is better than reason; Bergson
is nearer reality than Descartes. In consequence, the many mystic
systems enroll their armies of votaries with astounding ease. And
hatred grows apace. The Christian church, which long ago anath-
ematized the Encyclopedia, is hesitant and inarticulate when
the creed affirms the spiritual emancipation of dark people.
Eighteenth century France found the Holy Trinity incompatible
with reason, and substituted an earthly trinity of liberty, equality, and fraternity. The pages of *Le Noir* bear eloquent witness
to the humane effect of the new revelation. As we read them we
wonder if the goddess of reason who held her court in Notre
Dame de Paris was a wanton, after all.

V. B. Spratlin

Howard University, Washington, D. C.

The Evolution of the Negro College. By Dwight Oliver Wendell
Holmes, Ph.D. (New York: Bureau of Publications, Teachers
College, Columbia University. Contributions to Education,
No. 609. 1934. Pp. 221.)

The story of the development of the Negro college is one of
the most interesting phases in the history of American education.
Unlike other American colleges, the Negro college arose in response to needs which were urgent and immediate. It was intended not only to serve the generations of students who would
come to it after the period of its establishment and full development, but it was faced with the unusual situation, the immediate
emergency, demanding that instant service be rendered to the

multitudes, who, in the nature of the case, could not be kept waiting for its ministrations. It began with the missionary urge and
reached its height as a missionary crusade. Such a movement has
significance for American life in general as well as for Negro
life in particular; not only because Negroes are component parts
of the American population, but also because Americans recognizing these needs devoted themselves unselfishly to the planning
and the active participation in the operation of the Negro college.
When it is recalled that this service was not rendered to themselves or their children but to those who were the descendants of
another racial stock, it has more than a passing historical significance for all Americans.

The Negro College in its major development and expansion
belongs to the era which succeeded the War for Southern Independence. The period of Negro education prior to the war, including the beginnings of the efforts for the establishment of the
first colleges for Negroes, has been compactly covered in the excellent treatise by C. G. Woodson, *The Education of the Negro
Prior to 1861* (New York, 1915). This study pointed to the need
for a second volume which would cover the succeeding periods.
The surveys of the Negro college published in 1917 and 1929,
which were made under governmental auspices, the studies of individual colleges and the reports of denominational and philanthropic boards operating in the field of Negro education, have
directed further attention to the need for a comprehensive and
connected published account of the development of Negro education in the period following the abolition of slavery. This need
was particularly evident in the fields of the Negro Public School,
the Negro Secondary School and the Negro College. The effort to
contribute to one of these fields has resulted in this study by Dr.
Holmes. The other fields still await adequate treatment.

Dr. Holmes states that it is not his purpose to present the
events in the history of the Negro College in chronological order
but that it is his object "to interpret the events, the social forces
and the attitudes of individuals and groups which have affected
the establishment and development of these schools and thus determined the character of the opportunities for higher education
available to Negro youth today in segregated colleges, universities
and professional schools located mainly in the Southern states."

In his effort to trace this development, which the author terms "the evolution," the historical method was used.

The study is divided into four parts, containing twenty-six chapters. Part I includes preliminary statements concerning the historical background. Part II treats of the Federal Government and the Freedmen's Bureau. Howard University occupies a large place in this part of the discussion. Part III describes the major parts of the thesis under the title, "The Emergence of the College." The American Missionary Association, the Freedmen's Aid Society, the American Baptist Home Mission Society, the various denominational boards, the Negro denominations, the land-grant colleges and organized philanthropy are passed in review. Part IV contains the descriptions of progress from 1922 to 1932, with a presentation of the present status and trends towards consolidation, accreditation and changes in control.

The author endeavors to measure the significance of the historical background, in its socio-economic relationships, which is quite unlike some educators who venture into the historical field. As a rule, the tables, graphs, statistics and numerical data loom so large in these studies that the reader frequently has not been able to see the forests for the trees. The trappings of scholarship have been so often mistaken for the thing itself. Historical facts and figures must be evaluated and interpreted. They are not ends in themselves, and it is not sufficient to fasten them together in tabular form on a page with a tag attached, which is supposed to reveal the unseen mystery. The author of this work includes twenty-six tables, but they are not ends in themselves. They are intended as illustrations of factual materials presented in the textual matter.

The author's use of historical evidence, his effort to pursue the truth and his presentation of it follow the accepted rules of historical research. There are tendencies manifested at times to follow the popular views rather than the historian's view. One instance of this occurs in his discussion of the historical background of the Negro at the beginning of the war of 1861-1865, in which he states that "the Negro, generally considered, began his academic education at zero." However, he hastens to explain that there were numerous Negroes who were educated. In point of fact, this number was larger than most persons realize. The

Negro has been so flattered by his oratorical friends concerning his "remarkable progress since Emancipation," that he has been almost too willing to conclude that he began "at zero." There were thousands of free Negroes, north and south, who had freed themselves from the chains of ignorance as well as slavery prior to 1865. There were college graduates among this number and there were those who had been exposed at least to the processes of formal education. The author is not entirely forgetful of this group.

Another instance of the same tendency is manifested, when the statement is made that the slaves who thought about the issues of the war knew that they were the cause of the war and that their freedom was the issue of the war. There is very little reliable evidence, although there is much oratory and printed recollections for this conclusion. History must not be made dependent upon these sources alone. The confusion of issues reigned until they were clarified in 1863, with the approach of the Union armies; or else how shall one explain the Negroes who served in the Confederate army and who were inducted into the Confederate ranks in the closing days of the last year of the war? Moreover, the northern armies returned the fugitive slaves to their owners or regarded them as contraband property. And yet the author shows his acquaintance with some of the evidence bearing upon this confusion of the real issue of the war and reveals that there were stages of development on the question of the Negro as a war issue.

Entering directly into the educational history, the author is on surer ground. He divides the study into four periods. The first extends from 1860 to 1885, during which the Union armies, the Freedmen's Bureau, the Church, the volunteer and philanthropic boards were establishing colleges for the freedmen. There was the hasty duplication of efforts in many places and the introduction of that which seemed to border upon the impractical in education. Nevertheless the author concludes that "it was probably impossible for the work to be carried on in any other way that would have brought such speedy results." The second period extends from 1886 to 1916. This period was characterized by the increase in the number of schools and in the enrollment of students, the rise of industrial education and the beginnings of land-grant colleges. The addition of Negro teachers to the teaching staffs of the college was one of the characteristics of this period. The third period began in 1917 with the publication of the report of the Phelps-Stokes Fund concerning colleges and universities for Negroes. This report led to a critical evaluation of these schools. The interest of the foundations such as the General Education Board and the Julius Rosenwald Fund and the activities of the state governments gave adequate support and made possible systematic improvements. The author begins the fourth period in 1928, when the Survey of Negro Colleges was published by the United States Bureau of Education. Shortly afterwards, the Association of Colleges and Secondary Schools of the Southern States accepted the responsibility for the rating of the Negro colleges in the South.

The study shows that there were four groups of agencies which were responsible for the Negro College: (1) the Federal Government; (2) the Christian Church; (3) the state governments; (4) organized philanthropy. The work of these agencies resulted in the development of the number of institutions and in an increase in the college enrollment. In 1932 there were 109 institutions for Negroes doing college work. They were distributed among 19 states and the District of Columbia. They enrolled approximately 23,000 college students. The influence of the small college is evident when it is noted that 11 of the 19 institutions enrolled 500 or more students, 25 from 250 to 499 students, 29 from 100 to 249 students and 44 less than 100 students. The percentage of college students in these institutions arose from 15 in 1922 to 85 in 1932, showing that work on the secondary level was growing less important.

The author admits that the study is intended to be an historical investigation and that he does not intend to project his interest into the future. Nevertheless, in the last few pages he directs attention to several defects of the Negro College under the heading of "Recommendations." One is that the intense competition among colleges for students in those areas in which the opportunity for college education exceeds the demand should cease. The lack of objectives on the part of the colleges, the effort to operate a four-year college program on inadequate income and the relative scarcity of scholarship aids are cited. The final recommendation is that an organized survey should be undertaken for the purpose of planning the development of the Negro College for a period of twenty-five years or thereabouts. The author concludes with the expression of the belief that the time is ripe for an effective plan for the organization and administration of "the group of Negro colleges in a systematic way." This statement deserves further consideration.

Dr. Holmes has performed a worthwhile service in making the scattered materials and reports more readily accessible in a single volume. The book is a very important and useful contribution both to history and to education. The style is attractive and lucid. The treatment reflects careful and accurate scholarship. Historians and educators will find much valuable material in the book, and an eleven page bibliography adds to its usefulness. The omission of an index in a work of this type is a regrettable error. It impairs the practical use of the book as a reference for immediate purposes. As a concise survey of the field, however, this book will fill a need of long standing.

CHARLES H. WESLEY

The Antislavery Impulse, 1830-1844. By Gilbert H. Barnes. (New York: D. Appleton-Century Company, Inc., 1933. Pp. 199. Price, $3.50.)

The author, Professor of Economics at Ohio Wesleyan University, surveys the early stages of the antislavery movement and attempts to come nearer to a true understanding of its development because ". . . . contemporary records of the movement, especially outside New England, do not fit into the traditional story." Moreover, the author further points out in his preface that the contemporary records, ". . . . tell a different and incomparably more significant tale of a religious impulse which began in the west of 1830, was translated for a time into antislavery organization, then broadened into a sectional crusade against the South."

The author portrays Theodore D. Weld as the Urban II of the antislavery crusade. Despite the claim for Western origins the conversion of the leader took place in the East; however, the author clearly shows that his work of inaugurating the movement was carried on in the West where, with Tappan's money and Finney's doctrines, he was the moving spirit of Lane Seminary, and the man who did perhaps more than anyone else to open the doors of Oberlin College to women and Negroes. Professor Barnes further points out that a careful study of the sources indicates that ". . . . the movement of the thirties was not inconsiderable; it was a major factor in the rise of sectionalism and a prime cause of the final conflict."

In Chapter III the author depicts William Lloyd Garrison as an abolitionist whose radicalism had caused him to be disinherited by many friends of the cause. And further, as a man unfitted by his rashness to lead the great crusade against slavery, yet he was so powerful in his little New England group that he had to be handled with diplomacy.

Theodore Weld and his converts are described as being less prolific but more significant. As men who believed that liberalism rather than radicalism should be the philosophy of the movement and men who sensed the importance of spreading their antislavery propaganda through trained abolitionist ministers rather than through radical newspapers of the *Liberator* type.

From the Negro's point of view, Dr. Barnes presents a sympathetic picture of the free Negro in the North carrying the brunt of the support of Garrison's *Liberator* during lean years and possessing, even if at the expense of a white philanthropist, a representative in England who served as a precursor of the Frederick Douglass pleas in England for antislavery cooperation in the United States.

In the last half of the volume Theodore Weld is depicted as having emerged from the revivalist, antislavery society organizer and influential man in the brain trust of the movement, to the personal aide of John Q. Adams, during the gage rule controversy, and later to great though inconspicuous heights as foremost organizer of the powerful antislavery lobby. Thus the author presents the antislavery impulse as a two-fold battle; first, the fight to rid the scene of elements unfavorable to the antislavery movement, and second, the crusade to convince the people of the merits of the effort.

The book is filled with moving incidents that illuminate the work and lend to it the fascination of adventure; nevertheless, at the same time it is copiously documented and contains enough new material to alter considerably the traditional interpretations of the antislavery movement by showing the character and significance of the movement in the west.

JAMES B. BROWNING

Howard University.

The Racial Myth. By Paul Radin. (New York: 1934. Whittlesey House, McGraw-Hill Book Company, Inc. Pp. 141. Price, $1.50.)

This book is an acceptance of the challenge flung at anthropological scholarship by the intellectual vandals of contemporary Germany. Professor Radin is one of the matured American anthropologists. He writes with zest and vim. His style is clear and forceful. He is simple, direct and poignant. He does not exaggerate. Hardly does he filibuster. More remarkable is the fact that he is connected with the anthropology department at the University of California where Dr. A. L. Kroeber juggles to suit his fancy with facts as to the cultural nakedness of certain races, the Africans in particular.

The Racial Myth is dedicated "to the memory of my father, who was always in the vanguard of liberal movements and who understood, as he exemplified in his life, the dictum of the great Greek: *'Tis not in hate, but love, that men unite themselves'.*"

The thesis of the book is thus summed up in the author's preface: "In the crisis of civilization through which we are now passing, no thinking and feeling man can long remain untouched and unaffected. For that reason a brief review of the history of civilization and the contributions of the various races, mixed and unmixed, may possibly be of service and value. Such a survey indicates quite clearly that all specific racial pretensions to superiority are both illusory and unjustified."

Throughout the book there is an attempt to explode the myth of racial superiority. The factual presentation of the achievements of races and sub-races from time immemorial, although treated in a sketchy fashion, throws into discard the fantastic theories of Gobineau, Benjamin Kidd, Lothrop Stoddard, Mc-Dougall, Chamberlain, Grant, Lugard, Hitler, and the Nordico-philes.

Dr. Radin shows that racial nationalities tend to become ego-centric. The Jews claim to be the elect of God instead of "the rejected of God." The Greeks "substituted the children of light as opposed to the barbarians." The Romans passed "from ra-cial to national arrogance." Spaniards were glorified as "stern, uncompromising in valor and faith." The French represented themselves as "the epitome of rationality." The English "were credited with an inborn resistance and a rugged individualism that brooked no control." Italians possessed the "gift of beau-ty." Now comes "unhappy Germany, always on the periphery of the great movements that swept over Europe . . . . university professors, preached to a wondering world how civilization had once before been saved by a Germanic people and how it was to be saved again . . . . In a manner, of course, this was simply the old dream of a Golden Age refurbished in a smart Prussian uniform."

Chapter II deals with the Nordic doctrine. It is written ac-cording to the point of view of Professor F. H. Hankins' famous critique. The author believes that advocates of Nordic superiority are victims of the inferiority complex. "It is for this reason, therefore, that it behooves them to recognize the fact that a care-fully constructed theory of a German or Nordic race is but the compensation myth of confused late comers, of people whose his-torical rhythm has not synchronized with that of the rest of the world and who have, in consequence, always come to the table too late and with a poor appetite."

Chapter III considers "The Torch of Civilization from the Stone Age to Today." Despite the glorification of the civilization of the white and yellow races, "If a high degree of economic advance and efficiency, a rich artistic development, an amazing prose and poetry, and a complex religious development are the earmarks of a great and advanced civilization, the Negroes of West and East Africa, the Polynesians, and the American In-dians of Mexico and Peru possessed it. Surely it is a strange and thoroughly reprehensible artistic obscurantism that would extol the poetry, wisdom, and religiosity of the psalms and not give a high measure of praise to the following hymn of the Yoruba of West Africa:

> The sun shines and sends its burning rays down upon us,
> The moon rises in its glory.
> Rain will come and again the sun will shine.
> And over it all passes the eye of God.
> Nothing is hidden from him.
> Whether you be in your home,
> Whether you be on the water,
> Whether you rest in the shade of a tree in the open,
> He is there, your master . . . ."

The rest of the book is devoted to a study of the forces which are molding the arrogance of the races now dominating mankind. A world confederation where the myths of nationalism, rugged individualism, and racial superiority would be forgotten is suggested as a panacea to counteract the impending interracial Armageddon. It is the author's belief that the fundamental causes of racial intolerance are man's fondness for illusion, his unwillingness to progress, and his mania for extolling physical prowess.

Students of world affairs and interracial relations should read this book. Despite its brevity it is written with a scientific objectivity. It is not a scholarly dissertation with all the flare of academism. While Dr. Radin did not mention all the important contributions of the black races to civilization—for example: *the discovery and use of iron,* according to Boas, Torday, Hall and several ethnologists; *the naming of the stars,* according to Lucian, Volney, etc.; *the worship of one God,* according to Sir J. G. Wilkinson, Talbot, etc. (E. W. Smith quotes Sir James Frazer as asserting that Jews borrowed this idea of monotheism, while under the yoke of the Ethiopians and Egyptians, to institute their Jahweh— mistakenly called Jehovah—worship); *the conception of the four elements and their relations to the cosmos,* according to several Egyptologists (this idea was borrowed by the philosophers of the Milesian school, some of whom travelled to Egypt and Ethiopia); *the double spiral motiff* (copied by the Greek Minoan culture); *social institutions* such as theocracy, representative democracy, the jury system of judicial procedure, and several contributions mentioned by Herodotus, Strabo, Diodorus, Josephus, Volney, Erman, Prichard, Luschan, Champollion, Rosellini, Petrie, Sayce, Maspero and other archaeologists.

I believe that *The Racial Myth* is a fair presentation of the fallacy of Nordicophilism. All races have played a part in the history of civilization. To arrogate to one race this distinction is indicative of an unwillingness to tell the truth.

BEN N. AZIKIWE

Lincoln University, Pa.

NOTES

In Recent Books of American History

Treatises bearing upon the stormy period of the Civil War and Reconstruction are still freely flowing from the press. We are so close to that period that many of us have assumed the obligation of properly interpreting it for the generations unborn, and one interpreter does not please the other. Timely, however, is the publication of *The Diary of Edward Bates,* by Howard K. Beale (Government Printing Office, Washington, D. C., 1933). This is the record of a moderate antislavery Whig of Virginia, who became Lincoln's Attorney General and gave the Great Emancipator much advice which the latter did not take. *The Secession Movement in Virginia,* by Henry T. Shanks (Richmond, Garrett and Massie, 1934), is a work which does not add much to what we know from other well known treatments of that period. *The Irrepressible Conflict,* by Arthur Cole, the seventh volume of *A History of American Life* (New York, Macmillan and Company, 1934), continues an important series. *Louisiana in French Diplomacy,* 1759-1804, by E. Wilson Lyon (Norman, University of Oklahoma Press, 1934), has a suggestive title but the work is not an exhaustive production. *Unionism and Reconstruction in Tennessee, 1860-1865,* by James W. Patton (Chapel Hill, The University of North Carolina Press, 1934), has attracted some attention. The work gives a survey of Brownlow's rule, the Negro in politics, and the Freedman's Bureau. Limited almost exclusively to politics, however, the author fails to note the social and economic factors and to interpret them. It is a case of the old ground covered again. *The History of West Virginia,* by C. H. Ambler (New York, Prentice Hall, 1934), emphasizes unduly the history of Virginia as would be the case of an author who has made a special study of *Sectionalism in Virginia.* The author, of course, is more concerned with the part played by slavery in that upheaval than with that of the Negroes as makers of history in the new state to the west.

The more serious economic treatments in which the Negro figures as a factor, though smaller in number, are also appearing. *Plantation Slavery in Georgia,* by Ralph B. Flanders (Chapel Hill, University of North Carolina Press, 1933), is a factual study giving more details of the institution in that state than in U. B. Phillips' works, but not so well written. *Charleston Business on the Eve of the American Revolution,* by Leila Sellers (Chapel Hill, University of North Carolina Press, 1934), does not emphasize adequately the functions of the free people of color in the economic order of that city in those days. *Social and Economic History of the Unted States,* by Harry J. Carman (Boston, D. C. Heath and Company, 1934), is a work which in this the second volume, makes up for a lack in the first volume which did not give sufficient attention to the history of agriculture. Considerable space is given to slave labor.

A so-called new point of view has been shown in *The History of Agriculture in the Southern United States,* by Lewis C. Gray, assisted by Esther Katherine Thompson (Washington, Carnegie Institution of Washington, 1933). The author concludes that economic inferiority of the South rather than slavery was the cause of the Civil War. This, however, is an indirect statement that slavery was that cause, for the institution made the South economically inferior. *The Economic History of the South* (1934), by Emory I. Hawk, in a history series of Prentice Hall, edited by Carl Wittke, may serve well for information needed by average readers, but it falls short of being an adequate treatment of such a broad subject. There has appeared also *Salt as Factor in the Confederacy* by Ella Lonn, who among other productions has made a study of the Reconstruction of Louisiana (Baltimore, the author, vice Walter Neale, New York City, 1933).

IN ARTICLES IN AMERICAN MAGAZINES

In the American historical magazines frequent mention has been made of the Negro. Probably the most interesting have been the articles published from a thesis by W. A. Russ, Jr., who has made a study of disfranchisement during Reconstruction. In the *Journal of Negro History* for January, 1934, appeared an article entitled "Radical Disfranchisement and the Negro." In the September 1934 number of the *Mississippi Valley Historical Review* he published "Registration and Disfranchisement under Radical Reconstruction;" in the October issue of the *North Carolina*

Historical Review, "Radical Disfranchisement in North Carolina, 1867-1868;" and in the December issue of the *Maryland Magazine of History and Biography,* "Disfranchisement in Maryland, 1861-1867." Mr. Russ literally hates all the friends of freedom of that day. He seems to think that they were a very undesirable ilk and that they treated the Southerners unjustly. From most of these impositions, however, he exonerates the freedmen who cooperated with the "Radicals" of that day. His articles are weak from the point of view of interpretation. He misuses facts.

A number of articles have dealt especially with subjects closely related to slavery and reconstruction. For example, in the June issue of the *Mississippi Valley Historical Review* appears "Sections and Sectionalism in a Border State," by Jonas Viles; "Secession, Insurrection of the Negroes, and Northern Incendiarism," by S. A. Ashe and Lyon G. Tyler, in the July 1933 issue of *Tyler's Quarterly Historical and Genealogical Magazine;* "The Slavery Question and Mexico," by John D. P. Fuller, in the June 1934 issue of the *Mississippi Valley Historical Review;* "Hinton Rowan Helper," by D. R. Barbee, in *Tyler's Quarterly Historical and Genealogical Magazine* for January, 1933 and "Hinton Rowan Helper's Mendacity," by the same writer, in the April issue of the same magazine.

Other articles which concern the Negro, but of a more economic trend, are such as "The Origin and Early Spread of Iron Working," by Harold Peake, in the October 1933 issue of the *Geographical Review;* "The Tariff and the South," by M. Ogden Phillips, in the October 1933 issue of the *South Atlantic Quarterly;* and "The Introduction of East Indian Coolies into the British West Indies," by Edgar L. Erickson, in the June 1934 issue of the *Journal of Modern History.*

Articles bearing primarily upon social aspects are not wanting. Among these we find "Prudence Crandall and the Canterbury Experiment," by Alfred Thurston Child, Jr., in the *Bulletin of the Friends' Historical Association;* "Some Factors in the Development of Negro Social Institutions in the United States," by Guy B. Johnson, in the November 1934 issue of the *American Journal of Sociology;* "The Withdrawal from Haiti," by Ernest Gruening, in the July 1934 issue of *Foreign Affairs;* "Writing Vocabularies of Negro and White Children," by Fanny L. Segalla, in the December 1934 issue of *The School Review;* "The Educational Achievement of a group of Gifted Negro Children," by Paul A. Witly and Martin D. Jenkins, in the November 1934 issue of the *Journal of Educational Psychology.* In this last mentioned article the conclusion was reached that the greatest educational superiority of these gifted Negro children appeared in highly "verbal" subjects which appear not to depend greatly on school experience. This conclusion suggests the need for further study.

Addressing themselves to the study of the Negro scientifically, investigators report with such as "The Kerato-cricoid Muscle in the American White and Negro," by J. Hetherington; and the "Septal Apertures in the Humerus of American Whites and Negroes," by Mildred Trotter, both in the October issue of the *American Journal of Physical Anthropology;* "Patterns of the Aortic Arch in American White and Negro Stocks, with Comparative Notes on Certain other Mammals," by B. De Garis (C. F.), I. H. Black, and E. A. Riemenschneider in the *Journal of Anatomy,* Vol. XL, pages 599-619; and "The Calcification of the First Costal Cartilage among Whites and Negroes," by G. Bouck in the same publication.

In Books Dealing With Other Countries

We are often ignorant of what is being done in Africa to understand the natives. The Europeans may not be very sentimental about it except in the case of a few missionaries; but, if that continent is to be exploited, some use must be made of the natives. It will be impossible to exterminate most of them as was done in the case of the North American Indians. The native Africans, then, must be understood. Their customs and laws must be properly grasped. The first step in the process, then, is to learn their languages. Many of these languages have been reduced to writing; and grammars and dictionaries of these tongues are multiplying.

Among these significant productions of recent years one should note the *Outline of Nuer Grammar,* by J. P. Crazzolara (Wien, Anthropos Bibliothek, 1934); *Outlines of Tswa Grammar,* by J. A. Person (Cleveland, Central Mission Press, 1933); *The Gram-*

mar of the Tiv, a Bantu people, by Captain R. C. Abraham (London, 1933); *Grammatica della Lingua Scilluk,* by Padre K. Kohnen (Cairo, Missione dell'Africa); *A Comparative Study in Shona Phonetics,* by Clement M. Doke (Johannesburg, Research Grant Board, Union of South Africa, 1933); *A Vocabulary of the Dialects of Mashonaland,* by B. H. Barnes (London, Sheldon Press, 1933); Suaheli Wörterbuch, by Carl Velten (Leipzig, Kommissionsverlag von Otto Harrowitz, 1933); *Dictionary of the Asantee and Fante Language called Tshi,* by I. G. Christaller (Basel, Basel Evangelical Missionary Society, 1933); *Swahili Exercises,* by Edward Steere (London, Sheldon Press, 1933); *La Langue Songhay, Dialecte Dyerma,* by Ardant du Picq and *Une population Africaine, les Dyerma,* by the same author (Paris, Larose, 1933); *La Langue des Bozo, population des pêcheurs du Niger,* by Charles Monteil (Paris, Larose, 1933); *Die Völker und Sprachen Kameruns,* by G. Tressman (Gotha, Justus Perthes, 1933); *Contes d'Afrique,* by René Guillot sous la direction de M. Albert Charlton (Gorée, Imprimerie du Gouvernement General, 1933); *Myths and Legends of the Bantu,* by Alice Werner (London, George G. Harts and Company, 1933); and *Practical Phonetics for Students of African Languages,* by D. Westerman (Oxford University Press, 1934).

For recent works on Africa we are fortunately unfortunate in having accessible the *Bibliographie d'Historie Coloniale, 1900-1930,* by Alfred Martineau, M. Roussier, and M. J. Tramond. This work was produced with official stamp and therefore carefully planned so as not to offend any European nation. Each contributor of the bibliography of the colonies of a power had his own part to himself; and, if efficient and scholarly, his production might bear that stamp; and, if to the contrary, it might work out otherwise. It happened, for example, in the case of the Belgain colonies that the works excoriating the government for its atrocities in the Congo were not included. The same rule applied in the cases of other countries. Parts of this work, then, are ex parte.

Among these publications in French should be noted first those which appeared from the press of the Société d'Editions Géographiques, Maritimes et Coloniales in connection with the "Exposition Coloniale Internationale de 1931." While these productions

are primarily intended to portray the economic conditions of
these colonies they give information on the natives in showing
the extent to which their continent has been modernized. It
should be noted, too, that in 1927 this same press brought out
an interesting work, *L'Afrique Centrale: La Colonie du Niger*,
by Maurice Abadie, with an introduction by Maurice Delafosse.
These later productions of mainly commercial value are *Le
Niger, Le Sénégal, Le Soudan, La Côte d'Ivoire, La Mauritaine,
La Haute-Volta, La Guinée, Le Dahomey*, and *La Circonscription
de Darkar et Dépendances*. Two of these works of this society
are more informing with respect to the natives and more nearly
scientific than the others, namely *Afrique Occidentale Française*,
by Robert Delavignette, and *Afrique Equatoriale Française*, by
Julien Maigret, both of 1931.

The works of travellers in Africa still multiply. Many of
them unfortunately, are written to advertise the author or to
make money. In some instances, however, these books are informing as has been recently brought out in the case of Professor Frank Monaghan's *French Travellers in the United States
1765-1932*. Among those on Africa recently appearing we find
The Traveller in the East, by Thomas Mofolo (translated by H.
Ashton, the Society for the Promotion of Christian Knowledge,
London) ; *Africa*, a new edition, by Louis Bertrand del'Académie
Française (Paris, Albin Michel, 1933) ; *Nos Frères Noirs, Came-
roun-Dahomey*, by Henriette Celarié (Paris, Hachette, 1932) ; *The
Coast of Treasure*, by Lawrence C. Green (London, Putnams,
1933) ; and *L'Afrique Fantome*, by Michel Leiris (Paris, Librarie
Gallimard, 1934). This last mentioned work is a record of the
progress through Africa of the expedition headed by M. Griaule
across the continent from Darkar to Djbouti about two years ago.

In a serious vein certain writers have produced interesting
works on the political, social and economic aspects of Africa.
Such may be noted as *France et Afrique du Nord avant 1930: les
précurseurs de la conquête*, by F. Charles-Roux (Collection du
Centenaire de l'Algerie, Paris, Felix Alcan, 1932) ; *Fondation de
l'Etat Indépendant du Congo: un chapitre de l'histoire du par-
tage de l'Afrique*, by Robert Stanley Thompson, professeur d'histoire à Russell Sage College (Brussels, Publicity Office, 1933) ;
Native Administration in the Union of South Africa, by H. Rog-

ers (University Witwatersrand Press, 1933); *Modern Industry and the African*, by J. Merle Davis (London, 1933); *Histoire de la Colonisation Française*, by Georges Hardy (Paris, Larose, 1931); *Le Travail Obligatoire dans les colonies africaines*, by René Mercier (Paris, Larose, 1933); *L'Afrique champs d'expansion de l'Europe*, by E. L. Guernier (Paris, Librarie Armand Colin, 1933); *A la Recherche d'une politique indigène dans l'Ouest Africain*, by Henri Labouret (Paris, Editions du Comité de l'Afrique Française); *L'Ere des Négriers, 1714-1774, d'apres des documents inédits*, by Gaston-Martin (Paris, Librarie Felix Alcan, 1931).

Endeavoring to give a picture of Africa which may carry the impression of a large continent of many interests and possibilities, writers have brought out such works as *An African People in the Twentieth Century*, by L. P. Mair (London, George Routledge and Sons, 1933); *The African Today*, by D. Westerman (London, Sheldon Press, 1933); and *The Abyssinian at Home*, by C. H. Walker (London, Sheldon Press, 1933). Going into a detailed exposition of the tribes we observe such as *Bambuti, Die Zwerge von Congo*, by Paul Schebesta (Brockhaus, 1933); *Die Bafia und die Kultur der Mittelkamerun-Bantu*, by Gunter Tressman (Stuttgart, Strecker und Schröeder, 1934); *Die Afrikanischen Trommeln und ihre Ausserafrikanischen Beziehungen,* by H. Wieschoff (Stuttgart, Strecker und Schröeder, 1933); *Differenzierungserscheinungen in einigen Afrikanischen Gruppen*, by Sjoerd Hofstra (Amsterdam, Sheltema und Holkema's Boeckhandel, N. V., 1933), an empirical approach to a sociological and psychological problem; *Les Bayansi du Bas-Kwilu*, by R. de Beaucorps (Louvain, Editions de l'Aucam, 1933); and *Valenge Women, by E. Dora Earthy* (Oxford University Press, 1933).

Les Paysans Noirs, by R. Delavignette (Paris, Librarie Stock, 1931), is a sort of seasonal study. This is a story of natives of the Sudan arranged or based upon the life of each month of the year. *Les Jaga et les Bayaka du Kwango*, by M. Plancquaert (Bruxelles, Marcel Hayez, Imprimeur de l'Académie Royale de Belgique, 1932), is an historical and ethnographic work of a Jesuit who toiled some years among these natives. There appeared, too, *Les Peuples de l'Oubangui-Chari*, by Félix Eboué (Paris, Publications du Comité de l'Afrique Française, 1933); *Le*

Cameroun by J. Wilbois (Paris, Payot, 1934) ; *An Outline of Religious Dahoman Belief*, by M. J. and F. S. Herskovits (The American Anthropological Association, Menasha, Wisconsin, 1934) ; *Die Ursprung der Gottesidée: Eine Historisch-Kritische und Positive Studie*, by P. W. Schmidt (Munster und Westfalen, Verlag der Aschen-dorffischen der Urvölker Afrikas, 1933) ; *Das Einegeborenenrecht*, by Erich Schulz-Ewerth und Leonard Adam (Stuttgart, Strecker and Schröeder, 1930), dealing with Togo, Kameroon, Southwest Africa, and the South Sea Colonies; and *Coutumes Civiles des Baoulés de la region de Dimbokro*, by Marc Menalque (Paris, Larose, 1933). To these may be added some of a miscellaneous order as *Biene und Honig im Volksleben der Afrikaner mit Besonderer Berucksichtigung der Bienenzucht, ihrer Entstehung und Verbreitung*, by Carl Seyfert (Leipzig, 1930) ; *Der Islam in Ost-Afrika*, by Richard Rensch (Leipzig: Adolf Klein, 1931) ; *Ferro e Fuoco in Somalia*, by F. S. Caroselli (Roma, Sindicato Italiano, Arti Grfiche, 1933) ; *Il Cammello; I Reparti Cammellati*, von Massimo Adolfo Vitale (Rome, 1934).

In Works of Art and Archaeology

Still interested in the art and archaeology of Africa, new authors appear also in the field. Unfortunately most of them, with characteristic bias, try to explain why the natives of Africa should not be considered as the originators of these relics. Among the recent works to be noted in this sphere one observes *Contribution à l'Étude des Gravures Ruprestres et Inscriptions Tifnar du Sahara Central*, by M. Reygasse, (Alger, J. Carbonnel, 1932) ; *Paleolithic Man and the Nile Valley in Nubia and Upper Egypt*, a Study of the region during Pliocene and Pleistocene times, by K. S. Sandiford and W. J. Arkell (Chicago, The University of Chicago Press, 1933) ; *Kunst der Naturvölker*, by Eckart von Sydow (Berlin, Cassirer, 1933) ; *L'Ardrar Ahmet, Contribution à l'étude archéologique du District Saharien*, by Theodore Monod (Paris, Institut d'Ethnologie, 1933) ; and *The Rock Engraving of Griqualand and Bechuanaland, South Africa*, by M. Wilman (Cambridge, Deighton, Bell, and Company, Stationers, 1933).

In Articles in Magazines Dealing with Other Countries

In the January issue of *Journal of the African Society* appeared ''Labour Migration from a Bechuanaland Native Reserve,''

Part II (concluded), by Dr. I. Schapera; "Some Problems arising from the Part Played by Goats and Sheep in the Social Life of the Kikuyu," by I. S. B. Leaky in the same issue; "The Importance of the Educated African," by W. M. MacMillan, late Professor of History of the University of the Witwatersrand, Johannesburg, in the April issue; "How shall we Educate the African?" by B. N. Azikiwe in the same issue; "Liberia and the League of Nations," by Dr. M. D. Mackenzie in the October issue; "The Constitutional Relation of South African Protectorates," by Sir Clarkson Tredgold; and also "Native Affairs in Kenya," a report by a correspondent.

In *Africa,* the organ of the International Institute of African Languages and Cultures, appeared in January, 1934, "The Linguistic Situation in the Southern Sudan, by A. N. Tucker; "Mental Tests in the Study of the African," by Richard A. C. Oliver; "The Educational Work of Missionary Societies," by J. H. Oldham; "The Gold Coast, 1931," by H. A. Harman; "Die Buschmänner Südwestafrikas," by Viktor Lebzelter; "Arts en voie de disparition au Gabon," by F. Grébert; and "A Good Village," by T. Cullen Young.

In the April issue of *Africa* appeared "Die Afrikanischen Kulturkreise," by H. Baumann; "The Functions of Bride-Wealth in Ubena of the Rivers," by A. and T. and G. M. Culwick; "The Isoko Tribe," by James W. Welch; "L'Ethnologie de l'Afrique Centrale et le Musée du Congo-Belge," by J. Maes; "The Writing of History Textbooks for Africa," by W. E. Ward; "Some Notes on History and Geography Textbooks used in Africa," by D. G. Brackett and M. Wrong; and "East African Census Reports, 1931," by Frank Melland.

In the July issue of this publication appeared "The Kulu in Northern Nigeria," by C. K. Meek; "Les cas de possession et l'exorcisme chez les Vandau," by H. Ph. Junod; Die Bedeuting des Rindes bei den Nuer," by P. P. Crazzolora; "A Re-statement of Indirect Rule," by Margery Perham; "Methods of Study of Culture Contact," by Monica Hunter; "Lamba Literature," by C. M. Doke; "A Standard Hausa Dictionary," by D. Westerman.

In the October issue of *Africa* appeared "The Sociological Study of the Native Diet," by Reymond Firth; "The Study of Culture Contact as a Practical Problem," by L. P. Mair; "Indirect Rule and Education in East Africa," by C. C. Latham; "La Tribu Kwanyama en face de la civilisation Européenne," by P. C. Estermann; "The Problem of Relationship between Pygmies and Bushmen," by Walter Hirschberg; "Ibo Texts," selected, by R. F. G. Adams; "South African Publications relating to African Life and Languages," by I. Schapera.

In *Outre-Mer* have appeared such articles as "Ethnologie Coloniale," by Henri Labouret, in 1932; "Coutume Successorale des Sérères du Sine et du Saloum," by J. Bourgeau; "Notes sur le caractère des Peuls," by Gilbert Vieillard; "Folklore soudanais," by Dominique Traoré; "Ethnographie dahoméenne," by Guillaume Cyrille; Le Caiman sacré de Poun," by G. L. Ponton; "De la gaieté du Noir d'Afrique," by Mamby Sidibé; "Les problems posés par l'islamisation du Proche-Orient et de l'Afrique mediterranéenne," by Gaston Bouthoul; "Études sur quelques prénoms et noms de familles bambara," by Captain Delaforge, in 1932; and "Contribution à l'étude des coutumes des Balantes de Sedhiou," in 1933.

In the *Bulletin du Comité d'Études Historiques et Scientifiques* appeared some interesting articles in 1933: namely, "Mollusques terrestres et fluviales de l'Afrique Occidentale Française," by L. Germain; "Le Sénégal d'autrefois, Étude sur le Cayor," by R. Rousseau; "Contribution à l'histoire des Régueibat," by Ahmadou Ba; "Le Mahométisme daus le 'Hombori' en 1922," by Pol-Pagès; and "Araouan," by Commandant Péfontan. "The Routine of Commerce between Genoa and Northwest Africa during the late Twelfth Century," in the October 1933 issue of the *Mariner's Monthly,* may interest certain readers in this sphere.

Books for Teaching African Natives

The matter of teaching the native out of his own background has received some attention in Africa and at headquarters in home countries where they must safeguard the development of the African's mind. The matter of deciding upon history texts has proved to be a very difficult task. How can you teach the native the Crusades, one of these authors inquires, without leading him to regard as heroes Saladin and Almansour rather than so consider Richard Coeur de Lion and Saint Louis? One might have raised also the question as to how you can teach the native the history of Africa so as to lead him to admire such subjugators as Lugard, Faidherbe, and McCarthy rather than their own African patriots like El-Hadj Omar, Samori, and Chaka. To avoid such troubles a French author in discussing this difficulty advises that the teaching of African history should begin with the European penetration of the continent and that should be taught as a godsend for the people.

In view of these attitudes toward African education it may be profitable to notice *La Collaboration scolaire des Gouvernements Coloniaux et des Missions,* by J. Mazé (Maison Carrée, Alger, Imprimerie des P. P. Blancs, 1933); *British History for Overseas Students,* by E. E. Ward (London, Longmans, Green, 1934); *Moussa et Gi-Gla: Histoire de deuxs petits noirs,* a current reader used in instructing the natives in West Africa, by L. Sonolet and A. Pérès; *Suggested Methods for the African School,* by Harold Jowett (London, Longmans, Green and Company, 1933); *Les Femmes Médicins Missionaires,* by Arlette Butavand (Louvain, Edition de l'Aucam, 1933); *General Intelligence Tests for Africans, Manual of Directions* (Government Printer, Nairobi, Kenya Colony, 1932); and *Litafi Mai-tsarki, Tsofon Alkawali da Sabon Alkawali* (London-British and Foreign Bible Society, 1932). This last mentioned work is the Bible in Hausa.

Ezra Eziekel Smith

In 1877 the legislature of North Carolina established for the education of Negroes a State Normal School at Fayetteville. This school was opened that autumn under the principalship of Robert Harris, who served the institution efficiently until his death. Upon the passing of Mr. Harris, Charles W. Chesnut, a native of Ohio who had taught in North Carolina prior to this time, was chosen as principal of this school. After serving the institution for three years he went back to Cleveland in his native state where he became a law-reporter and achieved national fame for himself as a novelist portraying Negro life. Chesnut was succeeded by Ezra Eziekel Smith in August, 1883. In this position Smith served, with the exception of two interruptions, from that time until he died.

Ezra Eziekel Smith was born in Dublin County North Carolina, May 23, 1852. He attended school in Wilmington and Greensboro, but he completed his education at Shaw University in which he maintained his interest down to his death. He served the institution recently as trustee. He started out in life as a teacher in Wayne County, North Carolina, in a log schoolhouse which he built with his own hands. About this time, in 1875, he married Miss Willie A. Burnett, who bore him a son, Dr. E. E. Smith, Jr., a physician of Newport News. In 1879 Dr. Smith was ordained to preach in the Baptist Church, but his most serious effort in this sphere was that while devoting his attention mainly to education he pastored the First Baptist Church of Fayetteville six years. In 1908, a year after the death of his first wife, the educator married Nannie Louise Goode. To this union no children were born.

On the occasion of delivering an address on Liberia at Shaw University, he made such a favorable impression, that persons from afar sought copies of this discourse. Among those making this request was the executive of the American Colonization Society. Because of the new thought with respect to Africa and the vision which the speaker seemed to manifest, his prestige was thereby greatly enhanced wherever this address was read. Fortunately, when Grover Cleveland became President of the United States, he requested the American Colonization Society to recommend some exceptional Negro for the ministership to that country. This body, still retaining the impression which this teacher had made upon them with this address, highly recommended Ezra Eziekel Smith for the position, and he was appointed. He sailed for Liberia and presented his credentials to that government on July 21, 1888.

In this position Dr. Smith had been preceded by John J. Henry and Abraham Henson, with the title of Commissioner and Consul General, and by John Seys, Francis E. Dumas, James W. Mason, J. Milton Turner, John H. Smyth, Henry Highland Garnett, Moses A. Hopkins, and Charles H. J. Taylor, with the title of Minister Resident and Consul General. J. Milton Turner was the first Negro to serve in that position. The records of the State Department show that Dr. Smith discharged his functions well and reflected credit upon his race and his nation. Dr. Smith was called upon again as an interruption to his work at Fayetteville when he accepted the invitation to become Adjutant of the Third North Carolina Volunteer Infantry, during the Spanish-American War.

Although Dr. Smith accumulated considerable wealth, sufficient to lend his church once $10,000 for remodeling, the most constructive work of Dr. Smith was in connection with the school which he headed. What this institution accomplished is due in a large measure to his leadership and vision. It has developed from the occupancy of an up-stairs room in an old building on Gillespie Street to its ample site of fifty acres on which are twelve buildings valued at more than $400,000. He was virtually the founder of the Fayetteville State Normal School, the oldest institution of the kind for Negroes in the United States. In 1908 he purchased with his own money forty acres of land, which he deeded to the state, in order that the school might leave its cramped rented quarters in the city and move to its present beautiful site where it is unhampered in its expansion.

SIMON G. ATKINS

When the State of North Carolina sent an exhibit to the Sesqui-Centennial Exposition in Philadelphia in 1926, it included a display of the work of Negro education in North Carolina. In preparing this part of the exhibit, the State Department of Public Instruction requested the leading colored people of the State to name the fourteen persons of their race who had done most for Negro education in North Carolina during the twenty-five years preceding that time. Dr. Simon G. Atkins' name headed that list. This useful career ended June 28, 1934.

Dr. Simon G. Atkins was born in Haywood, Chatham County, North Carolina, June 11, 1863. He attended school in his home county, and in 1880 entered the Academic Department of St. Augustine's Normal and Collegiate Institute, Raleigh, N. C. There he was graduated with distinction in 1884. Later in life he traveled extensively in this country and abroad.

When he had finished college, he accepted the invitation of President J. C. Price of Livingstone College in Salisbury, to join the faculty of that institution. There he served in a most acceptable manner for six years, at the expiration of which he moved to Winston-Salem to take charge of and develop the colored public schools of that town. Livingstone regretted to part with such an unselfish worker and noted among its records the loss thereby sustained.

After five years of marked success as principal of the colored public school of Winston-Salem, Dr. Atkins gave up the work against the protest of the board of school commissioners, and made plans for the founding of the Slater Industrial and State Normal School, a private institution which has been made the Winston-Salem State Teachers College. One of his first steps in this direction was the founding of the settlement known as "Columbian Heights" in which the school is located. The community was started in 1891, with Dr. Atkins as the first settler. The institution was established in 1892, and has grown steadily since that time. From that date to the end of his life Dr. Atkins' labors were an inseparable part of its history. As head of the Slater State Normal School, now the Winston-Salem Teachers College, there radiated from him and the institution an influence for good among all the people of Winston-Salem and North Carolina. He had several opportunities to accept offers for higher compensation, like the presidency of Livingston and that of the Agricultural and Technical College, but he preferred to stay at his post of duty.

The Winston-Salem Teachers College became a standard normal school in 1920, and discontinued its high school work in 1923. This was made possible by an arrangement with the municipality of Winston-Salem by which the local high school for Negroes took over the high school work of the college after 1923. The Winston-Salem Teachers College thus became the first institution of higher learning for Negroes in North Carolina to restrict its work entirely to that of college grade. In 1925 the General Assembly gave the institution enlarged powers and extended its work from two years to four years above high school. For this expansion Dr. Atkins obtained not only increased appropriations from the State but grants from the General Education Board, the Rosenwald Fund, N. W. Reynolds, and the citizens of Winston-Salem.

Dr. Atkins, however, was not merely a servant of North Carolina. He was a man nationally known and sought after for co-operation in all things pertaining to the uplift of the Negroes of the United States. Although a layman, he held important positions in the A. M. E. Zion Church. For forty years he served as a delegate to its quadrennial conferences and once was a delegate to the Ecumenical Conference in London. He functioned, too, as the Secretary of Education of this connection, as its Secretary of Church Extension, and as a trustee of Livingstone College. All such movements as the National Association of Teachers in Colored Schools, the Association for the Study of Negro Life and History had his support and counted on his cooperation. North Carolina did not think of any citizen as being more highly respected than Simon G. Atkins.

LEVI J. ROWAN

In the death of L. J. Rowan passed out of action one of the outstanding Land-Grant College heads who have worked a revolution in the education of the Negroes of the United States since the World War. The same year, 1871, that the State of Mississippi purchased the historic Oakland College for the site of an institution for the higher education of the Negro, Rowan was born in Rodney, Louisiana, on the seventh of August. He studied there in the district school and in St. Joseph. Thus prepared, he entered Alcorn College and was graduated there in 1893. He then began his career as a teacher in a rural school in Lawrence County, Mississippi. To this rural section he took his wife (née Mattie Foote), whom he had just married. To this union were born: Victor, Ruth Inez, Mattie Hermione, Pearl Bernice, and Thelma Bee. In 1899 he was chosen to teach at Alcorn, his alma mater. In 1905 he was made president of the institution; and, with the exception of two years, he filled this position successfully until he passed away June 28, 1934.

Under his leadership Alcorn College witnessed a period of growth. There was improvement and expansion, both in its physical equipment and in the quality of the instruction given. From a few scattered and antiquated buildings, void of modern conveniences, and adequate for housing in any degree of health-giving comfort only a small group of students and instructors, the institution has developed into a model college community comprising more than twenty teachers' cottages, most of which are conveniently appointed, and fifteen public buildings with a capacity for the accommodation of a student group and faculty personnel of more than a thousand. "And from a loosely ill-integrated regime of non-cooperation, self-seeking, scheming, and intrigue, with all their attendant evils of inefficiency, the administration-faculty-student relationships were actually transformed into an efficient, cooperative, and harmonious educational effort."

Perhaps the greatest single achievement of the successful administration of the late President Rowan was the launching of what he took great pride in referring to as "The Greater Alcorn." This embraced among other phases of expansion a three hundred thousand dollar building program which added to the already greatly improved physical facilities a new dormitory for college women, an administration building, a science and agricultural building, all modernly appointed and fire-proof structures. This expansion included also three teachers' cottages, and a modern power, lighting, and heating plant. It meant, too, a thorough reorganization of the faculty to conform more closely to the latest requirements of modern college administrative procedure. As a natural sequence there came a revamping of academic, scientific, and industrial curricula to supply more adequately the present-day educational demands; and faculty members were required to further their academic and professional preparation by advanced study in the leading universities and colleges of the country.

CHARLES VICTOR ROMAN

Charles Victor Roman was born at Williamsport, Pennsylvania, on July 4, 1864. He died August 25, 1934. He was the son of Captain James William Roman and Anne Walker McGuin and was the fifth brother of the name. His father was a canal-boat owner, who moved to Canada where he married and finally settled at a place called Dundas in Ontario. Charles Victor, the son, worked first in a cotton mill and studied in a night school established for the mill boys by the Rev. Featherstone Osler, the father of the famous Sir William Osler.

An injury to his right knee and the surgical treatment of that day conspired to bring about the loss of one limb. The long convalescence gave him ample time to plan his future. His hungry, inquiring mind determined to answer the call of the blood; and upon his bed, he mapped out the steps that he followed, with extremely few digressions. As soon as he was able to get out on crutches, he entered the Hamilton Collegiate Institute, the four-year course of which he completed in three years.

The idea that next dominated the young Roman was to become a doctor of medicine. To obtain funds for this purpose he turned to teaching, and to do this he reversed the trip of his forbears and went from Canada to the Southland, where he remained. His early plan included medical study at McGill University in Montreal, but the threads of destiny made him a graduate of Meharry Medical College.

Upon completing his medical studies in 1890, he went to Clarksville, Tennessee, where he practiced for a short while. He settled in Dallas, Texas, and there well established himself as a physician. In 1891, he married Margaret Voorhees, who, like himself, had been of that gallant band of teachers in a time when means and methods were meager and difficult. Throughout his long and honourable career she was the steady and faithful consort upon whom he leaned heavily. They had no children.

In the setting of an arduous and busy professional life, Dr. Roman found time to read contemporaneous medical literature, to steep himself in the classics, to write numerous pamphlets, to keep up with every forward movement, to take post-graduate courses. He became interested in the diseases of the eye, ear, nose and throat. After fourteen years as a general practitioner he realized one of his dreams by going to Europe to study. On his return, he became the first man of his race, in that section, to limit his activities to the subject of his choice; at the same time, he was appointed to the faculty of Meharry Medical College as the first professor of ophthalmology, otology, rhinology and laryngology. He was one of the founders of the National Medical Association and for ten years editor-in-chief of its official journal. During the Great War, he was lecturer to troops of the United States Army. Fisk University made him its Director of Physiology and Hygiene.

His command of trenchant English, his wide acquaintance with the world, and his deep insight into the philosophy of life enabled him to present in striking and memorable phrases the essence of truth and to express his thought in an inimitable manner. In two of his books, *American Civilization and the Negro* and *Meharry Medical College—A History*, are these qualities brought to light. He was positive in his opinions, practical in his application of thought and progressive in his philosophy. A vigorous idealist for the fulfillment of human living, he possessed in the highest degree the imaginative, youthful and aspiring mind. He was a devotee at the Janus-faced shrine of Science, the Science of Art and Health; and his whole being was consecrated to the health of body, mind, and soul.

GEORGE CLINTON CLEMENT

George Clinton Clement, a bishop of the African Methodist Episcopal Zion Church, was born about four miles from the little village of Mocksville in Davie County, North Carolina, December 23, 1871. He died October 23, 1934. He was the youngest of six children, the only son of Albert Turner Clement and Eleanor Carter, both ex-slaves, the former an ordained and active minister of the A. M. E. Zion Church. He received his first formal instruction in the public schools of his home county; later he attended Livingstone College, Salisbury, North Carolina, from which he was graduated with the degree of Bachelor of Arts in May, 1898.

On the same day that he received his first baccalaureate degree from Livingstone College, May 25, 1898, he was joined in wedlock to Emma Clarissa Williams, another graduate of Livingstone College and a native of Providence, Rhode Island. To this union were born eight children: Abbie Evelyn, Rufus Early, Frederick Albert, John Clinton (deceased), Ruth Elizabeth, George Williams, James Addison and Emma Mills.

At an early age the youthful George accepted the Christian faith and expressed a desire to follow in his father's footsteps as a Methodist minister. Consequently, in 1893 he was ordained in the ministry of the African Methodist Episcopal Zion Church. There followed pastorates at Zebulon, Landis, Salisbury and Charlotte, North Carolina, and at Louisville, Kentucky. From this last pastorate he was elevated to the editorship of the *Star of Zion,* official paper of his denomination, by the General Conference meeting in Saint Louis, Missouri, in May, 1904. Dr. Clement served as editor of this church paper from 1904 to 1916; during the last years of this period he was also the manager of the A. M. E. Zion Publishing House at Charlotte, North Carolina.

The General Conference of 1916, meeting in Broadway Temple, Louisville, Kentucky, conferred the highest honor of his church upon him by elevating him to the bishopric. Under his supervision churches were purchased or erected at many places, including Chicago, Illinois; Chattanooga, Tennessee; Cleveland, Akron and Cincinnati, Ohio; High Point, Greensboro and Monroe, North Carolina; and Detroit, Michigan. For the past eight years and more he was the chairman of the Commission on Race Relations of the Federal Council of Churches of Christ in America, and a member of the Southern Inter-racial Commission.

One of the few Negroes wise and courageous enough to be a democrat in politics twenty years ago, he was strong enough to refuse a diplomatic post offered by President Woodrow Wilson, preferring to remain in America where he could actively interest himself in the welfare of his people. He could not leave his post of duty for the glare of such a position, for second only to his love of God was his love of his fellowman. Down to the end of his career he was known for his simple, kindly spirit, and his loving heart. No person was too low or poor or insignificant to receive the warm genuine friendship of George Clinton Clement.

Maintaining a Family Tradition—Ulysses Samuel Wharton

As people begin to advance they develop what is called traditions. Family traditions are highly prized; and the aristocratic element belonging to the exploiting and slaveholding classes have long ridiculed Negroes and poor whites who have no such traditions. Certain social scientists of our time, moreover, have entered upon the study of Negro life with the intent of enlarging upon the lack of proper background in the Negro family. It is well, then, to note the case of highly developed family traditions among Negroes as well as the lack of it among those unfortunately circumstanced. We sometimes forget that there were about 50,000 free Negro heads of families in the United States more than a century ago; and almost 4,000 of them, following in the foot-steps of the oppressors of the weak, had become slaveholders themselves. These half million free Negroes had taken their places in all walks of life as mechanics, artisans, business men, and professionals.

In no recent case is the family tradition among Negroes better maintained than in that of the Whartons of Averett, in Mecklenburg County, Virginia. George D. Wharton, a product of an enterprising Negro family, early educated himself in the fundamentals at Hampton and in law at Howard University. He entered upon life seriously. He endeavored to do at least as much as his forbears in impressing himself upon his generation not as a great man but as a useful citizen. In this community he began as a teacher and minister. There he acquired 1,800 acres of land and developed a model farm which gave tone to the community. His neighbors increased and the place assumed the aspect of a prosperous and happy district. He took up house construction and built comfortable homes for his neighbors. He opened a store there, engaged in real estate, served as postmaster, and functioned as the leader in all things social and economic which pertained to that community. At one time he was said to be worth a hundred thousand dollars. In this position he was respected far and wide, not only by the people of his own race, but by many others who had learned to know his worth.

George D. Wharton believed in education. He gave every opportunity, then, to his son, Ulysses Samuel Wharton, born to him and his wife (née Mary Craddock) December 6, 1885; and the son, appreciating the traditions of the family, tried to live up to what was required of him. At Hampton and Oberlin, where the young Wharton obtained his literary training, he grounded himself thoroughly in fundamentals which, with his medical education at Howard University, enabled him to lead a useful career. In this the youth was exceptional. Being the son a well-to-do man, he never faced that pecuniary embarrassment of so many students of his day. The traditions of his family were ever before him, however, and served as the guiding principle of his life. He felt that he could not be the son of George D. Wharton and be dishonorable. This thought was more deeply impressed than ever upon the son when the father passed away December 12, 1932.

Starting out in life as a physician, after serving an interneship at Freedman's Hospital in Washington, D. C., Dr. Wharton took with him to Altoona, his chosen field, Cordella Hughes Murdock, a product of one of the best families of North Carolina transplanted to the District of Columbia. In Altoona Dr. Wharton was on strange soil, for he was the first professional man of his race to settle in that city. He was fortunate in reaching Altoona, however, just before the time of the terrible epidemic of Influenza in 1917. Dr. Wharton easily convinced the white physicians of the city that he could more successfully treat this malady than any other doctor in those parts. He at once became idolized by them; and in spite of the usual racial barrier there was no professional courtesy which they would not gladly accord him. They made him a member of the Blair County Medical Association without his seeking the consideration and likewise placed him on the staff of the Altoona Hospital. This attitude remained unchanged down to the time of his death December 2, 1934.

Dr. Wharton, however, did not suffer on account of these recognitions. He spent some time daily in self-improvement, kept in touch with best and latest in the field of medicine, and worked indefatigably among his people to improve their health and happiness. When told that the effort to take care of such a large practice would undermine his health he would always reply that he wanted to serve the people down to the moment "that the bell rings." As a result he had a large practice which enabled him to keep his family above want and to provide for the education of his two sons, Murdock and Ulysses, who thus have the opportunity to maintain this family tradition of efficient service and lofty ideals.

MAGGIE LENA WALKER

In no recent case has the Negro race suffered a greater loss than in the death of Maggie Lena Walker, who passed away December 15, 1934. She belonged to that group of enterprising Negroes who, like W. W. Browne, the founder of the True Reformers, turned the Negro's penchant for secret societies into a business channel. From 1899 until her death she was the moving spirit of the Independent Order of St. Luke, an industrial insurance secret society, which up to the time she took charge had done little more than to have their annual meetings and display their regalia. This woman reorganized the order, systematized its business procedure, expanded the work, increased the benefits to members, accumulated assets, and established a bank at the headquarters in Richmond. As the president of the Saint Luke Penny Savings Bank she was the first woman of any race to occupy such a position in the modern world. Her life, then, offered the historian something new under the sun.

Maggie Lena Walker was born of William and Elizabeth Mitchell in Richmond, Virginia, July 15, 1865. Her mother's parents were Frederick and Peggie Draper. Her father died early, probably as a result of being robbed and drowned. The mother, an encumbered widow, struggling in domestic service to maintain a family, could not do much for the daughter. The young woman had to carve out her own future through hardships. In some way, however, she contrived to attend the public schools in Richmond and to undergo the training required then to teach. She entered upon this task with an enthusiasm which characterized her throughout life. She taught not only in the public school but, being an ardent worker in the religious sphere, she accomplished as much as an instructor in the Sunday School of the First Baptist Church with which she was connected.

During the three years which she taught, Mrs. Walker served also as a local insurance agent among her people in Richmond. For her, this experience was most fortunate. She saw unusual opportunities among her own people who had never been directed toward economic enterprise. She realized, too, that if this field is to be exploited, it must be done by efficient service. To equip herself further for such tasks as might be assigned her in the future, she took a business course, specializing especially in accounting and salesmanship. These qualifications enabled her to function further in the public life after she had married in 1890 Armistead Walker, a young man with whom she had become acquainted. To this union two children were born; but, although the cares of the household were sometimes taxing, Mrs. Walker never lost her interest in public affairs. Her husband passed away June 20, 1915.

Active for some time in the Independent Order of St. Luke, Mrs. Walker had worked up in the ranks to the position of national deputy and later to that of its executive secretary. In 1899 she became the actual head of the order, and held this post until her death. The work of the order grew not as agency for display but as an enterprise which impressed its worth upon both races of Virginia and the Eastern States into which it expanded. New opportunities were thereby afforded Mrs. Walker for helping the Negroes engaged in social uplift and economic enterprise; and she cheerfully responded to these appeals from various parts of the country. Virginia Union University in Richmond, Virginia Theological Seminary and College at Lynchburg, the Virginia Industrial School at Peaks, and the Manual Training School at Hanover were the recipients of her largest benefactions.

THE JOURNAL

OF

NEGRO HISTORY

Vol. XX—April, 1935—No. 2

NEGRO HISTORY WEEK THE TENTH YEAR

Negro History Week has undergone an evolution. Every year the public takes the celebration more seriously and approaches nearer and nearer the well defined objectives of the effort. Being gradually removed from the popular manifestations of eloquent speech laudatory of a few figures in history, the observance has become a sort of stock-taking period—one of inquiry into what has been revealed in the works of those who write with scientific objectivity and what use may be made of such data in the education of the youth. The public is becoming desirous of learning what the Negro African actually accomplished during the ancient and medieval times, how the race figured in the development of modern nations, and why its status is such as it is today in various parts of the modern world. While most of this thought may be traced to the minds of those engaged in the schoolroom the reports show that it has reached persons and circles in all walks of life.

One of the most successful and helpful means in sustaining this effort has been the use of tests on Negro life and history. These inquiries had to be conducted judiciously, however, because of the frequent embarrassment possible by the revelations therefrom resulting. Heads of schools and colleges for Negroes cannot always be called upon to test students on matters which they themselves do not know. It was easily discovered that most of these functionaries know less about the race than the children who have recently felt the impulse to learn something about themselves. With the exception of a knowledge of a few churchmen who have figured in the denomination to which they belong and some simple facts about Frederick Douglass, Booker T. Washington and Paul Lawrence Dunbar, the educators in charge of Negro schools know practically nothing of the racial or African background. They themselves were educated away from the race rather than to the race; and they have, therefore, mis-educated their students. Instead of teaching the Negro first about himself and then about other things in relation to himself, they have taught the Negro first about others and then about things in relation to others. It has been revealed, then, that the actual education of the Negro has not yet begun.

When there has been any opposition to the celebration of Negro History Week it has come from the misguiding administrators and instructors of Negroes who have been thus misdirected. They have gone so far in the wrong direction after taking the wrong road at the fork that they cannot easily come back to the point of divergence and pursue the right course. In the large Negro universities little thought is given to the celebration of Negro History Week or to the work of the Association for the Study of Negro Life and History. The persons in charge of these higher institutions have been so thoroughly trained and directed to teach the Negro only about others and things in relation to others that their minds are sealed against any other thought. In the smaller colleges and public schools where the minds are in the plastic stage greater success has been achieved in penetrating the background of the Negro and popularizing what the race has achieved. The misfits afflicting the Negro schools, however, are not only ignorant of the history of the Negro, but do not care to acquire such knowledge as that upon which these tests are based.

The first of the tests used during this celebration was the *Negro History Week Pamphlet* itself. Departing somewhat from the make-up of former years, this illustrated brochure dealt mainly with the Negroes' achievements in Africa as a key to the interpretation of the rôle played by the race elsewhere. The pamphlet showed the emergence of African culture from the prehistoric period through the stone age to the iron age, the rise of kingdoms like Ethiopia, Egypt, Ghana, Melle, Songhay, Bornu, Hausa, and Congo. This brief treatise presented Africa along with Asia as a forerunner of Europe, which was civilized by the Orient, and brought out the parallel in the history of the fall of the Roman Empire with that of the African kingdoms which were likewise destroyed by barbarian invaders to undergo modern development under similar conquerors. Enlightened by these revelations in the *Negro History Week Pamphlet,* distributed by the thousands, the people's interest in Africa greatly increased, and the study of that background by both races widely extended. The general public at last realized that it had neglected a large portion of the history of mankind.

The tests used on the students as a rule dealt mainly with the Negro in modern times and especially in the United States. Only in a few cases did teachers believe that we have advanced far enough in the study of the African background to hold the children responsible for what adults themselves have just begun to take into account. The most interesting of the tests thus used were reported from the Schoolmen's Club of Greater Cincinnati and from Wilberforce University. Following the principles for such projects established by educators concerned with other aspects of history, these instructors took up all ramifications of the present and past of this element in America. The results obtained, while more encouraging than in the case of previous reports, show how few Negro students are graduated from high school or college with any useful knowledge of what their people have done or may have the capacity to do. Where such inquiries tested the knowledge of whites in their own or mixed schools it was brought out more clearly than ever how their ignorance of the Negroes among them accounts for their attitudes in conformity to that tendency of man to hate those whom he does not know.

The next important feature of the observance of Negro History Week was the more extensive use of exhibits of Negro books and pictures by libraries. The Library of Congress led the way with a fair exhibit of books and graphs dealing mainly with history. In this exhibit were a few works presenting the development of the Negro in science; but there was little on poetry, music, painting or any other arts in which the Negro has excelled. The Public Library of Washington, D. C., it reported, might have had an exhibit but the staff lacked space and there was such a demand for books on the Negro during this History Week season that they had not sufficient works for such display. The libraries of Elizabeth, Newark, Jersey City, Cleveland, Detroit, and Chicago gave brief reports of similar exhibitions; and some of these took occasion to submit lists of books which are set apart on accessible shelves or brought otherwise to the attention of readers as informing works adequate to supply useful information frequently called for by perons recently becoming interested in the Negro.

While some of these books thus exhibited and recommended may be questionable because of the bias of the authors now picturing the Negro, the reading of these will doubtless stimulate the seekers to study those which are worth while. Some libraries have been unfortunate in regarding as authoritative almost all the productions of the large publishing houses when as a matter of fact such firms will publish falsehood as readily as they will the truth if these meretricious works will sell. It is fortunate, then, that a number of these libraries have learned to rely upon the Associated Publishers, Inc., a firm cooperating with the Association for the Study of Negro Life and History in supplying the public with only worth while books and pictures bearing upon the Negro. To such libraries, then, have found their way not only useful shelves of books in this field but pictures, portraits, and busts of Negroes and their coworkers who have figured in the past of this race.

In connection with the libraries thus interested and with the branches and clubs cooperating with the Association adult education has been given considerable stimulus. The study circles beyond the schools have increased, but additional organizations established for other purposes have taken up this work as a part of their program. A larger number of our radio stations carried out Negro History Week programs, ministers worked the thought into special sermons for those days, and an increasing number of clubs had their programs culminate with this celebration. In fact, it is difficult to find any group of Negroes meeting for mutual improvement without providing for some sort of dissemination of information of this kind. Negro business men say repeatedly that the most convincing argument which they can use in arousing the Negroes to economic enterprise is the rehearsal of the encouraging past of the race.

It is observed also that the schools now adopting textbooks for the study of the Negro are gradually reaching the desirable end of "Negro History Year," the study of the Negro throughout the school life of the child just as we have it in studying the Hebrew, the Greek, the Latin, and the Teuton. In Delaware and North Carolina the state boards of education have adopted such textbooks. In city systems like Tulsa, Dallas, New Orleans, Birmingham,

Columbia, and Atlanta the same official action has been taken with respect to Negro History. Carrying this program further there are those who would work out a special series of readers as textbooks for Negro schools only, but the majority of persons giving thought thereto believe that such readers should be made merely supplementary for all schools and as such only until the authors of our readers and geographies will become broad enough to include the whole truth about all the elements of our population.

All schools, however, have not yet been sufficiently awakened to have to tackle such problems of procedure as these. Many of the efforts first made to arouse the public must be kept up in reaching those who have not become interested except in passive fashion. Speakers for the celebration, then, are still in demand; and it is gratifying to learn of the increasing number now sufficiently informed and interested to carry a message to the people. L. P. Jackson in Virginia, Miles Mark Fisher in North Carolina, Rayford W. Logan in South Carolina and Georgia, Lorenzo J. Greene in Missouri and Kansas proved to be acceptable speakers. Most other points used local speakers as did Texas after failing to secure the expected services of Dr. Charles H. Wesley. Carter G. Woodson had time to go as far North as Detroit where he made thirteen speeches to meetings of citizens and assemblies of six of the largest high schools and had the Board of Education of Detroit consider the proposal of providing for an optional course of Negro history. A later speaking tour to West Virginia including the State College and Charleston, the capital, had virtually the same results among the educational authorities in that State.

The thought of Negro History Week reached certain unexpected groups. Chief among these were the Federal rehabilitation camps where educational advisers have had to deal with Negroes. In most of these cases either their advisers or the men with whom they had to work thought immediately of the beneficial results which might be obtained from teaching the salient facts of history as it has been influenced by the Negro. It is remarkable that this proposal should be suggested as a factor in the rehabilitation of men, most of whom have failed. If the teaching of a racial background can be helpful in rebuilding men from a low level certainly this is a strong argument for thus giving greater strength to those still in action on a higher plane. Be that as it may, the experiment was extensively made among these men not merely through public exercises for this particular week, but by using such dramatizations and exhibitions as the culmination of the actual study of the Negro in these camps. Lectures in this field have been given these men. Books bearing on the Negro have been extensively circulated among them, thanks to these far-sighted educational advisers. Pictures of distinguished Negroes, too, have likewise been drawn upon to enlighten these men and to stimulate them in the direction of trying life again with new hope and unwonted vigor.

Still other unexpected groups were reached among the whites. In the first place, additional schools which have not hitherto given the Negro's past a thought took some notice of this celebration. Religious and quasi-civic organizations also directed thereto the attention of their coworkers. Observing Negro History Week for the first time, however, some of these had difficulty in learning where to find proper materials and how to proceed, but the interest thus shown indicates that they will stage more impressive exercises another year. Instead of merely having some one to appear before them merely to explain what the celebration means these persons report that they have definitely planned for future cooperation in a systematic manner. It should be noted that most of the circles thus concerned are in the South where the thinking people believe that the intelligent elements of both races must work together for a new program of that section. A knowledge of history and the present status of the Negro is considered essential to the working out of this new method of attack. White men who know nothing about the Negro are regarded as belated and unprepared to function in the South.

COPPERHEAD NEWSPAPERS AND THE NEGRO

Historians writing about the Civil War period in American history have paid attention to the Abolition movement, the Underground Railroad, and the Emancipation Proclamation. But rarely, save in special studies, has much been said about the enormous opposition in the North to the Abolitionists and to the emancipation of the slaves, and the antagonistic attitude toward the Negroes which continued outspoken in the North throughout the Civil War itself. This opposition came, for the most part, from the Democrats and the hardy Democratic press—the Copperhead newspapers. Their hostility toward the Lincoln administration was in part political, but was also due to a dislike of abolition and the "sooty Ethiopians."

In Philadelphia, the best known Copperhead Journal was the *Age*. Though the first issue did not appear until right in the middle of the Civil War, in March 1863, the editorials were written with all the self-assurance and confidence of an editor who has had continuous public support and favor for decades. The attitude of the *Age* toward Lincoln, his policies, the prosecution of the War, the Abolitionists, and the Negroes, may be considered typical of the Copperhead press over the country.[1] This article will concern itself mainly with the attitude toward the Negro and the Abolitionists.

The editors agreed with the southern supporters of the slave system that the institution was a good thing.

In its mad antagonism to slavery, the fanatical Abolitionism of the North precipated a peaceful and prosperous land into all

---

[1] This statement is based on the reading and collecting of material from the files of a number of Copperhead newspapers. The many exchanges quoted in these papers reveal similar attitudes. *Vid.* "*The Jeffersonian,* Copperhead Newspaper" by the author in *The Pennsylvania Magazine of History and Biography,* Volume LVII, July 1933, pp. 260-283.

the horrors of an internecine strife. In this, from the commencement, it has clearly shown that it was fighting against God and
his decrees. Slavery was established on this continent for wise
purposes in the Divine mind—to make it the nursery of civilization, from which, in His own good time, should be taken the
instruments through which benighted Africa was to be colonized,
civilized, and Christianized.[2]

This doctrine was a favorite one in the South, of
course, but was also frequently voiced by Democratic leaders in the North. The Rev. Henry J. Van Dyke, father of
the late Dr. Henry J. Van Dyke, of Princeton, was an
ardent Jeffersonian Democrat, who argued from Scrip-
ture to prove the divine sanction for slavery. Preaching in the First Presbyterian Church, Brooklyn, December
9, 1860, he claimed that slavery was written in divine law:

When the Abolitionist tells me that slaveholding is sin, in the
simplicity of my faith in the Holy Scriptures, I point him to this
sacred record and tell him in all candor . . . that his teaching
blasphemes the name of God and His doctrine. . . .

Slavery is permitted and regulated by Divine Law, under both
the Jewish and Christian dispensations, not as the final destiny
of the enslaved, but as an important and necessary process in
their transition from heathenism to Christianity—a wheel in the
great machinery of Providence by which the final redemption is
to be accomplished . . . there are Christian families in the South
in which slaves are better fed and clothed and instructed, and
have a better opportunity for salvation, than the majority of
laboring people in the city of New York. . . . Fanaticism in the
North is one chief stumbling block in the way of the gospel in
the South.[3]

The editors of the *Age* contended that with the slave
system the United States had lived "in peace and prosperity, aye, such prosperity as the world had never seen,
until the spoiler of Abolitionism entered our Eden and
drove us from it."[4] That the Negro was in any way the
equal of a white man was a notion repugnant to this
journal, and it marshalled every possible argument to

[2] The *Age*, August 5, 1864.

[3] *Fast Day Sermons*, Rudd and Carleton (editors). New York, Rudd and
Carleton, 1861, pp. 139; 152-53.

[4] The *Age*, August 5, 1864.

prove the black man decidedly the inferior creature. When Lincoln quoted and interpreted the Declaration of Independence to mean literally that "all men are created free and equal," the *Age* maintained that, "This is precisely what the Declaration of Independence did not mean or George Washington would not have owned slaves. . . . Had the Negroes in those days been declared the equal of the white man, no union would have been formed and no constitution adopted."[5]

All of the attempts of the President to elevate the status of the blacks were of no avail, since the equality of the Negro to the white man was "a question of anthropology—a question of science, which cannot be determined by Presidential dictum." "Mr. Lincoln," asserted the editors, "will not change the law of nature in that respect, any more than Canute the Dane could bid the tide to stand still."[6]

In order to prove scientifically that colored people were the inferior the newspaper ran a column or two of anthropological lore on numerous occasions. These items consisted mainly of reprinting of articles from reviews or tales from pseudo-anthropologists. One Captain Speke is quoted from the London *Review:*

A large portion of the Negro race effect nudity, despising clothing as effeminate, but these are chiefly the boisterous, roving pastrals (sic) who are too lazy either to grow cotton, or to strip trees of their bark. The young women go naked, but the mothers suspend a little tail before and behind. . . .

How the Negro has lived so many ages without advancing seems marvelous, when all the country surrounding Africa are so forward in comparison; and judging from the progressive state of the world, one is led to either suppose that an African must either soon step out of his darkness or be superseded by a being superior to himself. . . . At present the African can neither help himself or be helped by others.[7]

[5] The *Age*, July 9, 1863.
[6] *Ibid.*, July 9, 1863.
[7] *Ibid.*, August 25, 1864.

Captain Speke told of characteristic practices such as flaying and roasting babies alive. Yet he seems to have found the natives good servants. In fact, said he, the natives return to slavery through choice in which condition they are better off than in freedom.[8]

From all this the *Age* concluded that "the three million blacks in the United States are infinitely better off than other Africans in all the world."[9] In another connection the statement is made that "impartial observation" has shown that the happiness and well-being of the Negro were "most promoted" where his subjugation remained "most complete." Hence the Negro as a slave in the South was much better off than the northern free Negro.

Another method of proving the Negro essentially a barbarian and attempting to arouse public sentiment against him was put into practice. This consisted in relaying of stories of attacks and rape by Negroes upon white women and girls. The Copperhead newspapers were filled with reports of this type. An editorial under the caption, "More Effects of Negro Equality," quotes from the Ohio *Statesman* of July 8, 1864:

The police of this city yesterday unearthed one of the most horrible cases of crime and brutality that has ever transpired in Columbus, in which an educated and virtuous white woman was betrayed and outraged by a Negro, who had succeeded in keeping his victim buried from the knowledge of her friends and most respectable connections. The woman in question is a widow named Mary McBride.[10]

Mrs. McBride, it seems, had come eight months before from Iowa to collect a debt due her husband. She transacted her business and was taken ill on her way home. Funds grew low and she sought, while waiting for more, a reasonable boarding place. A Negro, Henry Burns, volunteered to find her such a place. The story continues:

[8] The *Age*, August 25, 1864.
[9] *Ibid.*
[10] *Ibid.*, July 12, 1864

This African villain . . . then took her to his room in a frame
house near the corner of third street on the alley between Long
and Spring streets where he fastened her in a miserable chamber,
and that night by the use of drugs or some diabolical instru-
mentality effected her ruin after taking what money she had left.
The woman gave no explanation by what means this was effected,
but makes it clearly understood that this was done against her
will. She was completely overwhelmed by the audacity of the
villain, and her own shame, and Burns by a horrible system of
intimidation compelled her to keep in the house, and refused her
all communication with the outside world. The ferocious character
of the brute, and his threats that he would kill her if she exposed
him or anybody who came near her, terrified the sickly and weak-
minded woman with subjection, and she has thus remained his
prisoner ever since. He subjected her to the most beastly treatment, and not only subdued her spirit, but reduced her body to a
skeleton.

By some means . . . someone discovered the woman . . . and
reported the facts to the . . . police. They repaired to the house
and found a realization of the story which at first they had
deemed incredible. The woman was found in bed apparently at
the point of death. It appears that an abortion had been attempted by the Negro, or that she had been delivered of a Negro
child—no sign of which could be found. . . . She appeared en-
feebled in body and mind and her language was sometimes wild
and incoherent, but her conversation evinced a high degree of
education. She mentioned a number of families with whom she
was acquainted, and claimed that her own connections were of the
highest respectability. She said her parents were Abolitionists,
but she would revolt at the idea of amalgamation. There was
nothing about the surroundings of the chamber or her narrative
to relieve the affair of its hideous and revolting character.

The Negro Burns, as black, hideous, and ferocious a monster
as could be found in the country, was arrested by the police and
lodged in the city prison to await further investigation of the
affair. He is sullen and reserved, and evidently thinks that it
will go hard with him if all the facts can be produced in
evidence.[11]

The story has been given here at some length to show
the pattern which most of them followed. The technique
of reporting is evident at a glance—the emphasis on the
mysteriousness and horror of the crime, the blackness
and brutality of the Negro, the innocence, education, re-

[11] The *Age*, July 12, 1864.

spectability, and defencelessness of the white woman, with all the details appealing to the reader's sense of pity on the one hand, and sexual and sadistic impulses on the other.

The Negro soldiers, who for several reasons were a constant source of contention, were accused of numerous "barbarities" — "rapine, murder, and incendiarism" were, according to reports, daily occurrences. But these activities did not always have to be proved. For instance, in relating the story of the burning of Darien on the Georgian coast by Negro Union troops under Montgomery, the *Age* reprinted the account from the Chicago *Times,* which stated, "Of the unnamable outrages committed by these loosed fiends upon defenceless women and children while the plundering was in progress we have no account, but those who know the race and their instincts will not require verbal evidence to set the truth before them."[12] Montgomery was accused of encouraging these "outrages" and his removal demanded.

Other accounts of such "atrocities" were clipped from southern newspapers. The Richmond *Enquirer,* for example, furnished an account of "Horrible Crimes of Negro Soldiers." In July 1864, a Colonel Draper led four hundred Negro troops from the 2nd Massachusetts Infantry (with white commissioned officers), and fifty white cavalry into Westmoreland County and proceeded to destroy everything in the line of march. The *Enquirer* claimed that all of the property of Mr. Ben English was destroyed, save his house, and after this he was "stripped, tied up and given thirty-nine lashes with cow hide." Moreover, "twenty-five or thirty ladies were violated by this party of Negroes." "I could give names," said the reporter, "but deem it best not. Neither age nor color was spared by these demons who were encouraged by their white officers."

[12] The *Age,* July 8, 1863.

In further advance under Colonel Draper on his march to Richmond County, "six Negroes violated the person of Mrs. G. eleven times, she being the wife of a brave soldier of the 9th Virginia Cavalry, being also sick at the time, with a six months' old at her breast. This is only one instance of twenty like outrages. Mrs. Dr. Belfield whipped five Negroes from her rooms thus heroically defending herself."[13]

The *Christian Recorder,* the organ of the African Methodist Church in the United States, published a letter from a colored member of the Union army which was reprinted in the *Age* with the comment that any American who reads "must blush for his country."

Camp of 1st U. S. Colored Troops
Wilson's Landing, Charles City County
May 10, 1864

Mr. Editor:

You are aware that Wilson's Landing is on the James River a few miles above Jamestown, the very spot where the first sons of Africa were landed, in the year 1620 . . . and from that day up to the breaking of the rebellion, was looked upon as an inferior race by all civilized nations. But behold what has been revealed in the past three or four years: Why the colored men have ascended upon a platform of equality, and the slave can now apply the lash to the tender flesh of his master, for this day I am now an eye witness of the fact. The country being principally inhabited by wealthy farmers, there are a great many men in the regiment who are refugees from this place. While on a foraging expedition we captured a Mr. Clayton, a noted reb in this part of the country, and from his appearance, one of the F. F. V.'s; on the day before we captured several women who belonged to Mr. C. who had given them a most unmerciful whipping previous to their departure. On the arrival of Mr. C. in camp, the commanding officer determined to let the women have their revenge, and ordered Mr. C. to be tied to a tree in front of headquarters, and William Harris, a soldier in our regiment, and a member of Company E, who was acquainted with the gentleman, and who used to belong to him, was called upon to undress him and introduce him to the ladies that I mentioned before. Mr. Harris played his part conspicuously, bringing the blood from

[13] The *Age,* August 11, 1864.

his loins at every stroke, and not forgetting to remind the gentleman of days gone by. After giving him some fifteen or twenty
well-directed strokes, the ladies, one after another, came up and
gave him a like number, to remind him that *they* were no longer
his, but safely housed in Abraham's bosom, and under the protection of the Star-Spangled Banner, and guarded by their own
patriotic though down-trodden race. Oh! that I had the tongue
to express my feelings while standing on the banks of the James
River, on the soil of Virginia, the mother state of slavery, as a
witness of such a sudden reverse!

The day is clear, the fields of grain are beautiful, and the
birds are singing sweet melodious songs, while poor Mr. C. is
crying to his servant for mercy. Let all who sympathize with
the South take this narrative for a mirror.[14]

Yours truly,
G. W. H.

In addition to the alleged "atrocities," all of which
followed more or less the same pattern, the Negro troops
were accused of being high-handed with the use of
weapons. They shot down, it was claimed, civilians upon
the slightest provocation. Innocent people were thus
killed as the result of "the infernal policy of arming niggers and placing them in positions of trust and independence."[15]

The Abolitionists and much of the northern press
praised the bravery of these colored soldiers, thereby
further arousing the enmity of the Copperheads. At the
first assault of Port Hudson in May 1863 the news was
given out that the Negro troops charged over the ram-
parts, leaped over the siege guns, bayonneted the gunners,
and when their own muskets failed them, tore the flesh of
the enemy with their teeth before they were compelled to
retreat.[16] Six hundred out of a thousand Negroes had
been killed, according to some reports.[17] The *Age* discovered facts which led it to contend that practically the
entire story was a falsehood, prepared in advance in order

[14] The *Age*, June 8, 1864.
[15] *Ibid.*, August 24, 1864.
[16] *Ibid.*, September 26, 1863.
[17] *Ibid.*, August 13, 1863.

to "reconcile the North to the arming of the slaves." A letter from a Union white soldier present at the battle denying the unusual bravery of the Negro troops was printed,[18] and quotations were given from the New Orleans *Era,* the "personal organ of General Banks," to the effect that only twenty-eight out of 1,245 Negroes were killed and one hundred and twenty-three wounded by gunshots and forty-six by falling trees. "Many of the wounds were slight from which the sufferers have recovered." "And so," added the *Age,* "ends the romance of Negro valor at Port Hudson."[19]

According to the Chicago *Times,* Adjutant General Thomas announced in the beginning of his crusade down the Mississippi River that he had enlisted fifteen hundred Negroes. He was quoted as saying at Philadelphia, "I performed my mission without difficulty. The army made no opposition, and the blacks enlisted with alacrity. The able bodied of entire plantations came 'en masse,' and asked to be enrolled. And they make first rate soldiers; in some respects better than whites."[20]

The *Times* reported:

There should be some record of the achievements of these thousands of sable warriors. Beyond a skirmish or two, in which small bands of Negroes have been engaged, we have heard nothing of their existence. There has been so much enlistment of Negroes, as is reported, and their efficiency as soldiers is an unsolved problem. The New York *Tribune* says there have been twenty-five applications from white men to serve as officers in Negro regiments. We will wager a small amount, that if they were all appointed there would be an officer for every soldier in the field.[21]

It seems that the New York *Tribune* had said that "the 1st Kansas Colored Regiment was the best disciplined and the most perfectly drilled regiment in the American

---

[18] The *Age,* September 26, 1863.

[19] *Ibid.,* September 26, August 13, 1863.

[20] Quoted in the *Age,* July 15, 1863.

[21] *Ibid.*

army.''[22] The *Age* gave space to its opinion on this subject under the title of ''Negro Superiority:''

This, we suppose, is another confirmation of the truth of the Abolition doctrine that a Negro is as good as a white man! Our gallant *white* army—the soldiers who fought and conquered under McClelland, Grant, Meade, and other *white* generals—will not feel very highly complimented at this attempt to exalt the Negro over their heads. But it is evident, that the worship of the ''ebony idol'' is still to go on, while the interest of millions of free white men are to be entirely ignored in this cruel ''war for the African and his race!''[23]

The Negro soldiers had been the cause of further difficulty—the failure of the Petersburg mine affair was all due to the squabble over the use of Negro troops. According to the report of the Committee on the Conduct of the War, General Burnside had insisted that, in the words of the *Age,*

After the explosion of the mine the advance should be given to *raw Negro troops.* . . . This was objected to by Generals Grant and Meade, who knew the importance of having veterans in the advance on such a dangerous and trying occasion and General Burnside was ordered to designate by lot the advancing column which was done. This interference with the Negro programme of General Burnside threw him into a passion, and from that time, until he was ordered into his entrenchments after the affair had miscarried, he was like a sulky child seeking for excuses to avoid doing his duty, and allowing his brave men to be slaughtered by thousands, because a few regiments of raw Negro troops were not given the post of danger and honor in the assault. This is the true secret of the failure of the Petersburg mine affair.[24]

The New York *World* made much the same claim—that Burnside had lost interest in the affair after the refusal of Grant and Meade to allow Negro troops to be used and Burnside's indifference resulted in the loss of 4,500 men.[25] The Philadelphia journal further exclaimed:

Now what will the country think of a general who causes the failure of a grand military movement, and the loss of 4,500 brave

---

[22] The *Age*, July 29, 1863.
[23] The *Age*, July 29, 1863.
[24] *Ibid.*, March 24, 1865.
[25] Quoted in the *Age*, March 24, 1865.

fellows in one corps alone, because his Negro troops were not allowed to lead a "forlorn hope"; and what should they think of an administration which allows such conduct on the part of a superior officer? . . .

The truth is, the Negro mania has been as mischievous in the conduct of the war, as it has been in and is in politics. Men who are smitten with this disease can or will see through no other medium. The case of General Burnside is more than usually prominent and noticeable from its consequences, but there are hundreds of others which might be cited. . . . The effect of such a Negro policy upon the issue of the struggle cannot fail to be pernicious. If a corps commander is suffered to thwart an important movement, cause the butchery of 10,000 men, and bring disgrace upon the army, because Negro troops are not selected in preference to white, and if promotion rests, not upon deeds of gallantry, but in devotion to the Negro-equality dogma of a political party, then no man can tell where the demoralization of our army will end, or what calamity the future has in store for it.[26] . . .

The War and many events leading up to and connected with it, tended to push the Negroes into the limelight. While the issue between North and South was technically over States' Rights, Negro slavery was basically the outstanding cause of the War. And now, while the conflict was on, Negroes were receiving an amount of attention in speech and in print that they had, of course, never known before. The editors of the *Age* expressed themselves on this point:

Now-a-days the Negro, like flies in the summer time, is in every man's broth. He is the disturbing element in Church and State, in the family and in the nation, in the camp and in the cloister. There can be no movement contemplated or planned, into which some fidgetty humanitarian, or restless scheming politician, will not thrust the Negro. He is the stock in trade of that school of politicians whose birthplace was Yankee land, and they display him from their windows, and hang him on the sides of their political car, as their fathers did wooden clocks to cheat and humbug their honest, plain men or other sections of the country. For the ultimate fate of the Negro they care no more than they did for that of the Indian, after they had occupied his ground, burned his wigwam, and driven him from the territory they coveted. Until they were ready for the final extirpation of the red

[26] The *Age*, March 24, 1865.

man, they pretended with much concern for his temporal and spiritual welfare, but when the signal was given they exchanged the Bible for the rifle, the prayer book for the torch, and the work of butchery was consummated. History may repeat itself in the case of the Negro, if the same class of men are allowed a little longer to rule the nation and shape its policy.[27]

With the backing of the Abolition leaders, many Negroes, in their new sense of self-importance, made themselves obnoxious to white sections of the population. It would be strange if they had not, for with the amount of attention and praise they received, giving them the impression they were now the equal of whites, many of them expected to be admitted into social circles formerly closed to Africans. Equality on paper was one thing, and in practice quite another. In various sections of the country, particularly along the border states, the question of the continuation or promotion of segregation policies arose. Out in California, according to the *Alta Californian,* some Negroes were trying to force their way into a position of equality on the street cars, and almost caused a race riot.[28]

The *Age* was for segregation in clear terms. Surprisingly though, it argued that most of the colored people did not want to break down the various segregation bars. It was the "infernal" Abolitionists, "the champions of miscegnation," who were continuing "to thrust the African" upon the public.[29]

Some correspondence occurred about this time which illustrates several phases of class stratification and social relationships of that period. The editor of another Copperhead newspaper, the Easton (Pa.) *Argus,* had written an editorial, April 7, 1864, under the title, "Rowdies on Railroads," in which he said that ladies, travelling on the North Pennsylvania Railroad, had com-

[27] The *Age*, March 24, 1865.
[28] Quoted in the *Age*, November 23, 1864.
[29] The *Age*, March 22, 25, 1864.

plained of *"being thrown* into the same car with drunken soldiers, prostitutes, and Negroes."[30] The president of the railroad, Mr. F. A. Conley, wrote with reference to the editorial: "Presuming that you do not want to travel free over a road where you might be thrown in with a prostitute or Negro, I have directed our conductors to take up the annual pass issued in your name."[31]

To this decree the editor of the *Argus* replied:

You do not seem to relish the truth. The facts to which I called your attention, in a kind spirit, are well known to every person who has recently had occasion to travel over your road. They are the subject of daily complaint. I have myself seen the Ladies' Saloon of your Depot, at Philadelphia, so crowded with Negro women, that no white woman could find a seat, even if she felt disposed to associate with women of that color. I have heard intoxicated soldiers indulge in language so obscene, in your cars, that respectable ladies sought refuge on another part of the train. I have seen white men quarrel with Negroes for their right to a seat in your cars. I am well aware that the conductors, (from whom I have personally received gentlemanly treatment), cannot always prevent these things, but when your attention is called to an evil that is loudly condemned by the whole travelling public, it is your duty to make an effort to abate it. The people of this country, whatever may be their political predilections, are not quite willing to place themselves on the level with the "American citizen of African descent" and it is the universal opinion of that portion of the public who use your road, that there is entirely too much Negro equality in its management.

In order to save your conductors the trouble of taking up my pass, I herewith return it to you, and advise you to present it to one of the colored brethren for whom you seem to entertain such partiality. . . . Being thus relieved from any supposed obligation to you, I shall hereafter, speak of your management of the N. P. R. R., in such terms as I think it may deserve.[32]

Yours, etc.,

W. H. HUTTER.

It is worth nothing that the bodily odors of Negroes were occasionally referred to indirectly in accounts of their meetings and this gave added weight to the argu-

[30] Quoted in the *Age*, April 16, 1864.
[31] *Ibid.*
[32] *Ibid.*

ments for segregation on the cars and trains. In an account of a Negro mass meeting held on July 26, 1864, to express their indignation toward the various Passenger Railway Companies for their Jim Crow policies, the white reporter wrote, "As the hall had been sprinkled with *chloride of lime* (italics ours), previous to the organization, we ventured within the doors and, from the 'ums' and 'ahs,' for a while imagined we were at a darkey camp meeting. Then a 'cream colored fellow' was called to the chair and the meeting got under way."[33]

With the exception of rape, the most horrible thought to contemplate in the whole range of Negro-white relationships was racial intermixture. "Miscegenation," the editors of the Copperhead newspapers were fond of calling this social phenomenon. And they seemed never to miss an opportunity to play up every available story of such behavior. Even corner street embroglios between blacks and whites were labelled "miscegenation." The Detroit *Free Press* ran a number of these headliners: "A Negro Runs Away With the Wife of a White Man";[34] "Miscegenation in Detroit";[35] etc. The *Age* gave these lurid tales prominent space—from whatever source.

A typical one appeared under the caption, "Practical Miscegenation." A farmer in Southold, Michigan ("whose name is withheld as the parties are well known in the neighborhood where the circumstances transpired"), espoused the cause of Abolitionism and "believed in putting his doctrine into practice to the fullest extent." He employed "one of the blackest Africans he could find" and treated him as one of "his own offspring." The farmer's confidence in the Negro was such that he was entrusted with a share in the management and business of the farm. The Negro, in return for these favors, ran off

[33] The *Age*, July 27, 1864.
[34] Quoted in the *Age*, November 1, 1864.
[35] *Ibid.*, March 1, 1864.

with the farmer's sixteen-year-old daughter, who was "said to be intelligent and very prepossessing in appearance." The story continued:

> She could not be blamed for also admiring the sooty Ethiopian and with proper encouragement her admiration ripened into love. With the knowledge and consent of the parties the two were allowed to be much in each other's society. They took long strolls by moonlight and indulged in all those little delights which are properly supposed to make courtship so sweet. The affair culminated in an elopement, though there is no reason why they should have pursued this course, since it was not known their union was opposed by the parents.
>
> One night last week the farmer was disturbed by a noise outside the house. He got up and raised the window, but did not discover anything unusual. In the morning the Negro did not make his appearance, and the daughter was also missing. On going to her room, it was discovered that she had flown with her Negro paramour, taking her trunks and all her clothing. Since then nothing has been heard of them, and no effort has been made by the father to discover the whereabouts of his daughter. It is supposed that they have gone to Canada, probably on a wedding tour, and will yet return, when the doting parents will receive them with open arms and establish them in a home of their own, as a living illustration of the beauties of practical miscegenation.[36]

The Chicago *Times* described events in that city when the wives and sweethearts turned out to say farewell to a "Regiment of Africans on Their Way to War." A "vast throng of especial admirers" came to the depot to see them off. "White women were there in attendance to bid farewell to black husbands, around whose necks they clung long and fondly! Black women, too, and men almost white, were also locked in each other's arms, some weeping, while others were shouting, praying, and singing. . . ."[37]

In the meanwhile the dangers and horrors of "miscegenation" were freely depicted. Meetings were held about the subject. A mass meeting held in Pottstown, Pennsylvania, was reported, in which there appeared in proces-

---

[36] The *Age*, June 8, 1864.
[37] *Ibid.*, May 3, 1864.

sion from a nearby town, a wagon containing "thirty-four young ladies dressed in white" representing the states and territories. They carried a banner with the following words "containing a world of meaning," according to the *Age:*

FATHERS AND BROTHERS
PRESERVE US
FROM NEGRO EQUALITY[38]

All of these news items and editorials were printed for the purpose of arousing the disgust and horror of the reader, and creating opposition to the Republicans and Abolitionists as well as the too free intermingling of whites and blacks. That the slave system itself was responsible for more racial intermixture than all the doctrines of equality of the Abolitionists seems never to have occurred to the editors of the Copperhead newspapers. At least, the present writer has never seen any references in these journals to the real cause of the large mulatto population. Yet, every slurring remark and joke about the "cream-colored" Negroes, and the "near-whites" was a tacit acknowledgment that slavery did not prevent but rather promoted the "horrible" miscegenation.[39]

The responsibility for all this talk about and promotion of Negro equality was placed upon the Abolitionists and the Republicans. Phillips Brooks, the famous preacher, was held up to scorn and ridicule for his alleged expressed belief that the Negro was "intellectually and morally, quite equal to the white." This clergyman was also reported to have said that if a black man and a white woman were to "present themselves at the altar rail of the 'Holy

[38] The *Age*, October 2, 1863.

[39] For an account of miscegenation in the pre-bellum days, *vid.* Ralph Betts Flanders, *Plantation Slavery in Georgia*, University of North Carolina Press, Chapel Hill, N. C., 1933, p. 270.

Trinity' [Episcopalian Church]," he would "marry them without a scruple."[40]

There is no possible way in which to check up on the accuracy of many of these quotations, but the following will show, at least, the political and social distance between the Copperheads and the Republicans. The Governor of Iowa was quoted as saying: "I would rather eat with a nigger, drink with a nigger, live with a nigger, and sleep with a nigger, than with a Democrat."[41]

The Abolitionists, for years, according to the Democrats, had been running the country and bringing it to ruin with their subversive doctrines. And now the Civil War was directly due to their clamor. The *Age* calculated that by November, 1864, the War had already cost more than $4,000,000,000. The daily cost was at least $3,000,000 for the "emancipation of the Negro." This latter sum would pay "for the erection of 100,000 homes, so that every hundred days the war continues there is added to the load of taxation, a sum that would build another city like Philadelphia." It was also calculated that "this debt incurred in order to free the Negro, and raise him to an equality with the white man, would build 100,000 miles of railway, at a cost of $30,000 per mile, equal to the cost of four railways around the world." The purport of all these figures ran:

When these facts are well considered, and all the results pondered, we think that every man who is not entirely reckless in regard to the future [taxes, etc.], will pause, and consider whether the Slavery he is imposing on future generations of white men, will not be handled more galling and degrading than any evil that has befallen upon the Negro race in the United States.[42]

The readers of the newspaper were informed that the Negro equality movement was "one of the baldest and

[40] The *Age*, November 24, 1864.
[41] *Ibid.*, October 8, 1863.
[42] *Ibid.*, November 7, 1864.

most offensive humbugs ever attempted to be palmed upon
an intelligent and decent people." With the exception of
a few "crackbrained enthusiasts" and "harmless old
women," not one of the "whole gang" calling out "up
with the black man to a full level with the white race"
cared a tinker's dam what became of "Sambo and his
posterity." It was asserted that in the New England
states, whence came "the foul stream of Abolition treason
and fanaticism," the blacks were as badly off as in 1800,
"socially, morally, and intellectually." In the western
part of the United States where New England influence
predominated, the colored man was barred "from even an
approach to the rights and privileges of the white race."[43]

Hence the Abolitionists were hypocrites and their
meetings a farce. No pains were spared to describe these
in ludicrous fashion. In December, 1863, they held a meeting in Philadelphia, at which time such leaders as William
Lloyd Garrison, Lucretia Mott, and Lucy Stone were
present. The account was as follows:

THE ABOLITION CONVENTION
MEETING OF MUTUAL ADMIRATION CLUB
SEMI-FEMININE MEN AND STRONG-MINDED WOMEN
THE NEGRO! THE NEGRO! THE NEGRO!

. . . The hall had a gloomy appearance, and the audience which
half-filled its benches, was a queer one. On the platform, were
the great guns of the party—male and female, white and black
together. One old codger had uncombed hair flowing down to his
waist; and the females were unusually hard featured, reminding
one very much of the three old maids of mythology who had but
one eye and one tooth between them. On the floor, the rank and
file of the party, numbering about five hundred, peered up at
the platform, gathering inspiration. This rank and file deserves
description. The Negroes were thick in sky-blue bonnets and
ruffled skirts, pumps, and cast away stockings. The whites were
interspersed among the blacks—each one a representative of
philanthropy run mad. Tall women with long necks and long
tongues, came stalking in with babies togging after, and spread
themselves out on the benches, establishing a miniature nursery.
Forty-five-year-old misses, with long cork-screw curls, each one

[43] The *Age*, January 16, 1865.

redolent with grease, minced along the aisles, and languidly sank
down into a wilderness of calico. Men with carpet bags and
faded blue umbrellas, with sedgy ends, pounded along the floor,
staring about for seats. Abolition exhibited itself in all its phases.
Here sat a man who made it a point never to cut his beard; there
another who was conscientiously opposed to combs; and a third
who had a like aversion to soap and water. Women knit away
for dear life, only laying down their knitting to applaud the
speakers. Barnum and Kirkbride* out of that rank and file, could
each have enough specimens to stock their cabinets.[44] . . .

Since Abolitionism was said to be product of New
England "fanaticism," the Yankees were subjected to constant and bitter attacks from the vociferous *Age*. History was appealed to in an effort to show that from the
time of the Puritans to the present these people had made
money their god. The Yankees had profited from the
slave trade and had had it extended twenty years beyond
the time when the Southerners wanted the traffic stopped.
The Yankee had absolutely no conscience and was practically unaffected "by the ethical bearing of any question."[45]

There were four questions uppermost in his mind:

First. How can I make the most money out of the war?
Second. What can I do in my humble sphere to prolong it?
Third. Will my corns or weak eyes, or the colic I used to get
exempt me from the draft?
Fourth. If my infirmities fail me, what is the smallest percentage of my little earnings on shoddy for which one of my
fellow beings will agree to be shot in my stead?[46]

The Yankees were accused of making enormous profits
out of the Civil War, and of furnishing shoddy goods to
the Union forces.[47] News accounts were given of the smug-
gling of arms and ammunition into the South via the Ber-
mudas. This was carried on by Northerners, but the *Age*

---

* Kirkbride's was a private institution for the insane in Philadelphia.
[44] The *Age*, December 4, 1863.
[45] *Ibid.*, November 19, 1864.
[46] *Ibid.*, September 3, 1864.
[47] *Ibid.*, March 27, 1863.

did not have quite enough proof to pin this on to Yankee-dom,[48] though it would have been delighted to have had the opportunity. Much of the criticism about profits out of the war and shoddy goods was, of course, justified. But the Yankees were not by any means the only offenders.

The feeling against the people of New England is further revealed in an editorial which appeared directly after the defeat of Lee at Gettysburg.

It is a cause of great rejoicing that General Lee was outgen-eraled and defeated by General Meade *without the aid of Negroes or Yankee militia* (italics ours). The Negroes simply paraded our streets and fattened on the munificence of their friends and ad-mirers of the Jacobin League; while the Yankees, from their ele-vated position, took a bird's eye view of matters and things; philosophically pondering on the truth of the proverb that "it is an ill wind that blows nobody good." Thus, if Pennsylvania, which is a manufacturing as well as an agricultural state, should be seriously dealt with by the rebels, and Philadelphia itself destroyed by fire, a great number of contracts which are now filled in our beautiful Quaker city . . . would be taken in Bos-ton and other neatly painted New England towns, and thus the Negro philanthropy of Yankeedom would receive an additional reward. The fact that Pennsylvania produces coal and iron adds greatly to her manufacturing capacity and to the deteriment of the Yankee states, which have to purchase these commodities at a distance. A rebel raid into the heart of Pennsylvania would only give the Yankees a "fair chance," and help them to the monopoly of manufactured goods. The Venetians, who in their day, were as "cute" a people as the Yankees, said of themselves, that they were "first Venetians and then Christians"; their New England imitators are good Christians always (we are bound to admit that), but as regards patriotism, they are "Yankees first and Americans afterwards." Pennsylvanias ought to stick a pin in that, and remember it on all possible occasions.[49]

As for the future of the Africans in this country, the *Age* had great misgivings. Many of them as Federal troops had developed a sense of power and prestige that boded ill for the days to come after the War. The step from the former modes of life, "the chimney sweep, or

[48] The *Age*, December 28, 1863; January 13, 1864.
[49] *Ibid.*, July 6, 1863.

boot black, or hod carrier,'' could not be retraced. Furthermore, wrote the editors, ''The cesspool will never claim its own again.''[50]

Some of the Democrats contended that with the terrific slaughter of white soldiers on both sides of the line of battle, that when the War was finally brought to a close, the best man power of the nation would have been wiped out and the remaining population would be left entirely to the mercies of the blacks.[51] One correspondent suggested that since, according to calculations, the total population of the United States in 1930 would probably be about 200,000,000, with this tremendous increase the pressure and prejudice displayed toward the colored race would become more and more unbearable for them. In the course of time, the more intelligent blacks would emigrate to Liberia and the mass of them to tropical America ''lured by the advantages of a congenial climate and diminution of the prejudice of color.'' The gentleman made the further prediction that ''the columns of the census will not always be needed to enumerate the colored population of the Continent of North America.''[52]

As far as the place of the Negro in the society of the future was concerned, the *Age* believed that no amount of Emancipation Proclamations or enactments of legislatures would alter the real status of the people of black skin. Public opinion was the actual determiner of the position of the Negro in American civilization. It quoted an exchange, the Chicago *Times,* to prove this point. In a humorous and caustic vein the latter surveyed the current scene:

Our brethren of the boot-black, white washing and calcimining persuasion were out in force on Tuesday night to celebrate their glorious emancipation in Illinois. Night was made darker

[50] The *Age,* July 2, 1864.
[51] *Ibid.*
[52] *Ibid.,* July 14, 1863.

with the concentration of the shades; and gunpowder lent the enfranchised African its aid to give voice to their rejoicings.

Happy darkeys! In one moment the repeal of the "infamous black laws" has effected a miraculous change in their condition in this state. A week ago a Negro could not come into this state unless he wanted to, and now he is at liberty to come in as much as he pleases and in any way he pleases—on foot, on horseback, or in the cars—if he has the money to pay his passage. A week ago an Illinois Negro was an individual who practiced the menial pursuit of a boot-black; today by the repeal of the "infamous black laws" he is elevated to the dignified position of blackening boots. A week ago the unhappy colored man of the Negro race could not marry a white woman without her consent; today these same downtrodden serfs are free men who can now marry any white woman they choose provided she is not unwilling. . . . Last week thousands of people in this glorious state of Illinois were nothing but niggers; today bress de Lord, these same niggers are Africans, men of color, people of the colored persuasion.[53] . . .

Underneath this sarcasm there did lie a fundamental principle which history has since proved, namely, that the victory of the North and the liberation of the slaves could not and did not give the Negro real freedom, not to mention equality, economic or social. Minorities do not gain objectives in that way. In whatever light we may view the Copperhead press and its attitude toward the Negro, at least, it voiced the opinions and sentiments of a considerable portion of the North, and most of the South, in a period of transition so critical that two social and economic systems and two political parties saw no way to settle the controversy other than by civil war.

RAY H. ABRAMS

University of Pennsylvania

[53] Quoted in the *Age*, February 14, 1865.

PENAL SLAVERY AND SOUTHERN
RECONSTRUCTION

The Civil War fell like a huge boulder into the stream of American prison developments, sending large eddies across the main current that swept around to the north, and sharply diverting into a separate southern channel but a small portion of the old Auburn tradition. The remarkable penological stirrings in the post-war North— the rising agitation for prison reform, the culmination of the old Auburn system, and the birth of a new reformatory discipline[1]— had only an incidental relation to this bloody catastrophe.[2] On the other hand, the war and its aftermath were the dominant factors in separating the South from the Union in penological matters for at least half a century. Abruptly checked were the slow developments towards a penitentiary system, envisaged by Edward Livingston in Louisiana, and Francis Lieber in South Carolina.[3] The Black Belt, and in many respects the entire South, turned to a penal lease system that joined to the irresponsible control of poorly integrated states many of the worst features of the old slave traditions.

The Radical Republicans, with their schemes of reconstruction, seriously aggravated the Negro problem and

[1] E. C. Wines and T. Dwight's *Prisons in the United States and Canada* (N. Y., 1865), is an invaluable picture of the trends in the North at this date; see also, *The National Prison Association, Proceedings* (1870, 1873, 1877, and since 1884). See the author's *History of American Prison Developments* (1865-1910), a manuscript in Harvard College Library.

[2] The military prisons of the war period had no connection with this larger institutional development; see W. B. Hesseltine's *Civil War Prisons* (Columbus, O., 1930), for an unbiased treatment.

[3] Livingston, Edward, *Code of Reform and Penal Discipline* (Quebec, 1831); De Beaumont, G. A., and De Tocqueville, A., *The Penitentiary System in the United States* (Francis Lieber's translation, Philadelphia, 1833), with the added value due to Lieber's extended notes; Sneed, W. C., *The Kentucky Penitentiary* (Frankfort, Ky., 1860), giving a full account of the best prison in ante-bellum South.

disjointed the penal system. During the long years of slavery some of the blacks, it is said, had been protected from the rigors of the criminal laws by the patience as well as the interests of their masters.[4] Now the vicious character of the race conflict, and the restlessness and ignorance of the freedman, rapidly increased the number of Negroes in the criminal population until it exceeded ninety per cent of the total. Slave methods naturally suggested themselves as the logical patterns for penal discipline. Rare criers in the wilderness protested, but these years were hardly favorable to the growth of a humanitarian spirit in the South; there were no annual investigations by disinterested citizens, as in the North, to uncover the harsh realities.[5] Slave standards and race hatreds were to debase Southern penal practices for a generation.

The prostrate South had to rebuild its railroads as well as its prisons, both considerably demolished by Northern troops.[6] Out of the shocking corruption of the

[4] Phillips, U. B., *American Negro Slavery* (N. Y., 1918), pp. 454-88.

[5] Cable, George W., *The Silent South* (N. Y., 1885), p. 124: "It hardly need be said that the system is not in operation by reason of any malicious public intention. On the part of the lessees there is a most unadmirable spirit of enterprise. On the part of the state officials there is a very natural eagerness to report themselves as putting money into the treasury, and a low estimate of public sentiment and intelligence. In the people at large there is little more than listless oblivion. . . ."

[6] The South had only the beginnings of a penitentiary system before the war, for the administration of justice and correction had been largely a function of the counties, and they had relied largely on corporal punishments. The new constitutions of the sixties abolished these old practices, and the states as well as the counties found increasing numbers of criminals on their hands. While all but Florida and the Carolinas of the Southern states had provided some form of a state prison before the war, none of these were adequate now; indeed Northern troops had considerably demolished three of them.

Facts on the early history of Southern prisons are hard to find and verify; but it appears that the Richmond penitentiary, designed by Jefferson, was the first in the South and antedated the Auburn system; Kentucky and Georgia also had early prisons of a sort, but only that of the former, at Frankfort, was enlarged and improved until it became a worthy rival of Northern prisons. Tennessee probably started its wooden prison at Nash-

PENAL SLAVERY AND SOUTHERN RECONSTRUCTION   155

Carpetbag era emerged the penal lease system as a practical answer to both of these problems. By this scheme the states accommodated their increasing criminal populations without the expense of building great prisons—even, in several cases, reaping large profits for the state treasuries —at the same time they secured a large labor force for the reconstruction of the highways of commerce and the foundations of industry. As the South gradually got rid of the rule of Radical Republicanism and regained its freedom, conservative governments replaced liberal ones and rigid economy became the order of the day. Tax-laden citizens were only too eager to see the authorities contract honest leases, and there was no strong unionism as in the North to raise its voice and order the convict out of the construction field.[7] The triumphant Democrat gentry maintained its sway with the aid of hooded Ku Kluxers and red-shirted horsemen; the passions of the South were so hot that few troubled about the most damnable feature of this tyranny, the cruel system of penal slavery.

DARK DAYS IN THE BLACK BELT

With the exception of Alabama and Texas, all the Gulf States turned unreservedly towards the lease system. The Democrats determined in the seventies that extravagance and all legitimate state expenditures had to be checked. Self supporting, or better, profit earning, convicts became the goal of the prison authorities. At the

ville in 1831 slowly expanding it to 360 cells by 1874; Louisiana and Mississippi built prisons at their state capitals in the late thirties, and Alabama opened its prison at Wetumpka in 1841. Texas built a prison at Huntsville in 1847, providing 225 cells, which seems to have been greater than that of any other Southern prison before the war except Frankfort, Kentucky; Arkansas started a penitentiary with 84 cells in 1858.

[7] Lovely, C., *The Abuses of Prison Labor* (St. Louis, 1905). Even this Northern labor leader saw little to complain of on the grounds of competition with free labor, but he did condemn the cruelty of the conditions he found under the lease system.

start there was simply a desire to shift an inconvenient burden to other shoulders; but, as the great profits to be derived from prison labor became apparent, the states began to rival each other in exploiting their disorderly elements. This policy was to persist as long as the first era of material reconstruction continued unchecked.

In Georgia penal developments followed a relatively simple course. When the federal general, T. H. Ruger, disbanded the state government in 1867 he found one hundred convicts on his hands and the old prison in ruins —one result of Sherman's march. While waiting for a state convention to draft a new constitution, Ruger leased these convicts to an enterprising railroad builder. The first Carpetbag governor, Rufus Bullock, continued that policy, and his astute lieutenant, the demagogic H. I. Kimball, got some cheap labor for his railroads. In 1870, when Bullock lost his federal support, and the Democrats gained control, an investigation revealed shocking conditions. Only 380 prisoners could be located out of a total of 496 listed on the records. Nevertheless the major interest was in economy; the legislature hastened to indorse the lease system, and 500 were soon contracted to seven different lessees.[8] A permanent policy was finally adopted in 1876 as the prisoners, now numbering over 1,100, were distributed among three leasing companies. These leases extended for twenty years, and each lessee agreed to pay the state $25,000 a year. Governor J. M. Smith congratulated the state on its happy solution of a perplexing problem.[9]

Mississippi followed practically the same procedure. In 1867 the military government leased the convicts for

[8] McKelway, A. J., "Abolition of the Convict Lease System of Georgia," A. P. A., *Proceedings* (1908), pp. 219-26; Joint Committee of the Legislature, "Condition of the Georgia Penitentiary," Georgia General Assembly, *Report* (1870), pp. 195-200.

[9] Governor Smith's Message, *Georgia Assembly Documents* (1877), pp. 10-11.

three years, and the Carpetbaggers extended it. A partial
reorganization of the government in 1872 was the occasion
for some sharp criticism of this system, but the complaints
centered about the fact that the state paid the lessee $20,-
000 a year to keep the prisoners. An attempt was made to
return to a genuine penitentiary system, and a superintendent of prisons was appointed to take charge. The
prison had not been totally demolished by the troops, and
yet the destruction of all locks and machinery determined
that only the young, the infirm, and the sick could safely
be moved into what was left of the "walls," unless expensive repairs and enlargements were undertaken. The
superintendent decided to lease all the able-bodied to a
near-by railroad, this time at terms favorable to the
state.[10] When the Democrats gained full control in 1876
they voted down a proposal for a new penitentiary; instead they leased the entire prison population with full
authority to the Hamilton and Hebron Company. The
state had received what appeared to be favorable terms,
but the company found that it could sub-lease the men
at even more advantageous rates; there was no check
whatsoever on the cruel fate of these penal slaves.[11]

In a similar fashion Louisiana was forced to look for
a lease in 1868. It had become clear that General Benjamin F. Butler had sufficiently dismantled the prison at
Baton Rouge to make its repair economically impracti-
cable. A board of control was created. In the following
year this body proceeded to lease the prisoners for a
twenty year term at gradually increasing rates, reserving
to itself the authority to prescribe rules. This appeared to
be a satisfactory solution, but as the years rolled by the
board found it impossible to collect the payments or to
enforce its regulations. Nevertheless political favoritism

---

[10] Mississippi State Prison, *Report* (1872); (1874), pp. 85-90.

[11] Mississippi State Prison, *Report* (1876), pp. 3-9. The state received
$1.10 for each man over 140.

and popular indifference permitted the situation to continue throughout the century.[12]

Tennessee and Arkansas likewise turned their prisoners over to lessees at the close of the war. In each case at the start these companies worked their charges within the walls or in near-by mines, and thus maintained prisons comparable to those of Kentucky and Missouri. Arkansas even paid its lessee a small fee for each prisoner, and permitted him to pile up a huge debt for the enlargment of the prison. The lessee cannily filled the new cells with federal prisoners to increase his own profits. When the Democrats gained control they revised the system, compelling the lessee to pay an annual rental of $25,000, but permitting him to employ the convicts within or outside the walls as he chose.[13] Across the river to the east Tennessee likewise shifted for more favorable terms, finally in 1884 making a bargain with the Tennessee Coal and Iron Railway, giving the company complete control over the prisoners, and insuring an annual revenue of $100,000 to the state. No official attention was given to the serious overcrowding in the 350 cells of the Nashville prison, but the lessee partially relieved the situation by moving a large number of the prisoners to wooden stockades at Tracy City, Inman, and Coal Creek mining camps.[14]

[12] Wisner, E., *Public Welfare Administration in Louisiana* (Chicago, 1930), pp. 155-60. This board was composed of the same men as the board of railroad commissioners. The lease was supposed to bring in $5,000 the first year and this was to increase by $1,000 each year.

[13] Arkansas House of Representatives, *Journal* (1871), pp. 40-43; (1881), pp. 58 ff.; *Arkansas Public Documents* (1885-86), pp. 16-19; (1887-88), pp. 23-27.

[14] Moore, J. T., *Tennessee, The Volunteer State* (Nashville, 1923), I, 576, see note No. 6; N. P. A., *Proceedings* (1893), pp. 125-27; National Conference of Charities, *Proceedings* (1883), pp. 272-76. The 356 cells at Nashville were crowded with 658 in 1882 and already a large number in addition were scattered on railroads and mines. The total state convict population within and outside the prison walls had grown from 510 in 1868, to 997 in 1878, to 1,350 in 1888. See the Tennessee Penitentiary *Report* (1888), pp. 9-15.

Florida took the prize for cruelty in all the South. If more or less corrupt Carpetbaggers and Scalawags defiled justice in the other states during the early years of reconstruction, the prisoners of Florida were in the hands of plain scoundrels. The United States government had loaned the arsenal at Chattahoochee for a state prison and an average of eighty-two convicts had been housed here for eight years at a total cost of $234,473.[15] When President Hayes withdrew the federal troops that kept this government in power, it fell, and the new authorities quickly cut expenses by leasing all the prisoners for a nominal sum of $100 a year. In succeeding years the lessee changed almost every year, and while the state usually improved its bargain, the wretched convicts were thus shifted about in a haphazard fashion, with never any permanent quarters. They could only be held together by the most barbarous of disciplines, enforced at the point of the gun. The state well earned the title conferred by one of its own officers, "the American Siberia."[16]

Alabama and Texas revealed practically all of the forces active in the other Southern states in addition to a few Northern ones. Neither state had suffered so cruelly as their neighbors from war and reconstruction, and the voice of humanitarianism roused a greater response. Able leaders attempted to breast the trend towards the lease system, but in the end the great expansion of the criminal population rendered any other policy hopeless. The best they could achieve was a more careful state regulation of the living conditions of the convicts.

The first reconstruction government in Alabama hastened to lease the prison at Wetumpka for six years for the nominal fee of five dollars. When it was turned back in wretched condition in 1872 the state resolved to appoint

[15] Governor Bloxham's Message, *Messages and Documents of Florida* (1897), pp. 21-24. See also the other messages from 1881-98.

[16] Powell, J. C., *The American Siberia* (Philadelphia, 1891).

a warden and give him full charge.[17] But the legislature made only a very small appropriation for its maintenance and the warden in order to meet his expenses was forced to hire his able-bodied prisoners to several railroads.[18] The legislature sanctioned this but required that state officers retain full charge at each camp. The lessee proceeded to shirk all responsibility for guarding their charges and the state found its experiment at administration a most expensive undertaking. Escapes multiplied, and the attempted reform was dropped; after 1876 Alabama like its neighbors entrusted discipline to the lessees.

A striking hint of the origin of the technique of the lease system appeared as the warden in 1880 quoted prices on the three grades of prisoners: $5.00 per month for "full hands," $2.50 for "medium hands," nothing but keep for "dead hands,"[19] thus borrowing some well known terminology of slave days. J. H. Bankhead, the new warden in 1881, brought the influence of Northern reformers into Alabama as he condemned the conditions he found at both the walls and the mines. When Governor E. A. O'Neal indorsed the indictment, genuine reforms seemed at last probable. However, financial considerations, such as the cost of the construction of a new penitentiary, and the loss of income from the leases, defeated these Northern ideas. The best the conscientious warden could do was to move his headquarters to the Pratt mines where 400 of his men were employed, and, with the cooperation of the contractors, to erect some model log camps. Ala-

[17] Alabama Penitentiary, *Report* (1870), p. 3, p. 18. The inspectors report: "(we) deem it necessary to say that the prison is in every respect conducted by the lessees in a lawful and humane manner." At the same time their statistics report 97 received, 17 pardoned, 57 discharged, 6 escaped, and 92 dead.

[18] *Ibid.* (1873); (1878), pp. 3-7.

[19] *Alabama Governor's Message* (1884), pp. 20-21; (1884), pp. 354-56. This last is a special message by Governor Rufus W. Cobb on the penitentiary and contains a detailed history of developments since the war.

bama as a result provided living conditions far in advance of those found elsewhere in the South.[20] Bankhead, however, had worked himself out of a job, and the legislature abolished his office in 1885. Thus it was that Alabama, after a long struggle, frankly adopted the lease system. Fortunately the special board of inspectors with large powers of administration worked more satisfactorily than in most states. The labors of a decade of reformers earned at least the boast of maintaining the best living conditions in the South.[21]

Texas with its great area and rapidly growing population found the 225 cells at Huntsville prison pitiably inadequate in the first years after the war. The state at first attempted to solve the problem by employing the overflow on its own railroads. In 1871, as the railroads were being sold into private hands, this scheme had to be dropped, and the entire penal system was leased. The first lessee defaulted, convincing the state of the dangers of an inadequate prison. Cunningham and Ellis took a new lease and agreed to construct a second prison at Rusk as a part of their payment. Too many other profitable demands for the labor appeared, and the foundry and 400 cells at Rusk were barely completed twelve years later when the lease expired. Meanwhile more than 2,000 convicts had been scattered over a wide area, laboring at railroad construction, iron blasting, bridge building, and

---

[20] Alabama Inspectors of Penitentiary, *Report* (1884), pp. 70-71. These log structures contained four rooms 80 feet by 24 feet, and four 47 feet by 24 feet. Iron beds were suspended from the ceilings, each room had running water, a privy, and housed at least 35 men during the night. A bath house and dining room were attached to each structure.

[21] Alabama Inspectors of Penitentiary, *Report* (1886), pp. 3-6; National Conference of Charities, *Proceedings* (1883), pp. 265-301. Cable considered the conditions in Alabama and Texas greatly superior to those in the other states, with the Carolinas and Kentucky next best.

on large cotton plantations.[22] T. J. Goree, the able and progressive superintendent employed by the lessee, had taken an active interest in the best developments in England and in the North, and experimented with a system of progressive gradation, but this soon degenerated under his successor into a simple classification according to labor efficiency. The state authorities had not been idle; after considerable experimenting they finally achieved an efficient system of central inspection and roused the public to the responsibility of taking over the administration of the prisons. The task was too great, however, since no amount of doubling up could crowd all the prisoners into the 675 cells at the two prisons, even if the legislature had been willing to pay the bill. The new state superintendent was forced to contract with outside companies for the care and labor of large numbers of his prisoners. However he was able to maintain efficient inspection, even regulation, and secured for Texas a system rivalled in the South only by Alabama.[23]

PENAL SYSTEM IN THE BORDER STATES

Institutional developments in America had their sectional variations, but there were never any sharp boundary lines. This was particularly true of penal institutions, so much more closely identified with state politics than the educational and charitable developments. Thus there was a string of border states stretching from Virginia and the Carolinas to Kansas that scarcely fell in with the general penological trends of either the North or the South; yet they differed from each other in more striking

[22] Texas State Penitentiary, *Report* (1878-80). Huntsville had 342, 256 were at construction work at Rusk, 215 were cutting wood for railroads, 156 were constructing railroads, 104 were at an iron furnace, and 1,033 were employed on several cotton plantations.

[23] Texas Penitentiary Investigation Commission, *Report* (1913). This contains a fair account of the history of the developments since the war. Texas State Penitentiary, *Report* (1880); (1882); N. P. A., *Proceedings* (1897), pp. 131 ff.

ways, if possible, than from either of these two sections. Ambitious penitentiaries were built in the Carolinas after the war, but events converted them into little more than penal hospitals. The prisons in Virginia, Kentucky, and Missouri had many things in common with developments in both sections. Kansas applied many Southern methods in a Northern setting; on the other hand, West Virginia made slow progress toward building a typically Northern prison out of Southern materials. These prisons grouped together as penal mongrels rather than by virtue of any positive likeness.

The Carolinas before the war left the administration of justice entirely in the hands of the counties. After that struggle the Carpetbaggers, who hastened in to reconstruct these states with the backing of friends in Congress, readily determined to build respectable Northern penitentiaries. In spite of appalling corruption, the states persisted in these programs after the Republican yoke had been thrown off; but a variety of circumstances turned the majority of the criminals over to private lessees under conditions that closely resembled those of the Black Belt.

In keeping with the spirit of reconstruction the prison directors of North Carolina laid plans for a new penitentiary. In 1868 they persuaded the pliable Governor William Holden to pay $100,000 for 8,000 acres of worthless pine barrens which, acting in a private capacity, they had just purchased for a dollar an acre; rich with boodle, they hastened to their Northern homes.[24] A new commission chose another site with only 22 acres near Raleigh, and dispatched one of their number to study the latest plans in the North. An architect was hired in Ohio and the new cell-house at Pittsburgh was adopted as the model. When the Democrats captured the state they appointed

---

[24] North Carolina Commission of Inquiry, Report, *North Carolina Senate Documents* (1868-69), pp. 1-9; Ashe, S. A., *History of North Carolina* (Raleigh, 1925), II, 1087.

still a third commission; fortunately it was content to continue the old program, and even planned to expand the final capacity from 500 to 1,000 cells. Temporary wooden huts were built to house the increasing number of prisoners while construction slowly proceeded.[25]

This ambitious program was beyond the means of the state. While the directors waited for funds the convicts accumulated until over 400 were crowded into the thirty-six miserable log huts. The authorities were forced to resort to the lease system, and by 1877 they had let out over 500 of their able-bodied prisoners to two different railroads,[26] which further delayed the erection of the penitentiary, as only women, children, and feeble old men were now kept at the stockade. Nevertheless construction continued and by 1882 the wall and one of the cell houses were completed. Its 500 cells provided an excellent equipment for a Southern state. Unfortunately the failure of a halfhearted experiment with a shoe factory and the lack of any other employment discouraged a full use of the prison; it continued to function solely as a penal hospital. Meanwhile more than 800 convicts were scattered over six railroad systems, subject to such desperate conditions that 100 escaped in one year in spite of the fact that during the same period at least eleven others were shot down in such attempts. The directors had so completely lost their former inspiration that they were able to congratulate the state that the convicts had earned a surplus of $678 above the combined cost of their keep, the construction of the new prison, and the officers' salaries.[27]

[25] North Carolina Penitentiary Commission, *Report* (1869-70); (1873-74), p. 13.

[26] North Carolina Penitentiary, *Report* (1876-77), pp. 1-8.

[27] North Carolina Penitentiary, *Report* (1880); (1883), pp. 280-82.

South Carolina made as poor a start in the penitentiary business. The government of 1866 had decided to build a state prison, but nothing was done until the next year when the Radical Republicans took charge under Governor R. K. Scott. Amidst wholesale looting during the succeeding seven or eight years the prison proved to be about as big a drain on the state treasury as any other scheme of graft; $497,333 was spent on the institution and little of value remained when Theodore Parmele took charge under Governor D. H. Chamberlain's direction in 1875.[28] The population had been kept within the capicity of the prison by frequent pardon deliveries, and in times of stress this had been a convenient means of economy.[29] However in 1873, when the legislature cut appropriations in half, that scheme did not suffice, and the superintendent reported that he had been forced to lease some of the prisoners in order to feed them.[30] Governor Chamberlain secured a law to prevent competition with free labor and attempted to work the prisoners on a farm leased by the state but still failed to solve the financial problem. When in 1877 Governor Wade Hampton and the Democrats gained control they were determined to reduce the terrible weight of state taxes and thus demanded that the prisoners earn their full support. Parmele was forced against his protests to lease 150 of his men that year, and 200 more the next. So desperate were the conditions at the

[28] Oliphant, A. D., *Evolution of the Penal System in South Carolina* (Columbia, S. C., 1916), pp. 1-5; Commission to examine the Char. and Penal Institutions, Report, *South Carolina Reports* (1877-78), pp. 818-23. It is interesting to compare the cost of this poor structure with its 200 cells with the cost of Riverside's model equipment of over 1,100 cells which totalled just under $2,000,000; see Barnes, H. E., *The Evolution of Penology in Pennsylvania* (Indianapolis, 1927), pp. 211-13.

[29] Simkins, F. B., and Woody, R. H., *South Carolina in Reconstruction* (Chapel Hill, 1932), pp. 514-41. Governor Scott pardoned 579 in four years, Governor Moses pardoned 451 in two years, and Governor Chamberlain pardoned 73 in a year and a half.

[30] Superintendent of Prisons, Report, *South Carolina Reports* (1873), pp. 115-18; (1875).

several stockades that 153 men died and 82 escaped at these camps in two years.[31] Colonel T. J. Lipscomb displaced Parmele in 1879, and for the twelve years of his service continued to reiterate the protests of his predecessor against the methods of the lessees over whom he had no control. His only success was to maintain fairly decent conditions in the 200-cell prison, making it the hospital and clearing station for the rapidly expanding convict population.[32] Thus in spite of their grandiose efforts, the two Carolinas found themselves in the mid-eighties with much the same penal system as the states of the Black Belt.

Before the war Virginia and Kentucky had adapted their prisons to the Northern standards. The 170 outside cells at Richmond, designed by Thomas Jefferson, had never been converted into an Auburn cell block, but they had been sufficient during most of the slave era to afford one cell to each prisoner. This, together with an active industrial program, had made possible a fairly high standard of discipline.[33] Although Kentucky had leased its prison, the Auburn traditions had been maintained in other respects; throughout the pre-war period it had compared favorably with most of the prisons north of the Ohio.[34] It was the problems of the war and reconstruction that turned these institutions towards the Southern traditions.

Responsibility for the introduction of outside labor for Virginia convicts rests on the Northern or "Restored" government. While struggling to establish order in the war-torn state it had been forced to gather large numbers

[31] *Ibid.* (1878), pp. 475-78. Two railroads and a canal company received most of these, but some were sent to a large plantation.

[32] Oliphant, A. D., *Penal System of South Carolina*, pp. 6-8.

[33] Virginia Penitentiary Report, *Virginia Public Documents* (1855-56), Vol. i, No. 14. The warden this year reported with pride that he had only a deficit of $1.69, and urged that this compared very well with any Northern prison for those that reported surpluses had not paid the salaries out of the income.

[34] Sneed, W. C., *Kentucky Penitentiary*, passim.

of vagrant Negroes into the penal net. The state's interests in several of the railroads prompted the loan of these convicts to help reconstruct their lines.[35] As the state acquired a unified and stable government under the leadership of conservative Republicans this penal labor policy was continued until the legislature began to dispose of its railroad interests after 1870. Even then the state did not lose its desire for railroad expansion, and the authorities continued to loan the convicts to the private companies as a sort of subsidy. The government received no return from this labor; in fact it paid for the guarding of these outside convicts; justifying its action on the grounds that the 170 old cells at Richmond were totally inadequate to house the 600-odd state convicts.[36]

Virginia was enjoying an era of strange optimism. Not only were great hopes pinned on the railroads, but many things were expected from an industrial development. Unfortunately few of the new enterprises profited as richly as did the shoe factory opened at the penitentiary. The favored contractors encouraged the concentration of a larger portion of the convicts at the prison, and after 1876 around 700 men were continually crowded into its antiquated quarters.[37] A woman's building had been erected outside of the walls, close enough to permit the use of their labor in the shops, but the prison authorities were hesitant to call the legislature's attention to the crowded condition of the men for fear they would be ordered to send larger numbers to the railroads. It proved impossible to hide the desperate conditions. In 1889 the legislature directed that the prison lease all that it could

[35] Morton, R. L., *History of Virginia* (N. Y., 1924), Vol. iii, pp. 83-84, 364.

[36] *Ibid.*, pp. 364-65; Virginia Penitentiary, *Report* (1871).

[37] Virginia Penitentiary, *Report* (1880), pp. 8-9; (1882); (1886). At this last report 850 men and women were confined at the prison and less than a hundred of these were women. At this date only 189 men were working on railroads.

not comfortably hold, but stipulated that the lessess be required to pay the entire cost of supporting and guarding their men. Virginia was thus ready to follow the lead of its Southern neighbors, and she would have done so had it not been for the fact that outside demands for labor were not as urgent as those within the prison. In spite of her Southern intentions the old cell structure at Richmond remained jammed with hundreds of convicts laboring for the profit of the shoe contractors, and the authorities only succeeded in finding employment for a few hundred outside the walls.[38]

Kentucky, busy repenting of its alliance with the Yankees, paid little attention to the policies of H. I. Todd, lessee of its prison from 1863 to 1871. That gentleman managed to employ the majority in a hemp factory within the narrow confines of the prison and only worked a few trusties on a farm outside.[39] Another lessee out-bid Todd in 1871 by agreeing to enlarge the prison to a capacity of 700; by the end of his ten year lease he was crowding almost a thousand into very unsatisfactory quarters, and worrying chiefly over the 400 he was forced to support in idleness because of the lack of factory space.[40] Disturbing rumors of cruelty aroused Governor Luke P. Blackburn to demand that the legislature cancel the lease and take full charge of the prison. The state decided to build a second prison on the pattern of the new institution at Elmira, N. Y., just beginning to make its reputation, but Blackburn failed in his effort to have it designated a reformatory.[41] Meanwhile the state was not ready to operate its prison industries, and two contracts were let, one with a company to operate the prison, and another sup-

[38] Virginia Penitentiary, *Report* (1890), p. 7.

[39] Coulter, E. M., *The Civil War and Readjustment in Kentucky* (Chapel Hill, 1926), pp. 257-348; Kentucky Penitentiary, *Report* (1870), pp. 3-5.

[40] *Ibid.* (1880), pp. 3-8.

[41] Rule, L. V., *City of Dead Souls* (Louisville, 1920), pp. 153-57.

plying 250 men to a railroad. Under each contract the state was content to supply the guards and officers, surrendering all other functions to the contractors.[42] But the prison was still too crowded to permit its profitable operation; in two years the railroad had acquired both contracts and was greatly increasing the numbers at its construction camps. Terrible conditions developed at these stockades, and public indignation was aroused. A change in policy was forced on the authorities when the practice of displacing free labor on some of the railroads produced several riots at the camps.[43] The state made another attempt to take charge of its prison and sent some of the convicts to Eddyville to speed up the construction of the new prison. Overcrowding had meanwhile become extremely serious at Frankfort; a disastrous uprising among the idle prisoners destroyed Warden South's hopes of operating the prison for the state, and it was leased again in 1889. Thus Kentucky failed in its many attempts to break away from the Southern leasing methods. Not until the second prison was completed in the early nineties did the state finally assume full responsibility for the management of its penal system.[44]

By 1880 all the former Confederate states and Kentucky had surrendered a major part of their criminals into the hands of lessees interested chiefly in their private profits. Alabama and Texas were attempting to supervise the lease camps; Virginia, Kentucky, and the Carolinas were making efforts to maintain penitentiaries; but in all

[42] Kentucky Penitentiary, *Report* (1882), pp. 4-9.

[43] *Ibid.* (1885), pp. 19-23. The numbers at the prison fell from 700 to 500 while those on the railroads increased from 250 to 650 between 1882 and 1885. Rule, *op. cit.*, pp. 158-59. A mob of citizens gathered outside one of the largest camps in 1886 and shouted: "Our home people must live, hence we do this."

[44] Kentucky Penitentiary, Report on Outbreak, *Kentucky Documents* (1885), No. 18, pp. 1-83; Commission of Sinking Fund of Penitentiary, *Kentucky Documents* (1889-90), No. 19, pp. 4-5.

of these states, and in Missouri and Kansas as well, the
dictates of economy had given rise to wretched systems of
penal slavery that were little better than the worst ones
of the Black Belt. Occasionally the voice of a reformer
was heard above the sound of the money changers, but
the tax-payers soon reasserted their interests. If the most
critical years of poverty in the South were over by 1878,
the returning prosperity did not relieve the convicts for
at least another decade. Southern convicts were paying
full retribution for their own sins at a time when that old
principle was beginning to lose force in the North; but
they were also paying the penalty for the public crimes of
Civil War and reconstruction. Many thousands of happy-
go-lucky Negroes awoke from rosy dreams of freedom and
forty acres and a mule to find themselves shackled to the
task of reconstructing the South in hopeless penal
servitude.[45]

CONVICT LIFE IN THE SOUTH

In the days when Southern politics were full of bad
blood, and party rivalries took on the nature of personal
feuds, sentimental proposals for the reformation of criminals found little welcome. The convict's fate was a life
and death struggle. Vital statistics alone gained precedence over the treasurer's reports, and this only on rare
occasions. During the first years the struggle for the restoration of government by native whites was so fierce that
penal conditions could have aroused hardly any surprise.
In the eighties George Washington Cable urged that the
just treatment of the prisoners be recognized as a public

[45] Nevins, Allan, *Emergence of Modern America* (N. Y., 1930), p. 360,
also pp. 251-52. The public debts of eleven Southern States increased
$132,000,000 during the years of Negro-carpetbagger rule, 1867-72. The
efforts of later governments to lighten the heavy tax burden thus necessi-
tated, helps to explain their policy towards penal labor. National Conference
of Charities, *Proceedings* (1883), pp. 271-72. G. W. Cable could not see
the justice of "farming out into private hands whose single motive is
money, the most delicate and difficult task in the whole public service."

interest, but when public schools and charities received only niggardly support it was little wonder that the crimnial was expected to earn at least his keep.[46]

The old slave system provided many traditions and customs for Southern penology. Yet the penal lease camps lacked the saving grace of paternalism so characteristic of the old plantation slavery, and, at the same time, horror and brutality were unchecked by any concern for private property interests in the Negro. The new criminal laws gathered the most restless and independent from among the freedmen and gave them hopelessly long terms. The discipline which had kept the relatively docile slaves in the fields before the war could have no effect now; the penal slaves had to be herded about their camps by armed guards and shackled in the "cribs" at night. The lessee was interested in making as large returns as possible from the least outlay, and the interests of the lessee too frequently determined the policy of the state.

There were no standard living arrangements in the Southern prison camps. Yet one strong factor, the demand for economy, brought them all practically to a common level, scarcely that of subsistence. None of the lease camps ever tried to introduce any of the Auburn traditions, and the penitentiaries that did have individual cells

[46] Boyd, William K., ''Some Phases of Educational History in the South since 1865,'' *Studies in Southern History and Politics* (inscribed to W. A. Dunning, N. Y., 1914), pp. 262-65. In these early days the school funds were frequently diverted to other functions, and direct public support of these undertakings or of the charitable institutions was very meager until after the agitation of the Populists in the nineties. National Conference of Charities, *Proceedings* (1883), p. 268. Cable expressed in vivid terminology his belief that ''mistake springs from the indolent assumption that the call to make prisons what they ought to be is merely an appeal to public benevolence. It was so in their earlier turn, with public hospitals and public schools; and the effect was similar. For only here and there, if at all, did they find their best efficiency or a true public support until society rose to the noble modesty that recognized them not as public charities but as public interests.''

seldom attempted to apply rules of silence. Wooden huts
of one story usually housed a hundred or more on crude
bunks strung around the walls. The danger of escapes
frequently compelled the authorities to shut these up tight
at nightfall, and the atmosphere soon became indescrib-
ably foul. Water was usually scarce, and bathing almost
impossible; other sanitary arrangements were invariably
crude, and disease was rampant. Food was plentiful or
scarce as the economy of the lessee determined, and, if its
coarse nature and wretched preparation were little hardship to the majority of the victims, that brought no
pride to the state. Heat was usually lacking although
rickety stoves or open fires sometimes added much smoke
and a little warmth during the cold nights of the winter
months.[47] The fear of escapes was the controlling factor
in discipline. Various devices for shackling the feet were
tried, and in desperate cases heavy iron balls were added
to the chains. Striped garments were everywhere in use,
and the convicts had no picayune tastes regarding their
foot-wear as among the Northern prisoners—here they
were glad to get any at all.[48] Tobacco chewing was everywhere in evidence, but smoking was prohibited because of
the fire risk. Southern newspapers did not cry out, as in
the North, against the hotel accommodations of their prisoners, nevertheless this neglect did not seem to cause the
criminals to migrate north.

Religious influences, though not absent, had little significance. It was difficult to secure white chaplains, and it
was out of the question to hire Negroes. Plenty of the
latter turned up in the camps by legal proceedings, and
these dusky but fluent souls usually practiced their calling
without restraint on the one day of rest. Sunday schools

[47] Oliphant, A. D., *Evolution of Penology in South Carolina*, pp. 2-5.
Even the convicts at the penitentiary in South Carolina in 1875 had only
straw mattresses and no bunks.

[48] Alabama Inspectors of Convicts, *Report* (1884-86), pp. 354-66.

were popular among the prisoners, and occasionally out-side workers added to the value of these feeble attempts at regeneration.[49] When the religious forces did stir them-selves they usually attacked such popular devices of the devil as card playing. Arkansas passed a law against this vice in 1890, but the warden reported that he found it impossible to stamp out this most popular Sabbath pas-time.[50]

Such were the living conditions of the great majority of the Southern convicts in the first two decades following the war. Even when Alabama determined to make the lease system as respectable as possible, the model camps constructed at the mines did little more than improve the sanitary and eating arrangements.[51] After fourteen years' experience in charge of convict camps in Florida, Captain J. C. Powell was inspired to compare that system with the horrors of Siberia. If his information was limited to the very worst system of the South, his account certainly de-picted villainy that surpassed any responsible picture of the situation in Siberia.[52] Warden Bankhead in Alabama was more to the point when he called on local analogies:

I am prepared to demonstrate that our system is a better training school for criminals than any of the dens of iniquity that exist in our large cities. . . . The first lesson taught is that the state cares nothing for the criminal, nor his well being. . . . You may as well expect to instil decent habits into a hog as to reform a criminal whose habits and surroundings are as filthy as a pig's. To say there are any reformatory measures at our prison, or that any regard is had to similar subjects, is to state a false-hood.[53]

A small portion of the convicts avoided these hard-ships. The lessee had but little use for the feeble, the women, or the very young boys, and these were usually

[49] Kentucky Penitentiary, *Report* (1882), pp. 24-26. Governor Black-burn's wife was only one of the prominent women of the South to organize Sunday schools.

[50] Arkansas Inspectors of Convicts, *Report* (1890), p. 357.

[51] Alabama Penitentiary Inspectors, *Report* (1884), pp. 15-20.

[52] Powell, J. C., *The American Siberia* (Philadelphia, 1891).

[53] Alabama Penitentiary Inspectors, *Report* (1882), p. 15.

gathered at the walls along with the crippled and diseased transferred there from the camp. All of the states but Florida maintained these asylum prisons, but they lacked all features of a hospital except the suffering. Usually crowded beyond their capacity, with a wretched equipment of cells, frequently made only of wood, none of these prisons maintained a respectable discipline. Judged by Northern standards only, the prisons in the two Carolinas gradually assumed in the late eighties the character of penitentiaries.

Death or escape were the only quick methods of relief available to the convicts. Before the system was well established escapes were very frequent, and the disciplinary methods were primarily devised to check them. As late as 1882 a survey of the reports revealed that a total of 1,100 had made successful breaks for freedom in the two previous years.[54] The next year a study of mortality in prison disclosed the fact that while only four prisons north of the Ohio had a mortality of 25 in 1,000, only four prisons south of that river had a record of less than 50 in 1,000, while Louisiana exceeded one in ten.[55] These appalling facts, reacting on both the officers and the prisoners, were partly the result and partly the cause of the brutal conditions and practices of the lease system.

Southern discipline was not complicated by elaborate devices for reformation. It was "such as provides for efficiency in labor, and against insurrection and escape."[56] No rules of silence gave occasion for petty punishments.

[54] Alabama Inspectors of Convicts, *Report* (1886), p. 94; National Conference of Charities, *Proceedings* (1883), p. 274. Cable counted only 63 escapes out of 18,300 Northern convicts, while there were 49 escapes from 630 prisoners in Tennessee.

[55] National Conference of Charities, *Proceedings* (1883), pp. 262-63. North of the thirty-ninth parallel the average death rate of 28 prisons was 14.9 per thousand, south of the line there was an average mortality of 41.3 per thousand.

[56] *Ibid.* (1883), p. 275.

In fact there were no written rules of any sort in the many cases where complete control was intrusted to lessees. Such was the arrangement in all the states except Virginia and the Carolinas, although both Texas and Alabama were making attempts to control discipline. Punishment was usually with the lash or the strap, but ingenious guards sometimes devised other forms of torture. One method of "watering" a disorderly prisoner became quite notorious because of its dangerous consequences.[57] Alabama and Texas were the only states to regulate these punishments by law during this period; elsewhere the only check was the interest of the lessee in seeing that his punishments did not impair his labor force.[58]

The chief reliance for security was on the chains, the dogs, and the armed guards. In the early days guards did not always shoot at escaping prisoners. Fines were accordingly assessed on the lesee for every escape, and the guard's job was made to depend on his vigilance. Scores of fugitives were shot down every year in some of the states, and yet, with conditions as they were, there were always desperate men ready on the slightest occasion to "hang their life on a limb" in the hope of freedom.[59]

Cruel as was the fate of the convicts, Southern courts showed no sentimental hesitancy in meting out the full penalty of the law. There were no habitual criminal laws,

[57] Powell, *American Siberia*. "Watering" consisted of pouring a stream of water into the mouth of a convict stretched on his back; much of it got into the lungs and at best it produced a fit of choking. Georgia Legislature, *Joint Committee on Condition of Penitentiary* (1870), pp. 195-200. Whipping with a leather strap was the only punishment but there was no limit fixed by any rule.

[58] Texas State Penitentiary, *Report* (1882), pp. 12-13. Texas was one of the first to prohibit the use of trusties as guards.

[59] Wisner, *Public Welfare Administration in Louisiana*, p. 155: "The idea of reformation was totally abandoned. . . . The mortality rate was incredibly high, escapes common and the popular means of guarding prisoners were by chains, shotguns and dogs." Oliphant, *Evolution of Penology in South Carolina*, pp. 7-8.

or indeterminate sentence laws here; none were needed. Massachusetts courts might consider a twenty year sentence for a third felony too harsh to be applied, but out of 1,200 convicts in Georgia in 1880 only 150 had terms as short as three years, and over 500 had terms of ten years or more. Everywhere in the South sentences were unreasonably long, and the Negroes got more than their just share.[60] The social hatreds engendered by years of strife were still rampant; it continued to appear a social good to take idlers off to construction camps long after the notorious vagrancy laws were forgotten. There was no check available, as in the North, where cells rapidly became crowded and compelled the construction of costly Bastiles if convictions were too frequent. There were in fact no saving circumstances to protect the unfortunate Southern convict from hopeless oblivion until the first era of large-scale construction came to a close in the early nineties.

Even more than in the North the great majority of the prisoners remained under the control of the counties. These authorities had no more adequate housing equipments than the states when the new constitutions abolished branding, whipping, and the stocks, in favor of fines and imprisonment. While the states were experimenting with their leasing systems, the county sheriffs showed no lack of initiative in making use of their new labor forces.[61]

The large governmental responsibilities of Southern counties provided them with many outlets for labor. The employment of convicts in cleaning the streets was introduced by many cities at the close of the war, but the construction and repair of rural wagon roads soon became the chief task for such labor.[62] Counties in the North as well as the South had experimented with this plan from early

[60] National Conference of Charities, *Proceedings* (1883), p. 285.
[61] Steiner, J. F., and Brown, R. M., *North Carolina Chain Gang* (Chapel Hill, 1927), pp. 10-15.
[62] *Ibid.*, pp. 34-36.

times, but it did not become a normal procedure until the reconstruction days in the South. Carroll D. Wright found county convicts laboring on the public roads in eight Southern states in 1886. Even West Virginia, striving to develop a Northern penitentiary system, permitted its counties to labor twenty-five per cent of its total criminal population on the roads in that year.[63]

There was seldom any clear distinction in Southern law between state and county offenders. Judges usually had the discretion of committing their prisoners to the state prison or to the country chain-gang. North Carolina and a few other states limited the county sentences to ten years.[64] This flexible distribution usually worked to the advantage of the counties. In districts where local authorities were failing to make profitable use of this labor supply, the judges usually handed the great majority over to the state; but when a sheriff was building roads or leasing the men to advantage, the courts usually kept the able-bodied at home and sent only the aged and infirm to the state prison. The state authorities, eager to meet the largest demands of their lessees, made frequent protests against this distribution, but little was done until the states began to take over the responsibility of road construction at a much later date.[65]

This rivalry sometimes called forth damning indictments of the county systems. As their camps were less permanent or substantial than those of the state, and as the country authorities were more irresponsible, the conditions were if possible more wretched. Many of the sheriffs, rather than superintend the labor themselves,

[63] *Ibid.*, pp. 4-20; U. S. Commissioner of Labor, *Report* (1886). These states were Alabama, Arkansas, Florida, Georgia, Mississippi, North Carolina, Tennessee, and Texas. West Virginia should also be added according to Steiner.

[64] Steiner, *op. cit.*, p. 6.

[65] Alabama Inspectors of Convicts, *Report* (1886), pp. 23-27.

leased their charges to private companies to work the roads, drain swamps, operate lumber camps, or what not. There was no adequate regulation; acts of the legislatures of North Carolina and other states prohibiting county leases were never effective. Usually there was no provision for inspection, and there was no regular report on discipline or living accommodations; little enough attention was given to records of finances, escapes, or discharges. Chains, dogs, and guns were the mainstays for the security of the counties, but there were no provisions for safeguarding the interests of the prisoners.[66] The wretchedness of these camps more than rivaled that of the worst lease camps of the section.

Thus reconstruction and its aftermath witnessed the evolution of a vicious system of penal slavery throughout the South. Interests of economy and commercial reconstruction dominated the councils of the states. Open corruption had been stamped out, but favored enterprises continued to exploit the growing labor force; profits were shared with the states in most cases, but thousands of bewildered Negroes and unlucky whites were damned to hopeless slavery. There were occasional expressions of sympathy and bursts of indignation when the cruel facts were exposed, but there was no organization of public opinion comparable to the boards of charities in the North. While the rest of the nation was formulating, debating, and in several cases adopting parole and indeterminate sentence laws, and while progressive Northern states were establishing the first adult reformatories and checking the exploitation of convict labor by private

[66] Wager, P. W., *County Government and Administration in North Carolina* (Chapel Hill, 1928), pp. 270-74, 357-68. This gives an objective description of county penal administration. It is well to remember that the social and economic prostration of the South was a severe blow to the semi-aristocratic administration of county functions that was so much more satisfactory in many of the counties before the war.

contractors, the irresponsible lease system had gained undisputed sway in the South. Masquerading as it did under the cloak of justice, it perpetrated crueler brutalities than the old chattel slavery had been guilty of. But already a New South was emerging, and in the decade of the nineties some remarkable changes were to occur in its penal system.[67]

BLAKE McKELVEY

University of Chicago

[67] See the author's article ''A Half Century of Southern Penal Exploitation,'' *Social Forces* (October 1, 1934), for the continuation of this story.

ALPHA LODGE NO. 116, NEW JERSEY

(An extract from the Prince Hall Sodality)

It is seldom that the story of any private masonic lodge deserves notice in a general history unless it is of great antiquity, or has had a variety of singular experiences which give it prominence, or some peculiarity in origin or development which brings it conspicuity, and distinguishes it from the general run of lodges. A number of European lodges have received this historical treatment because of their antiquity, and because of the part they played in the formative period of the institution. A few American lodges must naturally be so treated because of their connection with the masonic colonization of this country. African Lodge No. 459 is likewise properly placed in this category because it represented the introduction of Freemasonry into a whole race of people, and also the projection of an enduring issue into the field of American masonic historiography.

The lodge which is the subject of this chapter has this distinctive feature of uniqueness. Its simple presence reflects and suggests many things of interest and moment. It touches the peculiar field of race relations from a different angle than is commonly seen by students of sociology; it brings to the foreground the whole question of the legitimacy of Negro masonry; it encroaches upon the doctrine of exclusive grand lodge jurisdiction; it gave an honored grand lodge the opportunity of making a sound and courageous decision on a matter of extreme delicacy, when considerations of expediency might have tempted it to do otherwise; and it has been the subject of much discussion, misrepresentation, and ignorance throughout the American masonic world. Moreover, its continuous and harmonious existence should give food for thought to those timid masons who have always feared that formal acknowledgment of their colored fraters would mean the Africanization of their lodges with its attendant social discord. All of these things Alpha Lodge caused, or became involved in without conscious effort on its own part, and for reasons not of its own making. It was a catalyctic agent in the family of lodges, creating commotion by its mere presence, and thus a masonic *cause célèbre*.[1]

The curious story of Alpha Lodge No. 116, of Newark, New Jersey, should be known to every student of masonic history in the United States, for it bears the unique distinction of being the only lodge here made up of both white and colored members and affiliated with a white grand lodge. Generally it is classed as a colored lodge. It has been charged that its charter was obtained by a species of trickery, but there is no doubt that the proceedings incident to its organization were quite regular. There is evidence, however, of a concealed design on the part of its sponsors, although they did nothing illegal.

At the 1870 communication of the Grand Lodge a petition from F. H. Sweres, Jeremiah Evans, and ten other Prince Hall masons asking for a warrant for Cushite Lodge, Newark, was received and referred to a special committee. The petition was denied in 1871 on recommendation of the committee, not, however, because of patent technical defects in the application, but rather on the theory that the masonic lineage of the applicants from African Lodge 459 was tainted with masonic vice, the vice being that Prince Hall had no authority to establish subordinates in Philadelphia and Providence, and then, later, to form a grand lodge from which the petitioners descended. The error in this reasoning and decision is apparent to those who have read the several chapters on grand lodge organization herein. The committee did as-

---

[1] *The Landmark* (New York), February 11, 18 and 25, and March 4, 1871; *New York Sun*, February 21, 22, 1871; *Newark Daily Journal*, March 11, 1871; *Newark Daily Advertiser*, March 16, 1871, February 16, 1872.

sert that race or color did not operate to bar membership in lodges in New Jersey, and pointed out the regular method to be pursued.

At the same session (1871) a dispensation was asked by a group of white masons to form Alpha Lodge, No. 116, and in due course a charter was issued. About a month after its constitution complaint was made that the charter had been obtained through fraud and misrepresentation, and the Grand Master summarily seized and impounded the charter, a rather high-handed action as it was based only on an ex parte accusation. The basis of the complaint was that Alpha Lodge had admitted, or contemplated admitting, colored men. This was not denied, and in fact, a number of the ''Cushite'' petitioners later became members of Alpha.

However, Alpha Lodge was not without masonic friends in Newark, and nearly one hundred of them promptly petitioned the Grand Master for the restoration of the charter. In the event their petition was denied they requested the Grand Master to call a special session of the Grand Lodge to consider the matter. Alpha Lodge officers also demanded a detailed statement of the charges against them. The Grand Master was unwilling to recede from the position he had taken, and equally unwilling to assemble the grand body. He referred the entire matter to the Committee on Petitions and Grievances. Upon their report he decided to withhold any further action until the next regular session of the Grand Lodge. At the communication held in 1872 the matter came up for consideration. That it was thoroughly debated, and that there were marked differences of opinion, is evident from the fact that discussion took place at two different sessions of the meeting. Finally a motion to restore the charter prevailed, and the incident was closed. No other honorable action was possible from the state of the record.[2]

[2] 1872, *N. J.*, p. 454. *Alpha Lodge No. 116*-Harold, V. B., *Voorhis-Nocalore*, Vol. ii, Part 3, p. 143.

In 1872, Trenton Lodge No. 5 adopted resolutions to the effect that the initiation of colored men into the fraternity would tend to disturb the harmony of the craft, and would be of no benefit to them. This was after Alpha Lodge had admitted several colored members. These resolutions were sent to every lodge in the jurisdiction, with the request that they take appropriate action to arrest the threatened peril.

On May 27, 1872, formal charges were filed against Alpha Lodge and its officers. They were read at the 1873 communication and referred to the Committee on Jurisprudence. This committee presented a report exonerating the accused, and which further stated that the action of Alpha Lodge, since the restoration of its charter, had been in accord with masonic law. The Grand Lodge adopted the report, and the resolutions of Trenton Lodge No. 5 were declared out of order. This decision was sound, as each lodge is the sole judge of the qualifications of its applicants.

Judging from the first colored initiates, Alpha Lodge was discriminating in the selection of candidates. Among them appear two Methodist ministers, several teachers, a baker and two engineers. In all its history, there has not been one expulsion for unmasonic conduct.

In furtherance of what we may now designate as a well-considered plan, nine of the colored members of Alpha Lodge demitted, and in 1873 applied for a warrant for Surgam Lodge to be also held in Newark. This petition was recommended by Alpha Lodge. The application appears not to have been pressed before the Committee on Warrants which recommended that action be postponed. A motion to postpone was lost by a large vote, and a second motion to reject the petition prevailed by a much larger vote. Thereafter, the colored petitioners for Surgam Lodge reaffiliated with their mother lodge.

It is currently reported that the white members demitted to other lodges, in accordance with a previous understanding, leaving the colored brethren in full control. The story is also current among white masons in the United States that a few white members remained in the lodge, to insure its natural extinction by blackballing all petitions for membership. Both of these are palpably untrue as the lodge still exists as Alpha Lodge No. 116, and its members are fraternally received by its sister lodges. A Past Master of Alpha Lodge, C. Lansing Nevius, a prominent colored attorney of Newark, New Jersey, advised that the membership is still mixed.

In this connection it is interesting to note that the Grand Lodge of New Jersey, carrying a mixed lodge on its roll, was one of the jurisdictions which severed fraternal relationship with the Grand Lodge of Washington for its attitude toward Negro Masonry.[3] In fact Grand Master Upton charges that New Jersey masons participated in a wide-spread conspiracy to discredit his Grand Lodge.[4]

Nearly forty years later the Grand Master of Mississippi learned, apparently for the first time, that colored men were initiated under the jurisdiction of New Jersey, for in 1909 he suspended fraternal relations with New Jersey. In 1927 these relations were restored by Mississippi, apparently of its own volition. The severance of relationship served one good purpose, however, as the Grand Master of New Jersey mentioned it in his address to the Grand Lodge, and in his review of the Alpha Lodge incident gave added publicity to an event which had been almost forgotten.[5] A new generation of masons thereby acquired a curious and interesting bit of historical information.

A review of the New Jersey proceedings for 1870,

[3] Upton, *Negro Masonry*, p. 6.
[4] Upton, *Negro Masonry*, p. 7. Note.
[5] 1909, New Jersey—*Grand Master's Address.*

1871, and 1872, indicates that a considerable group of white masons in Newark were favorably disposed to the recognition of Prince Hall masonry. St. John's Lodge No. 1 recommended the establishment of Alpha Lodge, and members of Eureka No. 39 supported the motion to restore the charter. Apparently the application for Alpha Lodge was prepared in anticipation of the rejection of the "Cushite" request, for it was presented at the same session in 1871. This is but a repetition of the experience of practically every Grand Lodge where the matter of recognition of Prince Hall masonry was considered. Although action on recognition was generally evaded, yet there was always a substantial minority who vigorously championed the cause of the colored frater.

The Committee on Petitions and Grievances to which was referred the Alpha case made a non-commital report in 1872 and handed the somewhat difficult matter back to the Grand Lodge without recommendation. This committee approved the Grand Master's action in arresting the charter, but at the same time was unable to show evidence of un-Masonic conduct to justify the act,—an apparent contradiction which is difficult to reconcile.

New Jersey should take honest pride in the fact that its Grand Lodge did restore the charter. Alpha Lodge was certainly innocent of any Masonic offense, and if its sponsors did conceal their real intent, they no doubt felt morally justified by the peculiar circumstances and conditions then in force. A revocation of the character would have meant that innocent masons would have been deprived of their legitimate status without benefit of trial in violation of the high ethical and legal tenets of the fraternity. New Jersey is to be congratulated for not permitting prejudice to override reason and masonic justice, even if it did later cause the temporary severance of fraternal relationship with Mississippi and Oklahoma, and some criticism from sister grand lodges whose action was based upon a persistent misunderstanding of the facts.

Alpha Lodge No. 116 still exists, a credit to itself, to its Grand Lodge and to the fraternity at large. Its growth has been modest but substantial, 79 members being enrolled as of January 1, 1931 and its work and internal harmony is beyond reproach. It is worthy to note that colored men of Newark did not rush to become members of Alpha in order to be connected with a white grand lodge. The great majority of colored masons preferred to affiliate with the three lodges of Prince Hall descent now functioning in that city.

Although the attempt to form Cushite Lodge died in its incipiency, yet the incident is noteworthy for other reasons than its mere novelty. The petitioners for this lodge made no attempt to conceal their racial identity or their masonic connections. The name selected, "Cushite," points to colored men with as much certainty as did the name "African" in Prince Hall's day. Moreover, their petition openly disclosed their lineage from Prince Hall and his first lodge, and the documents supporting the petition gave an abbreviated history of Negro Masonry in America. There was no attempt at fraud or deception in this effort, and this is typical of the conduct of Prince Hall masons in their varied contacts with their white fraters.[6]

The manner in which the petition was received by the Grand Lodge of New Jersey is worthy of comment. The Grand Master in his address, asked that it be given honest and respectful consideration. The special committee to which it was referred stated that it was couched in respectful language and was deserving of courteous treatment.

The committee's report indicates that the petition could have been denied peremptorily because of several

[6] Alpha Lodge No. 116, *David McGregor*, p. 13.

manifest defects. The application had not been approved
by any lodge; the petitioners failed to show by certificate
or otherwise that they were regular masons in good standing; and it was not affirmatively shown that the applicants
had demonstrated a masonic efficiency to the satisfaction
of any lodge. These requirements were a prerequisite to
a dispensation under the Grand Lodge regulations, and
the absence of any one was fatal to the application. However, the committee did not rely on these obvious infor-
malities, but chose to make a painstaking search to justify
a rejection on legal and historical grounds. In the state
of knowledge of Prince Hall masonry which existed at
that time, very little criticism can be made of the committee's final judgment. Today, however, in the light of
researches presented by John D. Caldwell,[7] Samuel W.
Clark,[8] and William H. Upton [9] the masonic student will
have no difficulty in seeing the fallacy in the objections
raised by the committee. These were, briefly, the method
by which masonry was transmitted by Prince Hall to his
successors, and the territorial argument, both of which
have been treated at length in this work.

The committee did make an obvious historical error
when it asserted that African Lodge died in 1808 at the
formation of Prince Hall Grand Lodge. It is difficult to
understand how such an erroneous statement could have
been made, even in 1871, as there were masons then living
who had been made in African Lodge. The committee
also raised the question of the right of African Lodge to
confer degrees because this power was not stated in
terms in the warrant. This was certainly a technical
quibble. The warrant to African Lodge was in the form
commonly used by the Grand Lodge of England at that
time, and no one has ever questioned the right of its sub-

[7] *New Day—New Duty.*
[8] *Negro Mason in Equity.*
[9] *Negro Masonry, Prince Hall's Letter Book.*

ordinates, acting under identical charters, to confer degrees. Moreover, the right to confer degrees is inherent
in every duly constituted lodge, and the doubt raised by
the committee shows a rather conspicuous lack of masonic
knowledge.

It is to be regretted that in all the writings concerning
Alpha Lodge, nothing appears from the hand of any of
the original colored members. It does not seem to have
occurred to any of the numerous white masons who have
devoted attention to this subject, that these colored members might have had impressions and attitudes worth
recording. They invariably treat the subject purely from
its effect on, and relation to, white masonry. Perhaps this
is better understood when we realize that it was a long
time before the Negro had a voice and a respectful hearing in the councils of those who were considering his
peculiar and most intimate problems.

The returns of Alpha Lodge No. 116 indicate that in
1872 twelve men were initiated as follows:

1872.
April 1.—Rev. John H. L. Sweres, (C) Pastor, Zion M. E.
    Church.
April 1.—Abram T. Cooke, (C) Baker.
April 8.—John M. O'Fake, (C) Music teacher.
April 15.—James M. Baxter, (C) School principal.
April 22.—Elias S. Ray, (C) Janitor.
April 29.—Thomas F. Washington, (C) Engineer.
May 6.—Jermiah G. Evans, (C) Engineer.
May 13.—Theodore M. Parker, (W) Machinist.
June 3.—Peter P. O'Fake, (C) Dancing teacher.
July 22.—William M. Clawson, (W) Engineer.
Oct. 28.—Alexander Singer, (C) Coachman.
Dec. 16.—George Healey, (W) Machinist.

In 1873 the process of gradually working the colored
members into the chairs was started, a Junior Warden

being elected and a Junior Deacon appointed, although the Master's seat was not occupied by a colored member until 1879. By 1881 all of the principal offices were filled by colored members. All of the charter members of Alpha, except one, gradually ceased their connection for one reason or another by 1885; the exception being Bro. Wm. Clarke, who remained a member until his death in 1920. As late as 1924 its membership was still reported as mixed, although Alpha Lodge is generally referred to as a colored lodge.

There is an obvious paradox in the story of Alpha Lodge which is not without a tinge of the ironical. The sovereign Grand Lodge of New Jersey voted decisively and emphatically on two separate occasions, not to admit colored masons into its fellowship. Yet, by a peculiar quirk of circumstances and events, it finds itself with a colored lodge on its register. And in all of this, the colored mason was, by the force of these same circumstances, merely a passive participant. All writers who have treated this subject are in accord in admitting that the conduct and attitude of the colored masons was in no wise censurable.

HARRY E. DAVIS

202 Engineers Building,
Cleveland, Ohio.

ATTITUDES OF THE IBERIAN PENINSULA

Not long after the Franco-Prussian War of 1870, the victors often reiterated the assertion that Africa begins at the Pyrennes. Others have said the Orient begins at Paris. The implication is that the Latin races are decadent. These "historical philosophers" asserted that the Spaniards, Portuguese, and probably a goodly number of French and Italians are not Europeans. They are not descendants of the tribes which swept down from Northern Europe, destroyed Rome, and laid the foundation of modern nations with a culture different from that of the Mediterranean race. To the extent that these remnants of the Roman Empire hold on to the culture of ancient days and thus continue primitive they are unprogressive and decadent. This was the new point of view of the Nordics who demonstrated their superiority in 1870 in the War between France and Germany. In other words, a victorious warlike people work out a new philosophy of history every time they succeed in an international conflict.

The argument underlying this aphorism that the Latin races are decadent is that they are older stock which, having matured earlier in a hot climate, have run their course. Nordics like the English and Germans in cold climates have matured slowly and are reaching the summit of their greatness at the time the Latins are declining. Of course, these theorists, while admitting that the logical outcome would be the subsequent decline of the Nordics, believed, nevertheless, that such a turn in their affairs was so remote that this particular aspect of the discussion had no particular value. The main point was to explain why the Nordices are destined to rule the world.

The argument was not based solely on the defeat of France in 1870. The triumph of Spanish arms in Africa in 1859, then, was explained as an insignificant feat, for in 1898 she lost her possessions to the United States. An upstart like Mussolini with sufficient force to disturb the calm of Europe and Africa was not expected from the ranks of the Latins; but his case may be explained by descent from an invading tribe from North Europe rather than from the decayed element in Southern Italy surviving at a "poor dying rate" the destruction of the Roman Empire. With respect to Spain it had to be conceded that the Celts and later Goths penetrated that area and the province of Asturias received a large infusion of Nordic blood. With these and many other exceptions the effort to group all stocks speaking Romance Languages and to classify them as decadent breaks down as an unscientific project. During later years racial classification has been worked out anthropologically, and scientists have recently reached the conclusion that there is no such thing as a race.

It is a fact, however, that isolated Portugal and Spain have received little infusion of new blood, and, like the Italians of Lower Italy and the natives of such islands as Sicily, Sardinia and Corsica, they are racially classified as "dark-complexioned white people or a Mediterranean race." L. A. Warren in discussing this matter in his *Modern Spanish Literature,* says that this original stock may have been an African race. He concedes that there is much evidence of Africa in Spain. Madrid shows some of it, and so does Andalucia. The Africanization, however, according to this author, is not to be taken literally. The reference is to the influence of the Moors who came into Spain from North Africa and left on the country their mark all of which did not disappear when these invaders were expelled. Spaniards, however, disclaim any such influence even from these Orientals inasmuch as they have been disconnected from the Iberian Peninsula for centuries. It is said that Spain is not Moorish except in the sense that the Moors and Spaniards both belong to the same Mediterranean race.[1]

"Is there much Moorish blood in Spain?" inquires L. A. Warren. "The Moors are inhabitants of north-west Africa and Morocco. There are two main races in Algeria and Morocco: the Arabs, descendants of the Mohammedan conquerors from Arabia, and the Berbers, the original inhabitants of North Africa all through history. The Moors, strictly speaking, should be used to denote a mixture of the Arabs and Berbers. But for the most part the Arabs and Berbers have not mixed, remaining separate races. The Berbers who, in Morocco, greatly outnumbered the Arabs, are of the Iberian race, that is to say, they are a European race and if put into European clothes would be undistinguishable from those generally known as Europeans; they have, however, of late centuries got, like the Portuguese, somewhat mixed with the Negro. The racial frontier between the European and African or Negro races is not the Mediterranean but the Sahara. The Berbers are of the same racial stock as the Spaniards. The result is that the inpouring of vast numbers of Berbers into southern Spain has not had the slightest effect in altering the physical make-up of the Spanish race, because the physical make-up of Berbers and Spaniards is almost identical. It is, therefore, impossible to judge from the study of the race today as to the proportion of African elements it contains. One has to form an estimate from historical data.

"The conquest of Spain by Tarik was made by an army of only about twelve thousand. But the conquest was permanent, and for several centuries Africans poured into the peninsula. There were two great influxes, one in the eleventh and another in the twelfth century. Of a population of about six millions in the south-eastern half

[1] Warren, L. A., *History of Spanish Literature* (London, 1929), Vol. ii, pp. 689-694.

perhaps from one and a half to two millions were of
African descent; but of these two-thirds would have been
Moors and not more than a third Syrians and Arabs.
The killings and expulsions must have removed about half
this population, leaving perhaps 750,000 of African descent, of whom 250,000 were from the East. These men
descended from invading stock were of the same Mediterranean race as the native Iberians, and have left therefore
no trace of their own in the physical composition of the
present Spanish race; that is to say, no trace that can be
disengaged from the Iberians.''[2]

Discussing the matter further, Warren says, ''Mohammedan Spain formed part of the Arabic and Moslem culture; so that though there was no different race, a different culture was stamping itself for centuries upon the
population. Now for centuries this process has been reversed, Christian and European culture having practically
obliterated that of Moslem and Arabic. The race in southern Spain is absolutely Mediterranean. Spain, therefore,
is a country of homogeneous Mediterranean race, with the
important exception of a large Celtic element along the
northern coast, strongest in Asturias; and with provinces
in the south and southeast carrying traces of former
Arabic culture. The difference between the north coast
and the rest of the peninsula is in part caused by the difference between the Celtic and Mediterranean races.
Otherwise the extraordinary difference between the provinces is due to geographical and climatic reasons.''[3]

In these fears expressed in the anthropological discussions of biased Europeans like Warren is apparent either
ignorance or intellectual dishonesty in arguing against
what scientists have well established as truth. We know
from experience that the crossing of different stocks does
produce definite physical and mental results in succeeding

[2] Warren, L. A., *op. cit.*, pp. 696-697.
[3] *Ibid.*, 697.

generations. Only prejudiced propagandists insist that
culture is determined by race. The entire theory of the
Nordic influence among the Latins breaks down, moreover, when we face the evidence of a large infusion of
Negro African blood in all the nations of Southern
Europe. Professor Sturgis contends that the Pelasgii
were of African origin. Sir Harry H. Johnston traced
Negro blood across India and the Malay states to Poly-
nesina. He contends that, according to recent discoveries,
"a Negroid race penetrated Italy and France and left
traces observed at the present time in the physiognomy of
the people of Southern Italy, Sicily, Sardinia, and Western France, and even in parts of the United Kingdom of
Great Britain and Ireland. Even today there are some examples of Keltiberian peoples of western Scotland and
western Wales and southern and western Ireland of distinctly Negroid type."[4]

It is evident, too, that Europeans are anxious to play
up the superiority of the Nordics, and where they find the
Latins manifesting a little evidence of progress they
eventually "discover" among such "exceptions" some
infusion of Teutonic blood. They would discount also the
contributions of the Orientals who lifted Europe out of
savagery. And so distasteful is the thought of being influenced by or racially mixed with the Negro African that
each pseudo-historian feels it his duty to minimize further
the traces of African influences in Europe so that in the
course of time it may pass from the memory of the coming
generations in keeping with the policy of making history
to order. Yet in their very assertions and discussions
intended to reach this end they give, as does L. A. Warren, the very facts which they would like to uproot. Every
one acquainted with the early Mediterranean history
knows that the Negro African, not to say any thing con-

---

[4] MacDonald, A. J., *Trade, Politics, and Christianity in Africa and the
East*, London, 1916; *The Journal of Negro History*, I, p. 330.

cerning the mulatto element, was a conspicuous factor in that sphere. Two important world movements, moreover, increased the contact of Europeans with Negro Africans, namely, the rise of Islam resulting in the Mohammedanization of parts of both Africa and Europe and the commercial expansion of Europe following the age of discovery and exploration.

The presence or pressure of the Mohammedans upon the people around the Mediterranean and the stimulus to trade and adventure finally extended the sphere of activity beyond that sea into the Atlantic Ocean. The people of the Iberian Peninsula naturally had been long thus concerned, and the first efforts toward this end developed in that area bordering on the two great waters. The Saracens were finally forced toward the South and out of the western part of the peninsula, leaving it clear for the emerging of Portugal by about 1300, much earlier than in the case of Spain. These Mohammedans, however, even when driven later out of Spain across the strait into Africa remained nevertheless a stumbling block to the slowly developing states trying to control the Mediterranean. The fruitless wars in which nations rising from the chaos of the Dark Ages had participated caused them to long for some other avenue in which their energy could be more profitably expended. The Genoese, Venetians and Normans, the first Europeans to have this vision, began to explore the west coast of Africa, but they were soon eliminated from the equation by the more adventurous Portuguese.[5]

Looking to Africa, the Portuguese crossed the Strait at Gibraltar and took Ceuta, although they later lost it to the Spanish. The Portuguese gained another strategic point on African soil in taking Tangier, which they later ceded to the British and the latter back to the Moors. The

[5] Monod, J. L., *Histoire de l'Afrique Occidentale Française*, Paris, 1931, pp. 147-150.

leader in these unusual adventures was Prince Henry, of Portugal, regarded as the "father of modern maritime discovery." He sent vessels to rediscover Madeira in 1420 and to touch later the Azores and the Cape Verde Islands. His explorers doubled the Cape Bojador in 1434, reached Senegal in 1445, and by the time that Prince Henry died in 1460 they had advanced around the westernmost point of Africa and explored the coast as far as between Gambia and Sierra Leone. These adventurers explored the Gulf of Guinea and crossed the Equator by 1471. After a brief cessation of efforts they dashed as far as the Congo. By 1486 Bartholomew Diaz unknowingly rounded the Cape of Good Hope on his way to Algoa Bay. In 1497 Vasco da Gama also doubled the Cape and explored the East Coast as far as Mombassa and Melinde and reached Calicut in India the following year. On the claims of these discoveries and explorations the Portuguese projected the first world-wide colonial empire set up by Europeans.

The greatest stimulus to these adventures of the Portuguese, however, was not the inspiration from Prince Henry, for he passed out of the picture in 1460. What had stimulated these later efforts was that the Portuguese had found gold dust and African slaves. Returning with supplies of these, the adventurers kindled the desire of others to enter upon or to finance such expeditions. The Portuguese had engaged in various wars which had profited the country nothing. Now they had men who went to sea and returned shortly with immense riches. Prince Henry himself, although defended by historians as interested in discovery rather than trade, accepted his share of the plunder brought back by his agents, and he actually participated in the African slave trade.[6]

Bringing Negroes to Portugal, moreover, was popular for two reasons. In the first place, the Negro was "a

[6]Helps, Sir Arthur, *Spanish Conquest of America*, I, pp. 23-25.

much more amenable person than the Mohammedan.''
Portuguese who held Moors as slaves placed them on the
market to be exchanged for Negroes. It is strange to say,
however, that in the first known instance of such an exchange two Moors brought ten Negroes, a target of buf-
falo hide and some ostrich eggs. This was a rather high
price, for in America the customary ratio became five Negroes for three whites. It was evidently considered a great
bargain, for the Portuguese, like the Spaniards, not only
desired to secure laborers at low cost but those who would
accept the Catholic religion. This the Latin had learned
from experience the Mohammedans would never willingly
do. These first Negro Africans brought as slaves to Portugal were introduced there by Gonçalvez in 1442.[7]

While these Portuguese traders met a little opposition
from sympathetic persons who showed some humanity to
man, they easily satisfied such objectors on the ground
that the importation of the Negroes would facilitate the
conversion of Africans and thus enable the church to fulfill its manifest destiny. It was understood, of course,
that in the carrying out of these plans that these unbaptized Negroes on accepting the faith of their captors
would become free in the operation of the unwritten law
that a Christian should not be held a slave. And there is
much to indicate that these Portuguese partly lived up to
what was expected of them, as is evidenced by numerous
favorable developments in that country during subsequent
years.

The introduction of African Negroes into the Iberian
Peninsula by Gonçalvez in 1442 may not have been the
actual beginning of the Negroes there. Negroes were
throughout the Mediterranean during the days of the
ancient Greeks and Romans; but in the course of time, to
be sure, were easily absorbed so as to be imperceptible
after the cutting off of the supply from Africa during the

[7] Helps, *op. cit.*, p. 24.

upheavals of the Middle Age. According to the *Ecclesi-astical and Secular Annals,* however, Negroes directly from Africa had already been introduced into certain parts of France and Spain. It is known that about a century before this the Normans, proceeding from Dieppe, had been trading along the West African Coast. This was about 1339, the time of Don Enrique the Third, when Bethencourt occupied the Canaries. The first slaves, however, were said not to be Negroes but Azengues. Yet these were persons produced in the melting pot by inter-breeding with Negroes. The Portuguese after driving the Normans from the African Coast settled Negroes upon the plantations of the grandees in the southern provinces of Estramadura, Alemtejo, and Algrave. With this cheap labor they so lowered the economic standard as to drive out many of the Portuguese peasants. With freedom of intermarriage, then, these Negroes actually Africanized a considerable portion of Portugal and left upon these people a stamp observed even today.

It seems certain, moreover, that Spaniards from Seville also had such early contact with Africans and had brought a number of them to that city. Discussing *Arabic Spain,* Bernard and Ellen M. Whishaw give evidence of this, saying, ''We find little mention of Nubians in Seville after this indirect hint of their presence in Moslem Spain, until the fourteenth and fifteenth centuries, when they are said to have been numerous. In 1475 the Catholic Kings had a Negro porter named Juan de Valladolid appointed Mayoral (Administrator) of the community in Seville with the title of the Negro count. A street in the city still bears the name of El Conde Negro in memory of him.''[8]

His nomination for this office ran thus: ''For the many good, loyal, and signal services which you have done us, and do each day, and because we know your sufficiency,

[8] Whishaw, Bernard, and Ellen, M., *op. cit.,* p. 129.

ability, and good disposition, we constitute you mayoral and judge of all the Negroes and mulattoes, free or slaves, which are in the very loyal and noble city of Seville, and throughout the whole archbishopric thereof, and that the said Negroes and mulattoes may not hold any festivals, nor pleadings amongst themselves, except before you Juan de Valladolid, Negro, our judge and mayoral of said Negroes and mulattoes; and we command that you, and you only, should take congnizance of the disputes, pleading marriages, and other things which may take place amongst them, forasmuch as you are a person sufficient for that office, and deserving of your power, and you know the laws and ordinances which ought to be kept, and we are informed that you are of noble lineage amongst the said Negroes.''[9]

Discussing further the Negroes of Seville, the Whishaws say, ''Among the various institutions supported by the Negroes was a religious Confraternity, founded in 1400, and still existing in 1852, with its own chapel in the parish church of San Roque. Over one of the altars in this chapel there were two antique paintings, one of which represented San Elesban (sic) King of Ethiopia, and the other Santa Efigenia. The legend of this saint relates that she was baptized by St. Matthew, when he was preaching in Ethiopia, and when the convent in which she shut herself up with two hundred maidens was set on fire by Hitaco (sic), St. Matthew appeared in the air and put out the flame. This was the incident represented in the picture of Santa Efigenia (*Glorias religiosas de Sevilla*, 391-99). Their choice of subjects for pictures strongly suggests that the Negroes of Seville claimed descent from the Nubians, otherwise they would hardly have depicted a king of Ethiopia and an Eastern Saint named Iphigenia. Thus they form a connecting link with the Nubians who

---

[9] Ortiz de Zuñiga, *Annales Eclesiasticos y Seculares de Sevilla*, Madrid, 1677, p. 374.

worshipped at the shrine of Santiago in the tenth century. There is still a Negro race at Niebla, in the province of Huelva, with the crisp black curly hair, the large liquid eyes, and the blueness under the finger nails which we associate with the Negro type, but without the thick lips of the African black. In complexion they are not darker than the average Gitano (Egyptian) of this region, but the type is entirely distinct. They are called Negritos by their neighbors. In the course of a few hours' stay in the town we saw at least a dozen children of the Negrito race.''[10]

The actual number of Negroes in Seville, although not known exactly, was considerable, for, says Sir Arthur Helps, the Negroes ''abounded there, and the fifties levied upon them produced considerable revenue.''[11] References to the Negroes in Seville both in the literature and history of Spain during later years tend to support this conclusion. The numbers there settled, however, were never so numerous as to be in prominence, or if larger than estimated these Africans must have been biologically attractive to the Spaniards who easily absorbed them.

There was another reason why the Latins would have this attitude toward these Africans. When the Portuguese first began to touch their shores the African Kingdoms were at their height of glory under the leadership of the Songhay Empire antedated by such political organizations as Kumbi-Kumbi (Ghana) and the Manding. The Portuguese were delighted to treat the representatives of these empires as equals. These African political aggregations, however, began to decline very soon because of innumerable wars among themselves; and they decided to call the Portuguese in as the arbiter in these conflicts. The Portuguese gladly rendered this service, for it gave them the opportunity to play the rôle of the animal which, ac-

---

[10] Whishaw, *op. cit.*, p. 129.
[11] Helps, Sir Arthur, *op. cit.*, p. 25.

cording to the fable, settled the dispute between the lion
and the lamb and ate the lamb for his fee.

These African kings began to go even to Portugal
itself to ask help of their country against their neighbors.
One of these kings was received on the condition that he
would first become a Christian, for the Portuguese would
not dare to give aid to any country of unbelievers. This
he agreed to do, and agents of the Portuguese king were
sent as escorts with him to Africa; but these adventurers
killed him for reasons of plunder and returned to their
home country without suffering therefrom. Other such
opportunities were used, of course, to gain a foothold
along the coast of Africa. In this way the Portuguese
took over the kingdom of the Congo, the name of which
was changed to San Salvador after the African ruler had
been taken to Portugal and Christianized. He has served
thereafter as a ruler of that empire under Christian influence in the name of Portugal.[12] The treaty of Tordesillas
allocating the African area to Portugal facilitated contacts and conquests of the Portuguese on that continent
from which came many other Negroes to Iberia.

Exactly what the treatment of the Negroes in the
Iberian Peninsula was when scattered from a center like
Sevilla so as to be subjected altogether to the will of the
various communities in which their lot might be cast is
not clear. Judging, however, from the following complaint
of Azurara when he first saw the ordeal the beginning
was as bad as it was in introducing the system elsewhere.
He piously exclaimed:

"O thou heavenly Father, who, with thy powerful
hand without movement of thy divine essence, govern-
est all the infinite company of the holy city, and who
drawest together all the axles of the upper worlds, divided into nine spheres, moving the times of their long

[12] For the details of this aspect of the story see R. P. Van Wing's
Etudes Bakongo, Brussells, 1932, passim.

and short periods as it pleases thee! I implore thee that my tears may not condemn my conscience, for not its law, but our common humanity constrains my humanity to lament piteously the suffering of the people (slaves). And if the brute animals, with their mere bestial sentiments, by a natural instinct, recognize the misfortunes of their like, what must this my human nature do, seeing thus before my eyes this wretched company, remembering that I myself am of the generation of the sons of Adam!

"The other day, which was the eighth of August, very early in the morning, by reason of the heat, the mariners began to bring-to their vessels, and, as they had been commanded, to draw forth those captives to take them out of the vessel: whom, placed together on that plain, it was a marvelous sight to behold, for amongst them there were some of a reasonable degree of whiteness, handsome and well made; others less white, resembling leopards in their color; others as black as Ethiopians, and so ill-formed, as well in their faces as their bodies, that it seemed to the beholders as if they saw the forms of a lower hemisphere.

"But what heart was that, how hard soever, which was not pierced with sorrow, seeing that company: for some had sunken cheeks, and their faces bathed in tears, looking at each other; others were groaning very dolorously, looking at the heights of the heavens, fixing their eyes upon them, crying out loudly, as if they were asking succour from the Father of nature; others struck their faces with their hands, throwing themselves on the earth; others made their lamentations in songs, according to the customs of their country, which, although we could not understand their language, we saw corresponded well to the height of their sorrow. But now, for the increase of their grief, came those who have the charge of the distribution, and they began to put them apart one from the other, in order to equalize the portions; wherefore it was necessary to part children and parents, husbands and wives, and brethren from each other. Neither in the partitions of friends and relations was any law kept, only each fell where the lot took him.

"O powerful fortune! who goest hither and thither with thy wheels, compassing the things of the world as it pleaseth thee, if thou canst, place before the eyes of this miserable nation some knowledge of the things that are to come after them, that they may receive some consolation in the midst of their great sadness! and you others who have the business of this partition, look with pity on such great misery, and consider how can those be parted whom you cannot disunite. Who will be able to make this partition without great difficulty? For while they were placing in one part the children that saw their parents in another, the children sprang up perseveringly and fled to them; the mothers enclosed their children in their arms and threw themselves with them on the ground, receiving wounds with little pity for their own flesh, so that their offspring might not be torn from them. And so, with labor and difficulty, they concluded the partition, for, besides the trouble they had with the captives, the plain was full of people, as well of the place as of the villages and neighborhood around, who in that day gave rest to their hands, the mainstay of their livelihood, only to see this novelty.

"And as they looked upon these things, some deploring, some reasoning upon them, they made such a riotous noise, as greatly to disturb those who had the management of this distribution. The Infante was there upon a powerful horse, accompanied by his people, looking out his share, but as a man who for his part did not care for gain, for, of the forty-six souls which fell to his fifth, he speedily made his choice, as all his principal riches were in his contentment, considering with great delight the salvation of those souls which before were lost. And certainly his thought was not vain, for as soon as they had knowledge of our language, they readily became Christians; and I, who have made this history in this volume, have seen in the town of Lagos young men and young women, the sons and grandsons of those very captives, born in this land, as good and as true Christians as if they had lineally descended, since the commencement of the law of Christ, from those who were first baptized.''[13]

The attitude of another distinguished churchman, Bartolomé de las Casas, was not so liberal with respect to the Africans. As Bishop of Chiapas, then in Guatemala but now in Mexico, this churchman had the opportunity to observe the Spanish cruelties practiced upon the Indians. They had been enslaved by the Spanish adventurers who were trying to become rich quickly in the exploitation of the plantations and mines in America. In 1552, therefore, las Casas published his *Brevisima relación de la destrucción de las Indias* to expose these atrocities. It was a case like that of the Belgians in the Congo. The gravest charge was that as many as fifteen millions of Indians had thus met their death at the hands of the Spaniards.

This book, however, proved to be more political than ameliorative of the conditions against which it complained. The other European exploiters, jealous of the success of Spaniards extending their sway into the New World, seized upon the book as a document with which they could discredit Spain. The work became so popular in such circles that during the sixteenth and seventeenth centuries it passed through three Italian editions, three Latin, four English, six French, eight German, and eighteen Dutch. As a matter of fact, however, these Latins, while much more inhumane than Bartolomé de las Casas believed that "Christians" should be, were surpassed by the Nordics in India, China, Guinea, Congo, and the United States, as pointed out by L. B. Simpson.[14]

[13] *Azarura*, cap. 25.

[14] Simpson, L. B., *The Encomienda in New Spain; forced native labor in the Spanish Colonies, 1492-1550*, Berkeley, 1929.

The point here noted, however, is that although Bishop de las Casas showed so much compassion for the aborigines in America, he did not apparently manifest any such compassion for the Africans. He was one of those who suggested the importation of Negroes from Africa to take the places of the overworked Indians. Doubtless, like others, he believed that the bodily vigor of the Negro was so much greater than that of the Indians that the former could easily endure the hardships and still live to partake of the benefits derived from a "Christian" land. The thought of converting the souls of Africans, too, had some weight with this churchman, but it is often asserted that he did not think of the African as being as worthy of preservation as the Indians. In the mind of that Churchman, according to some comments on his proposal, there was the thought that the aborigines in America represented a higher type than the Africans, and if some element had to be degraded with such drudgery it was better to impose this upon the lower rather than on the higher order of the human species. It is known that the Negroes thus imported were treated just as cruelly as had been the aborigines. Their souls, the bishop observed, could not be easily saved when their bodies were lost in the colonial treadmill. Yet he did not write a similar diatribe against the same class of exploiters in behalf of the Negro.

In thus discussing the attitude of Bishop Bartolomé de las Casas, however, it is well to note that he was not the only churchman who suggested the importation of Africans. The Jeronimite Fathers, Fray Bernadino especially, expressed the same opinion in the year 1518, and so did the judge of the *residencia*. The movements of that day indicated that slaves would have been introduced in New Spain even if the distinguished bishop had remained silent. It is well to observe, too, that in advocating the introduction of Negroes he had in mind those taken as captives in wars and, therefore, justly enslaved accord-

ing to the ethics of that day. The aborigines in America
had been enslaved by the wholesale whether captives or not.
This churchman repented of this error, according to his
Historia de las Indias.[15] "Of this advice which the Clerigo
gave," the story runs, "he very soon afterwards found
himself repentant, judging himself to have erred through
inadvertence. For after that he saw and had ascertained
as will appear, that the capture of Negroes is as unjust
as that of Indians, he perceived that the remedy which
he had advised—for Negroes to be brought hither in order
that Indians might be set free—was not a discreet remedy,
although he supposed at the time that the Negroes were
justly made captives. He has not, however, felt certain
that ignorance in this matter and his good intentions would
excuse him before the Divine judgment." The volume
says further, "This advice, that license should be given
to bring Negro slaves to these lands, the clerigo Casas
first gave, not considering the injustice with which the
Portuguese take them and make them slaves; which advice after he had apprehended the nature of the thing, he
would not have given for all he had in the world. For he
always held that they had been made slaves unjustly and
tyranically; for the same reason holds good of them as
of the Indians.[16]"

In trying to determine the attitude of the Latins toward the Negro African, moreover, one must bear in
mind the fact that their cruelties of the colonial era were
prompted by caste rather than by race prejudice which
characterizes the Nordic. In the cruel fashion in which
the Latin exploited the Negro he had exploited also the
Moslem, the Indian, or members of his own race of low
estate. The Latin did not proceed on the presumption that
black people were especially fitted to be their hewers of
wood and drawers of water. Negroes contriving to escape

[15] Bartolemé de las Casas, *op. cit.*, Vol. lxv, p. 30.
[16] *Ibid.*, Vol. lxv, p. 380.

the ordeal of slavery, as was always possible in various ways in Latin America, could work their way to the highest levels of the social order by industry, thrift, and mental ability; but among the Teutonic elements in the New World, as a rule, this door of opportunity was to be forever shut in the Negro's face because of his color. The race admixture which consequently followed in Latin America and the absence of a race problem in those parts, except so far as later contaminated by the Nordic, speak more eloquently for the record of the Latins than all the documents which have been compiled to picture the social order of these liberal people.

In view of this social leveling by miscegenation in Latin America it serves no purpose here, then, to undertake to point out the distinguished Latin Americans with an infusion of African blood. Negroes interbreeded with both Indians and Latins; and these when too fastidious to choose black companions, nevertheless intermarried with the mixed breeds and thus connected again with strains of diluted Negro blood. Yet in the evolution of this social order stood out a number of black men who attained distinction in Latin America. Becoming prominent in so many different spheres, too, these Negroes demonstrated by their careers not only their ability to achieve as others but the favorable attitude of the Latins with whom their lot had been cast in the New World.

A number of Negroes took an active part in the exploration of the country. Negroes were in the exploration of Guatemala, Chile, Peru, and Venezuela, in the company of Ponce de Leon in Florida, in the expedition of Ayllon northward from that place, with Cabeza de Vaca and Fray Marcos de Niza in the southwest, with Alarcon and Coronado in New Mexico, and with De Soto on the Mississippi. Nuflo de Olano distinguished himself as the faithful companion of Balboa to the Pacific Ocean. On the present site of Jamestown, where the Spaniards in 1526 made a settlement known as San Miguel de Gualdape, the Negroes rose in insurrection because of cruel treatment, broke up the colony, and returned to Santo Domingo. With the expedition of Cortez in Mexico was a Negro who, finding in his rations of rice some brown grains, planted them as an experiment, and thus made himself the pioneer in wheat raising in America. One of these Negroes wrote his name still higher in the hall of fame. This was Estevanico, or Little Stephen, the explorer of what is now New Mexico and Arizona.[17]

The larger freedom alloted the Negroes by the Latins doubtless accounts for their ambitious undertakings. The Nordic figured out that if slavery was to prove successful it would never do to treat the Negro as a human being. To keep a man down one must treat him as a person of such status. Probably for this reason the rebellious Negroes in Dutch Guiana could not maintain themselves free in any other way than to repair to the wilderness where white men could not easily exist. The Negro rebels in seventeenth century Jamaica could not keep up their spirits sufficiently to maintain very long their independent position in the hilly strongholds. Of the Portuguese in

[17] Estevanico was a member of the unfortunate expedition of Narvaez who undertook to get control of the country between Florida and the Rio de las Palmas, in Mexico. Estevanico was born in Azamor, Morocco, probably about the year 1500. He sailed first from Spain in 1527 along with 506 persons. They landed on the coast of Florida and undertook to explore the interior of the country. They were so frequently attacked by the Indians and suffered so many hardships, however, that their number diminished to 240 in about three months; and by the end of the year only four remained. These four, including Estevanico, finally reached the coast of Texas. For eight years they wandered among the Indians and became slaves. They finally made their lot easier by serving the Indians as "medicine men." These explorers knew so much more than the Indians about simple remedies that the red men marveled at their medical skill and came from afar in crowds to be cured. The Europeans finally returned to Spain, but Estevanico remained in Mexico, where he continued to learn more and more about the Indian languages and customs. Because of his knowledge of these things he was selected as the guide for the expedition northward to "Cibola" in 1539.

Brazil about the same time, however, the rebellious Negroes attained a more formidable, independent position in the province of Pernambuco and left the most striking example of what it means to breathe long the atmosphere of liberty and freedom. They established an actual monarchy and entered into relations with other settlements. Armies sent to conquer them were repeatedly cut to pieces. They were finally subdued only by directing against Palmares forces sufficient to batter down the defences of a well fortified kingdom.

The attitude of the Latins toward the Negro Africans, however, was not such as to require continuous battle against their masters. Many Negroes among them became free and arose to distinction in the service of their respective countries. A striking example of this was the brilliant career of Enriques Dias. He was born in Pernambuco, about the end of the sixteenth century. Not much is known about his boyhood. He developed into manhood about the time of the acute struggle of the Dutch in South America in the area which has become the United States of Brazil. Dias became the hero of this war. He participated in the defence of Bom Jesus in 1635. Wounded in his left hand in the battle of Port Salvo, Dias ordered immediately its amputation and returned to the fight. He further distinguished himself in winning the victory of San Salvador of Bahia in 1645. During twenty-one years of warfare he was routed only once. In appreciation of his services he was created an hidalgo by the king of Spain and Portugal and was honored with membership in the Orden de Cristo.[18]

Some liberalmindedness is evidenced also by the attitude of the Latin religious element. From the very be-

[18] For an account of the career of Dias consult the following: Francisco de Brito Freyre, *Nova Lusitania, Historia de la guerra brasilica*, Lisbao, 1675; Caspair Barlaci *Rerum per Octennium in Brasilica et alibi nuper gestarum Historia Amstelodami*, 1647; J. M. de Macedo, *Brazilian Biographical Annal*, Rio de Janeiro, Vol. ii, 1876.

ginning the Latins believed that the message of salvation
was to all men regardless of color. When the Anglican
clergy could not find time for the instruction and evangelization of Negroes in the Western Hemisphere the
Latin priestcraft of the colonies both as a result of their
own promptings and the decrees of the sovereigns of the
countries from which they came made the conversion of
the Negroes one of their first duties. The Latin clergy,
moreover, interfered in case of cruel treatment of slaves
and often effected the manumission of individuals that
they might enjoy the fulness of freedom. Unfortunately
the Catholic clerical orders were so organized and conducted as to be all but closed corporations so far as elevating the Negro to such positions was concerned. Yet it is
known that this situation changed somewhat with the rise
of the free mulatto class, the offspring of Negroes and
Europeans, who settled property upon this class and had
them elevated to the highest social level. Some members
of this higher order, of course, entered the priesthood.
Catholic churchmen themselves mention three instances of
such Negroes becoming bishops.

In spite of these attitudes, however, the cruelty of the
Spaniards has become proverbial.[19] Not much thought
was given to Portugal after its empire had crumbled in
international conflict and the country became so weak as
to be for a while attached to Spain. The persistence of
contemporaries in extending these charges of Spanish
cruelty, when they themselves had probably surpassed
those thus accused, is one of the outstanding exaggera-
tions in modern history. As already stated above, the
other European nations were jealous of Spain when it was
in its golden age. It seemed destined to control the whole
known civilized world by right of discovery, exploration
and development. The slogan of ''Down with the Spaniard'' because of their cruelty proved to be a convenient

[19] H. C. Morris in his *History of Colonization* sets forth this attitude.

rallying point for these commercial rivals. It served along with other forces to combine the enemies of Spain and to bring against that country such opposition as to effect its decline to the position of an insignificant power.

Some other experiences of the Spanish tended to substantiate to some extent the charges which these nations originally made with respect to their cruelties. The defence of the Catholic faith with such a fanatical agency as the Inquisition is certainly a blot on their escutcheon, but this was not an attitude with respect to race or distant subjects. The building up of the Spanish empire itself as it was under Charles V and Philip II meant not only the waging of vigorous wars for the unification of divergent provinces but first the ruthless expulsion of the Moslems who had built up an empire in Spain. To unify the people with the national purpose required rigorous treatment and thorough-going methods in the suppression of insurrections. To expel the Arabs, moreover, required the same cruelties as those the Spaniards had suffered at the hands of the Moslems. It is estimated that more than one half million Moslems were killed by the Spaniards in driving them from that country into Africa.

Thorough-going methods of Spain in extending its sway over certain parts of the people in Africa where it still had a small area under its control naturally required the same sort of drastic measures. During these years, both in Northern Africa and elsewhere in the Spanish possessions, the country became more exacting and more oppressive than formerly. In its decline Spain had less and less colonial territory upon which it could draw for revenue. The smaller area remaining still in the Spanish hands was called upon to supply the income which a world empire had once yielded. Inasmuch as the Spaniards would not revise downward their demands of these outlying possessions, they proved to be more and more onerous as the years rolled by.

A startling case of this is Cuba. Unfortunately historians of the United States and the American people in
general have exaggerated the evils of Spanish rule not
only on this island but thoroughout Latin America. The
independent people of the United States were naturally
interested in seeing the Latin American republics disconnected from their European overlords. The pro-
slavery element in the United States was especially resent-
ful with respect to Cuba because of their struggle for
extension into new slave territory. They had long dreamed
of acquiring various areas in Latin America, as they had
taken over Texas, and near the time of the Civil War in
this country these visionaries staked their last hope upon
Cuba as set forth in the Ostend Manifesto. The evils from
which the Cubans suffered are still kept fresh in the minds'
of Americans. Even the Negroes have been wont to
prate thus especially in rehearsing the deeds of the
martyred poet, Placido, and of Maceo, the hero of the war
for Cuban independence. The Negroes in Cuba, however,
have begun to realize that instead of being better off in
Cuba as a protectorate of the United States, they find
themselves daily approaching the status of their sable
brethren along the Atlantic, since race hate and segregation follow the United States flag.

In the Literature of the Iberian Peninsula

Spanish and Portuguese literature, like the history of
these people, early showed attitudes toward the Negro.
Following the example of historians, moreover, this first
notice was merely in allusions and remnants of myths and
fables like those connected with Song of Roland, the
Knights of the Round Table, the Holy Grail, and the Cid.
Some black knight was pictured in most of these circles
to give them color.[20] As Negroes did not come into Iberia

[20] Pedro Bohigas Balaguer, Los textos españoles y gallego-portugueses de
la demanda del Santo Grail, Madrid, 1925; The Journal of Negro History,
Vol. xviii, pp. 225-245.

in large numbers prior to the middle of the Fifteenth Century, however, no particular notice was taken of such an element in that out-of-way part of the world. True enough, as well authenticiated accounts prove, Negroes had touched the Peninsula just as they had other parts of Europe bordering upon the Mediterranean, but such infusions of Negro blood were so infrequent as to undergo dilution to the extent that it was not very noticeable prior to the preiod of discovery ushered in by Prince Henry of Portugal.

The very nature of the earliest literature of the Iberian Peninsula was such that little notice would be taken of the elements which were not permanently attached there. These first productions dealt with things, traditional, legendary and religious. There were such heroic exploits as those of Alphonso the Wise as king and scholar, but the larger number of these writings, under Italian influence, dealt with the mysticism of a religious order—miracles of the Virgin in response to prayer, others voluntarily performed by the Virgin, and those performed by images and relics of saints before which pilgrims from afar prayed for relief from their ills. Some of these images were black figures of Madonnas and saints. This literature dealt also with the devil and his work, divinations, omens, orgies, visions, and other manifestations. Emerging from this atmosphere, Spanish literature portrayed the church triumphant and later royalty with neither of which the Negroes living in that country had any conspicuous function. In some of the Spanish *romanceros,* the ballads, figured characters from Africa which gave them an Oriental setting.

Becoming absorbed with the problem of defending the Catholic faith to the extent that the Spanish established and perpetuated such an agency of persecution as the Inquisition, the literature naturally continued impregnated with religious sentiment. For a number of years authors of consequence could not freely express themselves because of the religious despotism under which they lived. The struggle against this, of course, concerned the writers of the time just as it did the statesmen and political theorists of Spain; and on account of some of their writings they suffered imprisonment, exile, and death. For a long time, then, Spanish literature was chiefly concerned with liberalism against Catholicism as well as freedom against absolutism. The movement commonly known elsewhere as romanticism in contradistinction to realism and classicism was delayed in Spain by these other problems which confronted its creators of thought.

The tracing of the notice taken of the Negro, moreover, is made more difficult in Spanish literature for the reason that both the Spanish and Portuguese had still other problems to solve. In the first place, these two nations of the same original stock with language and customs differing but little mutually hated each other and have never achieved unification which seems all but required for natural reasons. The Peninsula, moreover, was early overrun by the Moors upon whom both countries long had to vent their spleen. Like all other European nations, too, they had also on their hands the eternal Jew delving in all sorts of schemes even to the point of selling Christian slaves to the Turks. With these two elements to hate, to oppose, and finally to drive out of the Peninsula the people were too busily occupied to develop very much hostility toward the Negro African. That the Negro was first preferred to these undesirable elements may account not only for the comparatively large number of Negroes brought into these countries but also for the infrequent mention of the Negro in the literature of the Peninsula.

In the most interesting contributions to Spanish and Portuguese literature of a later period the notice taken of the Negro is often confused with references to the Moors. Some of the Moors had such a large infusion of

Negro African blood that they are referred to with the term *Negro* when as a matter of fact they were not actually black in spite of their having interbred with Africans. In these allusions, moreover, it appears that the word *Negro* was used often with contempt to express that pent-up feeling which these Latins felt for the Moors. The term is used with this feeling apparently less in later years after the expulsion of the invaders and the application of the word *Negro* solely to the blacks who were imported from Africa after the middle of the fifteenth century.

Drawn immediately into the circle of those sent to discover, explore and settle the New World, the Negro became a topic occasionally mentioned in historical literature. The efforts of the *Predictatores* and especially of Bartolomé de las Casas projected the Negro further into the foreground, and so did the frequent use of imported Africans by the *Conquistadores*. In addition to the works of Bartolomé de las Casas, already cited, one should note also José Antonio Saco's *Historia de la Esclavitud;* Gonzalo Fernandez de Oviedo's *Historia General;* Herrera's *Historia General;* Bernard Diaz del Castillo's *Conquista de Nueva Espana;* and Pedro de Casteñada's "Account of the Expedition to Cibola which took place in the year 1540," a translation in the series known as the *Spanish Explorers in the Southern United States.* Negroes in various numbers are noted in these enterprises in commendable rôles, but the most picturesque figures in this literature have already been noted above.

Throughout the period it should be borne in mind that the Portuguese writers generally followed the fortunes of the Spanish although their productions were inferior to those of the latter. The allusions made to the Negroes and Moors did not differ widely from those already cited in the case of the Spanish. The Moors to the Portuguese were always devils who ruined the land and the Christians

were always favored over the Moors, sometimes referred
to as black. Gil Vicente does this in urging Christians to
war against the Moors in his tragi-comedy *Exhortaçao da
guerra.* The thought of the author is that Africa was once
a Christian land, and it must now be redeemed.

The bringing of Negroes into Portugal to displace the
peasants and enrich the grandees, too, did not become
popular with all the Portuguese. Satirizing the pomp and
display of these plunderers, Gil Vicente in his *Romagem
de Aggravados* said:

> Que Ninguem não se contenta
> Da maneira que sohia,
> Tudo vai fóra de Termos.

Carrying the thought still further an anonymous verse
said:

> Em Africa á fome
> Morrem cavalleiros
> E cá nos palheiros
> O ouro se come.

In one of the popular songs of that day entitled *Levantar Ferro,* moreover, is an interesting refrain, "There's
plenty blacks in Africay." Evidently large numbers of
Negroes imported into Portugal had made the impression
that the supply was inexhaustible.

In the works of Sá de Miranda, Camões, and Almeida-
Garrett there were no outstanding allusions to the Negro.
The same may be said of the Spanish poets and novelists
of the nineteenth century and of today. Antonio C. G.
Crespo (1846-1883), referred to as a Portuguese Negro
himself, was one of the poets of that country who wrote
creditable verse. Neither he nor his Portuguese contemporaries, however, reached the level of the most representative literature of other lands.

The first important rôle played by the Negro in Spanish fiction appears in *El Zeloso Estremeño* or "The Jealous Estramaduran" by Cervantes, the author of *Don*

Quixote. Briefly told, "The Jealous Estremaduran" is the story of a prodigal son who wasted his wealth in riotous living and finally went to the Indies to recover his fortune. Rich again on returning to Spain, he considered many projects for happiness in his old age, all of which he rejected. He finally decided to marry a young woman who happened to be of a poor family although of noble birth. Convinced by his possession of a large fortune and the proffer of settling a portion of it upon the girl, the parents consented to the marriage.

Insanely jealous of the woman for knowing that in his advanced age he would not strikingly appeal to her and that she would have a natural preference for some younger man, he established her in a castle in which she was kept practically as a prisoner. Into this enclosure were to come no additional males except Luis, a Negro eunuch, employed to attend the old man's mule; and the African was daily locked in so as to have no communication with persons in the street and at the same time locked out of the inner part of the home so as to have no contact with the young wife. She was attended by a dueña, assisted by two Negro women servants and four white slave girls branded in their faces. All were cautioned to carry out religiously the rigid rules to permit no males to enter the house and to have no connection with the street whatever except when they would go to mass early in the morning when they could not be seen.

To make a long story short, a number of adventurous young men, seeing this building kept like a prison, found out upon inquiry the status of the attractive young woman who was therein incarcerated. Loyasa, one of these fellows, then, disguised himself as a lame beggar, and through the keyhole of the apartment in which the Negro eunuch was kept the youth so charmed him with his music from the street that the latter without a key effected some way of lifting the door from the hinges and permitted the

adventurer to enter his apartment in the loft. Becoming
the instructor of the Negro, the musican flattered him with
the thought that he was progressing much more rapidly
than he was and left him a guitar upon which he could
play certain tunes at an hour when they could not be
heard by the old man. The dueña and the servants,
charmed by this agreeable sound of music, a thing which
they had long wanted to hear, learned with much difficulty
that the Negro eunuch was being visited by this strange
person; and he finally contrived to enter the apartment of
these women, even that of Leonora herself.

She had ventured to participate in the festivities which
he had initiated in the house after being convinced that
a certain ointment and powder which the young man had
brought to treat her husband with after he had retired
would cause the septuagenarian to sleep soundly for several days while they were thus enjoying themselves. The
party proceeded without stint or limit one night until
interrupted by the false alarm of a Negro set to watch
over the old man to report any indications of his awakening. The party continued after the reassembling of the
participants. Unfortunately, however, earlier the next day
than was expected the elderly husband actually awoke to
find that the sanctity of his home had been destroyed in
seeing his wife in the arms of the handsome young man.
The play ends with the old gentleman realizing that youth
is attracted to youth and that he had wronged his wife in
thus imprisoning her. Before he died from the shock he
settled upon her his fortune with the understanding that
she should marry this man with whom she had thus dis-
honored herself; but he went away never to be invited
back, for he soon learned that she had taken the veil.

The point to be noted here with respect to the Negro
is that the author emphasizes in the play the Negro's love
of music and his aptitude in this art. The play turns
upon this particular point. In the street from which the

young man disguised as a beggar was trying with his
companions to win over the Negro eunuch the story says,
"The boys all made a ring around him when he sang and
Luis, the Negro, enchanted by the virote's music, would
have given one of his hands to be able to open the door,
and listen to him at his ease, such is the fondness for
music inherent in the Negro race." Playing upon this
trait of the Negro, Loaysa said further to Luis, "Among
my pupils I have three Negroes, slaves to three aldermen,
whom I have taught so well that they are fit to sing and
play at any dance or in any tavern." At another point,
Loaysa is pictured as "singing a sprightly ditty with such
good effect that the Negro was in ecstasy and felt as if the
time for opening the door would never arrive." It looked
very much like "social equality," too, when as he entered,
"Loaysa embraced his pupil, kissed him on the cheek, and
immediately put into his hands a big jar of wine, a box
of preserves and other sweet things with which his wallet
was well stored."

At the time of the interesting party finally staged in
the household, however, the author apparently puts the
two Negro women down at the end of the social ladder,
for he says, "After all the women, from the lady of
the house down to the negresses, had thus gratified their
eyes, Loaysa took his guitar, and played a song more be-
witchingly than ever." At another point the author says,
"The appointed hour having arrived, all the domestics,
great and small, black and white, repaired to the turning-
box, longing to see the señor musico fairly within their
seraglio." Yet in the arrangement of the household the
author speaks of the owner as providing it with four white
slave girls whom he branded in the face, but the two Negro
women occupying apparently the same status were not
thus treated as if they were cattle. In the next place
Guiomar, the Negro sent to watch over the old man lest
he might wake up during this party, is made to talk in a

brogue not much better than that spoken by Negroes trying to use other modern languages; and when the Negro
all but broke up the party with the false alarm that the old
man had awakened the wrath expressed would seem to
leave the impression of the Negro's inclination toward
mendacity.

And the author plays up again the Negro's love of
music when as a result of this alarm Luis is presented as
running, hugging his guitar, and he "hid himself in his
loft, where he huddled up under the bed-clothes, sweating
with terror; in spite of which he could not forbear from
tinkling the guitar from time to time, so inordinate—may
Satanas confound him!—was his love of music."

Cervantes, however, did not have as a dominant factor
in his make-up any sense of depreciation of the Negro as
certain allusions in his writings may seem to indicate. He
was rather hard on the Moors just as most Spanish
writers were; and, having suffered from capture and
enslavement among their kindred in North Africa, he may
have had an additional reason for this attitude. His language does not show the same attitude toward the
Negroes, some of whom were mixed with the Moors. The
word *Negro* was used in those days as we use black today
without any thought of race. As a Spanish author says in
his own language, "Es color infausta y triste, y como tal
vsamos desta palabra, diziendo: negra ventura, etc."—
Covarrubias. And we find "la negra orden de caualleria"
in Don Quijote, I, iii. It is known, however, that Cervantes
keenly appreciated the contribution of Juan Latino, the
most distinguished Negro in Spain at that time. In a
poem prefixed to *Don Quijote* the author took note of this
scholarly figure as did many others among his contemporaries. The lines thus giving the famous linguist
honorable mention were:

> Pues al cielo no le plu-
> Que salieses tan ladi-,
> Como el negro Juan Lati-,

Hablar latines rehu-.
No me despuntes de agu-,
No me alegues con filo-,
Porque, torciendo la bo-,
Dirá el que entiende la le-,
No un palmo de las ore-
¿Para que conmigo flo-?[21]

In his play *La Dama Boba,* Lope de Vega, the most productive of all Spanish writers, takes occasion also to refer to Juan Latino's status and courtship in saying:

No era tan blanco en Granada
Juan Latino, que la hija
de vn Beyntiquatro enseñaua;
y siendo negro y esclauo,
porque fue su madre esclaua
del claro duque de Seso,
honor de España y de Ytalia,
se vino a cassar con ella:
que gramatica estudiaua,
y la enseñó a conjugar
en llegando al *amo, amas;*
que asi llama el matrimonio
el latin.[22]

Juan Latino is otherwise known to fame. In thus rising in the world he owed much to Don John of Austria, whom he did not forget. "A vast number of tributes were paid by contemporary men of letters to Don John of Austria,"

[21] The thought here is:
Since Heaven it hath not pleased on thee
    Deep erudition to bestow,
Or black Latino's gift of tongues,
    No Latin let thy pages show.
Ape not philosophy or wit,
    Lest one who cannot comprehend,
Make a wry face at thee and ask
    Why offer flowers to me, my friend?
[22] Freely translated this means:
Not so white was Juan Latino of Grenada, who taught the daughter of a Venitecuatro (Alderman); and although a black slave, since his mother was the slave of the distinguished Duke of Sesa, an honor of Spain and Italy, succeeded in marrying her; for when she was studying grammar he taught her on reaching the verb to love, *amo, amas, ama,* by which the Latin meant romance.

says George Ticknor in his *History of Spanish Literature* (II, page 582) "but among them none is more curious than a Latin poem in two books containing seventeen or eighteen hundred hexameters, the work of a Negro, who had been brought as an infant from Africa, and who by his learning rose to be Professor of Latin and Greek in the school attached to the cathedral of Granada. He is the same person noted by Cervantes as "el Negro Juan Latino," in a poem prefixed to the *Don Quixote*. His volume of Latin verses on the birth of Ferdinand, the son of Philip II, on Pope Pius V, on Don John of Austria, and on the city of Grenada, making above a hundred and sixty pages in small quarto, printed at Granada in 1573, is not only one of the rarest books in the world, but is one of the most remarkable illustrations of the intellectual faculties and possible accomplishments of the African race."

Juan Latino himself says he was brought to Spain from Ethiopia, and until his manumission was a slave to the grandson of the famous Gonsalvo de Córdova. "His Latin verse is respectable," says Ticknor, "and, from his singular success as a scholar, he was commonly called Joannes Latinus, a *sobriquet* under which he is frequently mentioned. He was respectably married to a lady of Granada, who fell in love with him, as Eloise did with Abelard, while he was teaching her; and after his death, which occurred later than 1573, his wife and children erected a monument to his memory in the church of Sta. Ana, in that city, inscribing it with an epitaph, in which he is styled "Filius Aethiopum, prolesque nigerrima patrum."[23]

There is a play entitled "Juan Latino" by Diego

[23] Antonio, *Bib. Nov.*, Tom. 1. p. 716. *Don Quixote*, ed. Clemencin, Tom. L. p. Ix, note. Andreas Schottus in his *Hispaniae Bibliotheca sive de Academiis et Bibliothecis* (1608), speaking of the city of Granada, says: "Hic Joannes Latinus Aethiops, (res prodigiosa) nostra tempestate rhetoricam per multos annos publice docuit, juventutemque institui, et poema edidit in victoriam Joannis Austriaci navalem." p. 29.

Ximenez de Encisco, in the second volume of the *Come-dias Escogidas* (Madrid, 1652), which gives a full sketch of the Latin scholar. "In the first act," says Ticknor, "he is a slave of the Duke of Sesa, ill enough treated, kicked about and cuffed. In the second, he is tutor to Doña Ana de Carlobal, sister to an ecclesiastic of rank, and makes love to her through his Spanish verses, and in other ways after the Spanish fashion. In the third, he rises to distinction; obtains his chair in the University; and, favored by Don John of Austria, is enfranchised by the Duke of Sesa, who, however, manumits him very reluctantly, on the ground that it is his great glory to hold so distinguished a man as his property." Addressing Don John, Juan Latino is made to promise,[24] (f. 57) in the fervor of his gratitude:

> Yo prometo a vuestrad Alteza,
> Que he de quitar a la Fama
> Una pluma con que escriva
> Sus memorables hazanas.
> Y, como muchos poemas
> Toman nombre del que cantan,
> Llamaré Austriada mi libro,
> Pues Canta Don Juan de Austria[25]

With more detail we may add that in the first scene Dr. Carlobal, a clergyman, censures his sister, Ana, for her many flirtations, directing attention especially to the liberty with which she treats her suitors. In spirited and youthful fashion she reminds the doctor that he is her brother, not her husband, and that on St. John's Eve she proposes to enjoy herself abundantly. Her brother replies

---

[24] "This promise, of course," says Ticknor, "was made by the poet half a century or more after it had been fulfilled." Ticknor, *op. cit.*, Vol. ii, p. 582.

[25] The thought here is:

I promise your highness to take from Fame a pen with which I may write his memorable deeds. And, as many poems take their name from those of whom they sing I shall call my book Austriad since it sings of Don Juan of Austria.

with a threat to marry her off immediately, but he receives the response:

"¿Yo casarme con hombre que no sea
duque, marqués o conde? ¿Yo casada?
¿Doña Ana Carlobal, a quien desea
serurir el mundo, y festejar Granada?"[26]

The turning point is that while Ana is discussing her suitors with her servants, there reverberate sounds of music mingled with expressions of glee of numerous revellers. These passers-by are students among whom walked Juan Latino. The plot thickens when Juan picks up Ana's ribbon which had fallen from the window, for there was a taunting of Juan by the fellows in keeping with the superstition connected with thus becoming acquainted with a lady on St. John's Eve. It was said that Ana will marry Juan. Next comes the subplot in which develop the discontent of the Moors and their reform which brings Don Juan of Austria into the drama. This is followed by the more interesting taunts and jokes of his fellow students whose envy was excited by Juan's wearing Ana's ribbon. The first act closes with a session of the Academy at the Duke's house, where Juan wins popular applause with a scholarly disquistion on the invention of printing and the origin of writing. Having shown such great possibilities, Juan is thereafter entrusted to Dr. Carlobal to complete his education.

In the second act, Juan is presented as an aspirant at the university, for which he must compete with a certain Villanueva, already a scholar of experience and position. To qualify as a candidate to receive serious consideration Juan earnestly implores his master to manumit him only to be pacified with further promises of this forthcoming

[26] The meaning here is:

I to marry a man who is not a duke, marquis or count? I married? Doña Ana Carlobal, whom the world desires to serve and Granada to entertain?

generosity. The interest next shifts to Ana's eagerness to learn, which is rewarded by her brother in securing Juan Latino as her teacher. While instructing her, according to Lope de Vega, Juan taught the young lady the essentials of romance as well as the fundamentals of education. This act closes with the outcome of the candidacy of Juan Latino for the professorship for which his dignity, self-possession, and erudition are adjudged attainments far more desirable than the qualifications shown by his opponent, Villanueva.

The third act shows Juan advancing rapidly in quest of the heart of Ana whom Dr. Carlobal would have taught knowledge rather than love. The hero is next favored by Don Juan of Austria who showers many honors upon him, and uses his good offices to induce the Duke to manumit Juan. The attitude is further shown by the eulogy on Juan Latino by his distinguished friend in the following sonnet:

> "Hijo de esclauo soy; naci en Baena,
>   donde las letras aprendi primero;
>   creci siguiendo el centro verdadero,
>   premio que a la virtud el cielo ordena.
> No me ha estoruado mi amorosa pena
>   que sea de Granada Racionero,
>   Orfeo, Marte, Ciceron, Homero,
>   en voz, en armas, en Latin, en vena.
> Catredatico fui Griego excelente,
>   y, en fin, varon insigne, pues que llego
>   a ser deste lugar Colector digno.
> Y como le llamó por eminente
>   la antigua Roma a su Adriano, el Griego,
>   la noble Espana me llamó el Latino."[27]

[27] The thought here is:

I am the son of a slave. I was born in Baena, where I first learned the alphabet; I grew up seeking the true goal, the prize which heaven offers for virtue.

No burden was my pleasant task of a prebendary of Granada, with Orpheus, Mars, Cicero, Homer, in voice, in arms, in Latin, in poetry.

I was a professor, excellent in Greek and finally, distinguished man; then from this position I became a distinguished tax-collector. And as Ancient Rome designated Adrian as eminent in calling him Greek, noble Spain called me Latin.

Juan finally attains the honor of being made Doctor with all the ceremony marking the grant of the rights and privileges thereunto belonging. He attains also that still greater honor of winning the hand of the ardently loved Ana.[28]

The chief wit of the play, Castillo, then characterizes Juan Latino by weaving together in the following style the important incidents of the hero's career:

"... un dia naturaleza
tuuo ciertas combidadas,
Diosas de acquellos contornos,
que de camino passauan.
Era Sabado, y, muy triste
de no poder regalarlas,
se puso a hazer vn menudo,
y aun dizen que era de baca.
Tomo vna larga morcilla
la naturaleza sabia,
y comenco a echar en ella
letras, lenguas, esciencias varias,
nominatious, gerundios,
en fin, toda la gramatica,
la teologia, y las artes;
pero echo pimenta harta;
que al cozer esta morcilla,
salio como vna gualdrapa.
Minerua, diosa de guerra,
viendo que es rey de las armas
el claro Duque de Sesa
embiosela a su casa,
donde ha los anos que veis
que esta al humero colgada,
sin que la de libertad;
que aun ay morcillas esclaus.
Verdad es que el senor Duque,
sabiendo de Juan las gracias,
le dio estudio, que fue hazer
de vn cueruo vna aguila braua."

[28] "If these details are true," says Rudolph Schevill, "they give us new facts in Juan's career. We also learn that doña Ana had a brother who was *licenciado* and *alcalde* of Granada, while Dr. Carlobal, the clergyman, is called "fundador de la celebrada Universidad de Oscuna." Whether D. Juan Tellez Giron, fourth Count of Ureña, and founder of the University of Osuna (1548), called Carlobal to some important position I am unable to ascertain."—Rudolph Schevill, *The Dramatic Art of Lope de Vega*, Berkeley, 1918, page 308.

"These statements," says Rudolph Schevill, "do not agree with most of those made by Bermudez de Pedraza in his *Antiguedad y excelencias de Granada,* and quoted by Clemencin (edition of *Don Quixote,* note 10 to preliminary verses). In fact no two writers agree on the details of Juan Latino's life, which seem to have been handed down chiefly by word of mouth. One of the most interesting facts in the life of Juan Latino, and one which relates him more intimately to Lope, is the connection between their respective patrons. D. Gonzalo Fernández de Córdoba, third duke of Sessa, and grandson of *el Gran Capitán,* was the owner of the Negro scholar; while D. Luis Fernández de Córdoba Cardona y Aragón, sixth duke of Sessa, grandson of doña Beatriz de Córdoba y Figueroa, *nieta del Gran Capitán,* was Lope's patron and intimate friend.

"I cannot disentangle the confusion which seems to exist regarding doña Ana's brother and father, although the assertion of Pedraza, that the latter was *licenciado, y Gobernador del estado del duque de Sesa* lends some authority to Lope's statement that he was a *veinticuatro.* Encisco, we saw, gives doña Ana two brothers, one of whom is *licenciado* and *alcalde.* Pellicer, in his edition of *Don Quixote,* Madrid, 1787, p. 233, states briefly that Juan Latino died in Granada in 1573, while Ticknor and others guardedly say "after 1573." Nicholas Antonio may be responsible for this uncertainty. He says: 'Jacet in Sanctae Annae paroeciali ecclesia Granatensi, uti fert prae se lapidis titulus, quem ipse in ea urbe agens excripsit: Del Maestro Juan Latino, Catedratico de Granada, y doña Ana de Carleval su muger y herederos. MDLXXIII.''

"It may not be amiss here to add," says Ticknor, "that another Negro is celebrated in a play, written with skill in good Castilian, and claiming, at the end, to be founded in fact. It is called *El Valiente Negro en*

Flandes, by Andres de Claramonte, actor and play-wright, and is found in Tom. XXXI, 1638, of the *Collection of Comedies* printed at Barcelona and Sara-gossa. The Negro in question, however, was not, like Juan Latino, a native African, but was a slave born in Merida, and was distinguished only as a soldier, serving with great honor under the Duke of Alva, and enjoying the favor of that severe general.''[29]

Lope de Vega, as already herein referred to, thus brought the Negro into his writings. In most cases these were ordinary allusions of no particular literary sig-nificance but without prejudice. He frequently referred to the black saints and occasionally played up persons of this color in his comedies. In the discussion of the atti-tude of Lope de Vega, however, one must not be misled by the frequency of his mentioning the *Negro* in his writings. The way the *Negro* is thereby introduced is more important. In the works of this author all ele-ments figured. Lope de Vega brings Moors into several of his productions like the *Fundación de la Alhambra de Granada, El grao de Valencia, Quien bien ama tarde ol-vida, El Alcaide de Madrid, La devoción del Rosario, El Rey por semajanza, Guerras de amor y de honor, Ped-rino desposado, Las Burlas y enredos de Benito, Los Cau-tivos de Argel, La divina Vencedora,* and *El Favor agra-decido.* Hebrews appear also for their share in such plays as *La Octava maravilla;* and, of course, the ancient Jew in numerous plays of Biblical origin for a very different reason. All these elements have their place in using the stage to supply a picture of contemporary Spain.

In Lope de Vega neither the Moor nor the Jew of this time measured up to the level of the Spaniard.

---

[29] By Schevill we are referred to Gallardo's *Ensayo de una Biblioteca española,* III, no. 2627; and Rodríguez Marín's *Louis Barahona de Sotó* (Madrid, 1903), p. 35, and an article in *el Imparcial* (de Madrid), 1916, November 19, which adds practically nothing to previous information.

They were not militant Christians. The Negro with less mention than these other foreigners on the stage is treated more sympathetically. Lope de Vega had a special fondness for Negro music and dance, and he frequently introduced black characters to dramatize the achievements of the race in these spheres. In the closing of the *Nacimiento de Christo* (the Birth of Christ) he introduces with splendid effect the three kings preceded by dances of Gypsies and Negroes. In *La Vitoria de la honra,* Anton, Tiznado, and a Negro woman soloist together with a chorus of beautiful voices intersperse the production in most entertaining fashion; and no vileness is shown in the remark of Antonio in saying:

> Mil años le guarde el cielo
> que hoy quisiera que
> llevaras, toda una negra por higa;
> mas diérate gran fatiga
> si al cuello te la colgararas
> aunque una dama sospecho,
> y morena de color
> (pues los que tienen amor
> llevan su dama en el pecho)
> era la mejor de todas
> aqui, para entre los dos.

In the play called "El Mayor rey de los reyes" (King of Kings) we find the Negro given a still more prominent place by Lope de Vega. This play, however, or one bearing the same title, according to the editors of the works of Lope de Vega, has been attributed to Andres Claramonte, and a similar play to Calderon. These editors, however, find in this particular play certain embellishments and dramatic effects which they believe that only Lope de Vega could have produced. Among the kings who, according to the Biblical story of the Magi came to do honor to the Babe of Bethlehem was also the Negro King Melchor, frequently mentioned elsewhere in other modern literature and art of Europe.

Along with King Melchor appear Butifar, Zaydan, a
black queen, and a priest, all Negroes, who figured conspicuously throughout this play on a parity with others.

The next writer of consequence to project the Negro
into literature was Calderon. Calderon's attitude toward
the subordinated elements of the social order may be defined as still more favorable than that of his distinguished
predecessors. Certainly he had a softer attitude toward
both the Jews and the Moors than did Cervantes or
Lope de Vega. This is evident in the way that he
treated the Moors in his play entitled *Amar despues de la
muerte* (Love Survives Life). His more favorable attitude may be due to the fact that he was farther removed
from the conflict of the Spaniards and Moors and, therefore, had lost some of the rancor which had developed
between these two elements. With respect to the Negro
Calderon's writings not only show allusions to color with
reference to the Moors as in such plays as *El Gran
Principe de Fez, Don Baltasar de Loyola* and *La Nina
de Gomez Arias,* but he devotes one play especially to the
Negro in which black persons play important parts.
This is his *Sabila del Oriente y Gran Reina de Sabá.*

This play is based upon the famous theme of the
contacts of Solomon and the Queen of Sheba. It is at the
same time a contrast of one Oriental culture with that
of another or the contrast of the civilization of the Hami-
tes with that of the Semites. The play gives a contemporary conception of the ancient history of these people
with, of course, the exaggeration that a thing of this sort
naturally would have on the stage. It belongs to the
old classic drama. Nothing of any great consequence
is added to the story of this visit of one sovereign to the
other, but it is made sufficiently romantic to give further
ground for the claim of Abyssinians' being the descendants of the off-spring of Solomon and the Queen of
Sheba. It should be noted, too, that the important char-

acters in this play were not drawn exclusively from
Ethiopia and Judea. In the drama one finds Hiram, King
of Tyre; Candaces, King of Egypt; Libio, King of Pal-
myra; and Mandinga, together with a Negro gracioso,
and such Negro women as Irifile, Casimira, and Irene.
In conformity to the classic drama the author has conceived these as types into whose mouths he puts his own
words.

In another of Calderon's plays, *Los Hijos de la Fortuna, Teagenes y Cariclea* we have the Negro also occupying a conspicuous place in an international drama. This
is an effort to bring into play the conflict of the culture
of the Orient with that of the Occident. Here one sees
the Ethiopian, the Egyptian, and the Greek in action. The
play follows the rule of classicism. While Teagenes and
Cariclea are the chief characters in the story, the Negro
is projected into it sufficiently to give the drama color.
All of the Negroes brought into the picture, then, are
not servants. The author makes Idaspe, a black man,
speak for himself as an aristocrat, saying, "I am a noble
Satrap of Ethiopia, who, elevated by blood and fortune,
find few equals." There is also Persina, the Negro Queen
of Ethiopia, with black servants, nymphs and musicians,
who in their display of talent help to establish the claim
of the Negro to achievement in music even at that early
day. Here Calderon is following the example of Lope de
Vega in thus continuing Negro music and dance on the
Spanish stage. Evidently the Negro in the histrionic
sphere in Europe reached his first high level in Spain
during its golden age of the seventeenth century.

The details of *Los Hijos de la Fortuna* have no particular concern for us here. We are especially interested in the way these black characters were staged to
portray the status and history of that country in the
drama in which Ethiopians and Egyptians of diluted
Negro blood play their parts along with Greeks. The

Greeks greatly admired the Ethiopians as the leaders of ancient culture and referred to them as being so highly favored as to feast among the gods. While one does not find here the same picture as that set forth in such history of the Greeks as that recorded by Herodotus and in the poems of Homer and Aeschylus he does get sufficient glimpse of it to warrant the conclusion that in ancient times the Negro was one of the important factors in making an advanced world culture. This Oriental civilization was taken over by the Europeans who went into the Crusades as half savages and returned from the East with sufficient enlightenment to civilize their continent.

After the great masters of Spanish literature had passed out about the middle of the seventeenth century the literature of that country declined to a low level. Here and there were persons who undertook to follow the masters but did so feebly only. There were also poets of provincial beginnings and travellers who left realistic productions which reflected to a great extent the people among whom they moved. Some of these in temperament and thought were decidedly African. Of these writings a large number may be mentioned, but to no purpose here because of their unrepresentative character. Unfortunately, too, in this state of affairs writers of Spain failed to keep pace with the literary movements outside of their country and, therefore, were not contemporarily influenced by such stimuli as those which stirred the literary circles in France, Germany, and England. When these movements finally reached Spain the first efforts along these lines were poor imitations of what had been well expressed elsewhere.

About one century later, however, near the middle of the eighteenth century, we find better beginnings and, therefore, a literature more representative of a modern nation. Yet, inasmuch as Spain, like some other countries, had entered upon the program of ruthless exploitation of its colonies with the use of laboring elements most of whom were free people of color and Negro slaves, the Negro in that literature did not fare so well. Much bitterness developed thereafter with respect to these elements not because they were black but because they were the victims of a selfish colonial policy. In the production of Spanish realists, therefore, we find sometimes allusions which indicate that the Negro was regarded very much as he was in any other European country with such connections. The Negro is not frequently mentioned, but the attitude is curtly expressed.

In the case of *El Moro Exposito,* by Angel de Saavedra or the Duke of Rivas we find such an allusion. This poem, harking back to the Islamic occupation, contrasts the culture of two cities, Córdoba and Burgos, the former representing the civilization of the Moors, and the latter that of the Spaniards. It is a lengthy poem, styled a romance *heroico,* that is, a hendecasyllabic with assonance in alternate lines. There is not much plot to it, but it is picturesque. Of course, in contrast to the Christian civilization of the people of Burgos that of the Moors in Córdova naturally suffered. The Christian must be made superior to the "heathen" whether he is or not. One of the characters referred to in the poem as a Negro is denounced as an infamous black who should be dead.

In another play, *Guzman el Bueno,* by Don Antonio Gil y Zárate, the blacks are brought into the equation along with the Moors. Here the theme comes also from the days of Islam. The play deals with honor—such honor as was shown by the Spaniards when trying to drive out the Moors in order to preserve what they considered the true religion. One commenting on this, however, notes that this was not a struggle to maintain the stern honor of the Greek but Christian grace and fortitude. Yet the

author presents Aben-Comat of the Moors as "one of
the faithful who can serve a bad master with grace and
preserve his honor and integrity at the same time. He
inspires everybody with respect and admiration."[30] The
Moor here, however, is no longer a Negro.

References to the Negro in modern Spanish writings
grow less and less and tend to classify the race as unequal
to the European. For example, in Don Manuel Breton's
La Independencia the word *Negro* is used to denote a very
brown or black color of a member of a lower social order.
In *El Trovador,* Antonio Garcia Gutierez, with the same
attitude, makes an uncomplimentary allusion to the Negro.
He would have the term mean gloom, as in the *Negra
estrella.* In this way he makes use of the folktale of the
Cuevo Negro, on which is based Edgar Allan Poe's
"Raven." The presence of this dark species is considered as indicating misfortune or foreboding evil, which
tends to make the word *Negro* become more and more
synonymous with that which is impure, uninviting, and
undesirable. Whether this use of the term indicated the
attitude of Gutierez or merely something which he borrowed from another literature is not clear. It should be
remarked that this allusion to the "Raven" is found in
all great literatures like those of the Mesopotamians, the
Greeks, and the Romans. It may be added here, too, that
the word *Negro* was a name given in Spain to the mod-
erates of the Cortés of 1820 by the "exaltados," who
had provoked the provincial revolution.

The same sort of attitude is observed in Fernan Caballero's *La Familia de Alvareda.* To illustrate a point the
author reverts to the proverb characterizing one in a
peculiarly difficult situation out of which there are apparently ways of escape none of which can be used. The
illustration is the folk tale of a little Negro enamored
of another man's wife who finally informed her husband

---

[30] *Guzman el Bueno,* edited by an instructor.

of the African's unsolicited attentions. The husband
in collusion with the aggrieved wife plans a tryst for the
ardent lover with his wife in a room with three doors.
The Negro appeared upon the scene, overjoyed and
ladened with numerous gifts with which he would gladden
the heart of his now willing conquest. No sooner than he
had taken his seat and had begun to approach the wife
with affection, however, the husband seized upon the
little Negro and belabored him so terribly that, although
there were three doors in the room, he was not given
time to escape by either.

An American editor commenting on this novel, refers to
this tale as one of the weaknessess of Caballero's story because it adds nothing to the narrative, and serves merely
as a diversion which causes the movement to lag. This
criticism, however, seems a little severe, but it may be
explained by the usual bias of the Nordic commentator
who would hardly consider any such notice of a Negro as
in good taste. Doubtless if the allusion had been to a
Negro in the rôle of a clown rather than as paying court
to a Spanish lady it would not have been thus noticed
by the fastidious editor.

Juan Eugenio Hartzenbusch also stood among those
who could not escape bias. His attitude with respect to the
Negro is best shown in his very popular *Los Amantes de
Teruel*. This is a drama of love in which the hero, a
captive in prison, is being made love to by a dusky Moorish sultana. He resists the sultana's entreaties because
of his belief in his superiority as a Nordic. He pines
for the absent blonde heroine, although she is besieged
by many other suitors. The heroine, finally convinced
that the hero is dead or unworthy on some other account,
accepts one of her many suitors. In the meantime the
hero gets away from the dusky sultana only to fall into
the clutches of robbers. Finally he arrives at the home
of the heroine too late, and the lovers commit suicide.

The point in the play of Hartzenbusch is the contrast
of one race with the other. The dusky Arab of diluted
African blood was voluptuous, licentious. The Nordic of
the race to which Hartzenbusch belonged, for his father
was a German, although his mother was a native of
Spain and he developed in that country, was inherently
superior. In other words, in spite of itself it is almost
impossible for literature to be other than racially biased.
Europe was feeling its superiority over the Orient which
had civilized it, and this must now creep into the thought
of the best thinkers of the time. They thus used their
literary productions for propaganda.

In the case of Pedro Antonio Alarcon we see further
evidence of the attitude toward the *Negro* in the literature of that country. In his blood-and-thunder dime
novel, *El Final de Norma,* he makes a Negro the companion of one of the most important characters. Just
why this Negro should be taken out of his milieu to go as
far North as Greenland and Iceland requires a stretch of
the imagination of which only Alarcon himself is capable.
He has been charged with being a man of Moorish temperament, going to the extreme, seeking the gorgeous
and using the superlative to intensify brightness and
splendor, to strike the primitive eye, to increase the effect
of the story. And yet this Negro brought into the story
does not develop as a character. In one case the author
refers to his hiding *su caja de dientes.* The Negro is
also presented as lacking even in sufficient knowledge
to speak a modern language.

Alarcon took up Africa as a theme in 1860 in publishing his *Diario de un testigo de la guerra de Africa.* He
had participated in this conflict and used his unusual
ability to please the public in setting forth in bombastic
and colorful fashion what he observed and what he did
not observe in Africa. The book became unusually popular and sold to the number of a hundred thousand copies,
but it is not regarded as a highly literary production. It

has no particular bearing on the Negroes themselves with the exception of certain allusions to colored participants, who were Moors or not more than Moors with Negro blood. This diary was more of an account of the triumph of a vindictive people over the same elements of Orientals or their kindred who as Moors had once occupied Spain but had been driven to Africa where they were further humiliated. Numerous other writers of Spain also wrote on the African War of 1859 to glorify the Spanish victory which apparently stimulated the falling spirit of the rapidly decaying empire.

The same attitude, however, did not appear in the writings of all Spanish authors of this time. In spite of themselves some of them had an African temperament and could not easily get rid of that influence. In the case of Vicente Medina, a native of Murcia in Southern Spain, one of the most Africanized portions of that land, this color is evident in his writings. Sometimes it appears in the case of others where it is not expected. "The Tribute to the Dark Beauty," by Francisco Villaespesa, is a case in evidence. He wrote thus:

"Si me pierdo por el mundo
buscadme en Andalucía.
Allí donde haya guitarras
y cañas de manzanilla,

y mujeres con claveles
y mantones de Manila,
allí cantaré a mi tierra,
la de María Santísima.

Donde haya una calle blanca
y una reja florecida,
allí me veréis, hablando
con la morena más linda
de cuantas muestran sus ojos
a través de una mantilla."[31]

[31] Translated by L. A. Warren, this is: "If I am lost in the world seek me in Andalucia. Where there are guitars and glasses of manzanilla, and women with carnations and mantles from Manila, there I will sing to my land, the land of Maria Santisima.

"Wherever there is a white street and an iron screen covered with flowers, there you will see me talking with the prettiest dark beauty of those who show their eyes across a mantilla."

It should be noted, moreover, that some liberal movements did have the same effect in Spain as they had elsewhere. All Spaniards did not believe in the methods of
the Inquisition. *Uncle Tom's Cabin,* a realistic novel,
which portrayed the status of the Negro slaves in the
United States, stirred the whole world in being translated
into various languages and dramatized in Europe. Be it
said to the credit of Spain, however, that some ten years
before *Uncle Tom's Cabin* was brought out Gertrudis
Gomez de Avillaneda, essentially a Cuban, wrote and published in Spain in 1839, a novel called *Sab,* in which she
attacked slavery with much vigor. Lacking some of the
merits of her American compeer, she did not arouse
such popular interest as did Harriet Beecher Stowe, but
she did express her indignation against the abuses of the
system; and this work is still referred to as showing literary merit.

Into Spain, however, came the crimes of the exploitation which moved other parts of the world. Spain naturally felt bitter when in spite of its struggle to maintain
its empire she saw it gradually taken away in the making
of the Latin-American republics independent. The black
people themselves in these various republics were the oppressed not because they were Negroes, but because they
had once been slaves and had not been able to rise to the
level of the exploiting class. In most of these cases,
therefore, Spain naturally crushed the aspirations of
those whom we call people of African descent. Some few
of these, like Enriques Dias, who fought with Portugal,
helped to maintain the old order, but others resorted
to revolutionary efforts. Gabriel de la Concepcion Valdes,
called "Placido," distinguished himself in writings such
as *Jicotencal, Despidida a mi madre,* and finally *Plegaria a*

Dios,[32] which he recited when he was on the way to his execution in 1844. He, it was said, had tried to stir up a revolution of the blacks against Spain, but investigation

[32] PLEGARIA A DIOS

¡Ser de immensa bondad! ¡Dios poderoso!,
a Vos acudo en mi dolor vehemente . . .
¡extended vuestro brazo omnipotente,
rasgad de la calumnia el velo odioso,
y arrancad este sello ignominioso
con que el mundo manchar quiere mi frente!

¡Rey de los Reyes!, ¡Dios de mis abuelos!,
Vos sólo sois mi defensor, ¡Dios mío . . .!
Todo lo puede quien al mar sombrío
olas y peces dío, luz a los cielos,
fuego al Sol, giro al aire, al Norte hielos,
vida a las plantas, movimiento al rio.

Todo lo podéis Vos, todo fenece
o se reanima a vuestra voz sagrada;
fuera de Vos, Señor, el todo es nada
que en la insondable eternidad perece,
y aun esa misma nada os obedece,
pues de ella fue la humanidad creada.

Yo no os puedo engañar, Dios de clemencia,
y pues vuestra eternal sabiduría
ve al través de mi cuerpo el alma mía,
cual del aire a la clara transparencía
estorbad que, humillada la inocencia,
bata sus palmas la calumnia impía.

Estorbadlo, Senor, por la preciosa
sangre vertida, que la culpa sella
del pecado de Adán, o por aquella
madre cándida, dulce y amorosa,
cuando envuelta en pesar, mustia y llorosa,
siguío tu muerte como heliaca estrella.

Mas si cuadra a tu Suma Omnipotencia
que yo perezca cual malvado impío,
y que los hombres mi cadáver frío
ultrajen con maligna complacencia . . .
suene tu voz, acabe mi existencia . . .
¡Cúmplase en mí tu voluntad, Dios mio . . .!*

* José Manuel Carbonell y Rivero, *Evolución de la Cultura Cubana* (1608-1927) Vol. II, *La Poesía Lirica en Cuba*, pages 211-212.

has never revealed more than a general suspicion on account of which this promising author went to a martyr's grave. He was, then, the forerunner of Antonio Maceo.

The history of Spanish art supports these conclusions drawn from study of the literature of that country. Up to the time of El Greco the art of the Iberian Peninsula was under the dominating influence of Italy, just as the literature was during that time. With the coming of Velasquez and Murillo into the picture, artists caught the spirit of the country and began to deal with life as it was in Spain, although the religious motif was ever active. The Negro king is in evidence in Velasquez's *Adoration of the Magi;* and one of his productions is entitled *A Kitchen Maid* with distinctly Negroid features. Both Velasquez and Murillo, too, like Cervantes, Lope de Vega and Calderon, took the ambitious Negro into account. Juan de Pareja, a man of Negro African blood, the servant of Velasquez, was elevated by the distinguished painter who produced a striking portrait of his friend of color. Juan de Pareja became the outstanding disciple of the Velasquez school, and to him is attributed the striking painting known as *La vacación de San Mateo.*

Murillo, not blind to the Negro conspicuous at that time in Spain, produced a painting of a Negro boy along with two Spanish peasant lads typifying in realistic fashion those of low estate. Another fact in this painter's career, however, is still more interesting. He had a Negro servant, Sebastian Gomez, who while cleaning up the study for his master and his coworkers learned by dint of energy to portray the beautiful. Finding a striking painting hidden away where evidently an artist was retouching the work, Murillo inquired of his coworkers as to which one was producing this portrait with such evidence of a masterful touch. They knew nothing about it. Inquiring of Gomez as to those who might enter the study after office hours, Murillo forced from the young man the confession that he was this artist incognito. Overwhelmed with joy that without help a man of such low estate had developed so far with this art, Murillo liberated Gomez and accepted him as an understudy.

As in the case of Juan de Pareja, influenced by Velasquez, so was Sebastian Gomez, influenced in his work by Murillo. "In one of the churches of Seville," says A. F. Chamberlain, "are to be seen four beautiful pictures (Christ bound to a column, with St. Peter kneeling at his side; St. Joseph; St. Anne; Madonna and Child), the work of the mulatto, Sebastian Gomez, the slave, then the pupil, the companion and the equal of his master, the great painter Murillo, who had him made a free citizen of Spain, and at his death (in 1682), left him a part of his estate."[33]

As the art, like the literature of the Iberian Peninsula, suffered a decline about the middle of the seventeenth century we do not have many masters measuring up to the high European standard of other countries, and the Negro for a century is not frequently mentioned by those thus concerned. Coming to Goya, however, we find the Negro again in the picture, receiving attention from another great master. In Goya's *Carnival* (*El Entierro de la Sardina*) there are Negroid masks along with others of a different type. In the same artist's *A Miracle of St. Anthony* a Negroid figure is given a conspicuous position. In his *Duquesa de Alba con la negrita Maria de la Luz*, this woman of noble blood is portrayed as clasping most tenderly in her arms a little black girl. Such an attitude reminds one of that pictured in the *Jealous Estremaduran* by Cervantes in referring to the relations of Loaysa and Luis.

In the study of Sorolla and Zuloaga of a subsequent

[33] *The Journal of Race Development*, I, No. 4, p. 483.

period we do not find so much interest in the Negro as a subject of art, and the lesser artists of their day tended to follow this rule. In other Spanish speaking countries, influenced inevitably by the home country, the thought of the Negro was determined by so many other factors in their own national life that the treatment of the tendencies there found have no such direct bearing here as to require extended treatment. The absence of race prejudice in Latin America and the human solution of the so-called race problem by the application of the principle of brotherly love, rather than by pro-racial dictation, exploitation, and extermination followed by the Nordics, has given the Negro in such countries the same consideration in both literature and art as that of any other element of the population and without the designation of race. It is sufficient here to note that these beginnings in Spain account in part for this tendency in a sane direction.

We are not surprised, then, to observe that in traveling through Spain today one finds no evidence of racial discrimination based upon color. There are cases of persons being referred to occasionally as Negroes if they happen to be black or nearly so, but without prejudice. Negro actors touching Spain are warmly received in the best theatrical circles, as a recent production of the *Cronica* will show with respect to Josephine Baker and others. Recently there was on the Spanish stage a play by Insúa called the *Triangle,* in which is featured a black woman who in making a tour along with Spanish passengers is cordially received among them as their social equal. A leading periodical, *Estampa,* recently featured the banquet and popular reception given the admission to the bar of "El Primer Abogada Negro de España," Jorgé Dougan Linson. In the illustrations noting this event appear not only a most attractive cut of this Negro lawyer with his fellow attorneys on the street and in robes at his desk, but another representation of the banquet given him by the distinguished men of his profession of Barcelona in 1930. Spain evidently, then, is one of the countries which has been saved from the evils of race prejudice.

C. G. WOODSON

BOOK REVIEWS

Pedro de Alvarado, Conquistador. By John Eaghan Kelly. (Princeton University Press, 1932. Pp. 279. Price $3.50.)

In this volume Mr. Kelly has given an intensely readable account of the early life of Alvarado in the Spanish Province of Estremadura, the Juan de Grijalva expedition to Yucatan and Mexico, the rivalry between Cortés and Velásquez, and of more importance, the conquest of Mexico, Guatemala, Honduras and El Salvador. Moreover, the story does not end with the death of the conquistador but closes with a chapter which describes how in less than a year "his surviving children suffered poverty and the pangs of hunger." (p. 224).

The first part of the book tells the story of Alvarado as a lieutenant of Cortés between 1485 and 1523, the story of the exciting exploits of Cortés in Mexico, the Azetec Empire, (p. 25), the rise and fall of the Montezuma, the first entry into Mexico, and the *Noche triste* (p. 90). The final entry of Cortés and his Tlascalan allies flow along swiftly, with copious documentation and repeated disagreement with H. H. Bancroft's works.

The second part of the book gives the story of Pedro de Alvarado's explorations in his own right between 1524 and 1541 after the completion of his colorful apprenticeship under the tutelage of the masterful Hernán Cortés. However, even though Alvarado is in the sector (Guatemala) he has carved out for himself, the shadows of the greater *conquistadores,* Cortés, Pizarro and Almagro, loom across the borders to steal, at times, the limelight from the author's hero. In only three chapters of Part II does Alvarado stand out as the leading spirit of the conquest of Guatemala, Honduras and El Salvador; but he loses his position even here when "with indifferent success" (p. 200) he attempts to emulate the diplomatic traits of Cortés. Nevertheless, the author clearly shows that from beginning to end Alvarado even when not the leader was in the front rank of nearly every major campaign from Malalacia to Mexico City.

Earlier a diplomatic trait of Cortés had stood him in good stead, for it is pointed out that Alvarado like Cortés made extensive use of Indians to conquer other Indians. For example, the pacification of the Indians of Guatemala was accomplished largely through the cooperation of "- - - - two hundred Tlascalans newly arrived from Mexico to see further glory and spoils under the leadership of their white friends." (p. 162). However, the task of pacifying the Indians was a matter of grave concern, because the Indians of Guatemala were determined to keep the Spaniards out at all cost. This is shown in part by the fact that "although this was their first sight of horses, they fought furiously as the cavalry overwhelmed them, clinging desperately to the manes and tails of the animals and trying to overthrow them by main force." (p. 161).

From the point of view of the Negro it will be gratifying to some to see the capital "N" used in spelling the word, and the same folk will no doubt be surprised to see white dignified with a capital "W." (p. 162). The author includes appropriately in his work that "smallpox was introduced in Mexico by a Negro body servant of Narvaez" (p. 99) and that "- - - - many Negro servants - - -" perished in Alvarado's march across the frozen Andes mountains *en route* to Peru.

The chief merits of the book are its readableness of style throughout, especially the summary of the conquest of Mexico, and the appropriate use which the author makes of two hitherto unused letters written by Alvarado to Cortés. The book contains too much of Cortés to be a life of Alvarado (the preface to the contrary) and chapters seven, eight and nine suggest that the author has not written a very thorough discussion of the conquest of Guatemala. Professor Arthur S. Aiton has pointed out, moreover, that the materials available in Pacheo y Cordinas's *Documentos Inéditos,* which doubtless would have been of value, were not consulted by the author.

JAMES B. BROWNING

Howard University

The Odyssey of Cabeza de Vaca. By Morris Bishop, Assistant Professor of Romance Languages at Cornell University. (New York: The Century Company, 1933. Pp. vii, 306. Price $3.00.)

Alvar Nuñez Cabeza de Vaca is known widely as the first American to cross the North American continent and for having come within a relatively short distance of duplicating the achievement in South America (p. 177). His sustained efforts to demonstrate the practicability of a human Indian policy are less well understood. We know more about his explorations than of his other undertakings.

It is impossible here to single out more than the main features of this many-sided book because to an extent it is a discussion of the discovery, exploration and colonization of most of Latin America. The work is appropriately divided into two parts: North America and South America. In Part I the author lays before his reader life-like portraits of bits of Jerez de la Frontera, the Panfilo de Narváez expedition of 1527, and the seemingly endless but colorful overland journey of Alvar Nuñez from Florida by way of Galveston, Monterey, the Gulf of Mexico and thence across Mexico to the Gulf of California.

Of interest to the Negro reader is that one of the four pedestrians, who made their way across the continent, was "Estebanico of Azamor in Morocco (who may have been enslaved in the expedition against that city in 1513, in the course of which Magellan was lamed for life)" (p. 100). There are at least a dozen references to the cleverness, loyalty, passion and finally the stupidity of Estebanico. Moreover, it is suggested that at least in Mexico Estebanico found many other Negroes in the new world as the author states, on page 241, "meanwhile Estebanico swaggered among the Spanish negroes, who filled the capital."

Part II of the book contains a portrayal of the "decline and fall" of Alvar Nuñez Cabeza de Vaca in South America after a brief sojourn in Spain. Here in South America as in North America the author depicts phases of the Indian civilization, the attempts at colonization, the treatment of the Indians and the oversupply of intrigue in the colonies. Standing at times above and at other times below it all, however, is Alvar Nuñez hoping against odds to convince others that as governor he could demonstrate that a humane Indian policy was more practical than exploitation, and that Christian principles would end the apparently incessant strife in the Rio de la Plata region. In the end vice and corruption triumphed over honesty and decency, and the grand old man's fever-ridden body was sent back to Spain to await trial after trial, and then poverty, disgrace and death.

A few items in the book need to be checked. Alvar Nuñez is the correct name of the hero and Cabeza de Vaca is the honorary name of his family. The reader is apt to get the unfortunate impression that the sweeping statements about the cruel tendencies of the Spniards are typical of the Spanish colonial policy as a whole or that the Latins were especially cruel to Negroes when as a matter of fact these Latins in this respect were more humane than the English. Negro should be spelled with a capital "N" in keeping with a recent trend which is rapidly becoming a fixed policy.

In spite of these limitations Professor Bishop's work is a scholarly analysis of the colorful career of a man who, though a *conquistador,* tried to carry out the Indian policy of Bartolemé de las Casas. The painstaking care involved in documenting dubious points with source material and the achievement of telling the true story of Alvar Nuñez Cabeza de Vaca and his complex and varied experiences with so many different groups make the work a brilliant piece of historical research valuable for both the general reader and the specialist in the field.

James B. Browning

Howard University

Los Negros en Africa y America. By Luis Cincinato Bollo (Barcelona, Spain: Editorial Cervantes, 1932. Pp. 80.)

The author, who resides in Montevideo, Uruguay, has published previously *The Evolution of Man and Races* and a *Universal Geography.* He is qualified, therefore, to make a contribution to an impartial study of the Negro on account of his training, race, and place of origin. *Los Negros En Africa* may be used as a work for general circulation as reading text for Spanish classes in Negro schools and colleges, or as a reference book in classes in the social and biological sciences. In addition to the nine chapters there is an excellent bibliography followed by an index. A table of illustrations concludes the work and greatly enhances its value.

These titles of the nine chapters will suffice to give the reader an idea of the scope of this brief but comprehensive work: "The Races of North Africa;" "The Color of the Skin;" "A Secondary Character of all Races;" "Negroes in North America;" "The Pretended Incapacity of Negroes to Develop;" "Negroes in Brazil and the Antilles;" "Race Crossing;" "Hereditary and Evolutionary Laws;" "Geographical Distribution of the Africans," and "Blood-Color Groups in the Determination of Races." It is evident, then, that the author has touched every phase of this question which concerns those approaching the task scientifically.

The reader will find useful information in the discussion of anthropological and scientific laws dealing with the evolution of races and the Negro, and in references to such Latin-American Negroes as *Toussaint Louverture* of Haiti, *Antonio Maceo* and *Placido*, of Cuba, and *Simon Rivas* and *Escobar* of Panama. Certain passages translated reveal the author's historical, social, and scientific outlook on the evolution of the Negro. If the place of origin of the African Negroes is not in Africa, contends the author, "as the tradition of all the tribes of the Sudan says, but a land situated at the Southeast route of the two great Negro invasions, it must be supposed that their place or origin is the ancient continent of Gondwana, which unites Africa to India, Australia and South America in the secondary epoch, and whose remains existed in the form of great islands until the end of the tertiary epoch and even later. "The Negro after some hundreds of years," says the author further, "probably will lose his color and will become a dark reddish race without crossing with another race." "The anthropological element is very important, but it is not everything, because education and the social medium modify greatly the native qualities of every race."

Another point of interest in this study which helps the reader to appreciate the evolution of the race in Africa consists in the nine groups of illustrations including pictures of individuals of the Negroid races as the Hotentot, Bantu, Kaffir, Sudanese, and the like.

The wide acquaintance shown with the bibliography of forty-five well selected books, including works of such authorities as Lionel Decle, F. Ratzel, H. Bouchat, D'Obigny, and Dr. Kossovitch give further evidence of the value of Bollo's work. This book is an encouragement to the ever-increasing demand of the reading public both at home and abroad for comprehensive, historical, scientific and critical information on the Negro in Africa and America.

JAMES H. HUNT

Bishop College, Marshall, Texas

Economic History of the South. By Emory O. Hawk. (New York, Prentice-Hall, 1934. 557 pages. Price $5.00.)

This textbook is a convenient summary for undergraduates and will probably be widely used in both the South and North. For this very reason, it had best never have been written. For in its most vital part, the treatment of the Negro, it is such sheer propaganda that scholars must fear that Southern historians will never be able to maintain their balance once the Negro enters upon the scene.

If this appears to be an extreme statement, let the reader turn to page 506. There Professor Hawk says: "Many reformers have assumed that the negro population in the South has resulted in a problem based primarily upon racial prejudice. From an economic point of view, however, this opinion is not of supreme importance." What does the author mean by that extraordinary statement? "As a rule," he continues, "Southern people are not antagonistic to negroes so long as they remain segregated. Nor does the Southern negro, unless indoctrinated with what the Southerner regards as dangerous propaganda, desire racial equality. In the year 1919 while race riots occurred in Elaine, Arkansas; Charleston, South Carolina; Knoxville, Tennessee; and Longview, Texas, a serious race riot also took place in Chicago, Illinois." The clear import of these statements is that these riots were the result of the desire of Negroes for "racial equality," whatever that is. In fact, however, the Negroes of Elaine, Arkansas, to cite only one instance, wanted to engage an accountant to tell them how much the white landlords were cheating them. This attempt to show the desire for "racial equality" as the cause of race riots is unscientific, to say the least.

Again, we learn from the same page that the "so-called 'negro problem' of the South is practically the same as the racial problem which the North must face in dealing with many of its foreign immigrants—namely, illiteracy and its concomitant, a low standard of living.'' This statement is simply vicious. It clearly implies that a great majority of the Negroes in the South are illiterate, and that implication is untrue. Moreover, it purposely links the Negro with the foreigner so that the accumulated hatred against both can be used against each. Does this not smack more of the tactics of the Ku Klux Klan than it does of scholarly research?

Professor Hawk also justifies a lower wage differential for Negroes because of their alleged inefficiency which he takes for granted. Waiving this allegation, one would like to know what reason the author would give for the practice of paying Negro high school teachers in Atlanta and Birmingham fifty per cent of the salary paid to white teachers who are, not infrequently, inferior in training and ability to the colored teachers?

Even in his historical treatment of the Negro, the author reveals his clear bias. Thus, while he cites Jernegan's *Laboring and Dependent Classes in the American Colonies,* he omits entirely that historian's treatment of Negroes who had become so important in industry that white mechanics protested against their employment.

There yet remains to be written a textbook on the economic history of the South whose author will not cater to the fetish of white supremacy. Perhaps by that time, Prentice-Hall will have learned that the spelling of Negro with a small ''n'' indicates either ignorance or prejudice.

RAYFORD W. LOGAN

Atlanta University

Land-Grant Colleges for Negroes. By President John W. Davis, West Virginia State College (Publication of West Virginia State College, Institute, West Virginia, 1934. Pp. 73.)

This is a timely publication of an important chapter in the history of the education of the Negro in the United States, and it is fortunate that it has been produced by an outstanding educator who, during the last fifteen years, has been an important factor in this particular achievement. The most important development in the education of the Negro since the popularization of industrial training by Booker T. Washington is the development of the Land-Grant Colleges. Compared a generation ago with colleges maintained by philanthropists in the South, these institutions made a poor impression with their low curriculum, inadequate equipment, and untrained faculties. The South failed to support those Land-Grant Colleges. As the result of the social upheaval of the World War, which focused the attention of the country upon educational needs, however, both the administrative authorities in the South and the philanthropists supporting schools for Negroes decided that these Land-Grant Colleges should be reorganized and financed as higher institutions of learning. Supported by income from two sources, then, these institutions have easily outstripped during the last twenty years the privately maintained schools which once looked down upon the Land-Grant Colleges as questionable and inefficient. While some of such institutions formerly highly favored have had to close or be merged with others to continue their existence, the Land-Grant Colleges have made rapid strides toward recognition among the stand ardized institutions of the most advanced parts of the country.

President Davis, however, does not restrict his treatment to this particular aspect of such history. His story begins with the historical setting, the Morrill Act of 1862 and its operation as carried out by Congress in cooperation with the states. The author discusses also the period of uncertainty with respect to the status of the Land-Grant Colleges prior to 1890 and brings out the necessity for a second Morrill Act that year. This is further detailed with the action taken by the various state legislatures in pursuance of the provisions of the national measure. The data showing the amounts due under the Morrill Act and the amounts actually received further enlighten the reader in the study of this aspect of education. The author shows, moreover, the changing trends as the result of the need of the Land-Grant Colleges to direct their attention especially to the teaching of agriculture, mechanical arts, home economics, applied science, nursing and extension work for the general uplift of the people. The amounts received to carry out these purposes are also discussed in this monograph. This becomes further enlightening when studied in connection with other data showing the population of the Negroes in the various states, the percentage of Negro teachers and the like in comparison with those of the whites. Special attention is given to the operation of the Smith-Hughes Fund, and instructors and extension workers who have figured in carrying out these special programs of the Land-Grant Colleges have been given honorable mention in this work.

The author does not take the position that the whole problem has been solved. The work is intended to show how well the task at hand has been conceived and to what extent the efforts so far have been an encouragement in the right direction. The present needs, as well set forth on page forty with respect to the status of the high schools of the country from which Land-Grant Colleges must draw, clearly emphasize this particular aspect of the study. The "Addenda" and "Supporting Data" with numerous tables, graphs, and helpful bibliography further enhance the value of this work.

W. G. C.

Disloyalty in the Confederacy. By Georgia Lee Tatum. (Chapel Hill: The University of North Carolina Press. Pp. 176. Price $2.50.)

This compact but informative study is so closely related to other works on desertion, state rights, conscription, and peace movements in the Confederacy that a line of demarcation can scarcely be drawn, and there is unavoidably some overlapping. In the author's definition of terms, "disloyalty" refers to those who actively opposed the Confederate cause, "disaffection" applies to passive opponents, and "unionist" is reserved for those who never favored secession. She finds the origin of disaffection among the "coöperationists" who in 1861 wished to defer secession. That the lukewarm portion of the population was the first to lose its enthusiasm for the war is an obvious fact, but worthy of emphasis. A survey of the areas where disloyalty abounded shows them to be almost entirely coincident with the sectional divisions of the South. In general disloyalty flourished in the hill regions where slaves were few and poor whites and small farmers predominant. On this basis the author travels in her discussion from northwest Arkansas, through Texas, North Mississippi and Alabama, North Georgia, Western North and South Carolina, and East Tennessee.

Along with the negative attitude of disloyalty went a positive reaction, expressed in the formation of peace societies. While the author's survey of peace movements in the Confederacy is by no means exhaustive, yet her handling of it is quite sufficient for her purpose. Although she deals with its civil aspect, her emphasis is on its widespread existence in the army. The "Peace and Constitutional Society" west of the Mississippi, the "Peace Society" in North Alabama and Mississippi, and the "Heroes of America" in North and South Carolina honeycombed Confederate forces, undermining morale, and causing desertion. Conscription was a great contributing factor to disloyalty, for indifference often turned to active hostility only when the Confederate government attempted to force men into its armies.

The author has relied chiefly on the *Official Records of the War of the Rebellion*. Had she used manuscript materials to supplement the chief source, her story might have been made fuller in some respects. Her dependence on secondary materials at various points is somewhat greater than is desirable in a monograph. On the other hand, her failure to list in the bibliography such a closely related and important volume as Ella Lonn's *Desertion During the Civil War* seems at best to be a careless oversight.

Miss Tatum's work suffers from a want of literary style. An unfortunate tendency toward word-repetition, a too frequent use of "the" and "of the," together with unusually long and involved sentences mar the smoothness of the narrative. The index is irritatingly incomplete. These shortcomings do not, however, invalidate the work as a historical study, and the author is to be highly commended for the care, patience, and great amount of labor expended in undertaking a subject so beset with difficulties. The volume makes a useful addition to that growing list of monographs on the internal history of the Confederate States.

RUTH A. KETRING

Duke University Library,
Durham, N. C.

The Discovery and Re-Discovery of America. By T. P. Christensen. (Cedar Rapids, Iowa: Laurence Press Company, 1934. Pp. 133.)

The Discovery and Re-Discovery of America is every thing but what its title indicates. This treatment is inadequate either because of the ignorance or bias of the author. The book deals briefly with Indian discoverers and ancient mariners who are considered fabulous; but it treats in detail the supposed discovery of Eric the Red, the Zeno Brothers, the evidence of the Kensington Rune Stone, the work of John Scolvus and that of John Cabot as a forerunner of Columbus. The author while referring to the visit from "Atlantis" carefully ignores the African claims to the discovery of America. On reading this work one would conclude that the author is intellectually dishonest or that he has never heard of the three volumes produced by Leo Wiener.

Here we again see the shortcoming of the Nordic. He takes himself too seriously. Suppose these adventurers from Northern Europe did touch the shores of America and that Columbus must be denied the honor of being the first European to see land on this side of the Atlantic, that would not dispose of the case. The entire disquisition would not amount to any more than proof that these were the first Europeans to wake up and realize what the world is. Orientals had known America centuries before the Nordics ceased to fly at the throats of their enemies and drink water from their skull bones. Europe was in a state of savagery until the Crusades brought them into contact with the advanced nations of Africa and Asia by which the Nordics were civilized. We know now that Chinese and Japanese had contacts with Africa thousands of years ago and also that they touched America along the Pacific Coast. We know, moreover, that enterprising Africans on their West Coast had contact with America. And it was not merely an accidental visit. Skulls of Negroes found in caves on the Isthmus of Darien, African words taken into the language of the American aborigines, and the parallelism in the religion of these two peoples are far more convincing than any of the arguments for the Nordic claims set forth in this uninforming book.

The reviewer realizes that "discovery" here means to the Nordic the first sighting of this land by one of his own race. From this point of view America had not been discovered until some European stumbled upon it, and even he must now be deprived of that honor to award it to a descendant of a Northern tribe now dominant in the world. When the Nordics first learned, then, about the Western Hemisphere, explored it, conquered it, annihilated its natives, and brought into the new world Africans to exploit it—that was the grand discovery of America.

Other bias like this creeps thus into the entire fabric of so-called history. For example, Coster or Gutenberg is spoken of as the first to invent printing. He was the first of the Europeans to learn this when they were emerging from savagery; but the Chinese had been printing more than a thousand years prior to that time. Likewise pseudo-historians are now trying to find some branch of the Nordic stock that used iron at an early period; and in keeping with the custom of making history to order they will play up such a creation as the discovery of the use of iron. The reason for such industry in this particular case is that leading scientists have learned that Africans had discovered the use of iron when Europeans were in the bush. Europeans ought to become good sports and admit that they have not made civilization. Almost all we know except modern contrivances came from Africa and Asia. About the only thing the Europeans and their American descendants have done is to use these ideas of others to increase their power and dominion, to construct engines of war and destruction by which they have subjugated others standing in their path and by which they are now destroying themselves. This is what they designate as civilization.

C. G. WOODSON

NOTES

The Negro American, a mission investigation, has been distributed by the Catholic church as a study outline in response to many requests from Catholic schools and clubs for a plan of study on the Negro situation. This brochure of sixty-nine pages gives a general background for an appreciation of the difficulties which confront the Negro, the latest statistics of Catholic Negroes, and the work of the Catholic church for them. The pamphlet contains also suggestions for round table discussion, book reviews, and a brief bibliography. Copies of this work may be obtained from *The Colored Harvest,* 1130 North Calvert Street, Baltimore, Maryland, for fifty cents.

The Julius Rosenwald Fund has recently published *Every Tenth Pupil,* a brief sketch of the Negro schools in the South, by E. R. Embree, its director, and along with it *School Money in Black and White.* The latter is a series of maps, graphs, and charts showing the distribution of the wealth per capita of the total population, the income, the cost of the schools, the percentage of income expended for education for each pupil, the amount expended for educating Negro children in comparison with the much larger amount spent for the education of the white. The two together give a clear picture of the present status of Negro education and should be carefully studied by all persons who are interested in the future of this country.

The United States Bureau of the Census of the Department of Commerce has recently published a statistical report of the *Retail Business of the Negro in the United States, 1920-1932.* This is Chapter XVII of a larger report to be entitled *Retail Business.* The data consist of such facts as Negro proprietorship, Negroes in retail business, the scope of their retail trade, the analysis of some of the stores which they conduct, and general information with respect to establishments distributed according to sections throughout the United States. This particular part is the work of Charles E. Hall, a statistician recently promoted in that department to a position of usefulness to which his many years of long and efficient service entitle him. All persons who have made use of statistical reports of the Bureau of the Census during the last twenty-five or thirty years, especially the large work entitled *Negro Population in the United States,* 1790-1915, realize how much the public is indebted to the valuable data which have been computed and made available by Charles E. Hall and his coworkers.

Professor John G. Van Deusen, of Hobart College, Geneva, New York, has published a reprint of his article "Did Republicans 'Colonize' Indiana in 1879?" which appeared in the December issue of the *Indiana Magazine of History.* This discussion is indeed valuable in clearing up a dispute in the history of the Negro with respect to the first significant movement of the black population from the land of tenancy and peonage in the South to a "haven of rest" in the North. When they first started there arose a cry that these Negroes were being transplanted from the South where they could not vote to the North where politicians could use them in electing their candidates in 1880. Professor Van Deusen says in conclusion, however, "There were individual Republicans favoring 'colonization,' who perhaps assisted it to a moderate extent with funds, or encouraged it in other ways, but that the Republican organization, as such, was involved is absurd when one looks at the matter from the point of view of practical politics. One who studies the records of the period may discover the means by which Indiana was sometimes carried. The methods were not always above reproach, but they had the quality of being efficient. 'Colonization' of Negroes in Indiana would have been extravagant in price, the numbers insufficient, the plan unscientific from any point of view and altogether unworthy of the ingenuity of the men who are supposed to have executed it."

In the *Louisiana Historical Quarterly,* Volume XVIII, No. 1, January, 1935, have been published certain "Records of the Superior Council in Louisiana" in which will be found a number of documents throwing light on the Negroes in the early history of that state, especially during the eighteenth century. This particular number should be secured by all persons who are interested in the history of that country under the Latin element, the influence of which is still seen in those parts. The price of this particular issue is $1.00, and the valuable information which this particular one contains is well worth that price. *The Louisi-*

ana Historical Quarterly is located in the Cabildo, New Orleans.

A number of volumes bearing upon the Negro which will doubt-less be reviewed in these columns in the near future have re-cently appeared. Among these one notes Matthew T. Mellon's *Early American Views on Negro Slavery, from the Letters and Papers of the Republic,* brought out by the Meador Publishing Company, Boston, Massachusetts; James Truslow Adams's *America's Tragedy,* published by Charles Scribner's Sons, 1934; George Fort Milton's *Eve of Conflict,* by the Houghton Mifflin Company, 1934; D. S. Freeman's *Robert E. Lee,* by Charles Scribner's Sons, 1934.

It is clear from some of these titles that so many of our writers who style themselves historians are very militant. They are still fighting through the Civil War or grappling with the problems of the Reconstruction. The leaders of the Lost Cause are their heroes. Grant and Lincoln lost the battle for human rights, for the Negroes, now reduced to the low level of serfdom through tenancy and peonage, are regarded as occupying their ideal posi-tion in our social and economic order. Grant has been generally discredited; and if he could return to life and read some of these books about him he might regret that he had lived. Lincoln is beginning to receive his share of attention from those industrially fomenting this animus; and he, too, in all probability will soon be eliminated from the circle of the great. This historical writing reminds one of that characteristic of the decadence of the slavoc-racy which showed evidence of reversion to savagery.

ARTICLES IN AMERICAN MAGAZINES

In American scientific magazines on this side of the Atlantic the Negro has been occasionally mentioned. In the March number of the *American Journal of Sociology* of 1935 three interesting articles appear: "Race Consciousness among the South African Natives," by Professor W. O. Brown, of the University of Cin-cinnati; "Problems arising from Industrialization of Native Life in Central Africa," by Professor Charles W. Coulter, of the University of New Hampshire; "Cultural Participation and the Negro," by Sanford Winston, of the State College, University of North Carolina. To these may be added also three other articles in the March, 1935, number of *Progressive Education*: "Negro Children Study Culture," by Helen Adele Whiting; "Education for a Bi-Racial Community," by Pauline D. Knobbs; "Improving Race Relations through Social Studies," by Ruth Wanger.

The *American Journal of Physical Anthropology* in its first quarterly issue of 1934 has recently carried additional articles on the Negro, such as "Sweat Glands in the Negro and the European," by S. Glaser; "Histological Variability of Human Hair," by Leon Augustus Hausman; "Blood Group Classification," by A. L. Kroeber; "Syntosis between Manubrium and Body of the Sternum in Whites and Negroes," by Mildred Trotter. In the first quarterly issue of 1935 this same magazine carried notes on "Color-blindness among Negroes," by Kenneth B. M. Crooks, of Hampton Institute. Of interest also is "Fatal Poisoning with oil of Chenopodium in a Negro Child with Sickle Cell Anemia," by J. Wolf (*Archives of Pediatrics*, February, 1935). In the October 1934, issue of the *American Anthropologist* appeared "The Alleged Lack of Mental Diseases among Primitive Groups," by Ellen Winston.

RECENT BOOKS ON AFRICA

Among the recent publications of scientific pretension one finds many dealing with Africa. The Hogarth Press has published for W. G. Ballinger an interesting pamphlet entitled *Race and Economics in South Africa*. Through Simon Rivas and Escobar, of Panama, Luis Cincinnati Bollo has brought out *Los Negros en America y Africa*. From Paris has been published *Une Collection* "Cahiers d'art," by Leo Frobenius and Henri Breuil. The League of Coloured Peoples, of London, has published Charles Roden Buxton's brochure entitled *Impressions of Liberia, November, 1934*. In this the author discusses the persons with whom he came into contact, the inside factors in the government, the status of the native population, and the evils of the times.

Some other works in this field are: *Die Nyamwezi, Gesellschaft und Weltbild,* by Wilhelm Blohm (Hamburg, Frederichsen de Gruyter, 1933); Ernst W. Selmer's *Experimentalle Beiträge zur Phonetik* (Oslo, Kommissjon Hos Jacob Dybwad, 1933); R. P.

Trille's *Les Pygmées de l'Afrique Equatoriale* (Bloud, Editeur, Paris, 1933); L. Cipriani's *Le Antiche Rovine e Miniere della Rhodesia* (R. Bemporad, Edit., Florence, 1932); Paul German's *Die Volkerstämme im Nordern von Liberia* (Leipzig, R. Voigtlander, 1933); Reginald I. Lovell's *The Struggle for South Africa: A Study in Economic Imperialism* (New York, The Macmillan Company, 1934).

Other works dealing with various aspects of Africa and the Negro in general are still multiplying. On this list are found: *Language and race problems in South Africa,* by A. A. Barnouw ('S-Gravenhage Martinus Nijhoff, 1934, 89 pages); *Au Coeur du Hoggar mystérieux, Les Touareg tels que je les ai vus,* by E. Steinilder-Oberlin (Paris, P. Roger, 1934, 264 pages); *Man of Africa,* by Samuel Yosia Ntara, translated and arranged from the original Nyanja by T. Cullen Young, with a foreword by Julian Huxley (London, The Religious Tract Society, 1934); *Western Civilization and the natives of South Africa* (London, Routledge, 1934, XIV-312 pages); *Les martyrs africans,* by Louis Bertrand (Marseille, Edition Publiroc, 1933, 303 pages); *Niger: the life of Mungo Park,* by Lewis Grassic Gibbon (Edinburgh, The Porpoise Press; London, Faber and Faber, 1934, 308 pages); *L'Émir felon, Samory, roi du Soudan,* by Felix Leonnec (Paris, Tallandier, 1933, 124 pages); *L'hallucinante Afrique française,* by Pierre Weiss (Paris, L. Querelle, 214 pages); *L'enfer des Noirs; cannibalisme et fétichisme dans la brousse,* by J. Perrigault (Paris, Nouvelle librairie française, 1932, 220 pages); *Tanganyika without Prejudice: a Balanced Critical Review of the Territory and her Peoples,* by Eric Reid (London, "East Africa," 1934, x-240 pages); *Südwestafrika und sein Aussenhandel,* by Haro Brenner (Berlin, *Emil Ebering,* 1934, 87 pages).*

MAGAZINE ARTICLES ON AFRICA

Treating Africa from a general point of view are many articles in various periodicals. Among the most important of these are designated the following: "La relation du climat à la morpholo-

---

* Those who are interested in the scientific study of Africa will find very helpful the "Bibliographie Africaniste" by P. Lester in the *Journal de la Société des Africanistes,* tome iv, fascicule ii, pages 326-393.

gie nasale" by George Montandon (*Revue anthropologique*, Paris, XLIV, 5-17); "A Biometrician's View of Race in Man," by G. M. Morant (*Man*, London, XXXIV, 99-105); "Les races humaines," by Eugene Pittard in *L'evolution humaine des origines à nos jours* (*Quillet*, Paris, 1934, p. 231-280); "Les caracteristiques biologiques humaines," by Etienne Rebaud in *L'evolution humaine des origines à nos jours* (*Quillet*, Paris, 1934, p. 3-19); "Races blanches et races noires" (*La Terre et la Vie*, Paris, IV, 59-60); "La pensée primitive," by G. H. Loquet in *L'evolution humaine des origines à nos jours* (*Quillet*, Paris, I, 323-354); "The adaptation of intelligence tests to tropical Africa," by R. A. C. Oliver (*Oversea Education*, IV, 186-192); "Observations on the Dramatic Talent of Africans," by W. H. Taylor (*Oversea Education*, IV, 17-20); "Some Observations on Capt. R. S. Rattray's Paper, 'Present Tendencies of African Colonial Government,'" by Richmond Palmer (*Journal of the African Society*, London, XXXIII, 37-48); "La protection de l'enfance en Afrique tropicale," by Marquise de Noailles (*Le Monde colonial illustre*, Paris, 12th Year, No. 130, June 1934, pp. 91-92); "Missionary Work and Race Education in Africa," by Julius Richter (*International Review of Missions*, London, XVIII, 74-82); "The Position of Woman in Primitive Culture," by J. M. Cooper (*Primitive Man*, Washington, V, 32-47); "L'espece, la race, et le métissage en anthropologie," by H. Neuville (*Archives de Paléontologie Humaine, Memoir II*, 516 pages, Paris, 1933); "The African Standpoint," by Bruno Gutmann (*Africa*, January 1935); "Native Life in Johannesburg Slum Yard," by Ellen Hellman (*Africa*, January 1935).

The following bear chiefly upon North Africa: "Les arts decoratifs indigènes en Algerie," by Madame Bel (*Outre-Mer*, Paris, VI, 68-91); "Historic problems of the Libyan Desert," by Richard A. Bermann (*The Geographical Journal*, London, LXXXIII, 456-470); "Relazione della missione nel deserto della Cirenaica del prof. di Caporiacco," by Lodovico di Caporiacco (*Bollettino della reale Societe geografica italiana*, Rome, 6th series, XI, 127-129).

The following deal mainly with Northeast Africa: "Prehistoric Art in the Libyan Desert" (*Nature*, CXXXIII, No. 3349, January 6, 1934, p. 20); "Social Character of Bride-wealth, with

Special Reference to the Azande,'' by E. E. Evans-Pritchard (*Man,* London, XXXIV, 172-175); ''Survivals of the Throwing-knife in Darfur,'' by D. Olderogge (*Man,* London, XXXIV, 106-107); ''Village Handicrafts in the Sudan,'' by Powell-Cotton (*Man,* London, XXXIV, 90-91).

These, a still larger number, refer especially to West Africa: ''Contribution à l'étude anthropologique des Serères, documents recueillis par Ernest Chantre, by ''Eugene Pittard (*Archives suisses d'anthropologie générale,* Geneva, VI, 184-187); ''Versuch einer Neuartigen Typenanalyse an Westafrikanischen Negern. II,'' by Robert Routil (*Anthropologischer Anzeiger,* Stuttgart X, 51-73); ''Occurrence of 'Cleavers' of Lower Paleolithic Type in Northern Nigeria,'' by H. Balfour (*Man,* London XXXIV, 21-24); ''Northern Nigeria: Cleavers of Lower Paleolithic Type,'' by E. J. Wayland (*Man,* London XXXIV, 64); Collections africaines du departement de préhistoire exotique du Musée d'ethnographie du Trocadero, I, Harpons, ''Objects en os travaillés, et silex taillés de Taferjit et Tamaya Mellet (Sahara nigérien),'' by Harper Kelley (*Journal de la Société des Africanistes,* Paris IV, 135-143); ''Les témoines d'une civilisation ancienne dans le cercle de Tahoua'' by Y (*Bulletin du Comité d'études historiques et scientifiques de l'Afrique occidentale française,* Paris, XVI, 299-318); ''Documents pour l'ethnographie de la Côte d'Ivoire, Poids pour peser la poudre d'or Collections du Musée d'ethnographie de Genève, by Marguerite Dellenbach (*Archives suisses d'anthropologie générale,* Genève, VII, 58-72); ''The Conditions of Arts and Crafts in West-Africa,'' by K. C. Murray (*Oversea Education,* London, IV, 173-180; V, 1-8); ''Brief Notes on Pottery at Abuja and Kuta, Niger Province,'' by W. E. Nicholson (*Man,* London XXXIV, 70-71); ''Baked Clay Heads from Graves near Fomena, Ashanti,'' by R. P. Wild (*Man,* London, XXXIV, 1-4); ''Poésie du Bas-Dahomey,'' by Daniel Marquis-Sebie (*Les Annales coloniales,* Paris, 35th Year, No. 45, March, 1934, p. 14-15); ''Gabi Figures and Edegi, First King of the Nupe,'' (*Man,* London, XXXIV, 169-172); ''Sierra Leone in the Making,'' by F. Shelford (*Journal of the African Society,* London, XXVIII, 235-240); ''Comment j'ai vu la Guinée française,'' by Emile Taudière (*Le Monde colonial illustre,* Paris, 12th Year, No. 127, March 1934, p. 39); ''A Linguistic Tour in Southern Nigeria, Certain Problems Restated," by Ida C. Ward (*Africa,* January 1935); "L'Education des Masses en Afrique occidentale française," by H. Labouret (*Africa,* January 1935); Os Antigos Habitantes das Canarias, by E. Tamagnini (*Revista da Facultad de Ciencias da Universidade de Coimbra,* 1932); "Was sind Hamitensprachen?" by Werner Vycichl (*Africa,* January 1935).

Of Equatorial Africa the treatment in the scientific publications is as extensive as in the case of other parts of the continent. The most striking of those noticed are: "Etude comparée de crânes Kirdi et Moundan du Haut-Cameroun," by P. Royer and E. M. Buisson (*Journal de la Société des Africanistes,* Paris, IV, 129-133); "La préhistoire en pays Kirdi," by E. M. Buisson (*Togo-Cameroun,* Paris, April 1934, 115-116); "Notes de folklore lari," by R. P. Bonnefond and Jean Lombard (*Journal de la Société des Africanistes,* Paris, IV, 81-109); "Moundang," by E. M. Buisson (*Togo-Cameroun,* Paris, April 1934, 87-90); "Généralités sur les groupements Kirdi du Nord de Garoua," by the same author (*Togo-Cameroun,* Paris, April 1934, 92-97); "De la signification de certains tatouages en relief chez quelques tribus nègres du Cameroun," by the same author (*Revue anthropologique,* Paris, XLIV, 1934, 81-83); "Funèrailles d'un chef de village Kirdi," by the same author (*Togo-Cameroun,* Paris, April 1934, 111-113); "Le sel chez les Kirdi," by the same author (*Togo-Cameroun,* Paris, April 1934, 114); "Legende de Tinguelin," by the same author (*Togo-Cameroun,* Paris, April 1934, 117); "Les rapports des Noirs avec la nature," by Auguste Chevalier (*Journal de la Société des Africanistes,* Paris, IV, 123-127); "Esploratori italiani nell'Africa centrale," by Lidio Cipriania (*Le Vie d'Italia e del Mondo,* Milan, II, 970-990); "Les sociétés d'initiés en pays Banda," by Felix Eboué (*Afrique Equatoriale Française,* Paris, 10th Year, Number 34, January-April 1934, 19-21); "La fonte de la monnaie (croisettes) chez les Baluba du territoire de Musonoi (Haut-Katanga Ouest)," by Grégoire Gutzeit (*Archives suisses d'anthropologie générale,* Geneva, VIII, 73-81); "Rites de circoncision namchi," by Michel Leiris (*Journal de la Société des Africanistes,* Paris, IV, 63-79); "Le mariage indigène au Cameroun" (*Outre-Mer,* Paris, VI, 106-107); "Kotoko," by Lieurade (*Togo-Cameroun,* Paris, January

1934, 11-26) ; "Politique en pays Kirdi," by Jean Rezac (*Togo-Cameroun*, Paris, April 1934, 118-123) ; "Pêche chez les Kotoko," by Robin (*Togo-Cameroun*, Paris, January 1934, 27-29) ; "Sur les musiques du Haut Cameroun," by Leon Salasc (*Togo-Cameroun*, Paris, January 1934, 34-35) ; "Wanderungen de Neger am Ituri und ihre Verteilung," by Paul Schebesta (*Mitteilungen der anthropologischen Gesellschaft in Wien*, Vienna, LXIV, 1934, Sitzungsberichte, 12, 15) ; "Voyage au Gabon, 1864-1869," by Griffon du Bellay (*Afrique Equatoriale Française*, Paris, 10th Year, Number 34, January-April 1934, 12-13) ; "Un progetto di colonizzazione del Congo presentato a Vittorio Amedeo III di Savoia," by Carmelo Trasselli (*Rivista delle colonie italiane*, Bologne, VIII, 31-38) ; "Retour du Cameroun," by the same author (*Le Monde colonial illustre*, Paris 12th Year, Number 129, 77) ; "Les Chefs Indigènes au Mayombe, Hier, Aujourdhui, Demain," by N. de Cleene (*Africa*, January 1935) ; "Contribution a l'étude anthropologique du noir en Afrique Equatoriale Française," by Leon Pales (*L'Anthropologie*, XLIV, 45-76).

In still other articles there is much thought given to South Africa as in the following: "Recherches sur la grandeur du sphénoide et de la région temporale chez les Boschimans, les Hottentots et les Griquas," by Eugene Pittard and Marthe Aziz (*Archives suisses d'anthropologie générale*, Geneva, VII, 31-57) ; "Le sillon temporo-pariétal externe et le sillon sus-orbitaire chez les Boschimans, Hottentots et Griquas," by Eugene Pittard and J. J. Breitenbücher (*Archives suisses d'anthropologie générale*, Geneva, VI, 87-100) ; "Las misteriosas de la Rhodesia," by Lidio Cipriani (*Revista geografica americana*, Buenos Aires, I, 417-426) ; "La familia, la habitacion y la propriedad entre los Zulu, by the same author (*Revista geografica americana*, Buenos Aires, I, Number 7, April 1934, 517-540) ; "The Ovimbundu of Angola," by Wilfrid D. Hambly, Field Museum of Natural History, Chicago (*Anthropological Series*, Publication 329, XXI, 193-362) ; "Tridents, North Rhodesia," by D. Gordon Lancaster (*Man*, London, XXXIV, 184) ; "Midzimu Worship in a Village of the Wa-Barwe Tribe," by D. Shropshire (*Man*, London, XXXIV, 65-67) ; "The Wa-Sokile," by T. Cullen Young (*Man*, London, XXXIV, 32) ; *Beliefs and customs of the Xam Bushmen*, by D. F. Bleek, from material collected by Dr. W. H. I. Bleek and Miss L. C. Lloyd between 1870 and 1880, edited as Bantu Studies, Johannesburg, 297-312, 375-392; "La population indigène dans les villes du Sud-africain" (*Bulletin des Missions*, Lophem-lez-Bruges, XIII, Nos. 1-2, March-June 1934, 73); "Contribution a l'étude anthropologique au femur de Boschimans," by S. Gruntzesco (Thèse de science, Geneva, 1933); "Contribution à l'étude des dimensions et des formes de l'os unguis chez les Boschimans, Hottentots et Griquas." by E. Pittard (*Archives suisses de l'Anthropologie générale*, VI, 87-100); "Les dimension de lame horizontale du palatin chez les Boschimans, Hottentots et Griquas," by the same author (*Revue Anthropologique*, LXIII, 15).

With special bearing on East Africa others have made contributions. The most interesting and suggestive of these are: "The Brain of the Kenya Native," by F. W. Wint (*Journal of anatomy*, London, LXVIII, 216-222); "Vestigia di antiche civiltà in Eritrea e in Somalia," by E. Cerulli (*Rassegna italiana*, Rome, 1934, Special Number, 152-156); Description de la cérémonie dite Mohà (Côte française des Somalis)," by Maurice Bernard (*Journal de la Société des Africanistes*, Paris, IV, 33-34); "I 'tungi' della Somalia italiana," by Carlo Costa (*Le Vie d'Italia*, Milan, XL, 199-206); "Degeneration of a Wind Instrument," by G. M. Culwick (*Man*, London, XXXIV, 112); "Treatment of Fits by the Wambunga," by A. T. and G. M. Culwick (*Man*, London, XXXVI, 136); "Tribal Heirlooms among the Wabena of the Ulanga Valley," by the same authors (*Man*, London, XXXIV, 167); "Some Aspects of the Kimwani Fishing Culture, with Comparative Notes on Alien Methods, (Lake Victoria Nyanza, Tanganyika Territory)," by H. A. Fosbrooke (*Journal of the Royal Anthropological Institute of Great Britain and Ireland*, London, LXIV, 1-22); "Notes sur l'arithmomancie éthiopienne," by Marcel Griaule (*Journal de la Société des Africanistes*, Paris, IV, 25-31); "Un camp militaire abyssin," by the same author (*Journal of de la Société des Africanistes*, Paris, IV, 117-122); "Name-giving among the Wa-Sokile," by T. C. Hodson (*Man*, London, XXXIV, 16); "The Significance of Bride-price, with Special Reference to the Nandi," by G. W. B. Huntingford (*The Journal of the East Africa and Ugande Natural History Society*, Nairobi, Nos. 45-46, April-July 1932, 51-55); "Some Aspects of the Kikuyu Tribe," by L. S. B. Leakey (*Man*, London, XXXIV, 59); "Mental Tests of the African" (*Nature*, London, CXXXIII, No. 3355, February 17, 1934, 261); "The Hehe-Bena-Sangu Peoples of East Africa," by W. Bryant Mumford (*American Anthropologist*, Menasha, U. S. A., New Series, XXXVI, 202-222); "The Galla of East-Africa," by Arthur E. Robinson (*American Anthropologist*, Menasha, U. S. A., New Series, XXXVI, 313-314); "Le Musa ensete en Ethiopie," by de Scey-Montbéliard de Brun (*La Terre et la Vie*, Paris, IV, 21-28); "African Tribal Titles in 'The African People in the Twentieth Century,'" by A. Werner (*Man*, London, XXXIV, 80 pages); "East African Lacustrine Tribes: a Study in Adaptation," by E. B. Worthington (*Man*, London, XXXIV, 60 pages); "Les tone en Lonkundo (Congo belge)" by R. P. G., Hulstaert (*Anthropos*, St. Gabriel Mödling, XXIX, 75-97); "Les néologismes dans les idiomes gabonais," by A. Walker (*Journal de la Société des Africanistes*, Paris, III, 305-314); "La battaglia di Adua in alcune lettere del générale Lamberti," by Gian Lamberto Lamberti (*Rivista delle colonie italiane*, Bologna, VIII, 93-204); "Up Kenya in the rains," by James P. Chapin (*Natural History*, New York, XXXIII, 596-606; XXXIV, 83-94); "Climatology in Rhodesia and East Africa" (*Nature*, London, CXXXIII, No. 3352, January 27, 1934, 144); "C. M. L'Africa orientale italiana" (*Rivista delle colonie italiane*, Bologna, VIII, 50-55); "The Physiography of Uganda, the Evolution of the Great Lakes and the Victoria Nile Drainage System," by A. W. Groves (*Journal of the African Society*, London, XXXIII, 59-69); "Notes Ethnographiques sur les Kavirondo Septentrional et la colonie du Kenya," by G. Lindblom (*Revista del Instituo de Etnologia de Tucuman*, II, 395-440).

PERSONAL

CHARLES SUMNER WORMLEY

Dr. Charles Sumner Wormley, a life member of the Association, died on Monday, January 21, 1935, at his home in Washington, D. C. He was a son of G. Smith Wormley and Amelia Brent Wormley, a brother of Dr. James A. Wormley, deceased, of Newark, N. J., and a grandson of James Wormley, Senior, of the same city. The deceased was born in Washington, D. C., September 6, 1872. He was educated in the public schools of this city, and was graduated from the local high school of that day. After special preparation he entered the dental department of Howard University from which he was graduated with the degree of Doctor of Dental Surgery. While a student he had the honor of being awarded one of the coveted prizes offered by the Dental School. He entered upon his profession in this city and became one of the outstanding practitioners of Washington.

Dr. Wormley had many attainments among which were those in vocal music. He at one time collaborated with Roland Hayes in the Columbian Records; and Dr. Wormley's voice, a rich baritone, was heard on many occasions in concert halls, and at almost all the churches of his race in the city on festive occasions as well as at the rites of many church members and his friends. This service endeared him to thousands.

He was noted for his generosity and his geniality—the idol of his wide acquaintance not only in Washington but in the country at large. The most outstanding characteristic of Dr. Wormley beyond and above all was his unselfish devotion to his family to which he sacrificed his life that they too may spread sunshine to their less fortunate brothers. He was truly a Good Samaritan. He never married, but he maintained a home in which numbers of his relatives found refuge when overtaken by misfortune and old age.

Dr. Wormley's numerous social connections show his interest in all classes of people. He was a 33rd degree mason, and a member of a number of societies or organizations among which he counted the Benevolent Protective Order of Elks, the Young Men's Protective League, the Oldest Inhabitants, the Crispus Attucks Association, the Banneker Relief Association, the Musolit Club, and the Epsilon chapter of the Boule. For sometime he served as a member of the Board of Trustees of Howard University.

Evidently Dr. Wormley maintained the traditions of one of the most noted families developed in the United States. He certainly showed himself worthy of being named for Charles Sumner, the distinguished advocate of the rights of the Negro during those stormy days when he became closely attached to the grandfather of the deceased, James Wormley. Dr. Wormley's passing recalls the following which was said about his grandfather in the *Washington Star* fifty-one years ago and reprinted in that daily October 21, 1934:

"Mr. James Wormley, the well known hotel proprietor, died in Boston Saturday. The remains arrived here yesterday afternoon, accompanied by the members of the family, who were present at the death bed. The body was taken to Wormley's Hotel, corner of Fifteenth and H Streets, and placed in a room called the 'Sumner parlor' on account of the fact that the furniture in the room was purchased by Mr. Wormley from the residence of Senator Sumner after the latter's death. The esteem in which the deceased was held was manifested by the large number of prominent persons who called at the hotel yesterday to express their sympathy with the family. The flags on the hotels of the city yesterday were suspended at half mast in respect to the memory of the deceased. Arrangements have been made for holding the funeral at two o'clock tomorrow afternoon from the hotel.

"Mr. Wormley was one of the most remarkable colored men in the country and had a national reputation as a caterer. He was born in this city 64 years ago and began business as a driver of a hack; subsequently he served as steward on various naval vessels. Returning home, he was employed as steward of the Metropolitan Club. A little before the war he secured a house on I street near Fifteenth and went into business for himself. Among his patrons were many of the most prominent public men of the day. He accompanied Reverdy Johnson to England when Mr. Johnson went as Minister to the Court of St. James, and his skill as a caterer is said to have largely contributed to Mr. Johnson's diplomatic success. Mr. Wormley opened a hotel at the corner of Fifteenth and H streets, which bears his name, in 1871. The list of guests entertained there include many of the most eminent men of the day in every walk of life. The parlors of Wormley's have been the scene of many distinguished gatherings. His strict business integrity won for Mr. Wormley the confidence and friendship of the wealthy and influential citizens of Washington.

"The pallbearers will be as follows: Active—John F. Cook, John T. Given, Isaac Landis, M. W. Galt, James G. Berret, Hon. B. K. Bruce, Henry Birch and R. H. Gleaves. Honorary—T. E. Roessle, C. W.

Spofford, C. C. Willard, O. Y. Staples, Franklin Tinney, Theophile Felter, George S. Kraff and William Henry Smith. The following clergymen will officiate: Rev. William Waring, Berean Baptist Church; Rev. Byron Sunderland, Four-and-a-half Street Presbyterian Church, and Rev. Frank Grimké, Fifteenth Street Presbyterian Church."

In the editorial columns of *The Star* of October 25, 1884, the following appeared:

" 'Mr. Wormley's funeral was attended by two sets of pallbearers—one active and the other honorary. The first was colored and the last white. What folly at the grave.—*New York Graphic.*'

"This is an absurd and mischievous misstatement. There was no color line observable on the occasion referred to, the active pallbearers included both colored and white citizens of prominence, among the latter being the Chief Justice of the United States District Court, a mayor of the city at the beginning of the war, and leading business men, while the list of 'honoraries' was made up mostly of men in Mr. Wormley's occupation including also one or two of his own color. Both the esteem in which Mr. Wormley was held and the liberal and catholic spirit prevailing in Washington was shown by the fact that his funeral was attended by an imposing concourse of people, largely made up of men prominent in public and private life and their wives, including many gentlemen now or formerly occupying high positions in the civil, military and naval services of both the United States and the late Southern Confederacy."

This grandfather, James Wormley, had four children, William H. A., James Thompson, Garret Smith, and Anna M. Cole, all of whom are now dead. His second son, James Thompson, was the first graduate of the school of Pharmacy at Howard University, and it is so recorded on a bronze tablet in the new Medical School. Dr. Charles Sumner Wormley was the son of G. Smith Wormley and Amelia Brent Wormley. Of this family the oldest was James Augusta Wormley, deceased, who for many years was a successful physician with a large practice in Newark, New Jersey, among both colored and white citizens. Another brother, Dr. Roscoe C. Wormley, has been practicing dentistry for many years in Plainfield in the same State. His two sisters, Mrs. Edith Minton and Mrs. Alice Francis, were formerly teachers in the Washington Public Schools. His youngest brother, Leon S., is the pastor of a suburban church. G. Smith Wormley, the other brother, is the principal of the Randall Junior High School, of Washington, D. C. G. Smith Wormley's son, Dr. Lowell C. Wormley, is a successful practicing physician in New York City and assistant visiting surgeon of the Harlem Hospital.

MARTHA BAILEY BRIGGS

Miner Teachers College in dedicating its recent Founders Day exercises to the commemoration of the life and achievements of Martha Bailey Briggs, the third principal of the Miner Normal School, has happily restored the fast-fading likeness of a noble ancestor, and resuscitated the personality of an educational figure of the last century. Born March 31, 1838, in the Quaker environment of New Bedford, Massachusetts, of free parents, John Briggs and Fannie Bassett Briggs, of Martha's Vineyard, Massachusetts, at whose home the fugitive Frederick Douglas found refuge and through this family secured his first independent work, the daughter, Martha, in her early years absorbed in full measure a love of liberty, a penchant for simplicity, and a compassion for the forgotten ones of this world.

Miss Briggs' formal schooling included attendance at a private institution and at the public schools of her native town, culminating in her graduation in September 1850, in her twelfth year, as an honor student and the first Negro product of the New Bedford High School. In the remark of her god-child that to Miss Briggs "A child was never in the way," we have the key to the marvelous career of this pioneer teacher. From her childhood days Miss Briggs threw open the door of her heart to little children, so that an ever-recurring scene in her life is that of the tender mother, brooding over her circle of young children, "Even as a hen gathereth her chickens under her wings."

Most naturally then, did Miss Briggs assume the rôle of a teacher. Her first school was started in her father's home, but later she opened a private school, extending her classes into the night to serve the urgent needs of those pitiable ones of whom Wendell Phillips spoke as having only just graduated from the "southern institution." Later she taught in a school in Christiantown, Martha's Vineyard, in a private school, in the public schools of Newport, Rhode Island, and then, with two assistants, in a private school in a house loaned by Mr. George T. Downing in Newport. Significant it was that at this time, in 1859, Miss Briggs was summoned by Miss Myrtilla Miner to teach in her school in Washington, an invitation she then declined; and strangely guided again, it seems, were her steps to a new teaching experience in a school in Eastern Maryland, in what we might call the "Frederick Douglass Country." There she taught from 1867 to 1869.

On September 1, 1869, she was called to Washington, as the principal of the Anthony Bowen School, where she remained until 1873. In all of these school experiences Miss Briggs manifested rare power as a teacher, in the use of her background, in the maintenance of discipline, in the handling of the lesson, and in the inspiration of her personality. The crescent of eager young people pressing closely about her desk at the noon hour was a daily indication of the winning humanity of this benignant teacher.

With this antecedent rootage in educational experience Miss Briggs normally evolved into a teacher of teachers. Her career in teacher training began as principal of the Normal Department of Howard University in 1873, a department she virtually created during the years 1873 to 1879. At the latter date she was called to the principalship of the Miner Normal School, which she also served in this constructive capacity until 1883, when she returned to Howard. The Normal Department she continued to develop and dignify up to her untimely death on March 28, 1889. In view of her identification with the beginnings of this teacher training, Miss Briggs may not be unjustly regarded as a founder of both the Teachers College of Howard University and Miner Teachers College, and by this token a pioneer in teacher training in this country.

In her classroom she was an influential example. Clad in soft black silk, her matronly figure moved with dignity to her desk, at which she sat in simple poise, and with quiet hands folded before her, she related herself like a gracious queen to her respectful students. And so it was outside of the classroom. Her conviction, that education must touch the total life of the pupil and teacher, was given striking reality in her own home, where she lived surrounded by a group of promising young teachers, who with such mental and spiritual fortification went forth to teach with distinction in the schools of the community. These are but a few of the multitude of young men and women whose plastic youth her molding touch has shaped into characters of intellectual and social power.

In this work of teacher training Miss Briggs displayed superior fitness. Her love of children, which gave her an understanding of them, her supplementary studies in psychology and the history of education, her wide range of marginal knowledge, and her versatile adjustability to human contacts—all contributed to this signal mastery in the field of teacher training. In estimating the contribution of Martha B. Briggs to the educational life of her time, we might cite her own sheer example of the educability of Negro youth, her prophetic work in the field of teacher training, in that half a century ago she advocated a more careful selection of material for teacher training, and in that she so early laid unmistakable emphasis on culture and character in her students and teachers.

J. FRANCIS GREGORY

THE JOURNAL

OF

NEGRO HISTORY

Vol. XX—July, 1935—No. 3

THE TREATMENT OF COLORED UNION TROOPS
BY THE CONFEDERATES, 1861-1865

A question that arose during the second year of the American Civil War and became of increasing importance to both Union and Confederate authorities as the war progressed was whether colored Union troops when captured by the Confederates should be treated as prisoners of war or as slaves in insurrection. During the first year and a half of the war this was not a problem for, in spite of agitation for the enlistment of Negroes and several offers to raise Negro regiments, the Federal government declined to employ the colored man as a soldier. He was used as a laborer in connection with military camps and operations, but he was not permitted to bear arms.[1]

As the war progressed, however, a gradual change in the Federal policy took place. In the spring of 1862 General Hunter, though without clear authorization from the war department, began the enlistment of Negroes in South Carolina; a few months later Congress passed two acts authorizing the use of Negroes for any military or naval service for which they might be found competent;[2] and by the end of the year General Benjamin F. Butler had

---

[1] Shannon, Fred A., "The Federal Government and the Negro Soldier, 1861-1865," *Journal of Negro History*, xi (October 1926), 563-567.

[2] *Ibid.*, 572-575; Report of Provost Marshal J. B. Fry, March 17, 1866, *Official Records of the Union and Confederate Armies in the War of the Rebellion*, ser. iii, vol. v, 654-660.

raised a regiment, chiefly from the free black population of Louisiana, for his Corps d'Afrique, and in South Carolina General Saxton had organized a regiment composed of men who had been slaves until the arrival of the Federal troops.[3] Colored regiments were raised not only in the Southern regions as they fell under Union control, but also in the North. President Lincoln, who came to regard the aid of Negro troops as indispensable, encouraged their enlistment, and by the end of the war more than 186,000 Negroes had enlisted in the service of the United States.[4]

Although free Negroes had been serving in the militia of Southern States from the outset of the war,[5] the use of colored troops by the Federal government was bitterly denounced in the South and wild threats of retaliation were hurled at the black troops and their officers. The Confederate war department proclaimed General Hunter an outlaw and announced that if he "or any other commissioned officer employed in drilling, organizing, or instructing slaves, with a view to their armed service in this war" shall be captured, "he shall not be regarded as a prisoner of war, but held in close confinement for execution as a felon at such time and place as the President shall order."[6] Bills and resolutions calling for the severe punishment of persons of African descent found in the ranks of the enemy were introduced into the Confederate

[3] Fox, William F., *Regimental Losses in the American Civil War, 1861-1865* (Albany, 1889), 52-53. This South Carolina regiment was known at the outset as the First South Carolina but later as the Thirty-third United States Colored Infantry.

[4] *Official Records*, ser. iii, vol. v, 661-662.

[5] Order of M. Grivot, Adjutant and Inspector General of the Louisiana Militia, March 24, 1862, *ibid.*, ser. iv, vol. i, 1020; Act of the Tennessee Legislature, June 28, 1861, *ibid.*, 409; Wesley, Charles H., "The Employment of Negroes as Soldiers in the Confederate Army," *Journal of Negro History*, iv (July 1919), 243.

[6] General Orders No. 60, War Department, Adjutant and Inspector General's Office, Richmond, August 21, 1862, *Official Records*, ser. i, vol. xiv, 599.

congress.[7] Before long Northern newspapers were printing stories of the murder or sale into slavery of colored
soldiers who fell into the hands of the Confederates.[8]

The aim of this paper is to examine first the official
policy of the Confederate government as declared in proclamations of the President, acts of the congress, the correspondence of the executive departments with state and
military authorities, and in the correspondence of Union
and Confederate officers charged with the exchange of
prisoners of war, and secondly to consider certain Northern charges of cruel and barbarous treatment.

The first declaration of a policy on this subject is to
be found in an act of the Confederate congress of October
13, 1862, which provided that the secretary of war should
designate depots to which all slaves captured from the
enemy or otherwise than by lawful authority should be
delivered. When proof of ownership was presented these
recaptured slaves were to be returned to their masters.[9]
It was not clearly stated whether this law was to apply
only to non-combatant slaves or to Negro soldiers as well.
In 1864 Secretary of War Seddon disagreed with his assistant secretary who claimed that the act applied only
to non-combatant slaves, and in spite of more recent legislation by congress definitely providing for the disposition
of captured Negro troops, he applied this early act to
them.[10] But in the weeks immediately following the passage of this act Secretary Seddon and President Davis
either interpreted it as not applicable to slaves taken in

[7] *Journal of the Congress of the Confederate States of America, 1861-
1865* (Washington, 1904), v, 296, 329, 348, 543-547.

[8] Colonel Percy Howard, *The Barbarities of the Rebels* (Providence,
1863), *passim.*

[9] *Statutes at Large of the Confederate States of America* (Richmond,
1862), 89-90.

[10] Major Is. H. Carrington to Secretary Seddon, August 11, 1864, and
indorsement of Assistant Secretary Campbell, August 21, 1864, *Official
Records*, ser. ii, vol. vii, 583; Secretary Seddon to Governor M. L. Bonham,
August 31, 1864, *ibid.*, 703-704.

arms or they deliberately chose to ignore it. In the middle of November, General Mercer, commanding the District of Georgia, reported the capture of four Negroes wearing Federal uniforms and carrying muskets in their hands, and added:

If I may be permitted to express an opinion upon this subject I most earnestly request that these negroes be made an example of. They are slaves taken with arms in hand against their masters and wearing the abolition uniform. Some swift and terrible punishment should be inflicted that their fellows may be deterred from following their example.[11]

This report was referred to Secretary Seddon who, after conference with President Davis, wrote General Beauregard, Mercer's superior officer:

Slaves in flagrant rebellion are subject to death by the laws of every slave-holding State, and did circumstances admit without too great delays and military inconvenience might be handed over to the civil tribunals for condemnation. They cannot be recognized in any way as soldiers subject to the rules of war and to trial by military courts; yet for example and to repress any spirit of insubordination it is deemed essential that slaves in armed insurrection should meet condign punishment. Summary execution must therefore be inflicted on those taken, as with the slaves referred to by General Mercer, under circumstances indicative beyond doubt of actual rebellion. To guard, however, against the possible abuse of this grave power under the immediate excitement of capture or through over-zeal on the part of subordinate officers it is deemed judicious that the discretion of deciding and giving the order of execution should be reposed in the general commanding the special locality of the capture.

You will therefore instruct Brigadier-General Mercer to exercise this discretion of decision and summary execution in the case of the slaves referred to by him and any others hereafter captured under like circumstances.[12]

Three weeks after these instructions were sent, President Davis issued a proclamation, dated December 23, 1862, ordering that "all negro slaves captured in arms

[11] Brigadier-General H. W. Mercer to Brigadier-General Jordan, November 14, 1862, *ibid.*, vol. iv, 945-946.

[12] Secretary Seddon to General G. T. Beauregard, November 30, 1862, *ibid.*, 954.

be at once delivered over to the executive authorities of the respective States to which they belong to be dealt with according to the laws of said State.''[13] In the spring of the following year the Confederate congress considered various bills to deprive captured Negro soldiers of the rights and immunities of prisoners of war and finally adopted a joint resolution declaring that all Negroes, free as well as slave, taken in arms should be delivered to the authorities of the State or States in which they should be captured "to be dealt with according to the present or future law of such State or States.''[14] The only subsequent legislation on this subject was the repeal in February, 1865, of the specific provisions of this joint resolution, making it for the closing weeks of the war merely a general resolution of retaliation at the discretion of the President.[15]

Thus, if the law of October, 1862, applied to slaves taken in arms, there were three conflicting provisions for the disposition of such captives—one, that they should be sent to designated depots from which they would be returned to their masters; two, that they should be turned over to the authorities of the State to which they belonged; three, that they should be turned over to the authorities of the State in which they were captured. The latter two further provided that the captives should then be dealt with according to the laws of the State—which meant that as slaves in insurrection they were subject to the death penalty. The only provision affecting *free* Negroes taken in arms was that in the joint resolution of

[13]Richardson, J. D., *Messages and Papers of the Confederacy* (Nashville, 1906), i, 274.

[14]*Statutes at Large of the Confederate States of America* (Richmond, 1863), 167-168; *Journal of the Congress of the Confederate States*, iii, 203, 319, 333, 361, 386; vi, 486-488.

[15]*Ibid.*, iv, 501, 503, 507, 510, 520, 545; *Official Records*, ser. ii, vol. viii, 197.

congress that they should be turned over to the authorities of the State in which they were captured.

In view of these conflicting provisions it is not surprising that the execution of the laws was not free from confusion and vacillation. When in the summer of 1863 General Beauregard's forces captured fourteen Negro soldiers, some of whom claimed to be free, he sought instructions from the war department as to their disposition.[16] Secretary Seddon informed him that the joint resolutions of the last congress controlled the disposition of all Negroes taken in arms and that those in question should be turned over to the authorities of South Carolina, the State in which they were captured.[17] When these captives had been delivered to the South Carolina authorities Governor Bonham turned to Secretary Seddon for instructions concerning the free Negroes from the Northern States[18] and was informed that they should not be treated as regular prisoners of war. He was further advised that they should be promptly executed or held to hard labor during the war.[19] But the Confederate authorities did not continue to follow the terms of the joint resolution. In April, 1864, Governor Vance of North Carolina was instructed that the Negroes captured at Plymouth should be restored to their owners,[20] and in the following August Secretary Seddon informed Governor Bonham that "the embarrassments attending this question and the serious consequences which might ensue from the rigid enforcement of the act of congress originally passed on the subject, have co-operated with the objections which have been made by

[16] General G. T. Beauregard to Adjutant and Inspector General Cooper, July 17, 1863, *Official Records*, ser. ii, vol. vi, 125; same to same, July 21, 1863, *ibid.*, 134.

[17] Secretary Seddon to General Beauregard, July 22, 1863, *ibid.*, 139.

[18] Governor Bonham to Secretary Seddon, August 10, 1863, *ibid.*, 193.

[19] Secretary Seddon to Governor Bonham, Sept. 1, 1863, *ibid.*, 245-246.

[20] General Braxton Bragg to Governor Z. B. Vance, April 21, 1864, *ibid.*, vol. vii, 78-79.

the authorities of some of the States to receive Negroes directed to be turned over to them, and with the inability, when they have been turned over, to obtain criminal trials, to induce the Department to assume the responsibility of modifying the proposed action in relation to such Negroes.''[21] Henceforth Negroes taken in arms who could be identified as slaves were to be treated under the act of October 13, 1862, and returned to their owners. Free Negroes, though not yet recognized as prisoners of war, were to be turned over to the Confederate authorities who would hold them in strict confinement until their ultimate disposition should be decided upon.[22]

Except for their occasional employment as laborers on fortifications and trenches this continued to be the policy of the South in regard to recaptured slaves to the end of the war.[23] In spite of the efforts of the Union officers to secure treatment as prisoners of war for all captured Union troops regardless of color or previous condition of servitude, the Confederate authorities insisted that they would "die in the last ditch" before giving up the right to send slaves back to slavery as property recaptured. General Butler, Federal Commissioner for exchange, called into play his legal skill and in the summer of 1864 sent to the Confederate commissioner a lengthy argument denying the right of the South to restore recaptured slaves to their former owners.[24] Meeting the South on their own theory that slaves were property, he maintained that when in the course of the war movable property was captured not only the title thereto but also the *jus disponendi,* the right of disposing of that property, vested in the government making the capture. "Now, the United States have disposed of the property which

---

[21] Secretary Seddon to Governor Bonham, August 31, 1864, *ibid.,* 703-704.
[22] *Ibid.*
[23] Secretary Seddon to General R. E. Lee, October 15, 1864, *ibid.,* 990-991.
[24] Major General Benjamin F. Butler to Robert Ould, August 27, 1864, *ibid.,* 687-691.

they have acquired by capture in slaves taken by them,''
declared Butler, ''by giving that right of property to the
man himself, to the slave—i. e., by emancipating him and
declaring him free forever; so that if we have not mistaken the principles of international law and the laws of
war, we have no slaves in the armies of the United States.
All are free men. . . . Do the Confederate authorities
claim the right to reduce to a state of slavery freemen,
prisoners of war, captured by them? This claim our
fathers fought against under Bainbridge and Decatur
when set up by the Barbary powers on the northern shore
of Africa, about the year 1800, and in 1864 their children
will hardly yield it upon their own soil.'' The claim of the
Confederates that the *jus postliminii*, the principle of the
law of nations which rehabilitates the former owner with
his property taken by an enemy when such property is
recovered by the forces of his own country, justified their
restoration of slaves was denied by Butler on the ground
that it was a principle applicable only to immovable
property.

Butler's arguments did not persuade the Southern
officials to alter this policy. They insisted that the previous relations of slaves to their masters could not be
changed by the violence or seduction of an enemy and
that under the Confederate constitution it was incumbent
upon the central government to defend the relation of
master and slave established by state law and to sanction
the reclamation and return of all recaptured or fugitive
slaves. They maintained further that the United States
was estopped from denying this right to the Confederate
government because in the Revolutionary War and the
War of 1812 the United States had taken the very same
position now taken by the South.[25]

Though the officers of the Confederacy refused to the
end to treat recaptured slaves as prisoners of war they

[25] Secretary Seddon to General Lee, October 15, 1864, *ibid.*, 990-993.

finally agreed to accord this treatment to free Negroes taken in arms. In April, 1864, Butler informed Secretary of War Stanton that the Confederates were willing to make this concession,[26] but five months later Secretary Seddon declared that free Negroes were "not as yet formally recognized in any official dealings with the enemy as prisoners of war."[27] It was not until October 1864 that the Confederate authorities took a definite stand on this question. Following receipt of a clear statement of policy from Secretary Seddon,[28] General Lee informed General Grant that "all negroes in the military or naval service of the United States taken by us who are not identified as the property of citizens or residents of any of the Confederate States are regarded as prisoners of war, being held to be proper subjects of exchange . . . ."[29]

The willingness of the South to exchange free Negroes had little immediate consequence, for general exchange of prisoners had been suspended since the middle of 1863, due to the refusal of the South to treat white and colored prisoners on an equal basis and the unwillingness of the North to agree to any discrimination. This suspension continued until the closing weeks of the war and it was not until then that the exchange of any considerable number of Negro prisoners occurred, though meanwhile in connection with special exchanges a few Negro prisoners were delivered.[30] The decision of the Confederates to

[26] Major General Butler to Secretary Stanton, April 9, 1864, *ibid.*, 29-34.

[27] Secretary Seddon to Governor Bonham, August 31, 1864, *ibid.*, 703.

[28] Secretary Seddon to General Lee, October 15, 1864, *ibid.*, 990-993. This letter contains the surprising statement that "colored soldiers of the United States when captured have not, by the direction of the Department, been treated otherwise than as prisoners of war, unless identified or claimed to be recaptured slaves." This is clearly in conflict with his letter to Governor Bonham of September 1, 1863, noted above.

[29] General Lee to General Grant, October 19, 1864, *ibid.*, 1010.

[30] Major General E. A. Hitchcock's consolidated report of exchanged and parolled prisoners of war during the rebellion, December 6, 1865, *ibid.*, vol. viii, 821-832; *Record of the Services of the Seventh Regiment, U. S. Colored Troops from September 1863, to November 1866*, by an Officer of the Regiment (Providence, 1878), 112-136.

treat free Negroes as prisoners of war did mean, however, that they would no longer be held in close confinement but would be accorded the same general treatment as the white prisoners.[31] It may well be that some Negro prisoners were discriminated against as to food and shelter provided and prison duties assigned, but the reminiscences of prison life examined do not reveal that there was any such policy.

Closely connected with the question of the treatment of Negroes taken in arms is that of the treatment of white officers of colored troops. President Davis' proclamation of December, 1862, declared all commissioned officers in the command of General Butler robbers and criminals who, whenever captured, should be reserved for execution, and the joint resolution of congress stipulated that white commissioned officers of colored troops when captured should be put to death or otherwise punished at the discretion of the military court before which they should be tried.[32] These provisions, however, seem never to have been enforced, for there is no recorded case of such treatment being accorded officers of Negro troops while there are statements by such officers that they were treated in all respects as well as others. Some officers of colored troops when captured gave the number of some white regiment engaged in the fight, but others courageously gave their correct regiment and fared none the worse.[33]

[31] Occasionally subordinate officers claimed ignorance of this new policy and refused to treat free negroes as prisoners of war. Lt. F. Crocker to Commodore J. S. Palmer, February 7, 1865, *Official Records*, ser. ii, vol. viii, 316.

[32] Richardson, *Messages and Papers of the Confederacy*, i, 274; *Statutes at Large of the Confederate States* (1863), 167-168.

[33] Rickard, James H., *Services with Colored Troops in Burnside's Corps* [*Personal Narratives of Events in the War of the Rebellion, Being Papers Read Before the Rhode Island Soldiers and Sailors Historical Society*, ser. v, no. i] (Providence, 1894), 29; Sherman, George R., *Assault on Fort Gilmer and Reminiscences of Prison Life* [*Personal Narratives . . . Papers Read Before the Rhode Island Soldiers and Sailors Historical Society*, ser. v, no. vii] (Providence, 1897), 74.

One other phase of the treatment of Negro troops by the Confederates is the treatment on the field of battle or immediately after battle. What of the charges made by the North that the Confederates killed Negro soldiers rather than capture them and that when any were captured they were sold into slavery? Most reports of such treatment, like the usual stories of war atrocities, were as false as the reports in the Confederacy that Federal authorities were hanging South Carolina captives.[34] Yet there is some evidence that Negro troops were subjected to this cruel treatment.

The charge that captured Negroes were sold into slavery has least to support it. The only recorded case of such—overlooking the return of recaptured slaves to their masters—is that of two free Negroes, citizens of Massachusetts, who were acting as servants to the colonel and staff of a Massachusetts regiment when captured in Texas early in 1863. One of them was a member of a family that had been free for many generations and was the grandson of a revolutionary soldier, but he and his companion were seized and sold as slaves. The Federal government was powerless to aid them and they were not released until the close of the war.[35]

The Northern charge that Confederates killed Negro soldiers rather than capture them is true only in part. Because of the many variable factors involved it is difficult to draw any conclusions from the statistics of regimental losses, but these do not indicate that colored regiments suffered heavier losses than white regiments.[36] In support of this charge there is a letter from General Kirby Smith to General Taylor, in which he expressed the hope that it was not true that Taylor's troops had cap-

[34] Journal of the Congress of the Confederate States, i, 391-392, 399, 428.

[35] Official Records, ser. ii, vol. v, 455-456, 469-470, 484; vol. viii, 640, 703.

[36] Fox, Regimental Losses in the American Civil War, 48-49, 421-423, 426-461, 521-522.

tured Negroes in arms, but that the officers in command
of the capturing parties had "recognized the propriety
of giving no quarter to armed Negroes and their officers."
"In this way," stated Smith, "we may be relieved from a
disagreeable dilemma."[37] The Confederate secretary of
war did not fully approve this policy but he thought that
when Negroes were captured in arms "a few examples"
might be made.[38] At least one other Confederate officer
agreed with General Smith, for nearly a year later, March
6, 1864, Colonel W. P. Shingler, when reporting the capture of four Negro soldiers by a subordinate officer, stated
that he had directed that officer not to report any more
such captures.[39] Further evidence in support of this
Northern charge is the case of several Negro soldiers
captured near Jackson, Louisiana, in the summer of 1863
and shortly thereafter shot to death while being conducted
to camp by a back road. The Confederate officers admitted
the shooting but claimed that the prisoners had attempted
to escape.[40] The charge that the Confederates gave no
quarter to Negro troops seems to the writer to be supported also by the famous Fort Pillow affair. Although
the treatment accorded Negro troops in that engagement
is an extremely controversial subject, the mass of evidence
taken by the Union authorities following that battle seems
to show that the Confederates had little interest in the
taking of prisoners.[41]

If this evidence is sufficient to show that on occasion

[37] General E. Kirby Smith to Major General R. Taylor, June 13, 1863,
Official Records, ser. ii, vol. vi, 21-22.

[38] Assistant Adjutant General H. L. Clay to General E. Kirby Smith,
July 13, 1863, *ibid.*, 115.

[39] Colonel W. P. Shingler to Brigadier General Hunton, March 6, 1864,
ibid., 1022-1023.

[40] Colonel J. L. Logan to Colonel B. S. Ewell, September 3, 1863, and
inclosures, *ibid.*, 258-259; Brigadier General G. L. Andrews to Major General E. A. Hitchcock, February 7, 1864, *ibid.*, 924-925.

[41] *Ibid.*, ser. i, vol. xxxii, pt. i, 586-589, 518-533, 534-540; Brown, William Wells, *The Negro in the Rebellion* (Boston, 1867), 235-237.

Negro soldiers were killed rather than captured there is other evidence that on other occasions numerous colored troops were captured by the South. As early as November 1863 General Butler reported that some three thousand Negro troops were held as prisoners in the South.[42] Contrary to the sworn testimony of a Federal sergeant that when the Confederates captured Plymouth, North Carolina, in the spring of 1864, all Negroes found in blue uniform were killed by clubbing, shooting or hanging,[43] between three and four hundred Negro prisoners were listed in the report of that battle sent to President Davis.[44] Late in 1864 nearly a thousand captured Negroes were at work upon the Confederate fortifications of Mobile.[45] Not only did the Southerners usually capture Negro troops rather than kill them, but when the captives were wounded they were hospitalized and cared for until well enough to turn over to the Confederate authorities.[46]

In brief summary it may be said that though at the outset the Confederate authorities adopted a natural policy for a slave-holding society and decreed death for everyone engaged in what they regarded as armed insurrection by slaves, as the war progressed and the number so engaged increased, the policy was modified and thereafter no unusual cruelty was inflicted upon them; that in the heat of battle Negro soldiers, apparently because they were Negroes, were sometimes given no quarter; that to the end of the war the Confederate government insisted

[42] General Butler to Secretary Stanton, November 18, 1863, *Official Records*, ser. ii, vol. vi, 532-534.

[43] General Butler to General Grant, July 12, 1864, and inclosure, *ibid.*, vol. vii, 459-460.

[44] Colonel J. Taylor to President Davis, April 21, 1864, *ibid.*, ser. i, vol. li, pt. ii, 870.

[45] Major General E. A. Hitchcock to Secretary Stanton, November 22, 1865, *ibid.*, ser. ii, vol. viii, 803.

[46] Alfd. Roman to Brigadier General Thomas Jordan, August 7, 1863, *ibid.*, vol. vi, 187; Major and Provost-Marshal Is. H. Carrington to Secretary Seddon, August 11, 1864, *ibid.*, vol. vii, 583.

upon restoring recaptured slaves to their masters; and that in the contest over the treatment of Negro troops the two governments displayed their normally opposing views as to the status of the colored man. The South, as always, insisted that he was property and should be treated as such, though by the end of the war an exception was made in the case of free Negroes. The North, though reluctant to use the Negro as a soldier and slow to give him equal rights in the army, insisted with great firmness that every soldier was entitled to and should receive the same treatment—without discrimination—when taken prisoner by the enemy.

BRAINERD DYER

University of California
at Los Angeles

SARAH PARKER REMOND, ABOLITIONIST AND PHYSICIAN

Seventy years ago, the name of Sarah Parker Remond was well known on at least two continents to many thousands of persons who were interested in the movement for the abolition of slavery. A free Negro woman of remarkable ability and intellect, she was one of the few lecturers of her sex and race who, during the Garrisonian era, could command the attention of lords and mayors, as well as that of thousands of laymen, in behalf of the oppressed Negro slave.

Sarah Remond was born about 1815 in Salem, Massachusetts, of John and Nancy Remond. Her father, a native of the Island of Curaçoa, came to America at an early age. He later became a well-known hairdresser in Salem, and on May 2, 1811, he was admitted to citizenship in the Essex County Court.[1] Sarah Remond was well educated and probably received her early instruction in the schools of Salem, as did her brother Charles Lennox Remond. Negro children were able to attend the public schools in Salem much earlier than they were permitted to do so in some of the other cities.

Charles Lennox Remond, the first Negro to address American audiences on the abolition of slavery and the best known Negro before the time of Frederick Douglass, probably influenced his sister to become a public lecturer. In 1856, they were assigned to speak during an anti-slavery campaign in the state of New York by the Executive Committee of the American Anti-Slavery Society. A series of lectures was arranged which included many prominent speakers of the day. In many instances during these lecture tours Sarah and her brother were the

---

[1] Nell, William C., *The Colored Patriots of the American Revolution.* Boston, Robert F. Wallcut, 1855, p. 319.

recipients of many insults primarily because of their color. The hotels and boarding houses which admitted Susan B. Anthony refused to accommodate Sarah and Charles, in spite of their education and refinement. On one occasion when Charles Remond was in the home of an anti-slavery friend in Washington County, New York, a neighbor called and stated that a family in the vicinity was being neglected because it was suffering from small-pox. No one would go near them to help them. Mr. Remond expressed his sympathy and remarked, "To the colored people it is the same as having the smallpox all the time."[2]

During the early part of her lecture career, Sarah Remond spoke, for the most part, in the West with her brother. They were able to remove much of the prejudice which existed in this section against persons of color. Wherever and whenever possible she fought to overcome race discrimination and ill-feeling towards the Negro. In the year 1853 she was expelled from the Howard Athe-naeum in New York after she had purchased tickets of admission and had been admitted with two friends. An agent and officer forced her to leave the building and in so doing pushed her down the stairs. Miss Remond presented her case before the police court and an opinion sustaining the equal rights of colored persons was given by Justice Russell. The defendants were fined a small sum, and the agent was forced to pay the costs of the pro-ceedings. From that time on Miss Remond was permitted to occupy any seat at the Athenaeum she might choose to pay for.[3]

In September 1858, the editor of the *Anti-Slavery Advocate*, published in London, printed a letter written by

[2] Powell, Aaron M., *Personal Reminiscences of the Anti-Slavery and other Reforms and Reformers.* New York, 1899, p. 171.

[3] American and Foreign Anti-Slavery Society. *Thirteenth Annual Report.* New York, The Society, 1853, p. 154.

Sarah Remond to a friend of the editor. The letter was published primarily to prepare for the visit of Miss Remond in England the English people who were interested in the abolition of slavery. It is as follows:

Salem, Mass., Sept. 18, 1858.

Dear Friend,

Your letter dated August 18th, was received. It reached my home while I was absent attending an anti-slavery convention at Cape Cod, in the town of Harwich, in company with Parker Pillsbury, Mr. Foss and my brother. Our meetings, eight in number, were well attended. On Sunday, although we had a large hall, many were obliged to go away unable to obtain entrance. I never looked upon a more closely packed audience. We endeavored to speak the words of truth to them, and I am sure the meeting was a very successful one. I received last week a short but pleasant call from Mr. Garrison and an English gentleman, Mr. Robson, who has been traveling in America. Mr. Robson seems to understand the character of our nation and the spirit of slavery. He is bearing a very faithful testimony against the great crime of our age. There is a very strong effort being made on the part of the slave-holders and their allies to legalize the slave trade. Only think of it, in the nineteenth century, a nation which years ago declared the slave trade piracy, and at this time is making greater professions in favor of liberty and Christianity than any other nation in the world, endeavoring to legalize traffic in bodies and souls of men and women who are "made for little lower than angels." Is it not enough to make one's heart sick?

> Oh God! my every heart string cries,
> Doest thou these scenes behold
> In this our boasted Christian land,
> And must the truth be told?

It is true the traffic in slaves has always been carried on under the flag, but now there will be an attempt made to throw around this infamous crime the sanction of law. "And why not?" I may ask, "When the Supreme Court of the United States has declared that men and women with a dark complexion 'have no rights which white men are bound to respect.' " When I began to write to you I did not intend to write so much about the cause I feel so much interest in, but you know "out of the abundance of the heart the mouth speaketh." It gave me great satisfaction to hear of your safe arrival at Liverpool. To ride upon the waves of the ocean three thousand miles is really an event. I was exceedingly anxious to join you in your voyage; more so than I expressed in my letters to you. Feeling that you had no prejudice against color, I knew I should be sure of one person to speak a word now and then. I still hope to reach London before winter, but I dread starting for many reasons. I do not fear the wind nor the waves, but I know that no matter how I go, the spirit of prejudice will meet me. I shall take passage from Boston in an English steamer. You mentioned my brother's friend. It is a long time since he visited England, so I shall gather up all my courage, and endeavor to depend upon myself. Parker Pillsbury will write to a friend of his to meet me at Liverpool and I shall hope to get along very well. He wished me to remember him very kindly to you. He has visited me twice at my own home since I wrote to you last.

I am very truly yours,

SARAH PARKER REMOND.[4]

Sarah Remond made her voyage across the ocean late that year. She lectured in many of the large cities in Scotland, Ireland and England on the abolition of slavery, during the years 1859 and 1860.[5] Everywhere she was received with great enthusiasm by large, interested and sympathetic audiences. In Warrington, England, where she spoke in March 1859, her address was signed by the Mayor, the Rector of the Parish, a member of Parliament for the Borough and by three thousand five hundred twenty-two inhabitants of all ranks and classes. A donation of one hundred dollars was raised at this meeting and sent to William Lloyd Garrison for the aid of the American Anti-Slavery Society.[6]

That her presence in England was appreciated is shown by the fact that many prominent persons visited her; even Lord Henry Brougham who was eighty years of age at this time called on her while she was in London. For the most part she was presented to audiences in the different cities by the anti-slavery societies, male and female, which were organized in these various places.[7] The

---

[4] *Anti-Slavery Advocate*. London, 1858, vol. ii, no. xxiii, November 1858, p. 179-180.

[5] See *Anti-Slavery Advocate* for 1859-1860 for accounts of these lectures.

[6] *Anti-Slavery Advocate*, 1859, vol. ii, no. xxviii, April 1859, p. 221.

[7] See the reports of the various English anti-slavery societies, Leeds Young Men's Anti-Slavery society, Edinborough Ladies Emancipation society, etc.

newspapers of the day described her style of lecturing as being "well adapted to English audiences." It was "broad, comprehensive and impressive." Her presentation of the great questions of slavery were made intelligently—"Clear elucidation of just principles, no clap trap." According to these reports she did not play on the sympathies of her audiences by a long recital of the horrors of slavery. She applied her "rules of judgment to all persons, sects and classes."[8]

Her gentleness, refinement of manners, her fluent and clear-toned speech made her a popular lecturer. While on these speaking tours she had in mind certain aims which she hoped to fulfill. She desired preeminently to "extend the active sympathy of the whole British nation towards the cause of abolitionism in America." This she felt could be accomplished by money subscriptions which were to aid the work of the American Anti-Slavery societies, "public addresses from the English to the American people, especially from the English to the American churches, enunciating true Christian anti-slavery principles and feelings of sympathy with the abolitionists there in their patriotic and philanthropic labors." She further hoped to awaken the English people to a sense of the dangers that then threatened the "great principles of freedom hitherto maintained in one national policy through the so-called immigration scheme now in cooperation in the West Indies."[9] It is needless to say that with these purposes in mind much was accomplished to aid the cause which she so well represented.

Early in December in the year 1859 Sarah Remond desired to visit France. Accordingly, she went to the American Embassy to obtain the necessary visé on her passport. This was refused her by a Mr. Dallam, an official, upon the ground that colored persons are not citizens of

[8] *Anti-Slavery Advocate*, 1859, vol. ii, no. xxvii, March 1859, p. 211.
[9] *Ibid.*, p. 211.

the United States. Miss Remond's immediate remonstrance was answered with a threat of forcible removal from the office. A few days later she applied in writing to the minister respectfully insisting upon her right to have her passport viséd by the minister of her country. He replied by affirming a "manifest impossibility by law" that in her case "the indispensable qualification for an American passport was that of United States citizenship." He could not comply, therefore, with her desire. She later, however, obtained a passport from the British foreign secretary.[10] This was not the first time a colored person had been refused a passport on the ground of his color.

After the American Negro had been given his freedom, Sarah Remond continued working in his behalf. Again in 1867, she is found lecturing in England. This time before literary institutions and general audiences on such subjects as—"The Freeman or the Emancipated Negro of the Southern States of the United States."[11] Since some of her lectures were published many persons were able to read her plea for these needy people.[12] In 1864, she wrote a pamphlet of thirty pages entitled "The Negroes as Freedmen and Soldiers," which was published by the *Ladies London Emancipation Society,* stating the condition of the freedmen and telling of the services rendered by the Negro soldier in the war of the rebellion.

Still popular in London in 1867, she attended a large public breakfast given in honor of William Lloyd Garrison at St. James' Hall. The Duke of Argyll headed the list of a committee of fifty. There were many members of Parliament, philosophers, scientists, and literateurs present including Thomas F. Buxton, John Stuart Mill,

[10] American Anti-Slavery Society. *Annual Report by the Executive Committee for the Year Ending May the First, 1860,* New York, American Anti-Slavery Society, 1861, p. 222.

[11] *The Freedman.* London, A. Partridge, December 1, 1867, p. 121.

[12] *Ibid.,* p. 162.

Herbert Spencer, T. H. Huxley and William Howitt. The entire number present included about three hundred men and women. Other American Negroes present were Daniel A. Payne, J. Sella Martin, and William and Ellen Craft who were living at that time in London.[13]

An undated clipping states that Sarah Remond received the degree of Doctor of Medicine in 1871 from a leading medical school in Florence, Italy. Probably weariness with her fight against the race problem and the indifference displayed in regard to the rights of Negroes were some of the reasons which made her seek a new field of endeavor, in a new country where opportunity for self-expression and service would not be denied to her.

Mrs. Elizabeth Buffum Chace, a Quaker and friend of abolition, visited Florence, Italy, in 1873, and tells in her memoirs of her travels there. She mentions a visit and a tea with a Mrs. Putnam at which Sarah Remond was present. Mrs. Chace described Miss Remond as a "remarkable woman" and said that by her "indomitable energy and perseverance she had won a fine position in Florence as a physician and also socially." She quoted Miss Remond as saying that Americans had attempted to use their influence to prevent her success, "by bringing their hateful prejudices" to Italy.[14]

The name of Sarah Remond, then, should have a prominent place in the history of the Negro. The story of her life is an illustration of the untiring efforts of one who desired to help her race in every way and who suffered much mentally and physically in the long fight for the abolition of slavery and the betterment of race relations.

DOROTHY B. PORTER

[13] *William Lloyd Garrison, 1805-1879*. The story of his life as told by his children. New York Century Comany, 1889, vol. iv, p. 196-7.

[14] Lyman, Lillie B., and Arthur C. Wyman, *Elizabeth Buffum Chace, 1806-1899, Her Life and Environment*, (Boston, 1914) Volume II, p. 42.

OUT OF THE MOUTHS OF EX-SLAVES

After reading books on Negro life from the pens of such authors as Dubose Heyward, Julia Peterkin, Howard Odum and T. S. Stribling, some of us have had the feeling that Negroes themselves should step in and make contributions from the rich sources found in their background. We have hoped that men of talent and industry would assist in this task; and it has been attempted by a few outstanding writers like Carter G. Woodson, W. E. B. Dubois, Walter White, Langston Hughes and James Weldon Johnson. Lying waiting, however, there is so much more the sources of which are daily drying up that I have been prompted to participate in this effort.

After all the story of Negro life must be told—whether by white or by black or by both. At present, both are at work. From the pens of whites, we may get reflections of ideas and attitudes impossible from Negro authors. From these persons of the other race, when they are frank and loyal to truth, Negroes are able to find out just what is in the minds of their white neighbors. The Negroes may thus understand the basis of the white people's reaction to the blacks about them even though they may not agree with them as to attitudes. One can thereby trace lines of thought as they actually develop. Likewise, black authors may interpret their people to the world more faithfully than white authors. They are able to set forth the real black man as he was, is, and hopes to be. The one interpretation may counterbalance the other.

It may be argued that with two groups of writers dealing with the same or similar problems there is danger of controversy. This we must admit. However, the very heat of the argument will reveal what calm and deliberate judgment is likely to conceal. Further, these bickerings will cause judicious ones of each race to re-

pudiate their errant fellows and set forth what will be
nearer the facts. All these things grew and revolved
in the present writer's mind when in 1929 he invaded this
neglected field.

At that time the writer was head of the Extension
Department of Southern University, Scotlandville, Louisiana. His duties carried him off the campus every Saturday during the school year to such centers as St.
Joseph, Monroe, Bastrop, Minden and Ruston, in that
state. While teaching the topic of slavery in a class in
United States history he conceived the idea of securing
views of the institution from living ex-slaves and ex-
slave owners. In accordance with this plan, all students,
most of whom were teachers themselves, were requested to
interview as many of these persons as possible. Students
were asked to seek information regarding food, clothing, housing facilities, working conditions, amusements,
religious practices, educational opportunities, family life,
punishments and any other information obtainable. Every
member of the class entered enthusiastically into the
project, and thirty-six reported interviews totaling eighty-
two.

The passing of the years, the early age of witnesses
at the time, and the bitterness against the institution of
slavery might be arguments against the historical accuracy of everything which follows. Even the love to weave
a good story for attentive listeners bids us be cautious.
We notice, however, that other authors dealing with
American Negro Slavery quote from ex-slaves.[1] If it
is a fault, then we feel that we are in good company.

I. Shelter—Clothing—Food

The housing conditions of Negro slaves were set forth
in most of these reports. Slaves lived in one-roomed

[1] Phillips, U. B., *Negro Slavery in America;* Bancroft, Frederic, *Slave-
Trading in the Old South.*

log cabins with mud chimneys and dirt floors. The open-
ings between the logs were daubed with mud. Several of
these cabins were rowed off on each side of a road a short
distance from the owner's house. Such a group of houses
was commonly known as the "quarters."[2] "Their chimneys were made of sticks, mud and grass. The fireplaces
nearly took up the whole end of the cabin. The doors
were cut too low for one to stand upright while walking
in and out. The windows were small holes cut in the side
or end of the cabin with slide shutters somewhat similar
to those made for chickens to pass in and out of the hen
houses. Practically, the small door was the only entrance.
These quarters were built from one-half to one mile from
the planter's dwelling; some were much nearer. They
were mostly built in a circle, rainbow fashion . . . Sometimes holes were punched through the back of chimney
fireplaces so that overseers (by peeping through these
holes from the outside) could see when all persons were
present."[3] "Often a cabin was built about one hundred-
fifty yards from the mansion for the nigger drivers to
live in."[4] In this manner he could be easily communi-
cated with by his master.

"Generally there were no kitchens. Consequently, the
cooking, if carried on at all in the cabins, was done in the
big fireplace. The slaves ate and slept in the same room."[5]
"There was scarcely any furniture in the rude cabins.
Bedsteads were made of poles connected by boring holes
in each end and fastening them with wooden pegs. Planks

[2]L. M. Channell of Bastrop, referring to the J. Martin plantation of
Bayou Lafourche, La.; Mary L. Swearingan of Bastrop, quoting Martha
Washington, 92-year-old ex-slave.

[3]Mrs. L. J. Evans of Bastrop, quoting her Uncle Joseph Young of Lafayette County, Miss.

[4]Ella Alford of Bastrop, quoting testimony of Frank Roberson on a
Morehouse Parish Plantation.

[5]Gertrude Smith of Ruston, quoting Fannie White on a Texas Farm;
Willie R. Smith of Bastrop, quoting Rhiner Gardner, 85 years old; Callie J.
Harvey of Bastrop, quoting Roan Barnes.

formed the springs; hay or shucks the mattress. Sometimes these crude beds were fastened to the walls of the cabins."[6] "Children slept on the ground upon piles of hay or corn shucks."

"Although a cabin rarely contained more than one room, it was as much as a single, slave family was permitted to occupy no matter how large the family grew. Often more than one family lived in one cabin. W. S. Miles of St. Joseph, Louisiana, ex-slave in Alabama, told the writer that his father's family of seven lived in one room. Persons who were slaves in a low country stated that the cabins sometimes had rude floors. House slaves lived in the house of the master, but slept on the floor, winter and summer."[7]

Miss Rosa B. Johnson of Minden, giving the experiences of one ex-slave, Lee Henderson, "Just as they were related to her by him," says, "Slaves wore a heavy grade of cotton material made at home into garments. This material was very comfortable in the mild season; extremely hot when the season reached its hottest part; and very cold in the cold season of the year. Of course, they were bound to suffer. They were forced to adjust themselves to situations as best they could."

Another student, speaking of his father's experiences in slavery, says, "My father wore very coarse clothes made of crocus."[8] James Smith of Bastrop, thus gives eighty-five-year-old Mrs. Rhiner Gardner's description of slave clothing:

"The clothing of the slaves was as crude as the rest of the things which they were used to. All of their garments were made of heavy canvas. Some of their garments were dyed, and some

[6] *Ibid.*

[7] Johnnie B. Slaton of Ruston, quoting Mrs. Lue Bradford's experience on a plantation near Lexington, Ky.; Minnie J. Tims of Minden, quoting Melvin Elzy.

[8] J. E. Gray of Bastrop; Ella Alford of Bastrop, quoting Frank Roberson, says, "Every slave had two pairs of shoes a year, three pairs of pants and jumpers, or three dresses."

were not. It was not uncommon for the little boys and girls to have a one-piece garment made out of crocus bag by cutting a hole in the center of the bottom for the head and one in each side for the arms. The children wore no shoes until they were large enough to work. All the shoes for the slaves were coarse and hard. Every plantation maintained a cobbler to keep in repair the shoes which were worn by the slaves.''[9]

In this same vein another continues, ''The slaves wore a coarse kind of cloth called homespun. In winter the men and women were given a coarse kind of shoe made from horse hide. They were so hard that at times they would rub the skin from the feet. The children did not get shoes.''[10] Lue Taylor said that the women on her master's farm in Jefferson County, Mississippi, were given two dresses at Christmas time. W. S. Miles (born in 1854) reported that on his master's plantation in Pike County, Alabama, slaves wore homespun and very coarse red russet shoes. The little boys wore heavy linen dresses and ''Wahoo'' hats made from the bark of trees. Miles further stated that clothes were issued as needed; and upon occasions of marriage, slaves ''dressed out fine in their own clothes.''

For church wear and for the few parties allowed the slaves, calico and broad striped gingham dresses were occasionally issued to the women.[11] Clothes of the slaves were cleaned and mended at night on Sundays, or if the master was very kind, Saturday for the women and Saturday evening for the men.[12] It is to be supposed that house slaves were dressed much better than others; yet this custom is not brought out directly in the accounts. Details of issuing clothes are omitted from these narratives, a thing which is perhaps to be expected of those

[9] G. T. Griffin of St. Joseph.

[10] G. T. Griffin of St. Joseph.

[11] Sarah Skinner, *Recollection in Georgia and Louisiana;* Roan Barnes, ex-slave of Morehouse Parish, called this ''lowels''; he also says, ''when dey did gib shoes dey wus brogans wid brass on de toes.''

[12] Ella Alford, *op. cit.*

who were not past the adolescent stage during the period which they describe.

Statements regarding food are varied and interesting. Roan Barnes, ex-slave of Morehouse Parish, said:

"No cooking was done in de cabins, but all de slaves went to de cook house to eat. (No doubt he lived on a big plantation.) One woman did de cooking wid de chillun to hep her. We had greens, onions, meat and milk but never had any chicken or cake; only at Christmas time dey would give de slaves some flour and sugar to make cake. Some slaves got plenty to eat; some didn't. Some masters wouldn't give dey slaves enough to eat."

John Johnson, ex-slave of Morehouse Parish, evidently belonging to a small land owner, says:

"Food was of the poorest type and was given to the slaves from kitchen windows by hand. On days when company came, the children would claim the plates of each person. Usually the white visitors would leave some food on the plates and the lucky little black slaves would have a joyful time eating these scraps and left-overs."[13]

"Slaves on a plantation in Franklin Parish, Louisiana, were allowed to cook their breakfast and supper at home. Enough women were left at a big kitchen at the master's house to cook dinner for all the slaves. After the dinner was prepared it was sent to the field where it was eaten beneath shade trees."[14]

Jane Robinson, ex-slave in Jefferson County, Mississippi, says:[15]

"Our food was cooked at the big house during working days; on Sundays we were given food to cook in our cabins. We ate in the field when we were working. For breakfast we had milk and bread which were sent to the field in carts. For dinner we had vegetables, such as peas, cabbages and potatoes with bread. In winter we had pork, beef, and sausage."

Mrs. Sarah Skinner remarked:

"Cooking was done in an open fireplace. Food consisted of cornbread, molasses and meat in winter. There was a kind of hominy made for us from corn, which was used when vegetables were scarce. Pumpkins and sweet potatoes were often eaten.

[13]L. C. Griffin of Bastrop.
[14]Gertrude Smith of Ruston.
[15]Mamie Barkley of Bastrop.

Flour (bread) was seldom eaten by the slaves and sugar was unknown to them. Syrup was used to sweeten their foods where sugar was ordinarily used. They (the slaves) would parch corn, beat it and make a kind of coffee. Very few slaves owned chickens or hogs. Their masters would give them the fat part of the meat, but chickens and eggs were not given slaves except for sickness. Slaves often stole such things because of a desire for change.''

It is interesting to note some provisions for feeding of little slave children.[16]

''On a plantation in Franklin Parish, Louisiana, the children of the plantation were fed in a long trough with all their food put in at one time mixed together. The food consisted of vegetables, cornbread and milk. These troughs were located in the back yard of the master's house near the big kitchen.

''The children of the plantation were fed by some old woman who was too old for field work. They were fed in a trough or dug out made from the body of a tree. These poor little children ate with their hands or fingers and put their little heads down into the trough to sip up the milk or pot licker.''[17]

''We children ate at the big house. Our food was put in one big trough together; syrup, milk and other odd food were mixed in this trough and we children stood around eating like little pigs. Sometimes we would go to the creek and get mushel shell for spoons.''[18]

''The children were fed from troughs made from tupelo gum. These troughs were filled with milk and cornbread or with bread and pot liquor. The children ate with their hands, each one helping himself to all his heavenly spoons could dip. One master, Rainey of Texas, fed all his slaves, young and old from troughs.''[19]

Fannie White, who was a slave in Bowie County, Texas, says with regard to the amount of food to slaves, ''Food was weighed out weekly; six pounds of meal, three pounds of meat and a little lard for a man and his wife.'' This was ordinary food. Mae D. Moore of Minden, quoting her father, a Kentucky slave, says, ''Wheat bread was permitted Sunday mornings; a little sugar, coffee and

[16]Mamie Barkley of Bastrop.

[17]L. J. Evans of Bastrop, quoting Joseph Young.

[18]Mamie Barkley of Bastrop, quoting Sam Boykin.

[19]Mae D. Moore of Minden.

syrup would also be given on Sundays.''[20] Joseph Young, a slave in Lafayette County, Mississippi, says that ''meat was given on Sunday mornings but regular meals consisted of ash cakes made of corn meal baked in hot ashes and a quart of buttermilk.''[21] ''We slaves had plenty to eat,'' said another. ''Our master raised plenty to take care of his slaves.''[22] Hominy made of cracked corn was served for dinner on plantations near Bayou Lafourche, Louisiana.[23]

Lee Henderson states that his master fed his slaves well in order to keep them well and strong for work.[24] Frank Roberson, ex-slave of Morehouse Parish, says:

''Several cooks had to cook for seventy-five or a hundred head of people. The house where the food was cooked was not far from the mansion. In the 'big house' only the food for the master's family was cooked, as the mistress did not wish the odor of large amounts of food to penetrate the mansion. From this kitchen, the slaves carried their breakfast to the field where it was eaten up as soon as it became light enough to see. Dinner was sent to the field. Supper was taken from the cook house to cabins and formed the only meal normally eaten at home. No cooking was allowed in the cabin except on Sundays. Food was eaten either with the hands or sticks. I never saw a knife or spoon except in my master's house. Pickled pork, salt bacon, black molasses, cornbread, cabbages, peas and onions were the principal food of the slaves.''

Slaves often supplemented the food issued. ''Food for the slaves was usually kept in a storehouse commonly called the smoke-house. If an issue of food gave out before the alloted time, the slaves had to make shift as best they might. This led to petty theft and pilfering. Often they stole from smoke-house and chicken roost. Frequently pigs were taken and killed to repair a food shortage. The most skillful usually were able to secure through these means enough food to satisfy their own needs and

[20]Gertrude Smith of Ruston.
[21]Rosa B. Johnson of Minden.
[22]A. W. Casterman, quoting Ebleaux Washington.
[23]M. L. Channell of Bastrop.
[24]L. J. Evans of Bastrop.

those of fellow unfortunates as well.''[25] One Dan Robinson, who was a slave on the Bowie plantation, was a hunter for the Bowie family. Whenever he bagged more game than could be consumed by the master's family he was permitted to carry the excess home. In this manner he supplemented the weekly rations issued.[26] All slaves, however, were not permitted to hunt. This privilege was ordinarily granted only to old and trusted slaves.[27]

''A few house servants ate from the master's tables and fared well. House and yard slaves generally had the same kind of food that their masters ate.''[28] ''Lue Bradford, who was a house slave both in Kentucky and Alabama, states that it was very rare that any slave was permitted to eat cakes, pies, meats, or biscuit. She recites that in Alabama her master whipped his cook until the blood ran for eating two biscuit.''[29]

II. Family Life

In no phase of slavery do we find it more cruel and heartless than in family relationships. The utter helplessness of the slave both as regards the selection and retention of a bosom mate is clearly illustrated by these testimonies. Nor do we find lacking instances in which the lord and master took advantage of his authority to force his attentions upon the powerless slave women. The forced relationships to which these women had to submit were such as living with some Negro man without any type of ceremony, sustaining this relation after a broomstick ceremony, the reading of a passage from the Bible or other book, or an actual marriage ceremony, or cohabiting with varying degrees of intimacy as the para-

[25] James Smith of Bastrop.

[26] G. T. Griffin of St. Joseph.

[27] Ella Alford of Bastrop, quoting Patsy Larkin, a slave near Elma, Alabama.

[28] Mae D. Moore of Minden, quoting experience of her father.

[29] Related to Miss J. Slaton of Ruston.

mour or concubine of some white man or men. In every situation above save the last mentioned the slave woman was ordinarily expected to obey the catechismal injunction "replenish the earth" and thus satisfy if not glorify her lord and master.

Broomstick marriage may be regarded as the most elementary ceremony given to slaves.

"She was made to jump the broomstick as a form of marriage. Not understanding the marriage vow (she was fifteen years of age and had been brought up in Illinois and Missouri) one slave girl ran away that night to her mistress. There she remained and worked in the cotton fields until after the Civil War."[30]

"When anyone married, all they had to do was to jump over a broom and they were man and wife. Her mistress worried her about marrying. She did not want to marry. One night when she went to her room to retire, a large man had been locked in her room by her mistress. She managed to get away that night (she was just a young girl). The next night her mistress tied her in the room with the man who, she was told, was her husband."[31]

"Their masters would often select husbands for the women and wives for the men. Many and many a time they had never seen or heard of each other. The wedding was very simple. A broom, that was made from sedge straw, tied with a string, was thrown upon the ground or floor by the master; the man would catch the woman by the hand and both jumped across that broom at the same time whereupon the master would pronounce them man and wife."[32]

Mrs. Fannie White, ex-slave in Texas, says:

"The old master at times picked a wife for a man slave. At other times, he gave the Negro man the woman of his choice. They both had to jump over a broom together after which they were called man and wife. This was considered marriage for Negro slaves.

"The marriage was not the same on every plantation. Some places they would really marry and sometimes they would have a marriage feast. And some would marry by jumping over the broom. But if in case they would have a marriage feast it was

[30]M. M. Brown of Monroe.
[31]M. L. Leary of Minden.
[32]L. J. Evans of Bastrop.

just some feast—a hog, a cow, and everything that was enjoyed in those days by the people of that time.''[33]

Next we come to those ''reading'' from the Bible or other books and actual ceremonies. One reported: ''When anyone on this plantation wanted to marry the master would read a section from the Bible and declare them man and wife.''[34] ''Another ex-slave says that if his master heard a man say he liked a woman, he would call the two up and pronounce them man and wife. Sometimes one or two verses of the Bible or lines from another book were read.''[35] ''The master would perform the marriage ceremony by reading a portion from the Bible. If the husband lived on another plantation he could come to see his family on Sunday, sometimes, or nights in the week. Some children never saw their fathers.''[36]

Whenever the master allowed the marriage ceremony, a marriage (especially of a favored slave) meant a festive occasion. ''On certain occasions of a festive nature, the slaves were given dainty foods and sometimes wine by their owners. If a marriage between couples the owner liked occurred on the plantation he would treat the slaves to a big dinner consisting principally of pigs taken from the pasture.''[37] For such slaves the master showed respect for family ties, allowed slaves to marry and furnished the wedding usually at the big house.''[38]

It seems that the master's consent was usually necessary in all cases herein mentioned. Mrs. Sarah Skinner says:

''The masters had the say about their slaves marrying. A man slave would tell his master: I want to marry Sal over on Marse Jones place, and if the master thought it necessary he would consent. If Sal was a good work hand she would have to

[33]D. A. Franks of Minden.
[34]M. L. Leary of St. Joseph.
[35]J. H. Carter, *op. cit.*
[36]Ella Alford, *op. cit.*
[37]James Smith of Bastrop, quoting ex-slave, Mrs. Rhiner Gardner.
[38]A. W. Casterman, quoting Ebleaux Washington.

continue there with her own master and her husband could get a pass to go see her two or three times a week. Sometimes the masters would make exchange of slaves and let the man take his wife with him to his own master's place.''

''If Tom wanted Sallie for a wife, he would tell his master that he wanted her for his wife and if the master said that he might have her, Sallie had to become Tom's wife, regardless of her wishes. This constituted marriage.''[39]

''There were some marriages among the slaves but men and women often went together and considered themselves married when no ceremony had been performd. The master paid no attention to their relationship and reproduction unless it was in an extreme case wherein the parties involved became extremely rude. One man often claimed several wives. Little difference was shown as a man and his wife, or so-called wife, might have or might not have lived together in the huts. A man was not responsible for the support of the family as they all belonged to the owner; that is they belonged to the master of the slaves.''[40]

''No license was seen, yet you had to marry and live together as one happy family. Not a man was allowed to fight or mistreat his wife, whether she was in the wrong or right. Not a man was allowed to bring a girl to disgrace; for all men were made to stay in their places, or marry the girl and support her with a smile. As a whipping was the gift given without style. Old master read the matrimony from the book of God. They needed no witness to sign, for he was king and Lord; just you live together and do as he said or take the bull whip's lashes over your head.''[41]

The sanctity of this so-called slave family was not at all regarded by the master, as many witness.

''Rosetta Winn was sold from Virginia and brought into Louisiana. She was sold away from her little baby that was only nine months old. She never saw or heard from the child any more, though Rosetta lived to be about eighty-five years old.''

''Family ties were often broken when an owner decided to sell slaves. The relationship of the slaves was not regarded in the marketing process. On many occasions family unions were completely broken. Sometimes members of a family thus separated met again—many more did not and will never see each other again. These conditions led the slaves to have but little respect for each other as far as blood relationships went. Yet

[39]Mrs. L. M. Channell of Bastrop.

[40]Rosa B. Johnson of Minden, quoting Lee Henderson.

[41]S. M. E. Ewell of St. Joseph, quoting Mrs. Margaret Baker.

there were those who were warmly devoted to each other and strove to live in the bounds of one another and who cared for their young as much as they were permitted."[42]

Ann Eliza (née Riddle) Woodson, the mother of Dr. Carter G. Woodson, often related her experiences. In a slave pen in Richmond one day she saw a young Negro woman weeping as one dying of a bleeding heart. "Woman, why do you weep so?" the observer inquired. The reply was, "I am weeping because I am being sold away from my two little children. I'll never see them again!" Thereupon Ann Eliza said that for this very reason she should rejoice. She and her mother with several small children belonged to a poor farmer in Buckingham County, Virginia. Overwhelmed with debt from bad management, the owner had to dispose of either her or her mother to satisfy this claim. Ann, the oldest girl, but not yet grown up, begged the planter to sell her if possible that her mother might not be separated from her little children. Although put on the auction block three times and examined as one does a cow or mare for sale, however, the owner could not get the $1,100 asked for Ann Eliza; and he finally sold the mother with two of the youngest children of one and two years respectively, leaving those of five, seven, and nine years to scout for themselves.

Another ex-slave of bitter experience said:

"My grandmother, Mrs. Julian Wilcher, who is now ninety years, will cause tears to form in the listener's eyes if he will but listen to her tell how she was treated. She said only a few of the slaves were lawfully married. In fact, whenever a woman was an extraordinary breeder, she was mated by the master to his own accord. Only sometimes the couples were happily married, and occasionally when a couple was happy, the master separated them by selling one or the other; this I imagine caused many unhappy partings. These partings caused untold grief among the slaves, for usually when one was sold, he was carried to a plantation many miles away."[43]

"Mrs. Harriet Robinson, a Texas slave, was sold four times.

[42]Rosa B. Johnson of Minden.
[43]Mary L. Swearingan of Bastrop.

Being considered an excellent breeder, she always brought large prices and was always well cared for, was never whipped; but was with a broken heart constantly because she was used for breeding, as a lower animal, and was constantly separated from her children.''[44]

''One ex-slave owner of Texas, who fed his Negroes on such poorly cooked food from troughs that they often ran away, had them chased down with bad blood hounds. He bred and raised his own slaves. He would select three or four heavyweight men, force each to stay in a cabin with two or three women and serve them; in this way he bred his slaves as he did his stock. If one of these selected women did not breed, she was sent to do heavier work.''[45]

''Mr. Lyons also speaks of the value put upon a man and wife that had a large family, especially if the births of the children were close together. He said that man was exempted from work and the woman's only duty was the care for the children. Likewise, if a family failed to produce children they were forced to work especially hard and soon sold so as to get couples to produce children.''[46]

''If one man saw a fine woman or man on another plantation, he would buy him or her for breeding purposes in order to continue to have good able workers. If he didn't bring them on the same farm, he would arrange for them to breed from each other. When this man wanted to see his so-called wife, he had to get special order (permit) from the master. If a man was caught off the place without this order he was subject to be punished. He didn't enjoy the opportunity of being a help to his wife, only when his master saw fit for him to go to see her. She also said if the master or field master saw fit to whip this woman, her so-called husband could not go to her rescue at all, but could only stand back and look with eyes of tears, and listen to his poor wife suffer.''[47]

We have facts also regarding the relationships between slave women and men of the master class.

''Mr. Aaron Lyons, of Bastrop, La., another ex-slave, speaks of the moral conduct of some slave masters, imposing their masterly power upon slave women and then using their children as free slaves, but not allowing them to leave the plantation. Usually children of such unions were given a home; allowed choice marriages, and in many cases taught to read. The mothers of

[44] Mae D. Moore of Minden.
[45] *Ibid.*
[46] Ella Alford of Bastrop.
[47] Lueatha Mansfield of Bastrop.

these children were given better treatment after the children were born.''[48]

''Eliza Stokes, an Alabama slave and an excellent character, said that she was a field hand, but her master had her brought to the house for a house servant that he might make her his concubine. This she refused to be; he had her beaten in an attempt to force her into submission. She told her mistress about it; the mistress believed the story and sympathized with her. Later the mistress went to Texas to visit a sister, carrying the slave with her as a servant. Upon the mistress' return to Alabama, she left the slave woman with her sister, who was kind to her, teaching her to read and making her a cook.''[49]

''Luncendy Hall, a Kentucky slave girl—a house girl—was overpowered by her master, who was a lawyer. As a result, she gave birth to a baby girl, whose father was the master. The master's wife often tantalized the slave mother and child. The little slave girl's hair was kept cut short because they did not want it to be long like the mistress' little girl's hair. The mistress could not whip the slave woman—and the master would not—but the mistress would often hit her head with her fist. One day the slave filled her hair full of pins, heads down, points up; when the white woman hit the little mulatto slave girl, her fist was filled with pins. This slave had liberty to go where and when she pleased; lived in a room of the white people's house. However, she despised her master because he was the father of her child.''[50]

Mable O. Leary quotes Lettie Moonson as telling the following:

''There was a woman on the plantation who was to become a mother. The mistress thought that her husband was the father of the slave woman's girl because he did not beat the woman nor did he allow anyone else to whip her. Whenever the master left the mistress abused the slave woman. Finally the baby came. It was a little white baby. However, its father was a white man of an adjoining plantation. The mistress always believed her husband was the father. By the time the baby was six months old the mistress had beaten it to death. The mother prayed to the Lord to come and get the baby.''

III. THE SLAVE AND HIS WORK

Cheap labor was the reason for slavery—its justification. Had there not been an unusual amount of work to

---

[48]Ella Alford of Bastrop.
[49]M. J. Tims of Minden.
[50]*Ibid.*

be performed in the New World there would not have been any slavery. What do these eighty-two ex-slaves say regarding labor and working conditions of slaves? Mr. James Smith, member of Bastrop, and teacher in Morehouse Parish, introduces thus the experiences of Mrs. Rhiner Gardner, who was a slave on a South Carolina farm:

"Slaves were kept primarily for the work they could do in the production of cotton, corn, rice, tobacco and other staple farm crops. As cotton was 'king' in slavery time, the typical life of a slave centered around the plantation where cotton was the chief crop. Large crops of cotton made necessary immense stretches of farm land which sometimes had to be cleared and drained. Some of the heaviest work the slaves had to do consisted in clearing the farm of trees, logs, stumps, and in digging ditches, all of which was done in primitive fashion. The clearing was usually done in the late autumn and winter after the crops had been harvested and the slaves would otherwise be unemployed. Some of the more able-bodied women slaves sometimes lent a hand in this sort of work.

"Among the slaves, persons of all ages could be found. The young and able-bodied ones were employed to do the heavier farm work, while the old men and women were assigned the lighter tasks, such as sewing for the babies and the children too small to go to the field. They were frequently charged with the cooking for all the slaves so that no time would be lost by the field hands in the preparation of meals. At times they knitted socks for men and stockings for the women. Considerable time was spent in 'carding' cotton and wool.

"The old men usually had acquired some skill which they turned into useful service when they became too old to work in the field. Their work was to make baskets for the cotton and shuck collars for the teams. During the cultivating season, one or more of the old men would go along to the field with one other hand to file, sharpen the hoes, thus making it unnecessary for any of the laborers to cease work to sharpen hoes. It was their duty also to keep the plow points, hoes, and sweeps bright and ready for use by rubbing the rust with brick bats after pouring kerosene upon them. In unusually busy times, this work was done by children who remained at the houses. The feeding of the horses or farm animals also constituted a part of their work. While the horses and mules were at work in the fields, the old men would put their feed into troughs in the big farm barn which was separated into 'stalls' just large enough to admit one ani-

mal at a time. Blindness in both man and beast was not uncommon in slavery time.

"Every large plantation kept a blacksmith shop which took
care of the mending and making of a large part of the implements used on the farm. Many Negroes acquired considerable
skill in this art, some shops being able to turn out wagons and
respectable looking carriages. In such a shop, all handles for
axes, hatchets, hoes, shovels, and plows were made. All cutting
tools such as plow points, sweeps and mower blades were sharp-
ened in the local shops."

Speaking broadly, we may say that slaves fell into two
distinct classes. The first class constituted house and yard
slaves; the second class field slaves. Ordinarily the duties of a house slave kept him or her in contact and
proximity to master or mistress during the greater part
of the time. The very designation "field slave" is sufficiently descriptive. As a rule, house and yard slaves
had a much better time than field slaves, though not necessarily so. Lee Henderson states, "His duty was to make
whiskey for his master and the other whites. He says
that he enjoyed his work and drank as much whiskey as
he wished." Annie Terry, with whom the writer talked
in 1930, says that she was a little house girl who did nothing practically besides play with the little daughter and
son of her master. Her brother was the wagoner; consequently she went to town whenever she desired.

Mrs. Mae D. Moore of Minden says:

"My grandmother, who lived in Frankfort, Kentucky, was
a mid-wife, well cared for and was allowed a part of her earnings. When not engaged at her profession, she made ginger
cakes and sold them on the courthouse grounds. She finally
saved enough to buy her freedom and her husband's besides."

J. H. Carter of St. Joseph, Louisiana, speaking of his
father, relates the following:

"He said he was lucky to be bought by good owners. He did
everything they told him to do and did it by their orders, so it
was not long before he had a good job looking after the hogs,
catching and trapping wild hogs, and turkeys. He said the other
farm slaves would call him 'dat free nigger.'"

"Virginia Johnson was sold in Virginia and brought to Louisiana by her new master, as near as she can guess, at the age of eighteen—she was brought away from her father, mother, sisters and brothers. She was a house slave, but had to work about as hard as the field slaves. She had all of the work to do about the house except on Sundays, when she was given a little help from some of the women field slaves. She also states that her mistress was very mean to her, knocking her over the head many times with things until the blood would gush out."[51]

"The house girl or woman was taught to spin, weave, sew, knit, and do the best cooking. The men or boys who flunkied around for the master were used for carriage drivers, hostlers, taught carpentry, blacksmithing, painting and machinery. He said that Louisiana had an awful rough name and when the house or yard servants were disobedient they would threaten to send them down to New Orleans to be sold to hard taskmasters. These slaves would mourn and cry for many days until all was forgotten."[52]

Chock Archie, ex-slave in Alabama, told Miss Lucinda Cain of Bastrop, Texas:

"I was reared in my master's back yard, ate in his kitchen, sometimes along with his children. I did no field work, but cared for the small children and received absolutely good treatment. I knew nothing of the cruelty of slavery except when I would go to my mother's cabin, where I would hear talk about what had happened to the slaves; also at times I would hear crowds of white men pass, looking for Negroes who had escaped. Mr. Sam Scott, of Mer Rouge, my master's son, recognizes me today as his black pappy and gives me financial aid whenever I ask him."

"Louis Gaston, an ex-slave in Alabama, of over average intelligence, lost his sight at eighteen years of age. He was treated well by his master. Gaston sold corn for his master and kept an accurate account of all the money, which he collected. Often his meals were sent from the master's table. He was allowed to go to church when he desired, but was not allowed off the place at night. Once he was caught off by the patrols and whipped, being accused of having too much liberty."[53]

Of a Kentucky ex-slave, Mrs. Moore says:

"Fanny Johnson was used as a seamstress. Her mistress hired her services out to others. If she was mistreated, her mis-

[51]Lueatha Mansfield of Bastrop.
[52]L. J. Evans of Bastrop.
[53]M. J. Tims of Minden.

tress never allowed her to return to that place. In the run of a month, if Fanny had made a fair profit, the mistress would allow her to keep all she could earn in three days.''

Mrs. Lue Bradford tells of her experience in Kentucky, near Lexington:

"I was taken into the home as a little girl and taught first how to spin and card. Of course, I stayed in the house, but had to sleep on the floor winter and summer with only one quilt. Sometimes in the winter I would catch afire trying to keep warm, as the fire would get so low I had to roll so close that my clothes or quilt would catch afire.''[54]

Myrah Fisher, a Texas ex-slave, states:

"The master's cook was kindly treated and allowed to feed her children in the master's kitchen off such food as was left from the master's table. She attended church with the white people and had church-going clothes as well as plenty of work clothes.''

Mrs. Mary O'Guin, ex-slave of Webster Parish, tells thus her experience as a house slave:

"My mistress would surely work me around the house. I had to rise in the morning at four o'clock and sometimes couldn't retire when night came. I had to clean a six-room house and nurse three kids. When I grew older, cooking and the care of the yards were added to my duties.''[55]

Of the field slaves we have many reports, among which this from Mrs. Lue Bradford is interesting:

"The slaves had to work from sun to sun. The field boss would be in the field to see that they didn't play around. They would have to work until the horn sounded before they could stop for noon. In the morning, the field boss would have the record book and each person was supposed to report before starting for work and all were punished who were late. This encouraged punctuality. The slaves did not leave the field until dark. Upon arrival back home, the women had to cook supper and the men had to feed the stock and shuck corn for the next morning. Sometimes it would be ten o'clock before they finished all that was to be done at the 'big house' and stable.''[56]

[54]Johnnie B. Slaton of Ruston.
[55]Mrs. H. G. Lewis of Minden.
[56]Johnnie B. Slaton of Ruston.

"Linzy Scott was an ex-slave whose master, John Carter, lived in Tensas Parish. He was a field slave and had to work from Monday morning until Saturday night. The horn would blow every morning at four o'clock and the slaves would soon be on their way to the fields to begin work at daylight. Work was from then until twelve. If the weather were really hot, they were given one and a half hours for noon. The dinner was eaten, which they brought with them when they came from home in the morning; after which they worked until night and returned each one to his little cabin, where he would sometimes cook supper and other times go to bed hungry, too tired to cook."[57]

Sam Boykin, ex-slave in Morehouse Parish, speaking thus of field hands, says:

"I was a boy in slavery times but was large enough to work. We children were given tasks to do and when we finished our tasks our work was over for that day. In the fall, we would go to the field early before the frost was melted; our feet would get cold because we would not have on any shoes. To keep warm, we would wrap up in our sacks and hide under the cotton baskets but the overseer would find us and kick the baskets from over us and run us out to work in the frost. If you picked one or two hundred pounds of cotton one day, you had that amount to pick every day or get punished."[58]

Frank Roberson, ex-slave in Morehouse Parish, writing that "working hours were from sun to sun with no such thing as over time,"[59] says further:

"Children began field work at the age of seven years and toiled until they were unable to work. Then the disabled old men and women were left at the house to watch and attend to the babies and small children of the other slaves. Slave mothers during spring and summer months would nurse their babies in the morning about four o'clock, eat breakfast and go to the field. Up to four months old, babies were again nursed at eight or nine in the morning and again at noon. Older children were nursed only mornings, noon and nights. After the crops were 'laid by' the men were kept busy repairing fences and clearing new ground. The women were put at spinning, weaving and knitting."[60]

[57]Lueatha Mansfield of Bastrop.
[58]Mamie Barkley of Bastrop.
[59]Ella Alford, *op. cit.*; J. M. Simpson to Mrs. H. G. Lewis of Minden.
[60]Sarah Skinner, *op. cit.*

A Mrs. Nancy Young, born in Cairo, Illinois, and having experience as a slave in Illinois, Missouri, and Louisiana, while reporting that "Slaves often worked in the rain,"[61] says further:

"We slaves worked from sun to sun. The field boss would be in the field to see that we didn't play around. We had to work until the horn was heard before we could stop for noon. Sometimes we didn't have anything but bread to eat and water to drink. On Saturday nights we went up to the 'big house,' as we called it, to get our week's ration supply, which wasn't much. We went to work in the morning early just at good daybreak. Before we even went to work we had to go by the 'big house' and call the roll; this was done by each one calling his own name. For example, I would say: 'Jane, sir,' then I would go on to work. This was done to let them know who had gone to work on time or who had not gone."

Passing from work to the treatment of the slaves, one finds that, according to the testimonies of the slaves themselves, it was not so human. "On the larger plantations there was a man we called 'the Negro driver.' He would tell us what to do when we had finished one task. There was a driver with the hoe hands and one to go with the plow hands."[62] "As a rule, his treatment of Negro slaves was very harsh. If they failed to accomplish the amount of work ordinarily expected by their masters, they were reported by him to be whipped."[63] "In cotton picking time, everybody was given a certain limit to reach and if any person fell below his limit his clothes were stripped from his back and he was whipped on his naked body. There was one master who whipped until the blood ran from backs to ground. Three hundred pounds per day was the lowest for some masters. My master would let a slave who picked six hundred pounds of cotton each day for three days walk around idle during the remaining three days of the week."

[61] Miss M. M. Brown of Monroe.
[62] Mamie Barkley of Bastrop.
[63] Sarah Skinner, *op. cit.*

"Mrs. Martha Washington reported that some of the conditions of slavery were horrible."[64] "Burton Davis, a Georgia slave, field hand, plowed from daybreak until dark. When time was rushing, he was forced to work on moonshine nights. The horses were changed and rested but he had to keep on plowing."[65] One Mrs. Emma Gray, ex-slave in Morehouse Parish, says:

"Our old master was supposed to be the best in the neighborhood, but he sometimes whipped. When he did, the men would have to pull off their shirts and the women would have to pull down their waists to receive the whippings upon naked skin. My old master whipped one lady about walking with a stiff leg until her back bled. I was whipped several times in slavery—one morning for being late. When I was about sixteen years old, the overseer attempted to whip me about plowing. I had become tired of being whipped. Old Bumpus (the overseer) hit me with a bull whip—drawing blood. I grabbed it; he changed ends and hit me on the head. I then snatched the whip and struck him on the head. This drew blood, making both of us bleed. After fifteen minutes of hard tussling, he let me go and never attempted to whip me again."[66]

"Alex Johnson was a slave whose master was Huey Young, and he lived on the Young plantation. Uncle Alex was a field slave and sometimes his work was very hard; he was his mother's girl for four years. He washed, cooked, spun, knitted and nursed in order to help his mother, who had certain tasks to finish in a limited time.

"By daylight, each one had to be ready to begin and work until noon, when they ate their dinner which had been brought along with them in the morning and some would bring their breakfast, for they wouldn't have time to eat before leaving home. The length of the noon hour depended upon the amount of work to be done. After noon, they worked until night. Then they would go to the cabin, get supper and go to bed. If they would stay up a good while, old master would knock and order everyone to bed.

"Huey Young was very cruel to his slaves, although his wife was very kind. He had a bench with holes bored in it through which yokes fitted. When he got ready to whip a slave, he would place one of these yokes over his head to hold him. He would simply beat him with a paddle having holes in it. One

[64] M. I. Swearingan of Bastrop.
[65] Mae D. Moore of Minden.
[66] J. E. Gray of Bastrop.

day, Uncle Alex says, he whipped a woman until the wagoners had to carry her home in a wagon. The man (ex-master) died a few years ago and Uncle Alex just knows he was lost. During his last sickness, he didn't want anyone to do anything for him but Uncle Alex's wife, who is still living. She was a very small child when the war ended.''[67]

"Mrs. Pricilla Owens reported that her master treated her fairly well. He was her father. Most of the meanness was done by overseers. If the right report reached the master, he would sometimes send his overseer away. Upon one occasion, an overseer whipped a woman until the blood ran on the floor. She had not been on the plantation very long. The master had given all the slaves passes to another plantation to attend a dance. After reaching there and having so much fun, they decided to dance all night. The overseer liked this particular woman and thought she was away with some of the slaves and whipped her almost to death. For this act, the overseer was sent away to another place.''[68]

IV. PUNISHMENTS AND SLAVE-TRADING

Around the question of punishment hinges the most frequent bases for the argument regarding the inhumanity of slavery. Much has been said concerning cruel punishment of men and women held in bondage. Negro men and women who passed through the ordeal of slavery dwell upon this feature of punishment more than any other. It is no surprise, then, to find that statements regarding the corrections of slaves have been full and frequent in these accounts.

Lee Henderson told Mrs. Rosa B. Johnson that, "Punishment was not so severe on his master's plantation unless the slave was very unruly. Most of the whipping was done with a strap. In extreme cases persons were whipped so severly that the skin was taken off the body in spots and the clothes were discolored with blood. On some occasions one slave was forced to whip another slave." In this connection, Mrs. Patsy Larkin tells the following story:

[67]Lueatha Mansfield of Bastrop.
[68]Mable L. Leary of Minden.

"My Uncle was a 'nigger driver' and just before we were set free, my mother made my mistress angry and the mistress told my Uncle to give my mother a good whipping; he whipped her good for which I hated him although he could not help himself."[69]

Mrs. Mae Dee Moore of Minden, set forth the cruelty of a Texas slave owner in these words:

"A very cruel slave owner who lived in Harrison County, Texas, owned about forty or fifty slaves and kept a hired overseer. Slaves were beaten for the least offense. Oftentimes when a slave was tied down and beaten almost to death, this man who weighed about one hundred and eighty-five or two hundred pounds, would get on the slave and walk up and down his back, stamping, occasionally saying, 'if there is anything I like better than my drink, it is whipping a nigger.' Many times he would have slaves whipped to death, have a hole dug and kick the dead slaves into it."

The following tale is related not only to illustrate a type of punishment but also to show to what extremities helplessness will lead.

"During the time of slavery, there were two women by the names of Betty and Molly. Molly was tall with coal black hair, about the age of thirty. Betty was a slave brought from Alabama and sold in Louisiana. She was very high-tempered. She weighed about one hundred and eighty-five pounds. Betty was treated very cruelly by the overseer on account of her temper. On one occasion, her punishment was to be whipped every morning for one month. This she thought horrible. She was the mother of one child named Simon.

"One day Aunt Betty and Molly got into a dispute over a cotton row in a field where they were chopping cotton. Betty struck Molly with her hoe, cutting the flesh from her face. Her punishment was so severe, she decided that she would stand it no longer. She threw her little son, Simon, in the well. They whipped her terribly about the disappearance of the child. She would never tell where the child was. There was one old slave who felt sorry for her and begged her to tell where the child was because he had heard the overseer say that night would be his last time to whip her because he was going to kill her. So she told this old slave man where her little son was. He rushed to the lot where the well was and pulled him out.

[69] Ella Alford of Bastrop.

"Aunt Betty was brought to Homer and tried by the court and was condemned to die.

"On the day that she was hanged they asked her what she had to say. She only said, 'I want to eat breakfast in hell tomorrow morning with Molly McAmore!' "[70]

Some ex-slaves dwelt upon the unusual practices and features of punishments. "Mrs. Monson said that women were whipped until they bled and then forced to bathe in brine."[71] J. H. Carter giving reminiscences of his father recalls that:

"Many were treated as brutes, whipped and put in stocks, and I am told that some slave owners after putting them in stocks would build a fire of bark and chunk the bark while burning and let the small pieces drop on the slave while in the stocks.

"About once a year when the white folks were away, a gang of the slaves would come together and have the big time of their lives; sometimes they would get caught, which meant a good punishment, usually ending in a sound beating upon nude bodies draped across logs."[72]

"All the slaves were checked upon at night and if one were missing, the overseer would call for him and if he (slave) had not been visiting the hut of someone on that plantation, he was hunted and if caught before he could reach his own hut, he would be given from fifty to one hundred lashes on his naked back with a big plaited leather whip made of rawhide leather. Some of these whips, he said, had nine small ends plaited; this was called a cat-o-nine-tails which would bring nine blisters at each stroke. He also said that some of the overseers were so cruel that they would pour turpentine over blisters to make the pains more severe. They thought that this would make the slaves fear such cruel punishment and not venture to leave the plantation without a written permit."[73]

"Louisa Harris said if a slave began learning to write and let it be known, his fingers were cut off. There was a colored church on the plantation. They were never given money and just enough clothes to work in. Women were whipped as children. Their clothes were turned over their heads and they were whipped so that they couldn't move."[74]

[70] Minnie J. Tims of Minden.
[71] Mary L. Swearingan of Bastrop, quoting Bertha Pillars.
[72] Related to M. L. Leary of Minden.
[73] L. J. Evans of Bastrop, quoting Joseph Young.
[74] Mable L. Leary of Minden.

Dr. Carter G. Woodson gives the testimony of his grandfather, Carter Woodson, a slave in Fluvanna County, Virginia. Being an excellent mechanic and cabinetmaker, he was permitted to go from plantation to plantation and make contracts for work in his own name and report periodically to his master. Functioning in this capacity, the old gentleman thought of himself as free rather than a slave. One day, then, when the overseer of the plantation undertook to whip Carter Woodson he turned the tables on the former and whipped him. His master, therefore, had him caught and tied up to afflict him with the punishment adequate for such a bold deed. On approaching the accused, the master said, "When I get through with you, Carter Woodson, you will be sorry that you ever struck a white man." Thereupon the sufferer replied, "You don't have to get through with this for me to feel that way, for I am sorry now, sir."

George Woodson, the son of Carter Woodson, and the uncle of Dr. Carter G. Woodson, had more of the invincible spirit than his father. This chip of the old block was what was called in those days an unruly slave. George grew tired of being punished even after having performed his duties faithfully, and began to strike back. One day he whipped the overseer for trying to punish him without justification; and when his master appeared upon the scene George whipped him also. This the slave knew to be tantamount to servile insurrection. George escaped to the woods and endeavored to induce other slaves to join him. Run down by blood hounds, however, he was soon apprehended and returned to the plantation, where he was so severely beaten as to bleed profusely and to have scars on almost every part of the body. To heal his wounds he was washed down in brine or what the slaves referred to as "salt and water." When George finally recovered sufficiently to go to the auction block he was taken to Richmond and sold into Louisiana, and his relatives never heard of him again. George's brother, James Henry

Woodson, the father of Dr. Carter G. Woodson, carried with him to his grave the grievance against that institution which thus deprived him of his oldest brother.

It is not at all surprising to note that much of the punishment centered around the problem of work. Hannah Towns told Mrs. M. J. Tims, of Minden, that, "If a slave were found to be stubborn he had a real hard time. The men especially were whipped if they were found not wanting to work or were sold from their family." Mrs. H. G. Lewis of Minden, quotes Tessie Moore as saying: "My mother was whipped nearly to death for not reporting to work on time. Besides, she was not allowed to eat for a day."

Another slave quaintly sets forth thus his narrative in dialect:

"My master wus name Bunkie. He wus not so mean to his slaves. He whipped only dem dat wus lazy and contrary. Some marsters wus very mean to dem. De overseer would whup de slaves if dey didn't work to suit him. Sometimes he would whup de slaves till de blood run. He would tie um and stake um out by tying each hand and foot to four stakes drove in de ground. De slaves had to work from sun to sun. Cotton picking time each slave had to fetch so much cotton or git a whuppin. When I wus bout thirteen, de overseer ask me fur my shirt case (because) I didn't pick de mount (amount) of cotton he did. I begged him to let me off an' I'd git it next time; en I did. Loter (lot of) old men and women would git whuppins case dey would let me beat um picking cotton."[75]

"If a slave felt ill, the master usually gave what medicine he thought necessary. The doctor was seldom called in. The master prized a horse more than some slaves and often whipped a slave to death about abusing his horse. If a master moved, he carried his slave just as he did his household materials."[76]

Mrs. Lizzie Shelton told Mrs. M. L. Leary of Minden, that:

"She would just as soon have been in hell as in slavery. Every day she had to clean the silver and her mistress would find some fault for which she was daily beaten."

[75]Callie Harvey of Bastrop.
[76]G. T. Griffin of St. Joseph, quoting ex-slave Robinson, of Louisiana.

"Our master would punish us by putting us into stocks. If a slave committed a bad crime, he would be put into the stocks by his head; that is, his head was put through the hole so that it would fasten around his neck. If the crime was not bad, he would be put in by the feet. Someone carried water and food to him. We were also punished by whipping with a whip made from cow hide; or a large whip called a bull whip. When a mother was sent to attend to her baby, she had a certain time to stay; if she stayed over that time she was whipped."[77]

In view of the preceding the following cases revolving around stealing will not astonish the readers. Joe Caldwell, ex-slave of Louisiana, says:

"If a slave stole anything he was whipped. The punishment for a minor offense was ten lashes on bare back. When resistance was offered, punishment was doubled or trebled; the flesh was raw and blood streamed."[78]

Lue Bradford of the same slaveholding area, says:

"My second master, a Mr. Heard, and his wife were very cruel to their cook. One day she cooked some biscuits and brought them to the table. Mrs. Heard decided that she had kept one or two for herself. Now she (the slave) was not allowed to eat biscuits at all, consequently Mr. and Mrs. Heard began questioning the cook. Of course the cook had eaten the biscuits, but forgot to wash the pan in which they had been cooked. Mr. Heard counted the number of biscuits on the table then went into the kitchen where he could see the signs in the pan; from which he was able to judge that the cook had misplaced two biscuits. Mr. Heard finished his dinner, then took the cook out and whipped the blood out of her."[79]

"Rosa Tims had a very cruel master who whipped his slaves often to keep them smart. The slaves were allowed to sing while working; but they had to turn down a wash-pot to retain the sound when they sang and prayed at home. They were not allowed to visit without a pass. If they slipped off, the hounds found them, then a dreadful whipping followed."[80]

Not all slaves were whipped as witness the following stories:

[77]Mamie Barkley of Bastrop, quoting Jane Robinson.
[78]Lucinda Cabin of Bastrop.
[79]Johnnie B. Slaton of Ruston.
[80]Minnie J. Tims of Minden.

"Mr. Johnson was a water boy in the days of slavery; he states that he was one who could talk so fast and say so many funny things that his mistress could never whip him."[81]

"Mrs. Mary Frances, an ex-slave woman about ninety years of age, states that during slavery time many of the slaves endured all kinds of torture in order to escape the hard punishments inflicted upon them. She tells of an instance when an uncle of her's resisted one of the overseers and struck his master a severe blow when the master attempted to beat him with a cow hide whip for not working fast enough for him. After having this encounter with the master the poor slave knew that it meant death if he remained on the place and that if he ran away the hounds would be sent in pursuit. Thus, he had to think fast of a means to escape.

"Immediately he set out for the woods. After crossing a small stream in a dense forest he came to a spot where there was a large hole in the ground. This was the place for him. He took trees, leaves and branches to cover it over in order that he might be protected from wild animals and storms. He made a bed of leaves upon which to sleep, and kept near him a large club which was his only weapon. He killed birds and game and other wild animals of this forest for food. He seized every opportunity to slip back to the plantation to visit the cabin in which his mother lived, so as to stay in touch with her and family. No one knew of his whereabouts but her, and she kept it strictly a secret. This particular slave remained in the forest until the hair covered his body and he looked like the animals about him.

"When freedom came, he revealed himself, went to his wife and children, who to their utmost surprise, and fright, greeted him, although they were not thoroughly convinced that he was whom he claimed to be."[82]

Lue Bradford, who was a slave near Lexington, Kentucky, suggests that cruel masters were not always regarded with favor by their white neighbors. She says, "The Heard people were so cruel and did so many disgraceful things to their slaves that their neighbors stopped visiting them, looking upon them as a set of dirty people not even good enough to visit."[83]

Not all punishment was administered by the masters, overseers and drivers. Patrols had a very definite hand

[81] L. J. Evans of Bastrop.
[82] Minnie J. Tims of Minden.
[83] Johnnie Slaton of Ruston.

and part in keeping the Negro slaves confined to plantations and properly terrified. Negro hunting, Negro catching, Negro watching and Negro whipping constituted the
greatest sport of many youthful whites. Ex-slaves refer
to them as "patty-rolls," the "patter-rollers," "patter-
roses," or "paddle rollers."

"Sometimes all those who were out without a pass were
caught by the patrols, severely whipped and carried to their
masters. Whenever a slave tried to escape or run away from
his master, he was hunted down by bulldogs or blood hounds.
Sometimes slaves would be so badly lacerated by the dogs that
they would bleed to death, being located by the presence of
vultures in unusual numbers hovering over some lonely spot."[84]

"Once in a while, they would give a frolic, and if anyone
from another plantation was caught there by the patter-roses
without a pass, he was beaten and sent home."[85]

"The slaves didn't have any privileges. If dey wanted to
go from one plantation to de udder, dey had to ask. If a young
man wanted to go to see a girl, he had to ask. If he slipped
away and the Paddle Rollers (they were the men that watched
the plantation at night) caught him, he wus whupped with a
bull whup. It wus pleated rawhide. Some of de slaves wud
holler so mournful when dey git a whuppin."[86]

Not the least inhuman phase of slavery was the domestic slave trade, and that practice did not fail to leave its
impression upon those most affected. We were able to
secure accounts of procedure from those actually involved—from those who had actually traveled in the slave
coffles and experienced their hardships—from those who
had been sold away from family and loved ones. Slaves
were sold to clear accumulated debts and to effect a division of property among heirs. Stubborn and unruly
slaves were sold as a punishment, and some because they
bore blood relationship to the master. Mr. James Smith,
of Bastrop, says:

"One of the saddest pictures of slave life was that presented
by the wanton disregard of family ties by the owners. The

[84]Mrs. L. J. Evans of Bastrop, quoting her uncle, Joseph Young.
[85]M. M. Brown of Monroe.
[86]Callie F. Harvey of Bastrop, quoting Roan Barnes.

buying and selling of slaves was as common as the buying and selling of horses and cattle. Families were separated never again to be seen or heard from. The fear of being sold away from the family or of having the family sold kept the slaves in constant uneasiness. If a slave was called to the house by the owner or overseer and the cause was not known by the rest of the slaves they invariably guessed that a 'deal' had been made and the person in question had been sold.''

Mrs. Amelia Armstrong stated that she had "seen children sold from their mothers and husbands sold from wives." "Frank Jones, who was a slave in Macon, Georgia, was sold from his wife and three children. He never saw them again."[87] "Myrah Fisher, an ex-slave in Texas, says that when her mistress and master died, the slaves were divided and sold. She was sold from her children into Louisiana, the children being sold into North Carolina and Georgia."[88] "Often brothers and sisters were sold from each other right in the presence of their mothers and were not allowed to cry at the parting."[89]

"Mrs. Bradford relates that she was sold to a slave speculator. She was brought with a drove of slaves from Kentucky to Alabama. At night the men (speculators) rented a stable for them to stay just as we see horse stables of today with no protection at all. There were seventy-five in the drove. If one would get too hot and die on the way or anything happened that would cause one to die, they would dig a hole and put him into it, put a little dirt over him and go on."[90]

"Often fathers were sold from their families or mothers from their children and children from their parents' arms. Knowing they would never see each other again, this was heart breaking to both the ones leaving and the ones left behind. Slaves, who were good workers or who could read and write, were often sold for large sums, or given in exchange for some debt."[91]

"My mother was upon the block to be sold at one time but her mistress, Minder Cox, would not let her be sold. After the death of my mistress' father, the slaves were divided. My father

[87]Minnie J. Tims, P. O. Box 493, Homer, Louisiana, of Minden.

[88]Mae Dee Moore of Minden.

[89]Ella Alford of Bastrop, quoting Patsy Larkin, ex-slave, near Selma, Alabama.

[90]Johnnie Slaton of Ruston.

[91]G. L. Griffin of St. Joseph, quoting ex-slave, Robinson.

belonged to my mistress' stepmother. He was allowed to come to see us, but sometimes he had a mean overseer, who would not let him come; then he would have to slip off to see us."[92]

"I was born about the year of 1845 in Bossier Parish near Plainsdealing. My mother was a Mulatoo—the daughter of her master, who gave to her, her sister and mother their freedom which was legal in the state of Virginia; but after the master's death, his son (white and the new master) came to the Negro quarters and asked my grandmother to let him see the papers his father had given her. The papers, once in his hands, he burned them (the papers) in the presence of my grandmother and ran from the house. Soon thereafter he sold them to the Negro trader, who took them to New Orleans and sold them from the block."[93]

"When dey sold slaves dey wud carry them in droves just like dey do cattle and horses today. A man would be riding in front and one behind. Natchez, Mississippi, was one of the big slave markets. Dey would take chillun from dey mothers. Dey would never see each other again. Dey would examine men, women, and chillun just like dey would cattle and horses before buying um. Sometimes dey would give $1,500; $1,800 for one slave."[94]

Just when and how many times a slave could change hands and did, may be judged from the experience of Mrs. Young, an ex-slave.

"When Mrs. Young was about sixteen years old, Mr. Bert sold her to Mr. William Gipson of Plattsburg, Mo., and finally Mr. Gipson sold her to Mr. Pratt of Plattsburg, Mo. Mr. Pratt put her in the traders yard and sold her to General Dodge. Then General Dodge sold her to a southern slave owner, Mr. Dirge Sandford. Mr. Dirge Sandford brought her from Plattsburg, Mo., to Monroe, La. This was a tiresome journey. They walked two by two, the men being chained two by two, legs and arms. They brought with them provisions to eat on the way, a herd of horses and a herd of mules. When transferred across the rivers, they were made to stand among the horses and mules. She was fifteen years old when she arrived in Monroe, La., and there were only two stores in Monroe, on the Ouachita river. Mr. Sandford put her on a block and sold her off to Mr. Tannel Hatheway of Log Town, La., in the pine hills."[95]

[92]Mamie M. Barkley of Bastrop, quoting Jane Robinson, ex-slave of Jefferson County, Mississippi.

[93]J. E. Gray of Bastrop, quoting Mrs. Emma Gray.

[94]Callie Harvey of Bastrop, quoting Roan Barnes.

[95]M. M. Brown of Monroe.

"When a planter owed a debt and was not able to meet it, all of his slaves were called to the yard, placed in a circle and the creditor allowed to select from that number enough slaves to settle the debt. In some instances, the men would be ordered to pull off their shirts, the women to pull off their shirt waists, that prospective buyers might see if they had healthy looking muscles or if their backs were scarred."[96]

At all times during slavery, there seemed to have been those high-spirited souls (called "bad" by their masters) who chafed under the yoke of bondage to such a degree that they were willing to risk life and limb by running away. This study enables us to give the testimony of a few who attempted to find freedom in flight and the results of such attempts.

"Burton Davis, Georgia ex-slave, a farm hand, plowing from day-break until dark and on moonshine nights says, 'Once he ran away, was overtaken and beaten until his back was gashed. As a treatment, strong salt water was thrown on his back; while unable to go to meals, he was fed pot licker and bread crumbs."[97]

"One morning, my boss came around and told me, since I was such an able bodied giant, more work was expected of me. He put a task which was impossible for me to complete in the few hours alloted. When he returned, he found I had not finished it. His anger had no bounds; he struck me, drawing blood as usual; suddenly I turned upon him giving him a sound thrashing and made my escape by the help of the Lord to another far-off plantation. I found the master there not near as cruel as my former one. I worked faithfully for the new master until the Negroes were freed."[98]

"Bob Jones belonged to a man who owned a plantation on Bayou Lafourche. Bob continued to run away from his master despite the hounds and the cruel beatings. So a kind of iron halter with a bell attached to it was placed upon Bob's head so that he might easily be caught."[99]

"I remember one morning during the slavery period, I saw a colored man on the back of our plantation, who seemed to be running away. It wasn't long before he was lost to my sight. About five hours later, we heard some dogs barking. I was told that they were 'nigger' hounds. They trailed that man, I was

[96]L. J. Evans of Bastrop, quoting Joseph Young.
[97]Mae Dee Moore of Minden.
[98]Lucinda Cain of Bastrop, quoting Jeff Barnes, ex-slave in Alabama.
[99]L. M. Channell of Bastrop.

told, to the present site of Spyker Carbon plant where he killed two of the dogs in a fight with them. It was the custom for the dogs to taste Negro blood when they had trailed well. The Negro man was brought back by our field washed down in blood. This was done to make us afraid to run away."[100]

"Sometimes a slave and the overseer would get into a fuss or fight and the slave would run away to keep from being punished. Then he would be chased by the blood hounds; sometimes they would get away. I have seen a number of slaves hiding in the woods around my master's plantation. At night they would slip to the quarters and beg for our food."[101]

V. Religion and Recreation Activities

Accounts of religious conditions and opportunities for slaves vary. Some ex-slaves insist that every opportunity for worship was given; others claim that even the privilege of free worship was denied. Worship was a fact. The seeds of Christianity found ripe soil in breasts of black slaves often denied the right of open public worship. Negro slaves seemed to have fallen upon the most ingenious plans to gratify their desire to "Take their burdens to the Lord." Slaves attended the same churches attended by the whites, listening to the same sermons, the same songs, and the same prayers.

"On a Bowie County, Texas, farm, slaves were allowed to hold church services on Wednesday nights, Sunday and Sunday nights. They were not allowed to preach or sing loud for fear of disturbing their mistress. The old master would read the Negro Parson a chapter in the Bible, select his text, and give him some instructions about handling the subject."[102]

Mrs. Rhiner Gardner of Morehouse Parish, says:

"A few slaves were usually present at most of the religious services held for the whites. They were, the carriage drivers, who after driving the white people to church were given seats at the service."[103]

[100]Emma Gray to J. E. Gray of Bastrop.
[101]Mamie Barkley of Bastrop, quoting Jane Robinson.
[102]Gertrude Smith of Ruston, quoting Fanny White.
[103]James Smith of Bastrop.

"Slaves went to church with their masters but there were no seats in the churches for them. They sat on the floor of the church or steps and peeped in. They did not understand any way just where or why it was the master carried them."[104]

"The only time slaves were allowed to attend church was on Sunday and they had to have a pass before they could go. In the morning they would attend the white folks church and in the afternoon, the church for the slaves."[105]

"There would be church service on Sunday. In the morning the slaves would attend church with their masters—upstairs— where a white preacher would preach. In the evening there would be service downstairs for the slaves, where sometimes a white preacher would preach and sometimes a colored one."[106]

"On Sunday evening, we would have church. A white preacher would preach; one was named Mr. Muller. He would teach us from the Catechism and preach. In his sermon, he would tell us how to obey our mistress and masters. Sometimes we would slip out in the bushes and have church; then we would have a colored preacher to preach for us."[107]

"The white minister preached to the slaves on Sunday afternoons. His text was always the same, namely: 'Servants obey your masters.' "[108]

"Mrs. Pricilla Owens, who was born in Georgia and was run off to Texas to escape the Union soldiers, says that slaves were allowed to have church to themselves. They had it in the quarters. The Negro slaves were sometimes forced to attend church with their masters and other times the white preacher would preach for the whites in the morning and for the slaves in the evening. He would use such expressions as 'Don't steal your master's chickens,' 'Obey your masters,' 'Don't run away, don't lie.' This kind of preaching was given in the afternoon."[109]

"On some Sundays, the white preacher would preach to the slaves, the slaves kneeling on the ground in front of the mansion porch, while he (the preacher) and the white family together with a Nigger preacher sat on the porch. Of course, the Nigger preacher, as he was called, sat on one end of the porch while old master's family sat at the other end. We had preaching very seldom."[110]

[104] A. W. Casterman, quoting Annie Washington.

[105] Lueatha Mansfield of Bastrop, from Uncle Alex.

[106] *Ibid.*, from Uncle Linzy.

[107] Mamie Barkley of Bastrop, quoting Jane Robinson.

[108] M. J. Tims of Minden, quoting Melvina Elzy.

[109] A. W. Casterman of Minden.

[110] Ella Alford of Bastrop.

An ex-slave gives us the gist of a typical sermon for the Negro slaves of his section. By comparison with other accounts, the sermon seems to have been universal.

"You slaves will go to heaven if you are good, but don't ever think that you will be close to your mistress and master. No! No! there will be a wall between you; but there will be holes in it that will permit you to look out and see your mistress when she passes by. If you want to sit behind this wall, you must do the language of the text 'Obey your masters.'

"Now don't you steal your master's chickens, turkeys; don't you steal your master's hogs, and don't you run away; don't talk about your mistress and master. If you do, you will not get a chance to go to heaven and sit behind the glorious wall, because here is the language of the text—on these points—then he would reach upon the porch and get a long steel strap or bullwhip and show it to the slaves saying, that is what you will get if you disobey.

"Now I will let Parson Tom preach to you because you can understand his talk.

"Parson Tom would get up and repeat everything that the white preacher had said, because he was afraid to say anything different."[111]

Statements which follow lead one to believe that at times worship of any nature was denied to the slaves.

"The slaves did not have churches as we have now. They made arbors of small pine trees. Some of them didn't have arbors. When they wanted to sing and pray, they would steal off into the woods. During that time, most of the masters were cruel. If they would hear them (slaves) singing, they would get their whips and whip them all the way home. Whipping did not stop them from having meetings. When one place was located they would find another one. They didn't have many preachers. Everyone was so anxious to have a word to say that a preacher did not have a chance. All of them would sing and pray."[112]

"If dey had prayer meeting dey would turn a wash pot down to ketch de sound to keep de marsters from hearing um. Didn't have no church; sometimes a white man would go around through the quarters preaching to de slaves telling dem to obey dey marsters and missus and dey would be good to dem."[113]

"Slaves were not allowed to have church, but they would have

[111]Ella Alford of Bastrop, quoting Frank Roberson.
[112]M. J. Jones of Minden, quoting Hannah Lowery.
[113]Callie Harvey of Bastrop, quoting Roan Barnes.

prayer meetings secretly. They would place pots in the door to keep the sound in the house to prevent their masters from hearing them.''[114]

Mrs. L. J. Evans, quoting Joseph Young, says:

''They (slaves) sang and prayed around their fireplaces. Someone would exhort if there was a preacher among them. This was all done by permission. The overseer would always be present to know what was being said or done.''

''Andrew Jackson, ex-slave of Louisiana, says they went to church services on Sundays. The Negroes met in one or another of the cabins and held these services.''[115]

''On Sunday they (the slaves) would have services after the white people had had theirs. Most times, however, the slaves held their meetings in the woods under (brush) arbors made by them. The preacher came from some other plantation; he preached about heaven and hell. There they were not allowed to pray for freedom, but sometimes the slaves would steal away at night and go into cane thickets and pray for deliverance; they always prayed in a prostrate position with the face close to the ground so that no sound could escape to warn the master or the overseer.''[116]

''There were no churches as such for Negro slaves. At times the slaves would be called together by a white minister who would exhort the servants to be subject unto their masters. If there happened to be a church located on or near the master's plantation, he would allow the slaves to be called together there on special occasions and instructed by a minister. If there chanced to be among the slaves a man of their own race who could read and write, he generally preached and would, at times and places unknown to the master, call his fellow slaves together and hold religious services with them. It was to such leaders as these that the slaves owed much of their religious instructions.''[117]

Mr. Kalvin Woods, who is about ninety-five or a hundred years old, says:

''When he was a slave, he always would try to preach to the other slaves and would slip about from plantation to plantation preaching. However, the women slaves would take old quilts and rags and wet them thoroughly; then hang them up in the form of a little room and the slaves who were interested about it would huddle up behind these quilts to do their praying, preaching and

[114]M. M. Brown of Monroe, quoting Nancy Young.
[115]M. J. Tims of Minden.
[116]Ella Alford of Minden, quoting Patsy Larkin.
[117]James Smith of Bastrop, quoting Rhiner Gardner.

singing. These wet rags and quilts were used to keep the sound of their voices from penetrating the air. They didn't want their masters to hear them, for they knew it meant a punishment for them. Mr. Woods says many a happy meeting was carried on behind these quilts and rags.''[118]

Referring to a plantation located in Louisiana, Mrs. Channel says:

''On this plantation, there were about one hundred and fifty slaves. Of this number, only about ten were Christians. We can easily account for this, for religious services among slaves were strictly forbidden. But the slaves would steal away into the woods at night and hold services. They would form a circle on their knees around the speaker who would also be on his knees. He would bend forward and speak into or over a vessel of water to drown the sound. If anyone became animated and cried out, the others would quickly stop the noise by placing their hands over the offender's mouth.''

In some localities and communities, masters allowed slaves privilege to earn and spend money of their own; others permitted the slaves to own chickens, pigs, and the like, or to have garden patches. ''An ex-slave told the writer that his master willingly gave some of the slaves patches for themselves which they worked on Sundays and at night. When the crop was harvested he (the master) would sell if for them and give the slaves the money.''[119] Jane Robinson, who was a slave in Jefferson County, Mississippi, says:

''We were not given any money, but sometimes we were given patches on which to raise some truck; this (truck) would be sold and the money given to us. The truck patch had to be worked at night. I used to hold a light for my grandfather as he worked in his truck patch.''[120]

''Mrs. Channell says that on the Martin plantation, thrifty slaves were allowed to work at night and make a little garden for themselves.''

[118]Mary L. Swearingan of Bastrop.
[119]Sarah Skinner.
[120]Mamie Barkley of Bastrop.

"Many of the slaves had money which some would bury. A man by the name of Allen Jones had a shoe shop. He would fix shoes, for which he was paid well. Some had stores. They sold beer and ginger snaps. They had to fix shoes and sell in their stores at night, between times, or on Saturday evenings. Many of the slaves also had patches. They worked for the master during day and in the little patches at night. Sometimes the master would give time off from work. The most that they would plant on these patches were things to eat. If they raised more than they could eat, the rest was sold and the money given to the slaves. As they grew in finance, they were then able to buy better shoes, dresses or hats."[121]

Mr. Crawford Martin of this very plantation, says, "They (slaves) got money sometimes by working on the time that was given to them, such as Saturday evening and sometimes all day Saturday. They (slaves) used this money to buy nice things that the master did not give, such as shoes and (better) clothing."[122] Another ex-slave says: "On some Louisiana plantations, it was permissible for slaves to raise chickens and to work small gardens during leisure. Only thrifty favorite slaves were allowed this privilege. This was called the edge of slavery."[123] "Money was got by working out for white folks who did not have slaves. This was done when they were off for the week-end."[124] "During sickness, a mistress or some old slave who could not do much work attended to the sick. In very serious sickness, a physician was called."[125]

Even in the dark house of bondage means of lightening the burden through recreation and amusement were not lacking. The customs of granting Sundays to slaves as a day of rest was practically universal. It was a practice rarely varied except in cases of extreme emergency. Our investigation showed that work was not required of

[121]Mary Jones of Bastrop, quoting Mrs. Hannah Lowry.
[122]A. W. Casterman of Minden.
[123]A. W. Casterman, quoting Annie Washington.
[124]Sarah Skinner, *op. cit.*
[125]Ella Herson of Bastrop.

slaves on Saturday afternoons and evenings. Occasionally, exceptionally good masters would allow slaves all of
Saturday. Besides the foregoing, all recognized state and
national holidays normally called for suspension of regular daily duties.

"Mrs. Amelia Armstrong, an ex-slave in Columbus, Mississippi, states that she was a servant in the home of her master
and was granted permission to leave the plantation along with
other slaves upon several occasions for pleasure visits. They
never had any work to do on Sunday as they had a Christian
hearted master."[126]
"For entertainment slaves were always given a big dinner
on the 4th of July; all had picnics on some occasions. Those who
liked frolics could have them on special occasions."
"The slaves had little time or occasion for amusement. However, after the accomplishment of a particularly heavy task, such
as the harvesting of a bumper crop, or the clearing of a large
piece of land, if the slaves had worked to the satisfaction of the
overseer, the master was usually induced to permit a big dance
to the slaves."

"Mrs. Nancy Young said slaves had very few amusements. They visited on Sundays and once in a while they
would give a frolic."[127] Mrs. L. J. Evans of Bastrop
quotes her Uncle Joseph Young as saying, "The only
amusements the slaves had were boxing, wrestling, jumping and dancing." "It was stated by this man that
slaves usually amused themselves by boxing, foot races,
dancing (secretly), playing music on tin cans, Jew's
harps, or any kind of instrument which they could get
that would produce sound. On many occasions, the whites
enjoyed looking at the Negroes perform."[128]
"Some of the slave owners would allow their slaves to
stage ring plays and go from house to house on Sundays."[129] "For amusement, dancing was allowed; the overseer would give them passes from house to house on the

[126]H. A. Dillon of Bastrop.
[127]M. M. Brown of Monroe.
[128]Rosa B. Johnson of Minden, quoting Lee Henderson.
[129]J. H. Carter of St. Joseph, quoting father.

plantation, and they would dance themselves down. Dancing seemed to be the only amusement for the slaves.''[130]

"Usually when a slave holder gave a big festival, slaves from all neighboring farms would be invited. At times, festivals would be given for the sole benefit of the slaves of one slave holder. At this festival, the Negroes would sing and dance. Some would march and dance by the music of a banjo, others by the beating of a tin-pan. The ladies would dress in white towel dresses, with white rags on their heads. The men would dress in white duckings and shirts. Their pantaloons would be rolled up to the knees, and all would dance barefooted.''[131]

"The slaves were allowed to have socials or balls occasionally. At times, the mistress and master would come out to see the Negroes dance and enjoy themselves; the dances that were done in those days were quadrille and other square dances. An accordion often furnished the music. On rare occasions, there were fiddles, fifes, and sometimes a drum. This same music was often carried to the home of the master when company came.''[132]

"Frequently, these slaves were permitted to have a ball or dance. Some would play ring plays, such as 'Git around Napper and git out ob de way' or 'Where yo gwine buzzard, Where you gwine crow? Ise gwine down to de new groun to jump Jim Crow. Wheel aroun and turn aroun and do jes so. Evy time you turn aroun, you jump Jim Crow.' ''[133]

"De most pledger the slaves had wus playing ball, shooting marbles and playing de fiddle. Sometimes, dey would slip off to give a dance.''[134]

"There was nothing ever given for their enjoyment, Uncle Alex says, unless it was a big watermelon eating. There were always four or five acres planted in watermelons and during the season, they would have a big feast out under the trees. There would be plenty of whisky at all times, but they would have that to buy. They never had any money not even as much as a dollar given to them by their masters.''[135]

"For entertainment, they (slaves) were given big dinners on some occasions, such as the 4th of July, when they were through or up with the crops.''[136]

[130] Gertrude Smith of Ruston, quoting Fanny White.

[131] Gertrude Smith of Ruston.

[132] G. T. Griffin of St. Joseph, quoting Robinson.

[133] L. M. Channell of Bastrop.

[134] Roan Barnes to Callie F. Harvey of Bastrop.

[135] Lueatha Mansfield of Bastrop.

[136] A. W. Casterman of Minden, quoting Annie Washington, ex-slave in Webster Parish.

VI. Did They Find Their Burdens Hard?

We are not without positive reactions from ex-slaves regarding slavery. Although the majority of those questioned did not express themselves upon the institution, fourteen delivered themselves in no uncertain terms. What might be surprising to some is the fact that several ex-slaves not only feel no animus but actually long for the "good old times." The statements follow—the pro-slavery sentiments first and the anti-slavery sentiments thereafter.

One of the investigators closed his account of an interview with an ex-slave who "says that slaves fared much better than Negroes do now. He said we would be much better treated were we slaves."[137] "Lee Henderson states that he admires those days as he got along very nicely and did not have to work very hard."[138] "Some would have much better time if they were in slavery now."[139] "Priscilla Owens says, the slaves on their plantation had a much better time than most Negroes are having now."[140] "One old gentleman said his master was simply fine in every way. Since surrender, he has often wished for slavery again because he surely had a really splendid time."[141]

No less positive and emphatic are the statements from the other side. "Mrs. Martha Washington, aged 92 years, said to the writer not long ago that some of the conditions of slaves were horrible and the majority of masters were cruel."[142] Lettie Stephens remarked to Mrs. Callie Harvey of Bastrop, "Slaves had a hard time where I was." "As a whole, I did not see much cruelty to slaves but heard of a lot. For my part, I do not care to see such

[137]A. W. Casterman of Minden, quoting Elex Washington, ex-slave, near Jackson, Miss.
[138]Rosa B. Johnson of Minden.
[139]A. W. Casterman of Minden, quoting Crawford Martin.
[140]A. W. Casterman of Minden.
[141]Mrs. D. A. Franks of Minden.
[142]Mary L. Swearingan of Bastrop.

again. I was fourteen years old when we were set free.''[143]
''All of my days during the time of slavery were dark,
seemingly.''[144] ''All the ex-slaves with whom I have
talked, say that slavery at its best was terrible. There was
no freedom, no privileges, nothing but hard labor and deprivations.''[145] ''Mrs. Lettie Monson said that all she
knew of slavery was mean and unjust. She bears out the
statement of others. Women were whipped until they
bled and then were forced to bathe in brine. One was
just about dead when permitted to stop for sickness.''[146]
''I consider the days of slavery as the darkest days of the
world to my people—I mean to the Negro race. We were
sold just as our masters would see fit, and many of us
were driven and kicked about like dogs.''[147] ''Mrs. Lizzie
Shelton reported that she would just as soon be in Hell
as to live as she did in slavery.''[148]

And yet, ''Lucy Hamilton, born in Claiborne Parish,
four miles north of Athens, Louisiana, says that she has
seen more slavery since surrender than before.''[149]

[143]Sarah Skinner.
[144]Mrs. H. S. Lewis of Minden, quoting Tessie Moore.
[145]Callie F. Harvey of Bastrop.
[146]Mable L. Leary of Minden.
[147]Mrs. H. G. Lewis of Minden, quoting Mr. J. M. Simpson.
[148]Mable L. Leary of Minden.
[149]M. J. Tims of Minden.

It is quite interesting to read the opinions of such white persons as
will express themselves to Negroes regarding slavery as they saw the institution either as children of slave owners or slave owners themselves. A. L.
Osbin, one such person who lived in Tennessee during the days of slavery
says:

"My father owned fifty or sixty slaves, and worked them very hard
every day in the week. On Sundays women would prepare meals for the
mistress, and clean the house. My father was very cruel to his slaves in
every respect. I was a sympathetic boy, and my father finally listened to my
plea for better treatment of slaves and improved.''

Another, according to Booker T. Wagney, recalls the old days in these
words:

''I was quite a kid during that time, but old enough to realize how
conditions should be. My dad was a slave-holder and he did not have the
feeling that people should have for people in that condition. When I was

And stepping aside to allow one of the student inter-viewers have the floor as the curtain is drawn on our report:

"May I add here that even though slavery has been abolished, it still exists in parts of our country. To go about and visit the large plantations where Negroes toil day after day in the fields till the end of the year when they are told by the owners that they are yet in debt—which means that they must toil yet another year, only to find themselves where they started—is indeed sad to behold. However, we as a whole have done exceedingly well as we have only had sixty-five years to get where we now stand. 'Watch us grow.'"

JOHN B. CADE

Prairie View College,
Prairie View, Texas.

at the age of ten, my father had me as one of the overseers in his field because he owned so much money and land, and so many slaves."

A very old man who was a slave owner said about two years ago that during slavery he gave each one of his "Nigger" (Negro) slaves about two pecks of meal and three or four pounds of bacon a week. Most of his slaves slept on the floor and after breakfast, at sunrise, the slaves went to the fields where they worked practically all day. He gave them about one hour and a half rest for noon. He is classed as a very mean man and even now most of the Negroes fear him. He hates Negroes and does everything in his power to harm them. It would make one's blood boil to hear him sit and talk about what he has done to Negroes.

A. W. Casterman of Minden, quotes one Lawyer Stewart who recalled that his father owned a few slaves but borrowed slaves from folks around town who did not need them. To do this, contracts had to be made, which were quite rigid. He remembered his father hiring a man and woman under many restrictions, such as, they must have so many suits a year, must be given plenty to eat; the woman must not be put to heavy work, such as plowing, rolling logs. She could do house work or hoe; she also could pick cotton.

Slaves seldom lived together unmarried. The man might live on one plantation and the woman on another. The masters saw to it that the man went to see his wife on week-ends, but he was compelled to report for work Monday. Marriage was binding. He remembered that many of them lived together until death.

Slaves ate in the kitchen. At supper hour they ate the clearings and anything they could get. The same waitress served both master and slaves, with only a door separating the eating (or should I say dining) rooms.

SOME DATA ON OCCUPATIONS AMONG NEGROES IN ST. LOUIS FROM 1866 TO 1897

From 1866 to 1897 the St. Louis Board of Education printed in its *Annual Reports* the occupations of the parents of children enrolled in the public schools. This information was reported for each school separately, and because of segregation of Negroes in St. Louis a study of the occupations of Negro parents as compared with white parents is possible. These data do not give a complete picture of all the gainfully employed persons in St. Louis, nor is it an unbiased sample. Since employed persons included in the tabulation must have children attending the public schools, the sample is particularly biased with respect to very young workers and very old workers. However, we may assume that this bias operates the same with regard to Negro workers as with white workers and that comparison may be made between the two races. No distinction is made by sex, and a large number of parents remain unclassified with regard to occupation.

In Table I we present the data on occupations of Negro parents as recorded for the Negro schools each year by the Board of Education. In Table II the percentage distribution for white and Negro parents is given for five-year intervals. The second period beginning in 1871 comprises only four years because occupational statistics were not reported in 1875. Likewise the period beginning in 1891 is for four years because the classification of occupations was changed in 1895. The material for 1895 to 1897 when the School Board discontinued reporting on the occupations of the parents of school children is presented in Table III.

TABLE I.—OCCUPATIONS OF PARENTS OF NEGRO CHILDREN ENROLLED IN ST. LOUIS PUBLIC SCHOOLS FROM 1866 TO 1894

School year beginning	Agents	Artists	Boardinghouse Keepers	Boatmen	Butchers	Clerks	Confectioners	Draymen	Farmers	Laborers	Laundresses	Manufacturers	Mechanics	Merchants	Professionals	Public Officers	Saloonkeepers	Seamstresses	Unclassified	Totals
1866			10	53		2		69	8	107	87	9	3	6	2		8	20	83	437
1867			11	76	4			79	22	255	183	10	25	5	7	2	8	15	218	924
1868			13	98	5	2		90	26	255	136	22	54	14	21		8	17	160	917
1869			8	112		2		174	74	329	200	11	23	2	13		2	30	277	1,249
1870	1		15	113	3	7		116	50	567	339	12	33	9	13	1	6	21	253	1,560
1871	1	1	12	98	4	7	1	107	61	294	426	15	61	8	22	3	12	37	412	1,568
1872	5		9	104	18	12	1	170	57	510	445	11	44	10	23	2	7	42	305	1,774
1873	1		22	82	2	10	8	145	40	590	519	2	24	34	24	1	10	21	184	1,727
1874	1			84	2	5		156	39	531	438		74	2	35	1	11	19	212	1,634
1875																				
1876	1		10	88		7	3		43	722	471		50	3	64	4	6		184	1,831
1877	1	3	9	132		4	3	158	87	1,109	551	1	73	2	67	2	16	21	193	2,484
1878	1	5	12	97	8	8	2	205	150	902	708	1	77	4	31	8	18	36	645	2,934
1879	3	3	11	167	5	5	5	215	124	1,482	822	4	145	19	40	5	35	50	450	3,670
1880	6		21	96	4	6	3	297	79	1,720	804	12	132	9	66	8	24	54	321	3,652
1881	7	1	17	88	4	3	6	272	72	1,918	864	17	139	7	70	5	31	35	433	4,055
1882	8		16	169	7	11	5	339	106	1,844	812	12	182	6	42	3	26	54	418	4,224
1883	8	1	22	187	1	7	1	507	140	1,903	974	3	125	9	70	5	35	57	251	4,366
1884	10		14	228	3	13	4	562	92	1,956	836	3	145	15	69	2	24	41	368	4,391
1885	4		9	188	6	13	12	563	119	2,192	796	3	167	15	47	9	31	29	218	4,411
1886	3	1	27	229	5	5	5	570	102	2,079	1,049	4	85	6	44	24	26	36	237	4,497
1887	4		12	130	1	7	3	526	63	2,172	840		91	8	65	18	25	34	539	4,645
1888	6	14	12	139	1	6	3	634	72	2,301	1,157	3	83	8	54	6	34	93	607	5,079
1889	3		38	63	6	13	4	462	99	2,333	816	6	94	6	67		16	71	931	5,022
1890	2		22	79	1	10	10	427	114	2,259	970	104	73	24	69	11	3	41	648	4,874
1891	11	2	28	68	6	12	6	468	101	2,277	1,192	1	112	5	81	2	12	35	681	5,092
1892	5		18	75		15	9	619	36	2,473	1,090	6	85	11	93	4	12	115	477	5,145
1893	9		14	57	1	17	7	483	32	2,744	1,340	17	109	16	93	14	16	139	571	5,672
1894	9		30	65	3	18	9	675	94	2,491	1,258	11	70	18	78	8	11	157	653	5,658

There is evidently a typographical error in the School Board Report.

TABLE II.—THE PERCENTAGE OF PARENTS ENGAGED IN VARIOUS OCCUPATIONS FROM 1866 TO 1894, CLASSIFIED BY RACE.

Occupations	1866 to 70 Negro	White	1871 to 75 Negro	White	1876 to 80 Negro	White	1881 to 85 Negro	White	1886 to 90 Negro	White	1891 to 94 Negro	White
Agents		2.6	.1	2.7	.1	3.3	.2	3.0	.1	3.4	.1	3.6
Artists		.6	.9	.5	.1	.7	.4	.5	.5	1.1	.4	1.1
Boardinghouse Keepers	.8	1.4	5.5	1.5	.4	1.0	4.0	.9	2.7	.5	1.2	.4
Boatmen	8.9	3.6	.4	2.1	4.0	1.2	.1	.8	.1	1.7		1.8
Butchers	.2	1.6	.5	1.7	.2	1.8	.2	1.8	.2	8.0	.3	9.8
Clerks	.3	3.8	.1	4.1	.1	5.2	.1	6.7	.1	.7	.2	.9
Confectioners	10.4	.1	8.6	.7	7.9	.7	11.8	.6	10.4	3.9	10.4	4.0
Draymen	3.5	3.2	2.9	3.7	3.4	3.5	2.5	3.7	1.9	1.5	1.2	.9
Farmers	29.7	2.0	28.7	2.2	40.7	1.9	45.7	1.6	46.2	14.4	46.3	14.4
Laborers	18.6	11.7	27.3	12.2	23.0	14.1	20.0	13.9	20.0	1.7	22.6	1.5
Laundresses		2.1	.4	2.2	.2	2.2	.2	1.6	.5	6.5	.2	6.1
Manufacturers	1.3	6.9	3.0	8.2	3.3	8.3	3.5	6.8	1.8	26.1	1.8	25.0
Mechanics	2.7	23.8	.8	24.3	.3	23.6	.2	25.9	.2	10.8	.2	10.0
Merchants	.7	12.8	1.6	12.4	1.8	13.3	1.4	11.5	1.2	3.4	1.6	3.6
Professionals	1.1	3.7	.1	3.8	.2	4.2	.1	4.1	.2	2.8	.1	2.8
Public Officers	.1	3.0	.6	2.7	.7	2.9	.7	2.9	.4	1.9	.2	1.8
Saloonkeepers	.6	2.1	1.9	2.5	1.2	2.2	1.0	2.0	1.1	1.8	2.1	1.5
Seamstresses	1.6	2.9		2.8		2.2		1.7				
Unclassified	19.5	12.1	16.6	9.5	12.3	7.9	7.9	10.0	12.3	9.4	11.1	10.3

TABLE III.—OCCUPATIONS OF PARENTS OF NEGRO CHILDREN IN ST. LOUIS PUBLIC SCHOOLS FROM 1895 TO 1897

	1895	Negro 1896	1897	Per cent: 1895-97 Negro	White
Agricultural, etc.	42	43	58	.8	1.2
Electric Service	3	9	7	.1	1.0
Manufacturing and Mechanical					
Proprietors	14	38	38	.5	6.5
Employees	167	191	86	2.6	25.2
Mercantile					
Proprietors	22	51	49	.7	10.6
Employees	93	71	9	1.0	14.5
Personal Service	2,631	2,946	3,030	49.5	10.7
Professional Service	188	160	172	3.0	3.7
Public Employment	353	24	48	2.4	3.5
Transportation	339	479	535	7.8	6.6
Unskilled	1,527	1,671	1,557	27.3	10.0
Unclassified	363	191	196	4.3	6.5

RALPH AND MILDRED FLETCHER

BOOK REVIEWS

The Negro Citizen of West Virginia. By Thomas E. Posey.
(The Press of West Virginia State College, Institute, West
Virginia, 1935. Pp. 119. Price, $1.00.)

By many people who have never lived in West Virginia, that
state is regarded as a region of mountain feuds, terrible mining camps, and questionable black-and-white politics; by many
who have never lived out of that state, it is regarded as a sort
of *ne plus ultra*—a reasonably limited democracy in which Negroes have not too great nor yet too small a share. For all
such persons Mr. Thomas E. Posey's recently published *The
Negro Citizen of West Virginia* ought to be both a boon and
a remedy—a boon for enlightenment and a remedy for false
beliefs—and to all who are seriously interested in the study of
Negro life and history, it should prove profoundly interesting.

In nine short but interesting chapters there are discussions
of the part played by the Negro—rather, the part played *with*
him—in the movement that culminated in the disruption of
Virginia and the formation of the State of West Virginia, of
the Negro's struggles to win and maintain the full rights of
citizenship in the new state, and of the political, economic, educational, and general social progress of the Negro in the state
within recent years. Some phases of these topics, such as those
considered under the headings "Making the Negro a Citizen"
and "Significant Social Legislation for Negroes," have been
clearly and thoroughly treated; while others, such as those headed
"Industrial Expansion and Population Increase" and "The
Negro Prominent in Politics," have not been fully analyzed nor
adequately discussed. Under the last-mentioned chapter head
Mr. Posey dwelt too much on the individual biographies of the
near-great and too little on the *influence* of Negro citizens as a
group on the course of political affairs in the state. In the
opinion of the present reviewer at least, he gave too much attention to the *politicians* and not enough to the *politics*, when, obviously, the latter is of much greater significance.

Inasmuch as Mr. Posey's chief interest is economics, it would be surprising to find that his discussion of the economic life of the Negro in West Virginia is no more extensive than it is if one were not aware of the difficulties that are ever attendant upon impartial efforts to study the economic problems of Negroes, especially where the racial difficulties of these problems are further complicated by troublesome odds between labor and capital. One can not help wishing, nevertheless, that this discussion had thrown more light on the economic status of the Negro in the state, not only with regard to Negro wage-earners but also with regard to the ownership of land by Negroes, their activities in business, and their standards of living.

In addition to the chapters dealing with the political and economic life of the Negroes in the state, there is a chapter on "The Negro in the Courts," which gives an account of five important legal battles, each of which served to establish or safeguard some particular right of Negro citizens; there is a chapter on "The Education of the Negro," which records the progress of Negro education in the state, especially since 1914; and there is a final chapter on "Social and Recreational Facilities for Negroes," in which is set forth the need for further improvements in the social service and recreational facilities now provided for these people. All three of these chapters are illuminating, especially in that, along with the chapters dealing with matters economic, they indicate some of the important things for which Negroes must continue to strive in West Virginia; but all of them are to a considerable extent wanting in sufficient factual data and critical interpretation of them.

In spite of the more or less noticeable defects in the treatment of its subject, however, and in spite of some detracting elements of style, such as occasional awkwardness of expression and haziness of thought, Mr. Posey's book is a valuable contribution to the history of the Negro in American life. It represents the first attempt made by a Negro to make a comprehensive, historical survey of Negro life in West Virginia, or, with the exception of Mr. A. H. Gordon's *Sketches of Negro Life and History in South Carolina* (1929), of Negro life in any other separate state. One hopes that in the revision promised in the foreword of the work Mr. Posey will not only deal more thoroughly with all of the important phases of his subject but will also project his treatment of it against a broader background of the larger history of the United States.

W. EDWARD FARRISON

Agricultural and Technical College,
Greensboro, N. C.

Letters of Theodore Dwight Weld, Angelina Grimké Weld, and Sarah Grimké, 1822-1844. Edited by Gilbert H. Barnes and Dwight L. Dumond, and prepared and published under the direction of the American Historical Association from the income of the Albert J. Beveridge Memorial Fund. (New York: D. Appleton-Century Company, 1934. Volume I, pp. xxxvii+510. Volume II, pp. x+512. Calendar of letters and notes. Price, $10.00.)

In these portraits, largely self-penned, one meets in a peculiarly intimate way the American reformer of a century ago with his aspirations, heroisms, and infirmities. Although attention is focused upon Weld and the Grimké sisters, it falls, in lesser degrees, upon highly illuminating facts about Charles Stuart, Lewis Tappan, James Thome, James G. Birney, and about a score of others.

We re-encounter in the introduction to the letters, the thesis of Professor Barnes' earlier book, *The Anti-Slavery Impulse,* 1830-1844 (D. Appleton-Century Co., 1933). It is stated here, however, with slightly less exuberance. Instead of locating the origins of the anti-slavery movement in the crusade of William Lloyd Garrison and his New England followers, Professor Barnes found it originating in the benevolent activities of the American churches and Arthur and Lewis Tappan. In 1830 the movement received fresh impetus in the teaching and methods of Charles G. Finney, the famous Presbyterian revivalist, and was sustained largely by Weld, who, according to the book now being reviewed, was "the movement's man of power, the greatest individual factor in its triumph."

Weld, a son of a Congregational minister of western New York, was sent at the age of seventeen to an academy to prepare for college. When study injured his eyes, he left school and wandered for two years in the West and South, lecturing on the "Science of Mnemonics." Upon his return home he was converted by Finney, and spent the years 1827-1830 at Oneida Institute preparing for the ministry. The institution was a pioneer in the manual labor movement, and Weld as "monitor general" of the school's farm earned a part of his expenses; the rest was paid by Charles Stuart—a bachelor and pietist, who ate no meat, avoided alcohol, tea and coffee, and bathed daily in cold water. Stuart left for England in 1829 to agitate for the abolition of slavery in the West Indies; and during the next two years, by letter and pamphlet, he persuaded Weld to devote his life to the anti-slavery cause. Weld brought to the cause the convictions of a reformer, a fine melodious voice, and a constitution that somehow withstood years of frontier travel, the Graham diet, and strenuous lecturing.

With these talents and an ability to arouse practical enthusiasm in others for making gifts and loans to him, Weld's influence became wide. He was the moving spirit in a council of reformers which met at New York City in the spring of 1831 to consider the organization of a national anti-slavery society. Under his leadership the students almost to a man seceded from Lane Seminary, when in 1834 the trustees forbade any discussion of the slavery question. Eventually he and the Tappans found shelter for the students at Oberlin. To compensate the school for harboring the Lane Rebels and for opening her doors to Negroes, Oberlin received a princely endowment and Finney. These events started Oberlin on her long career of reform. After this master stroke Weld became a regular anti-slavery lecturer, and "the most mobbed man in America," as he said of himself. He also wrote *The Bible Against Slavery; The Power of Congress over the District of Columbia,* and *Slavery As It Is.* The last dealt in a vivid manner with the cruelties of slavery reported to him, and was the source book of the anti-slavery movement for a decade, supplying Harriet Beecher Stowe with her ideas of slavery. James Thome wrote Weld that after wading through the book he came out dripping with blood. Weld ended his career in the early forties by leading the anti-slavery lobby in the nation's capital.

As early as 1836 Weld began to correspond with the Grimké sisters, who had forsaken a fine home in Charleston, and had attracted national attention by the anti-slavery sentiments expressed in such works as an *Appeal to the Christian Women of the South*, which was publicly burned by the southern postmasters. They too had given offense by lecturing to "promiscuous" audiences of men and women on the subjects of slavery and woman's rights. Indeed, Angelina was so sensitive about the equality of the sexes that she refused to answer Weld's letters until he ceased to write them in pencil. Weld replied, with a bit of humor lacking in his letters, that he also believed in the rights of women, and that thereafter he would carry an ink bottle in his pocket "though it might put my temperance good name in jeopardy." It would be hard to imagine a more serious, impractical courtship. One letter might strongly censure the sisters for their rashness in advocating the rights of their sex or pacificism, a second might praise their courage, a third, fourth and fifth might be given over to heart searchings and self-examinations. Weld actually mentions his aversion to dirt, and his daily cold baths, as reasons for not marrying. Both Weld and Angelina feared that marriage would conflict with duty. The common opinion was that by her independent feminism Angelina had unsexed herself, and was unfitted for marriage. Eventually in 1838, after two years of ecstatic correspondence Weld, as James Thome put it, "showed great moral courage" by marrying. Their marriage ceremony was symbolic. Neither would consent to be married by a clergyman, nor would they bind themselves by the words usually spoken at marriage. Weld spoke of the unrighteous legal powers vested in a husband: Angelina uttered a few words of devotion. A colored minister then prayed for them, and Garrison read the marriage certificate which was signed by those present. Angelina was excommunicated from the Quaker church for marrying Weld, who was a Presbyterian, and Sarah for attending the service. Whittier, who wished to remain a Quaker, remained outside the room until the ceremony was over. After Angelina's marriage both sisters dropped into relative obscurity as teachers in Weld's liberal school at Belleville, New Jersey, Angelina from poor health, and Sarah from motives that one can only surmise.

For making these letters easily accessible, and for a scholarly accuracy in annotation, the editors deserve the gratitude of the students of American humanitarianism. Although entirely relevant, many of the letters are repetitious and leave one wondering whether by a severe pruning the letters might not have been compressed with more effectiveness into one volume. The letters demonstrate the importance of Weld, but they do not justify the unfavorable opinion of Garrison that Professor Barnes holds.

CLAYTON S. ELLSWORTH

College of Wooster,
Wooster, Ohio

Le Cameroun. By J. Wilbois. (Paris, Payot, 1934. 255 pages).

Prior to the World War Germany had exploited her colonies with just about the same callous brutality as had the other colonial Powers. To assure better treatment to these colonies, which were taken from Germany at the end of the War, Woodrow Wilson insisted that they be given in trusteeship to various European nations that were to administer them under the supervision of the League of Nations.

To what extent have these Mandatory Powers lived up to this ideal of trusteeship set forth in Article XXII of the Covenant of the League of Nations? To just about the same extent that they have lived up to any other ideal—that is, they have honored it more in the breach than in the observance. How was it, indeed, to be expected that a colonial power would practice a dual set of ethics: exploitation of natives in the colonies and paramountcy of native rights in the adjoining mandated area? The inevitable has happened in spite of generally earnest efforts on the part of the Permanent Mandates Commission of the League of Nations. The mandated areas have been more and more assimilated to the colonies.

This study of the French Cameroons, one of a series of similar studies of French African possessions, is the most valu-

able case study of mandated areas since Dr. Raymond Buell
included this same area in his notable *The Native Problem in
Africa*. Unfortunately, however, Wilbois confines his study
almost entirely to the southern part, which has a population
of about 1,000,000 inhabitants. During the "Lotus Decade" that
followed the World War this region enjoyed a certain prosperity. Some native chiefs had an income of about $4,000 a
year. With the decline in the price of palm oil from 1,600
francs a ton to 300 francs a ton, this prosperity has largely
disappeared. But, says the author (p. 31): "A Negro in the
Cameroons gets along one hundred times better than does an unemployed worker in the United States." The impact of European
civilization on Africa is further revealed in the disappearance
of native artisans, blacksmiths for example, since the importation
of foreign articles supplants the native craft.

The author's discussion of family life is particularly enlightening because of his analysis of the so-called "bride purchase,"
the traditional basis for denunciation by missionaries of African
"savages." Supporting the conclusions of Torday in the magazine, *Africa*, Wilbois points out that it is just as ridiculous to
call the Cameroon wife the slave of her husband "as it is to say
that a Frenchman is the slave of his wife because she pays
for him with her dowry" (p. 43). This reviewer suggests that
in some American social circles also it is not unknown for
women to buy themselves a husband or a title. To the equally
irritating accusation of general polygamy the author replies
that, since there were 672,161 men aged fourteen to fifty-nine
and 751,863 women of the same age, it is obviously impossible
for polygamy to be general. In one place, of sixteen men, six
had one wife and five were bachelors.

Probably the most severe indictment of French rule is her
policy of leaving education largely in the hands of missions.
These missions have the two objects of preventing the spread of
Mohammedanism and of making paganism impossible. In non-
recognized mission schools with an enrollment of 55,000 natives little is taught except the catechism. In the recognized mission schools, in which the use of the French language is oblig-
atory, there were only 8,000 pupils in 1932. In the entire
area (population close to 3,000,000) the French government

itself had in 1932 one superior school with seventy-three pupils; seven regional schools with 1,953 pupils; fifty-six village schools with 4,531 pupils instructed by African monitors. Some 200 students had attended vocational schools. Thus, some 15,000 students, or one-half of one per cent of the total population, were receiving an education in the government and recognized mission schools. The government spent 1,800,000 francs for educational purposes, or about three cents per capita at the rate of exchange in 1932. If this is trusteeship, what is exploitation? Of course, the missions spent considerable sums, but the Cameroons were given in trust to the French government, not to religious enterprise.

For sanitation and health the Government in 1932 spent 14,415,000 francs, or about $576,600. This is most commendable. The expenditure has not, however, succeeded in completely eradicating sleeping sickness. It is interesting to note that venereal diseases constitute less than fifteen per cent of the diseases treated.

In administering the territory the French follow the principles of both direct and indirect rule. In the "civilized" part 1800 African functionaries aid 600 Frenchmen. These Africans have practically no part in formulating policies. They are employed as interpreters, monitors, hospital assistants, road supervisors, custom agents, policemen, bookkeepers, stenographers and secretaries. African "notables" sit on agricultural commissions, sanitary commissions, chambers of commerce, and even on the territorial administrative council, but they are little more than observers and sources of information. In the interior, native chiefs are permitted to settle minor disputes, keep up the roads, and levy taxes. It is to be hoped that the author is correct in his statement that in the future they will be given more extensive powers.

To American Negroes who remember pleasantly the almost total absence of race prejudice in France, it is disheartening to learn that on the railways in the Cameroons first and second class coaches are reserved for whites and that the Negro conductors zealously expel blacks who try to ride in them.

J. Wilbois, who is the *Directeur de l'Ecole d'Administration et d'Affaires* in Paris, has given us an authoritative and objective study. The Negro does not appear as a savage, nor does the white man strut with the vainglorious nonsense of Kipling's bearers of "The White Man's Burden." France's shortcomings are revealed in a way that must make the government realize more fully than ever that she has betrayed her trust. Since France has practically ignored the League in her administration of the French Cameroons, enthusiastic supporters of the mandate system must reluctantly conclude that another ideal born of the World War has perished.

RAYFORD W. LOGAN

Atlanta University

Crusader and Feminist, Letters of Jane Grey Swisshelm, 1858-1865. By Arthur J. Larsen. St. Paul. (The Minnesota Historical Society, 1934. Pp. 327).

This book is an important volume based upon the source material of an interesting career. Jane Grey Swisshelm was an editor in Western Pennsylvania, on the Minnesota frontier, and in the national capital. She became famous in doing the unusual thing of embarking upon a professional career as an editor, lecturer, abolitionist, and an advocate of women's rights long before the public came to the position of feeling that a woman should function in such spheres. Mr. Larsen, the author, is of the opinion that her greatest achievement was that of a controversialist—"A flaming anti-slavery crusader and a dauntless champion of woman's rights." The author believes that the material collected affords him a sufficiently clear vision to make the proper estimate of this unusual character.

In this study Mr. Larsen had access to files of the *St. Cloud Visitor* and the *St. Cloud Democrat*, which she edited. He obtained also from her daughters and relatives a number of portraits and manuscripts, and a partial file of the *Pittsburgh Saturday Visitor*. The letters, he believes, have their chief value in the description of places, the characterization of the people, the accounts of frontier travel, the comments on pioneer journalism, the reflections of public opinion, and the echoing of current, although sometimes baseless, gossip. With respect to the Minnesota history itself he finds that she voiced something of the popular psychology as to the bloody crises of the Civil and Sioux wars. "Her letters offer, in a sense, a cinematographic view of rapidly changing scenes in a period of important happenings, with a talking accompaniment—trenchant and not infrequently ironical comments by an observer who, whatever the degree of her information, was never in doubt about her own mind."

The contents of the book give further details as to how the author has tried to paint this picture from the sources studied. He is able thereby to construct a picture of Central Minnesota in the fifties, the mode of living at that time, and the general conditions obtaining on the eve of the conflict between the North and South. From these sources also he develops a more vivid panorama of the stirring scenes of '62, the war time aspects of things in Washington, the gossip in restricted circles— in fact, an inside view of many things hitherto unknown. Into the picture, of course, there is much about hospital service during the war, references to various incidents connected with the unionists and secessionists, and the closing scenes of the drama with special emphasis upon women workers.

With respect to Negroes themselves we see special mention of a school in Washington, the attitude of the Negroes toward the whites, the project for colonization revived by Lincoln, the enlistment of the freedmen as soldiers and their services in the Union army. In thus giving the public this work the author has rendered historical scholarship a distinct service.

W. G. C.

Liberia in World Politics. By Nnamdi Azikiwe, Former Head of the Department of History and Political Science of Lincoln University in Pennsylvania. (London: Arthur H. Stockwell, Ltd., 1935. Pp. 406. Price 7s 6d.)

Americans pay little attention to Liberia, and most Europeans think of the country as a joke. The recent suggestion that Liberia be given to Germany to satisfy its demand for African colonies shows the contempt of these exploiters for "this pretense of a black republic on the West Coast of Africa." In case of apparently friendly relations between that country and European powers there has usually come to the surface some design to deprive Liberia of its territory or to secure some economic advantage. The American's endorsement of the Firestone invasion of that African area shows that on this side of the Atlantic the same attitude has developed.

Mr. Azikiwe, the author of this volume, a native African educated in the United States, however, does not share this snobbish attitude toward the black republic. He is of the opinion that Liberia deserves much credit for its skillful diplomacy and ability to measure up in great crises. Compared with other nations less handicapped, Liberia does not fall below the standard expected of small powers struggling against odds. The book, then, is written in conformity to the requirement to treat the past sympathetically.

In conformity to the title the book deals primarily with politics. The author does not tarry long with the historic background. Only two chapters "Digging into the Past" and "Self-Determination" deal mainly with the history of the country. The brief summary thus afforded, however, is clear and sufficiently detailed for the average student of politics. After devoting another chapter to the aborigines of that country the author plunges into his main problem in portraying Liberia as the remaining spot in Africa to which are directed the eyes of land-grabbing Europeans in the scramble for that continent.

Addressing himself to this main task, the author discusses the relations of the Germans and Liberians, imperialism, Liberian loans, forced labor, the Firestone lease, the proposed international commission, the capacity of Liberia for self-government, the reconstruction of Liberia, the resurgence of Kru militarism, the League of Nations as it concerns itself about Liberia, the present economic crisis, and the possibilities for the country to advance. In the development of these thoughts the author has used numerous sources found in both European and American libraries.

After discussing in detail the trend of European and even American diplomacy toward the dismemberment of Liberia, the author discloses the purposes of his book in saying, "By all means, this last vestige of hope for African nationality should be safeguarded and revitalized by every true son and daughter of African descent. The position of Liberia in world politics is a question mark, whether Europe and America should be allowed to annihilate this lone star on the wide African expanse—by vilifications in their press, in their national legislatures, and in their stock exchanges. It is also a challenge to the manhood of the race, as it is to all Liberians and to those who are interested in maintaining its corporate existence, to contribute their share for the salvation of this "Sick man of Africa," and inject into its veins and arteries a new life and a national awakening." Mr. Azikiwe agrees with President Cheeseman's historic challenge, "If by our neglect and indifference, we bring the 'Lone Star' to disgrace, and fail in preserving our national institutions, we shall not only confirm the prejudices and opinions of those who are not in sympathy with the Negro's advancement, but shall bring upon the race a stigma which generations will not obliterate."

C. G. WOODSON.

The Education of the Negro in the American Social Order. By Horace Mann Bond. (New York: Prentice Hall, 1934).

This book is a general treatise which covers unscientifically much ground. The author undertakes to give the setting of the Negro as a result of the social and industrial revolution, referring particularly to the revolution which has brought things to the point where they are today. He confines most of his treatment to the situation since the general emancipation of the race. He becomes more serious with the treatment of the "Origin of the Tax-Supported Schools during the Reconstruction Period." The effect of the undertaking of a systematic reconstruction of education is also noted. He gives attention to the popularization of industrial education by Booker T. Washington, and the work of the Julius Rosenwald Fund. Next he discusses "Inequality in Education for the Two Races," "The Progress Made Toward Equality," "The Effect of Migration, Industrialization, Urbanization, and the Burden of the Dual System Throughout the South."

The author then proceeds to the discussion of the educational problems in the other part of his book. These are problems which concern the operation of the school as it functions through teachers and pupils. He discusses the capacity of the Negro to learn, the achievement of children, their education in certain centers in the North, and special problems of administration which have resulted in recent years. In this respect the book deals with education as it is today and may be useful in the study of the history of education of the Negro as it is reflected by its present status.

From the usual point of view of dealing with and noting the progress of education of the Negro from without, this book is regarded as a contribution. The method of treatment in vogue in our colleges of education which produce works of this sort is carefully observed in this effort to give such a picture of the education of the Negro as that which we have of various elements otherwise circumstanced. When you have finished reading the book you may thoughtlessly get the impression that with certain exceptions the education of the Negro is a simple process very much like that of the others and the only thing we need to do now is to remove the inequalities that everything may run along smoothly in the usual way. This is what we have been hoping and working for during the last three generations, but we find ourselves about as far from the goal as we were in 1865. The Negro produced by his educational system is unable to take care of himself in this social order. The mentally undeveloped class of Negroes, as a rule, has shown greater possibilities for leadership than the so-called educated American of African descent. This the author denies as an untruth, brushes the fact aside, and fails to deal with truth because he insists that truth is not truth.

It does seem reasonable that education should have some direct bearing on the grave problems which people have to solve in order to endure. The so-called enlightened element ought to be equal to the demands upon it for efficient leadership; but about as far as the educated Negro has been able to go is to preach a sermon as his oppressor tells him to preach, to teach principles set up by his traducers for the advantage of the oppressor, and to cooperate with the exploiter in keeping the Negro in his place. The so-called educated Negro has never learned to think and therefore does not know how to do. It has been asserted that his education is at fault. It is strikingly evident that he has been educated from without rather than from within. He is educated to be a white man and forced to live a Negro. Trained to be an American and forced to remain an African. The education of the Negro should be made to bear upon the solution of this problem as it is rather than deal with the imagination of things as they should be.

C. G. WOODSON

NOTES

The contribution of the Catholics toward the religious uplift and general welfare of the Negro is attested in the production entitled *A Saint in the Slave Trade, 1581 to 1654, Saint Peter Claver,* brought out by Sheed and Ward in New York City. This is an interesting and valuable biography of a Jesuit missionary to Africa. One thereby learns not only what this religious order did for the comfort and welfare of the tribes reached but useful facts of scientific value. The book should find its way to all collections dealing especially with the Negro.

In Bennet Champ Clark's *John Quincy Adams, "Old Man Eloquent,"* a publication of Little, Brown and Company, of Boston, one will be surprised not only to know that the author knew little of importance in connection with the life of this American, but that he failed also to note adequately the significant battle of Adams for free speech in the struggle for a hearing on slavery in Congress. Frederick H. Gillett's *George Frisbie Hoar,* published by Houghton, Mifflin Company, Boston, gives opportunity for further study of this man and measures in which he participated. Many of the movements connected with the name of this statesman vitally concerned the Negro.

In the *Growth of the American People,* a textbook of American history for high schools, under the authorship of Marcus W. Jernegan, H. E. Carlson and A. C. Ross, published by Longmans, Green and Company, of New York, there is unfortunately the usual propaganda about *Uncle Tom's Cabin.* It is ignorantly stated that this production was an unfair attack on slavery. It is surprising that a man of Professor Jernegan's scholarship should attach his name to such a work. *Uncle Tom's Cabin* was never published as a definitive history. It was, however, an historical romance founded in fact, as anyone who has taken the time to examine the documentary evidence will concede. Such evidence is accessible in Frederic Bancroft's *Slave-trading in the Old South,* in Elizabeth Donan's *Documents Illustrative of the History of the Slave Trade,* and in H. T. Catterall's *Judicial Cases Concerning American Slavery and the*

Negro. It looks like selling one's soul when an author, to have his book adopted in certain quarters, will incorporate therein the local views with respect to men and measures. History should not be made to order.

In Professor Charles M. Andrews' *The Colonial Period of American History,* a Pulitzer Prize production of the year 1934, published by the Yale University Press, we are somewhat disappointed that it does not cover all America. The work does not deal in detail with the colonization of the Latins to the south of us and therefore does not teem with facts of history in which the Negro Americans participated more freely in that sphere than they were permitted to do in what is now the United States. This book, then, is chiefly the history of British colonization along the Atlantic. American writers should refrain from using unscientifically the word *American* to apply solely to the United States. The People of Argentina and Ecuador are just as much Americans as those of the United States.

Professor A. C. McLaughlin's recent *Constitutional History of the United States* is the product of long experience as a teacher in this field at Michigan and the University of Chicago. The author is of the opinion that the Constitution and the Union grew rather than developed by making. The country grew into the Union held together by a fundamental law which the majority of the citizens of the United States learned to respect in spite of such efforts to the contrary as nullification and secession. Early in his career Professor McLaughlin dealt more with the vital questions of freedom and slavery as the underlying causes of most of what happened throughout that crisis; but during later years he has given more attention to the economic problems which showed clashes of various elements of the social order and the cleavage between the East and the West. Does this show liberalmindedness or narrowness?

Along with Douglass Southall Freeman's *R. E. Lee,* awarded the Pulitzer Prize this year, have appeared the biographies of other distinguished men of that time. In William Starr Myers' *George B. McClellan; A Study in Personality,* brought out by the D. Appleton-Century Company, of New York, we do not find much new light on this failure of the Civil War in spite of the effort to manufacture from his remains a great character. Robert R. McCormick has published through the D. Appleton-Century Company, *Ulysses S. Grant: The Great Soldier of America.* Dodd, Mead and Company have brought out David S. Muzzey's *James G. Blaine: A Political Idol of Other Days.*

D. B. Chidsey's *The Gentleman From New York, A Life of Roscoe Conkling* has been published by the Yale University Press, New Haven. The questions of import especially those dealing with the reconstruction are treated in this work as they revolve around this character seen by the author mainly as a political boss. Through Harrison Smith and Robert Haas, of New York City, has been published Fletcher Pratt's *Ordeal by Fire,* a history of the Civil War. In this same field has written Mary Merwin Phelps the life story of a brilliant woman and her distinguished father, *Kate Chase: Dominant Daughter of Salmon P. Chase.*

Works of various sorts dealing with sections are rapidly multiplying as usual. This we see in W. W. Ryle's *Missouri: Union or Secession,* brought out by the George Peabody College, of Nashville. Alfred B. Williams' *Hampton and His Red Shirts,* another work of this type, published by the Evans and Cogswell Company, of Charleston, South Carolina, has already passed to its second printing because of the great demand for this account of an eyewitness of Hampton's campaign against Carpetbag rule in 1876. "A Southern Gentleman" comes into the foreground in a work of fiction entitled *Bottom Rail on Top,* by H. J. Eckenrode, published by Greenberg in New York City.

In this connection should be mentioned also William S. Jenkins' *Pro-Slavery Thought in the Old South,* published by the University of North Carolina Press at Chapel Hill, and *The Fifteenth Amendment, An Account of Its Enactment,* by A. Caperton Braxton, from the press of J. B. Bell and Company of Lynchburg, Virginia, 1934.

Books dealing with race and culture have also come at the usual pace. E. B. Reuter, a prolific writer on racial matters in the United States, has undertaken to broaden the scope of his efforts in producing *Race and Culture Contacts,* a publication of McGraw-Hill and Company, New York, 1934. Joseph J. Williams, S. J., the author of *Hebrewisms of West Africa, Voodoos and Obeahs, Whence the Black Irish of Jamaica?* and *Whisperings of the Caribbean,* has brought out through the Dial Press of New York *Psychic Phenomena of Jamaica,* a study of witchcraft, applied magic, the belief in ghosts, funeral customs, and poltergeist. Professor Benjamin Brawley, of Howard University, has published through the University of North Carolina Press at Chapel Hill his *Early Negro American Writers,* an effort to improve upon Vernon Loggins' *Negro Author.* The Johns Hopkins Press, of Baltimore, Maryland, has just announced *A Study of the Development of Negro Education under Catholic Auspices in Maryland and the District of Columbia,* by Michael Francis Rouse.

In American Magazines

Certain articles in American magazines are of interest. "Negro Suffrage and Fusion Rule in North Carolina," by W. A. Mabry, in *The North Carolina Historical Review,* April 1935; "Malthusianism and the Debate on Slavery," by J. J. Spengler, *The South Atlantic Quarterly,* April 1935; "The Underground Railroad in Southern Chautauqua County," by W. S. Bailey, *New York History,* January 1935; "White Spirituals in the Southern Uplands," by James W. Patton, *Tennessee Historical Magazine,* January 1935; "Dorothy Dodd, the Schooner *Emperor,* an Incident of the Illegal Slave Trade in Florida," *Florida Historical Society Quarterly,* January 1935; "Sectional Ambition the Cause of the War in 1861," a letter by Lyon G. Tyler, *Tyler's Quarterly Historical and Genealogical Magazine,* April 1935; "Slavery Propaganda turning the Mexican War," by John D. P. Fuller, *Southwestern Historical Magazine,* April 1935; "The Concept of Race," by Julian Huxley, *Harper's,* May 1935; "The Technic of Mob Rule," by George Boas, in the same periodical; "Negroes and the Fur Trade," by Kenneth W. Porter, in *Minnesota History,* December 1935; "Henry A. Wise and the Virginia Fire Eaters of 1856," *The Mississippi Valley Historical Review,* March 1935; "Black Man's Art," by H. I. Brock, *New York Times Magazine,* May 5, 1935.

Books on Africa

D. Appleton-Century Company has published Captain R. S. Rattray's *The Leopard Priestess,* a sort of novel which at the same time is an elementary treatise on Central African anthropology. This firm has published also a less interesting work of adventures in Africa called *The Yellow Diamond*, by George Gibbs. Through A. Stokes and Company, F. G. Carnochan and Hans Christian Adamson have produced *The Empire of Snakes*, an unusual account of primitive people in Central Africa.

Leo Frobenius's *Madsimu Dsangara, Chronique d'art rupestre sud-African, t. II, Les styles ethnographiques, prehistoriques,* has been published. The unfailing interest of this German scholar in the scientific approach to Africa is further attested by this work. Unfortunately, Europeans must bring into their works the theory of the high culture of some mythical ancient race which accomplished great things in Africa before the coming of the present "belated natives," even when the yarn seems more remote than ever.

Egypt and Negro Africa, by C. G. Seligman, is a 1933 publication of Routledge, London. The author is inclined to think that Egyptian ideas went into the interior only when there is just as much evidence that ideas migrated from the interior northward into Egypt. What actual facts the author collected should be carefully noted, but his unwarranted bias in his comments should be just as carefully avoided.

The Religious Tract Society has published Cullen Young's translation of Samuel Y. Ntara's book. The author is a native of Africa. Miss Alice Werner and William Hichens, also interested in penetrating the native's mind, have published through the Azania Press the first literary composition by an East African Native woman to be published in Great Britain. This was a poem of a Swahili woman of two generations ago, *The Advice of Mwana Kupona upon the Wifely Duty*.

Dr. L. S. B. Leakey has published a thought-awakening book on *The Stone Age Races of Kenya*, dealing with findings of the Middle Pleistocene Period. This book will evidently force a reconstruction of certain authors' theories, for several have taken the position that in this particular area iron was discovered at such an ancient epoch that the natives did not have a prolonged stone age and "skipped over" the bronze age to that of iron.

There has been recently published *Etiopia Occidentale*, by

Enrico Cèrulli (Collezione di Opere e di Monografie a cura del Ministero delle Colonie) Sindicato Italiano degli Arti Grafiche, Editore in Roma. In view of what is now going on in Europe with respect to Northeast Africa, this work may seem timely and informing. It shows the continuation of the European effort to make Africa altogether a dependent continent. Two other works in this field throw light on the same movements. One is *The 1820 Settlers in South Africa, A Study in British Colonial Policy,* by I. E. Edwards, published by Longmans. The other appeared through the Macmillan Company as J. Merle Davis' *Modern Industry and the African.* Still another such work is *The Anglo-Egyptian Sudan,* by Sir Harold MacMichael, published by Faber and Faber. To these may be added Ifor L. Evans' *Native Policy in South Africa* from the press of Cambridge University in 1934; and Von Erwin Mai's *Die Kakaokultur an der Goldküste und ihre Socialgeographischen Wirkungen.*

Some of these recent publications on Africa deal primarily with the natives. Such is in part Albert Helser's *Education of Primitive People,* published in New York, London, and Edinburgh in 1934, by Fleming H. Revel. In Arthur E. Southron's *Gold Coast Methodism, the First Hundred Years,* London, 1934, the modernization of the natives again comes into the foreground. Of a different stamp are a few other recent works like Fr. C. Cagnolo's *The Akikuyu: Their Customs, Traditions, and Folklore,* published at Nyeri, Kenya, through the Mission of the Consolata Fathers in 1933; I. Schapera's *Western Civilization and Natives of South Africa,* from the press of G. Routledge and Sons, London, 1934; Von Ernst Strasser's *Der Eine Gott im Bewusstsein der Völker,* brought out in Leipzig, 1934; a work on the natives of Bornu by L. M. Mamadi entitled *Kitabuwa Kanuribe Kitabu Kendegami,* from Yerwa, Bornu Province, for the Bornu Native Administration, by the C. M. S. Bookshops, Lagos, 1934; and another such production by M. K. Malem entitled *Kitabuwa Kanuribe, Kitabu, Kenuguimi, Kitabu, gargam, Kanem-wa Bornowabe kasargata, Faida tatawa magaranti badigaram Bornobaro, Lagos,* 1934.

ARTICLES ON AFRICA IN MAGAZINES

In the vein of one who glories in the triumph of force over weakness, which is now considered justifiable throughout the

Christian world, Brooke Claxton writes in the Spring issue of *Queen's Quarterly* "The Commonwealth of South Africa;" in the April issue of *The Fortnightly* Captain R. S. Rattray has a similar article on "The Maker of Nigeria," Sir George Taubman Goldie. "Italy in Abyssinia," by Robert Gale Woolbert, has appeared in *Foreign Affairs*, April 1935.

Approaching the social order from the natural science point of view, Allison Davis has contributed "The Distribution of the Blood-Groups and its Bearing upon the Concept of Race, Part II," *The Sociological Review*, April 1935. *Europe*, for March 1935, carried "Chefs Noirs," by Robert Delavignette. In the April issue of *Blackwood's Magazine* Mrs. R. F. Carnegie has an article entitled "A Kenya 'Rain-Making.'"

In *The Journal of the African Society*, April 1935, are the following: "Criminal Justice in East Africa," by H. Grattan Bushe; "Negro Art: Sculpture from West Africa," by Dora Clarke; "Sir George Goldie on Africa," by Major Leonard Darwin; "The Problem of Liberia," by F. M. Dyke; reports for 1933 of various dependencies, among which are "The Sudan Annual Report," by E. N. Corbyn; "Native Affairs in Northern Rhodesia;" "Uganda Protectorate," by Major G. T. Keane; "Tanganyika Territory;" "Education in Tanganyika," by W. Bryant Mumford; "Some Problems of Indirect Rule in Africa," by Margery Perham.

In the April issue of *Africa* appeared the following articles: "Charakter und Einteilung der Sudansprachen," by Diedrich Westermann; "Some Aspects of the Subtribes of the Edo People of Southern Nigeria," by H. L. M. Butcher; "Culture Contact on the Fringe of Civilization," by A. T. and G. M. Culwick; "La Lutte contre les Maladies Sociales au Cameroun," by Dr. Millous; "Vernacular Texts in South African Native Schools," by Clement Doke; "How far Can African Ceremonial be Incorporated in the Christian System?" by T. Cullen Young.

THE JOURNAL

OF

NEGRO HISTORY

Vol. XX—October, 1935—No. 4

ANNUAL REPORT OF THE DIRECTOR

Although no longer assisted by any of the large foundations the Association with its limited income has continued to grow and expand its sphere of influence. Throughout the past twenty years, the celebration of which takes place in Chicago on the ninth of September, the work has steadily developed. The Association has carried forward with meager means what it did during its early years when it depended almost altogether on the financial support of the founder and director of the organization. The financial statement of the Secretary-Treasurer herein given speaks for itself with respect to the fiscal year closing June 30, 1935.

FINANCIAL STATEMENT, JULY 1, 1934, TO JUNE 30, 1935

RECEIPTS		DISBURSEMENTS	
Subscriptions	$1,219.50	Research	$ 800.00
Memberships	552.75	Printing	2,005.37
Contributions	2,358.43	Stenographic Service	1,481.00
Publications	642.00	Traveling Expenses	123.20
Sundry Income	50.27	Rent	275.00
		History Prizes	225.00
		Postage	85.77
		Sundry Expenditures	105.54
	$4,822.95		$5,200.88
Balance on hand July 1, 1934	1,325.94	Balance on hand June 30	948.01
Grand Total	$6,148.89		$6,148.89

The total income of the Association for this period, amounting to less than seven thousand dollars, is much less than it was during the years when the foundations freely granted sums for research. Yet when it is taken into account that the amount thus raised has come chiefly from the impoverished Negro element of the United States it must strike the observer as a fine demonstration of selfhelp. Because the foundations during the depression have had to discontinue some of their benefactions, and because the Association is fearlessly opposed by certain "pro-racial or interracial" workers for the race, the Negroes deeply interested in their past have redoubled their efforts to support the work in giving now more than ever before in the history of the undertaking. This, of course, is still a small amount. Yet if the Negroes can give seven thousand dollars to such work during these troublous times they can easily give fifteen thousand dollars when things are normal, and this will support a moderate research program as well as maintain the Journal of Negro History. Toward this as a goal the Association will strive.

The Association could have a larger income if it formed some of the attachments which boards and foundations often exact to control agencies. Recently the Director with the advice of the Executive Council refused an offer of five thousand dollars a year presented with such conditions. The Director has always taken the position that to do the work of this organization with scientific objectivity and to restrict it to the special field in which it has served efficiently the management must continue untrammelled. To swerve from this course might bring the Association to the position of producing history to order. The treatment of the past of the Negro does not require more extensive writing but less of what has been dictated by propaganda. There should be more of that writing which results from actual research. The Association will continue in this fashion at its post of duty as it has been conceived and is now being performed. Rather than diverge from this chosen way it would discontinue the effort and declare the task ended. In this way only can the truth of the past be revealed and the generations unborn be properly enlightened.

RESEARCH

The Director has stimulated research in various parts. Instructors and students in graduate schools in this country and Europe have frequently called upon him for guidance in the field and such assistance has been freely given both by mail and by visits to and from persons and institutions thus concerned. Among these should be mentioned Mr. M. Brachwitz of Berlin, Germany; M. Pierre de Lanux, of Paris, France; and Miss Alice Werner, of England. Special studies begun by Europeans have been somewhat upset by the unsettled state of affairs in both Italy and Germany, but it is still believed that the projected studies of the Negro in the European mind will be completed at an early date. The researches into the past of Spain and England have resulted in the publication of "Some Attitudes in English Literature" and "Attitudes of the Iberian Peninsula."

In Europe where the Director spends about three months annually in the furtherance of research with respect to the Negro definite tasks have been undertaken and are going forward. The special study of the natives of Africa has progressed satisfactorily with the accumulation of valuable data, some of which will soon be compiled and put into literary form. This task has been facilitated by the purchase of practically all works on Africa considered useful to the staff of the Association. Renewed contact with European scholars has greatly aided the staff in grasping what we know about the so-called Dark Continent and how we know it, and what we do not know about that land and why we do not know it. From Europe it has been possible to reach an additional number of intelligent Africans who have been educated sufficiently to appreciate their own background and to write thereupon scientifically.

This greatly increased body of facts and observations has delayed but at the same time enriched the work entitled the *African Background Outlined or Handbook for the Study of the Negro.* This work was once reported as finished, but additional information at the last hour compelled an amplification of the work to cover aspects which in recent years have become more relatively important. Instead of being restricted to such phases as history, literature, art, and religion, the work as it is now being printed will embrace much of diplomacy and economic imperialism. The first part of the work, as formerly stated, however, is a narrative dealing with the past and present in Africa from the point of view of the modern historian who visions a whole world, while the second portion of the volume is an effort to outline for schools and clubs the actual courses now in demand in many circles.

In taking up problems in American History the Association has been equally attentive. Some assistance has been given Mr. Thomas H. Posey in the revision of his *Negro Citizen of West Virginia.* Similar guidance has been given Mr. E. D. Preston in his study of the early history of Education in the District of Columbia. The results of his first effort will appear as an article in the October issue of THE JOURNAL OF NEGRO HISTORY. The most important task of all was assisting Mrs. Maud Cuney Hare in the arrangement and compiling of the data she has collected in the study of *Negro Musicians and Their Music.* This book is now being published by the Associated Publishers as a volume supplying a long-felt need of an account of the achievements of Negroes in a sphere in which they are probably at their best. This work, however, is not restricted in its treatment to American Negroes. It deals with the artists of this type of all times and all places.

At present the Director is engaged in making available in readable form brief biographical sketches of *African Heroes and Heroines,* those who defied the Europeans and made the last stand for their native land. This task has been exceedingly difficult because of the bias found in the sources available in Europe. The natives themselves did not always preserve their own records, and those who did wrote in languages and dialects with which the average European or American is not familiar. These African characters, then, are seen only through eyes of the foreigner whose attitude was that of contempt for any native who did not willingly accept his religion or political domination. Only by approaching these historical figures negatively through European sources can the truth be revealed, and then only in scattered fragments which make the path of the investigator rather difficult. The present study of the Negro from the point of view of ethnology and anthropology throws little light on the natives themselves except to prove in "Nordic" fashion how those in advance of the backward tribes "took over their culture" from the Caucasian in some mysterious manner which has no foundation in things factual.

The Research Department has been concerned also in the matter of local research in special communities. As the purposes of the Association unfold themselves from year to year various communities become interested in doing in their respective spheres what the Association has endeavored to do as a nation-wide task. Schools, churches, and fraternities have become more history-conscious. These agencies have begun to appoint actual historians who are paid to engage in research with respect to the past of the institutions concerned; and some of them, working in cooperation with the Association for the Study of Negro Life and History or under the supervision of the Director, have produced reports and volumes of considerable value.

EDUCATIONAL WORK

The Educational Work of the Association has shown the usual growth without any particular change in the plans carried out. Schools visited and assisted have proceeded along various lines, clubs have continued to extend their efforts into neglected aspects of the life and history of the Negro under the guidance of the Association, and young

people's religious societies have tended to incorporate into
their annual outlines much more of the treatment of the
past of the Negro than what has been heretofore customary. These recent endeavors indicate devoting longer
periods and doing more systematic work than has been
usual with those who first directed attention this way. Not
many extensive plans have been made to take up this
work, but by giving more attention to it from year to
year it has become a larger interest of the institutions
which thereby supply the Association a wider field.

Through clubs the Association has done much in adult
education. The needs of these circles differ somewhat
from those of the schools. Members of clubs desire ready
information but often of a serious and important kind.
Such organizations have to be encouraged to go directly
to the point at issue for the enlightenment earnestly desired
to fill a want experienced in the life of mature and busy
people. In rendering such groups assistance the Association has had to be careful not to suggest too brief treatment while avoiding at the same time the long drawn-out
story by which the patience of the adult may be taxed. In
some cases, of course, the Association has missed the
mark, but in most instances the seekers thus organized
have been properly taken care of by a member of the staff
or by some friend cooperating with the Association. The
Association does not claim to be omniscient or omnipotent
in this field, but as a rule the staff can help almost any
student thus concerned or direct him to some one who can.

The fact that the young people's religious societies have
become so history-conscious as to take up the study of the
Negro is evidence of the growth of the educational work
of the Association. The Association in this case, however,
has always endeavored to proceed wisely in guiding the
efforts of the youth in the churches. The management has
ever borne in mind that any attempt to substitute altogether the secular for the spiritual would result in failure.
While encouraging such young people to study the Ne-

gro the staff has always suggested those aspects of the history of the race which articulate with the religious work already outlined. *The History of the Negro Church* is fraught with stories of men and movements which well illustrate the great Christian virtues emphasized in religious circles. Leaders of these groups are learning to draw more frequently upon this new and interesting data which, so closely connected with the youth thus trained, serves them as an ennobling and inspiring force. Preachers thus inclined are beginning to take into consideration this new literature now being made available, and improvement in their sermons has been generally noted in the most advanced centers of thought.

NEGRO HISTORY WEEK

Of Negro History Week little needs to be said, and yet this annual celebration must be recorded as the most popular effort ever made by the Association. Persons who have never heard of the Association as such and are unacquainted with the career of the founder have nevertheless heard of and felt the impulse of Negro History Week. Nothing initiated in recent years has become more popular. Not every church, school or club participates in this celebration, but there is hardly any community of Negroes and white persons in sympathy with them in which most of the institutions in good standing do not take a part in this celebration.

Fortunately, too, the interest in the celebration has not grown more rapidly than the people have learned to make proper use of it. The selfish, the misguided, and the uninformed often become troublesome factors in any new movement, and great precaution has to be taken against those who thus mar the plot. Rarely, however, has experience in this particular case shown much difficulty from these sources. The very seriousness of the purpose of the movement has doubtless been the deterrent force operating against injecting any undesirable factor into this work.

Sometimes, however, precaution is urged by the staff also against becoming too race-conscious. The Negro must learn to look upon his past as creditable as that of any other people, but he must not become embittered against others who have wronged the weak. Such an attitude, the staff always emphasizes, is the result from misunderstanding history and the distortion of the lessons taught by the past and would place the Negro on the level with his oppressor.

The celebration of Negro History Week has long since become the time when institutions have done most for their own circles in purchasing books and pictures bearing upon the race. Recently these schools and clubs have begun to do something for the Association for the study of Negro Life and History, but it has been done mainly voluntarily. For a number of years representatives at the annual meetings of the Association have insisted that the institutions be asked to appeal to their teachers and students for funds to support the work of the Association, but the Director has seriously objected to such an appeal lest it might make Negro History Week assume the aspect of a scheme to exploit the public. In this case, however, the Director was recently outvoted, and the appeal has been sent to the people. Considerable income has thereby been raised, and the much feared result has not materialized. It seems that the more the people have done for this cause the more they have appreciated its worth.

BRANCHES OF THE ASSOCIATION

The local branches of the Association have continued along the usual course without increase. It is still the policy of the Association not to multiply these local organizations during these days when matters literary and scientific are being neglected. In the case of Detroit, however, the Association in cooperation with the Civic Association under Mr. Snow F. Grigsby, has revived the work there formerly undertaken by a defunct circle which unsuccessfully attempted the same task. For three days the Director addressed high school students, teachers' organizations and official groups in the interest of the study of the Negro, and much interest was manifested in the plans and purposes which he outlined. That interest has deepened there into a conviction that the public authorities should provide for the study of the Negro along with others.

Under Mr. L. F. Palmer was organized the Newport News Branch of the Association, which has done much to direct attention to the study of the Negro and to inculcate an appreciation of his contribution to civilization. With a loyal high school teaching staff similarly interested the moving spirit of this branch has undertaken the study of the Negro under the guidance of the Director; and he has brought before this body at times men well informed on the Negro in Africa and America. With extensive plans for resuming the work where it was temporarily abandoned last spring this circle hopes to enjoy further study of the African background and the development of the Negro in America. In less systematic manner other groups in Virginia are very active.

Several branches, it must be noted, moreover, have not permitted the problems of the time to dampen their ardor. The work in Philadelphia has done fairly well under the handicap from the prolonged sickness of Miss Marie Chase, its efficient secretary. The local research group under Mr. L. P. Jackson in Petersburg is still active. Mr. Harry E. Davis holds together the same circle for systematic work in Cleveland. Mr. Herman Dreer has greatly expanded his work in St. Louis. Mr. W. L. Davis is still laboring with the state-wide commission for the study of the Negro in Texas. Miss Gertrude Greene sends favorable reports from the circle of coworkers in New Orleans.

THE JOURNAL OF NEGRO HISTORY

THE JOURNAL OF NEGRO HISTORY lost a number of subscribers during the lean years which have recently passed, but the subscription list is gradually being rebuilt and now bids fair to reach a much higher number. The format and policies of the magazine have not undergone any change to appeal to those who have not been interested, but the fact that this magazine has been published regularly every quarter since January, 1916, has attracted subscribers who might not have been interested in the publication during its early years. The evaluation of the first twenty volumes of this magazine on the basis of its conformity to scientific objectivity has been another of its assets.

Some of the new subscribers to this magazine are persons who desire to support the publication, not every time because they will have need for the data published, but for the good the review may do in other circles. Subscriptions are sometimes given to persons who have never heard of the publication and are thereby made sufficiently interested to subscribe. A few friends of the work have been sufficiently philanthropic to pay subscriptions for institutions which have had difficulties in meeting their obligations.

CARTER G. WOODSON

PROCEEDINGS OF THE ANNUAL MEETING AND THE CELEBRATION OF THE TWENTIETH ANNIVERSARY OF THE ASSOCIATION FOR THE STUDY OF NEGRO LIFE AND HISTORY IN CHICAGO, SEPTEMBER 9-11, 1935

Amid the downpour of rain, the sweeping of high winds, and flooding of streets a representative element of Chicago joined with the delegates to the conference for the celebration of the Twentieth Anniversary of the Association on Sunday afternoon, on the 8th of September, at the New Wendell Phillips High School, to witness the demonstration of the achievements of the Negro in music. A most interesting program had been worked out under Mrs. Maude Roberts George, chairman of the Music Committee; and the artists creditably performed their parts. Among these were Shelby Nichols, Miss Maude Roberts Walker, Miss Margaret Bonds, Mrs. Elsie Breeding, Miss Florence B. Price and the Umbrian Glee Club, of Chicago; and Mrs. Roena Muckleroy Savage, of Jefferson City, Missouri. Mrs. Clara E. Hutchison gave a survey of the Negro in music, and Mrs. Lucy Harth Smith of Lexington, Kentucky, delivered in an impressive manner an appreciation of the Negro in this art.

At six o'clock on the same day the professional and business men of Chicago entertained at dinner at International House the visitors present at this conference. At the close of the repast Mr. A. L. Jackson, chairman of the General Committee in charge, introduced for short welcome addresses Dr. M. O. Bousfield, Miss Vivian Harsh, Mr. Robert S. Abbott, Mr. George R. Arthur, Mr. C. R. Rorem, Professor A. E. Holt, Miss Mary E. McDowell, Dr. Mary F. Waring, Mrs. Helen Brascher, Mr. Harry M. Englestein, Mr. Richard L. Jones, Dr. A. L. Scott, Dr. Arthur G. Falls, and Mr. Morris Lewis. Brief responses were made by Mr. Snow F. Grigsby, of Detroit; Mr. A. G. Lindsay, of St. Louis; Mr. Laurence C. Jones, of Piney

Woods, Mississippi; Prof. R. R. Brazeal of Morehouse College; Dr. N. O. Calloway of Tuskegee; Mrs. Louise H. Pack of Washington, D. C.; and Miss Juanita Howard of the same city. The one hundred and eighty persons who enjoyed this dinner and the thirty-four who for lack of seats could only observe the party from an adjoining room testify that it was an enjoyable occasion.

At ten o'clock Monday morning, the 9th, at the St. Mark's M. E. Church, the history of the Association was rehearsed. Bishop Randall A. Carter, a member of the Executive Council, presided. Dr. W. Sherman Savage, of Lincoln University in Missouri, began the program with a paper on "Twenty Years of the Association for the Study of Negro Life and History." He was followed by Professor Luther P. Jackson with a paper on "The Work of the Association and the People." After these two gentlemen had reviewed in detail the record of the organization those interested participated in a general discussion opened by Dr. E. W. Moore, of Columbus, Ohio. Special efforts of the Association were commended, and inviting fields for the extension of its usefulness were pointed out by various speakers.

The afternoon session took place in the same place with Professor Lloyd O. Lewis, of Morehouse College, presiding. Professor Rayford W. Logan, of Atlanta University, read a paper entitled "An Evaluation of the First Twenty Volumes of The Journal of Negro History." Following him appeared Judge Albert B. George, of Chicago, with an address on "The Negro and the Public Mind Today." He endeavored to show how this and other movements have influenced the thought of the people. During the general discussion interesting and valuable suggestions came from Mr. H. Theo. Tatum of the Roosevelt High School, of Gary, Indiana, and from Mr. Herman Dreer, vice-principal of the Summer High School of St. Louis. Among others, Professor E. M. Booker, of Morris College, of South Carolina, made remarks.

At the evening session at the New Wendell Phillips High School on the same day Dr. A. L. Scott presided. The Mayor of Chicago could not be present as planned, but sent Maj. Adam E. Patterson to make a few remarks. The first speaker of the evening was President Mary McLeod Bethune, of Bethune-Cookman College, Daytona, Florida. She spoke both interestingly and informingly on "The Association for the Study of Negro Life and History: Its Contribution to Our Modern Life." Her main thought was that after spending the past twenty years in saving and publishing in scientific form the records of the Negro, the Association in the future must devote more time to interpreting these facts to the people. The program for the evening closed with an address by Carter G. Woodson, on "The Call of the Neglected Race." The speaker endeavored to show that this call for service in discovering and popularizing the truth is being answered by the Association. In this way the Association is trying to emancipate the Negro in mind.

On Tuesday morning with the Director of the Association in the chair Professor W. B. Hesseltine, of the University of Wisconsin, spoke on "Some New Aspects of the Pro-Slavery Argument." Professor Lorenzo J. Greene, of Lincoln University in Missouri, followed him with a survey of "Slavery in New England." Both of these well-prepared and effectively read papers evoked a prolonged general discussion which, with the exception of one or two diversions, proved immensely stimulating. The speakers were adequately prepared to answer intelligently the most searching questions on the movements of the ante bellum period as they connected with slavery or were determined by that system.

On Tuesday afternoon with Dr. John M. Gandy, of Virginia State College, in the chair the session settled down to "Looking at West Africa from the Point of View of the Scholar." Professor Melville J. Herskovits, of Northwestern University, delivered an address on "The Significance of West Africa for Negro Research," and Dr. W. D. Hambly, of the Field Museum of Natural History, gave an illustrated lecture on "African Art and Handicraft." Both speakers showed that they had collected an abundance of valuable data while exploring Africa, and this enabled them to speak convincingly. The general discussion evoked further inquiry into aspects which seemed to be especially interesting to the large and sympathetic audience.

The evening assembly on Tuesday at the New Wendell Phillips High School was the most largely attended of all the sessions. President J. R. E. Lee, of Florida Agricultural and Mechanical College, introduced President R. R. Wright, of Wilberforce University, as the presiding officer. After a few remarks on the importance of the effort and the significance of it at this hour, President Wright presented Mrs. Laura Boulton, of Chicago. After a brief lecture on African music she used native instruments and an electric phonograph to reproduce various types of African music collected on that continent. Professor Ralph J. Bunche, of Howard University, was next presented to discuss from first-hand information "French and British Imperialism in West Africa." The last speaker was Dr. F. Ernest Work, of Muskingum College, New Concord, Ohio, who spoke on "Ethiopia, or Abyssinia as a Pawn in European Diplomacy." Inasmuch as these speakers had all traveled and studied in Africa and Dr. Work had served as educational adviser to the Negus of Abyssinia, this proved to be the most popular session of the conference. The audience of about sixteen hundred people patiently listened to the long discourses and enthusiastically applauded these informants on that distant land to which international complications have directed the attention of the entire world.

On Wednesday morning came the business session. In the absence of the president, Captain Louis R. Mehlinger, secretary-treasurer of the Association, presided. Prof. L. O. Lewis served as secretary. The reports of the officers of the organization were submitted, discussed, and approved. By motion the secretary was instructed to cast the unanimous ballot of the Association for the reelection of the entire corps of officers. The chief matter of new business which followed was that of making the support of the Association nation-wide. A motion prevailed to appoint a large committee with one or more representatives from each state with a steering committee composed of those in and near Washington. Persons from various parts were suggested, and their names will be published as soon as the number willing to serve can be ascertained. The matter of the next meeting place was left to the judgment of the Executive Council inasmuch as there was a difference of opinion as to whether the Association should favor Detroit or Richmond, Virginia.

The final session was held in Evanston in Harris Hall of Northwestern University for "Presenting the Work of the Association to the North Shore." Dr. Walter Dill Scott, president of the University, presided. Alderman E. B. Jourdain briefly but intelligently discussed "What the Negro May Learn from History." Dr. Charles H. Wesley, of Howard University, then delivered a scholarly and eloquent address on "The Reconstruction of History" as the thing necessary to give the Negro credit for his glorious past and to induce the biased of other races to treat the Negro as a citizen. The address left a lasting impression and served as a fitting climax of the celebration of the Twentieth Anniversary of the Association. The meeting adjourned after some remarks by Captain L. R. Mehlinger, secretary-treasurer of the Association.

Thus passed into history the most largely attended and the most impressive assembly ever held by the Association. To this success the unselfish efforts of the General Committee in charge of the celebration with A. L. Jackson as chairman and Morris Lewis as secretary made a large

contribution. These public spirited citizens were warmly
supported by others from various walks in the city of
Chicago and workers from afar who met the challenge of
the Rosenwald Family Association that appropriated $750
toward the expenses of the conference on the condition
that an equal amount be raised elsewhere. Mr. George R.
Arthur who made this suggestion to this foundation was
prompted by the remembrance of the fact that Mr. Julius
Rosenwald early became interested in the Association,
contributed to its support, and served as a member of its
Executive Council.

The interest during the week became city-wide, and sessions near the end of the conference were crowded beyond
the seating capacity of the auditoriums in which they were
held. To supply the information required it became necessary for the officers and visitors to remain in the city after
the conference to address institutions and circles of citizens desiring to learn more of the message of the Association for the Study of Negro Life and History. The
persons thus moved represented the best elements of both
races in and near the city of Chicago.

TWENTY YEARS OF THE ASSOCIATION FOR THE STUDY OF NEGRO LIFE AND HISTORY[1]

The Association for the Study of Negro Life and History was organized in Chicago by Carter G. Woodson on September 9, 1915, with the assistance of George C. Hall, J. E. Stamps, W. B. Hartgrove and A. L. Jackson. The minutes of this first meeting read as follows:

9/9/15

A meeting called by Dr. Woodson for the purpose of considering definite plans for organization of a society, which should publish a magazine devoted to the study of the Negro, was held in the office of the Executive Secretary of the Wabash Avenue Department of the Chicago Y. M. C. A. Those present were C. G. Woodson, G. C. Hall, A. L. Jackson, W. B. Hartgrove, and J. E. Stamps. Dr. Hall was elected temporary chairman, J. E. Stamps, temporary secretary. The proposed constitution was read, and after alterations, adopted. A permanent organization was formed, and the following officers elected: Dr. G. C. Hall, President, J. E. Moorland, Secretary-Treasurer, C. G. Woodson, Director of Research and Editor. In addition to the above named officers the Executive Council will be J. A. Bigham, A. L. Jackson, Miss S. P. Breckinridge, G. N. Grisham.

The editorial staff will consist of six or eight persons to be selected by the editor and approved by the Executive Council.

A motion prevailed that in a reply to a request from Dr. Moorland we offer to cooperate with Howard University along lines satisfactory to the Executive Council.[2]

J. E. STAMPS.

[1] An address delivered on the occasion of the celebration of the Twentieth Anniversary of the Association for the Study of Negro Life and History in Chicago, Illinois, September 9, 1935.

[2] Some of these officers failed to function in these capacities. Mr. G. N. Grisham, of Kansas City, retiring at that time from public life, refused to serve although he gave some financial aid. This position was filled by the appointment of Mr. Garnet C. Wilkinson. Dr. J. E. Moorland, who was not at this meeting which launched the movement, nevertheless served with J. A. Bigham and C. G. Woodson as the incorporators of the Association under

We are here then to celebrate the twentieth anniversary of the organization in the city where it was established. What had been accomplished in the first decade of the Association's history was reviewed by the Director at the tenth celebration in the city of Washington on September 9, 1925, under the title "Ten Years of Collecting and Publishing the Records of the Negro." At that time he commented upon the struggles and difficulties which the Association faced in getting started with this work. There is no necessity for covering that ground again. This paper, then, will deal largely with the work which has been done since 1925 and its relation to what has gone before.

One will naturally ask the question: What has the society accomplished during these years? Those who organized the Association claimed as its objective the following: "The collection of sociological and historical data on the Negro, the study of peoples of African blood, the publishing of books in this field and the promotion of harmony between the races by acquainting one with the achievements of the other," that is, familiarizing the whites with the accomplishments of the Negro. Throughout these twenty years the Association has been striving to carry forward the object it set for itself in 1915. The organization has lived up to these ideals.

One of the outstanding achievements during this period has been the publication of The Journal of Negro History. This magazine very early took its place among the scientific reviews of the learned societies. The high standard maintained in this magazine has encouraged research by American and foreign scholars, and it has done much to develop the young Negro scholars, some of whom would

the laws of the District of Columbia on October 2, 1915. Dr. Moorland cooperated as Secretary-Treasurer until 1921 when he had moved from Washington to New York City. Dr. G. C. Hall was president for two years. The staff of editors invited to participate consisted of Monroe N. Work, Benjamin Brawley, George E. Haynes, Walter Dyson, Robert E. Park, and Kelly Miller, none of whom were present at the first meeting. With two exceptions, these gentlemen never cooperated as a staff, and this part of the plan was soon abandoned.

have been a long time securing a hearing but for THE
JOURNAL OF NEGRO HISTORY. When the Association first
came into the field there were few competent historical
writers in the race. Today there are many able workers.
It is reasonable to think that THE JOURNAL OF NEGRO HIS-
TORY has had a great influence upon this movement. There
are at the present nineteen bulky volumes of this publication already completed and the twentieth is now in progress.
THE JOURNAL OF NEGRO HISTORY is scientific. Its articles
as a rule show original treatment or independent research.
The magazine publishes also many valuable documents
with facts which otherwise never would have become
widely known. There was praise for this magazine from
the beginning by men scientifically trained, and it has
found its way into most of the important libraries in this
country and abroad.

Another activity of the Association through the last two
decades has been its interest in research, not only by providing a medium through which scholars might publish
the results of their efforts but by promoting definite projects of its own. One study was directed toward Reconstruction History. This investigation was carried on by
Dean A. A. Taylor, when he was associated with Dr.
Woodson, and the results were published as *The Negro in
South Carolina during the Reconstruction* and *The Negro
in the Reconstruction of Virginia*. At the same time Dr.
Woodson was producing on his own account *The Mind of
the Negro, Free Negro Heads of Families in the United
States in 1830,* and *Free Negro Owners of Slaves in
the United States in 1830*.

During these years, too, the economic and social interest
of the Negro has claimed the attention of the Association
and such studies have been brought out during the period.
Some of these are *The Employment of Negroes in the
District of Columbia,* by Lorenzo J. Greene and Myra Col-
son Callis, *The Negro Wage Earner,* by Lorenzo J. Greene
and Carter G. Woodson; *The Rural Negro,* also by the Director of the Association, and *Negro Professional Man and*

the Community, by the same author. The Association has also studied the relation of the races, especially as they have come into contact with the Negro. The studies of the relation of the Negroes and Indians, by Dean J. H. Johnston and Kenneth W. Porter, have been productive of good results.

The Association has made a very definite effort, in recent years, to study the Negro out of the bounds of the United States, the purpose being to find what contributions these Negroes have made toward culture and how they are living at the present day. The Association definitely turned its attention to this phase of work in 1927. The Director, in his annual report of that year, could say that research in foreign parts has been productive of good results, the book on African myths and proverbs had been published and Miss Ruth A. Fisher had extracted items bearing on the Negro from the archives of England. From foreign scholars have come such contributions as "The Society for the Propagation of the Gospel in Foreign Parts: Its Work Among the Negroes of North America to 1783" by Faith Virbert; "The Negro Race in French Literature" by Fernand Masse; "Montesquieu's Influence on Anti-Slavery Opinion in England," by T. F. H. Fletcher. The Director himself, working in the same field, has produced "Attitudes in English Literature" and "Attitudes in the Iberian Peninsula." Arrangements have been made to carry this particular part of the work much further with the assistance of investigators employed in the archives of England, France, Spain, Italy, and Germany.

At the same time interest in this new phase of study developed among American Negro scholars, who have carried out such projects. Dr. V. B. Spratlin, of Howard University, has written articles of this stamp, and he has produced a book which traces in much detail the contact of the Spanish with the African. Dr. W. N. Rivers of Miner Teachers College in Washington, D. C., and Professor John F. Matheus, of West Virginia State College, have cooperated with the Director for the purpose of translating books in other languages, bearing on the Negro, and thus making them available for the English reading public. Professor Mercer Cook, of Howard University, has compiled references to Negroes in French literature in order to supply stimulating reading matter for classes in French.

The collection of manuscript materials bearing on the Negro has been the task of the Association during this period. The Social Science Research Council supplied $4,000 for the exploratory effort. Appeal was made to persons who had in their possession letters, wills, diaries, bills of sale of slaves, receipts and the like, to give them to the Association that they might be preserved for the benefit of workers in history bearing on the Negro. These documents, now numbering more than four thousand, are housed in the Library of Congress in the manuscript division of that institution and are being used in studying all phases of the Negro. Because of the depression, the collecting of documents as a definite project had to cease. The Association, however, has continued this important task through workers carrying on other activities.

The organization from the beginning has served as a free bureau for those making studies of various kinds on the Negro. Some universities have insisted that before a subject bearing on the Negro could be selected for dissertation or thesis, it must be submitted to the Director of this Association for his approval. The Association has had to serve schools and colleges as a clearing house for questions relating to the Negro. The organization has furnished bibliographies for courses on Negro history and race relations. The search for rare books bearing upon the race has been a task of the Association. This has enabled the society to fill a need which the college libraries have experienced. Reprints of some of these have been produced at small cost to the schools as in the case of Delafosse's *Negroes of Africa*. With Negro History Week the Association has popularized its work throughout America.

During these twenty years the Association has done much in making the contributions of the Negro known to the foreign world, and it is still going on and broadening its influence as the years go by. It has become an important member of the learned societies. It is bringing to view new facts and gathering new documents so that the scholars may write with more authority on the Negro. Each year it is pushing the frontier of fact bearing on the Negro back further and further.

The problem of financing the Association has been a trying one from the very beginning. When we note the work done by the various learned societies (especially the historical societies) and the amount available for their work, one wonders how the Association for the Study of Negro Life and History has been able to do so much with such a little money. We observe the following report of receipts and expenditures for these twenty years from 1915 to 1935:

FINANCIAL STATEMENT FROM SEPTEMBER 9, 1915, TO SEPTEMBER 9, 1935

RECEIPTS		DISBURSEMENTS	
Research Fund	$133,336.53	Research	$ 94,556.14
Subscriptions	28,608.09	Printing	86,561.97
Membership	12,986.20	Stenographic Service	13,343.57
Contributions	78,708.55	Rent	11,242.11
Advertising	3,476.50	Salaries	30,578.37
Sundry Income	16,419.07	Traveling Expenses	21,043.70
		Sundry Expenditures	15,180.13
		Balance on hand	953.95
Totals	$273,534.94		$273,534.94

It can be seen that as great a work as the Association has been able to do it could have done better if more funds had been available. During recent years the Association has had to depend largely upon the contributions given by interested Negroes such as teachers, preachers and school children. Boards which once aided the work are now unable to give further aid or refused to do so because of the independent character of the Association. The work which it has carried has had to be somewhat curtailed, but the organization is still very active and out of debt. It is to be hoped that the Association can soon secure the financial aid it deserves to carry on its larger program.

W. SHERMAN SAVAGE

THE WORK OF THE ASSOCIATION
AND THE PEOPLE[1]

The twenty years of the Association for the Study of Negro Life and History may be divided into two periods of ten each. The first of these periods represents a time when the Association was largely a scholarly organization with a very limited influence on the people at large; the second period continued with the program of the first, but at the same time it reached the people. This organization, then, unlike most historical societies, is unique in that it has played a double role, and played both very successfully. The treatment of the scholarly activities of the Association has been assigned to other persons on this program. My discussion lays emphasis on the second period of the Association's existence—the period when the organization reached the general public.

The establishment of the Association for the Study of Negro Life and History twenty years ago today by Dr. Carter G. Woodson with four others thus interested was a significant event in the life of the Negro and the nation. The significance of this event is well summed up in the words of the Boston *Herald* of 1915, which said, "When men of any race begin to show pride in their own antecedents we have one of the surest signs of prosperity and rising civilization." *"Begin* to show pride in their own antecedents" was a correct expression since the Association to which this paper referred was then in its infancy. During these twenty years the organization has passed out of the infant stage into a full grown institution, into an institution which has a popular backing and following. Its influence has extended from Washington, D. C., to every state in the union and to foreign countries. The Association, today, we must repeat, is a thing of the people.

[1] An address delivered on the occasion of the celebration of the Twentieth Anniversary of the Association for the Study of Negro Life and History, Chicago, Illinois, September 9, 1935.

The function of the scholar is to create. Such has been
the place fulfilled by Dr. Carter G. Woodson, a staff of
collaborators, and contributors to THE JOURNAL OF NEGRO
HISTORY. The productions of the scholar pass on to teachers and the educated class. The knowledge of this group
in turn passes on to school children, who eventually make
such knowledge the common possession of all the people.
The enlightened classes also in meeting among themselves
for their mutual edification project themselves beyond
their own group and beyond school children into the
masses. This orderly succession of steps in the trans-
mission of knowledge represents the experience of the
Association for the Study of Negro Life and History. In
so doing it has reached the people.

The agencies involved in these successive steps are
represented in THE JOURNAL OF NEGRO HISTORY, clubs and
branches of young and old, the annual meetings of the Association, speaking tours of the Director and other persons, and finally, Negro History Week. This discussion
excludes THE JOURNAL OF NEGRO HISTORY, which is mentioned in extenso elsewhere. It gives passing reference to
the clubs, the annual meeting, and the speaking tours of
the Director; it lays emphasis on Negro History Week,
the agency which has done most in reaching the people.

Negro history clubs have operated through such agencies as schools, churches, and social welfare organizations.
They are confined almost altogether to the larger urban
centers of the country. Some of these clubs scattered over
the country have maintained an official connection with
the Association at Washington and have therefore been
known as "branches." These clubs and branches make
use of the publications of the Association, and, in some instances, have delved into the research field by bringing out
facts respecting Negro achievement in their own localities.
They have aided also in collecting documents and manuscripts for publication at Washington.

Clubs and branches have had a checkered career. A number of them have arisen during the twenty years of the Association, but after maintaining an existence of a year or more they have then reported themselves as dormant. On the other hand, however, the Association has always maintained a small band of tireless workers all over the country at strategic points. One of the most notable instances of continuous efforts along this line has been the work of Mr. Herman Dreer at St. Louis. Negro history is a matter of such importance to this man that he has organized in his city at the Poro College the Carter G. Woodson School of Negro History, an organization of children which meets weekly on Saturdays throughout the year. There are other Dreers situated in almost every state of the country. At Lexington, Kentucky, for example, the efforts of Mrs. Lucy Harth Smith have been very creditable. In recent years Newport News, Virginia, under the leadership of Mr. L. F. Palmer, has done much to keep the Negro history idea alive.

Of much importance in reaching the people is the annual meeting of the Association for the Study of Negro Life and History. Continuity in annual meetings begins with the year 1920, prior to which they were sometimes officially restricted. In that year the Association met at Washington, D. C.; in 1921, Lynchburg, Virginia; 1922, Louisville; 1923, Atlanta; 1924, Richmond, Virginia; 1925, Washington; 1926, Baltimore; 1927, Pittsburgh; 1928, St. Louis; 1929, Washington; 1930, Cleveland; 1931, New York City; 1932, Atlanta; 1933, Washington again; 1934, Houston, Texas; and 1935, at the place of its origin, Chicago, Illinois. For five years the Association staged, in addition to these annual meetings, an assembly known as the Spring Conference. From 1923 to 1927 these conferences were held successively at Baltimore, Philadelphia, Durham in North Carolina, Petersburg in Virginia, and Jacksonville in Florida. In the twenty years of its existence the Association has thus gone around the country.

Some reference to these annual meetings as a popularizing force is worth while at this point. Each one appears as a step in advance over the preceding one so that today the annual meeting of this body attracts nation-wide attention. The metropolitan newspapers report its activities. Signs of growth were first noted at the meeting held at Lynchburg in 1921. This gathering, the Director reported, was a success "above and beyond that of any other hitherto held. The attendance was large, the enthusiasm ran higher, and the financial support secured far exceeded that of other meetings." Similarly at Louisville, the next year, the same authority reported success from both the local and national point of view. "Persons from afar," he said, "came to take an active part, and citizens of Louisville and nearby cities of Kentucky attended in considerable numbers." At St. Louis, in 1928, was a similar occurrence. In this instance, as in the others, "there was a representative attendance from the cities and towns nearby, and a considerable number of persons came from afar to participate in this conference. Persons came from places as distant as Texas, Georgia, and New England. Pittsburgh proved to be a record breaker from the standpoint of local attendance. At this conference we have the report—"The evening sessions were so well attended that the people had to be turned away for the lack of seating capacity in the large auditorium of the Ebenezer Baptist Church." Our conclusion from these statements is that the annual meeting of the Association has been a factor in drawing the Association to the people and the people to the organization.

Similar in effect to the annual meetings have been the frequent tours of the Director of the Association and other persons. As the chief promoter of the Association and Negro history, Dr. Woodson has naturally been the source of attracting the people. He has spoken in the schools and colleges, churches, social welfare circles, and business institutions of practically every state in the country where there is considerable Negro population. In 1928 he made a survey of the whole state of Florida which he characterized as "thorough." In 1933 the tour of the Director in the Southwest and Middle West took on all the proportions of "a swing around the circle." Included in this itinerary were New Orleans, Baton Rouge, most of the larger centers and schools in Texas, Fort Smith and Pine Bluff in Arkansas, St. Louis, Jefferson City and Kansas City in Missouri, and Wichita in Kansas. In all of these places Dr. Woodson reached the people; and, in some instances, great crowds of them. In his path were left newly created clubs, branches, the incorporation of Negro history in the curriculum of schools, a firmer basis of financial support, a cementing of the races, and general good will. As for the white people in Texas at certain points, the Director of the Association found that they were just as anxious and more anxious to hear the story of the achievements of the Negro than the Negroes themselves. On this occasion, as on others, Dr. Woodson addressed several white colleges.

The annual meetings of the Association and the occasional tours of the Director have been agencies for reaching the people, but, after all, at best such efforts could reach but a limited few. Some channel needed to be discovered by which the Association might touch the country at large all at one time. "The Negro has a glorious past," so one Negro weekly declared, "but to keep this knowledge confined to a restricted few (would) not serve any useful purpose." This paper further stated in effect that unless a change was made "the vast majority of white folk will continue to believe that the Negro has no history worthy of the name and Negroes will continue to hide their faces in shame." In short, from 1915 to 1925, the valuable contributions of the Association remained almost altogether in the possession of the limited few of this country. Despite all that had been done and despite all which this address indicates to this point, the Association by 1925 had not affected the rank and file of the people.

Happily, the condition just referred to did not continue, for in 1926 this organization instituted an annual national celebration which has proved to be a popular device of immense proportions. The annual celebration we refer to is Negro History Week which comes the second week in February. In the opinion of the founder of the Association, the originator of this celebration, the "observance of Negro History Week, proved to be one of the most fortunate steps ever taken by the Association."

For several years the observance of Negro History Week was confined to colleges, accredited high schools, and the people of the urban centers of the country. As in the case of the clubs and branches referred to above such cities as Baltimore, Wilmington in Delaware, Washington, Richmond, Petersburg, Raleigh, Charleston, Jacksonville, Montgomery, Jackson in Mississippi, New Orleans, the cities of Texas, Nashville, Louisville, Lexington in Kentucky, St. Louis, and Kansas City all figured prominently in this observance. In like manner centers of the North and East, like Chicago, Cleveland, New York, Philadelphia and Pittsburgh also observed this week. In the latter group of urban centers the celebration was carried out not so much through schools, as was the case of the cities in the South and West, but rather through churches, clubs, and various social welfare agencies.

The extension of the Association to the people through Negro History Week in the *urban* centers of the country was a notable achievement, but the urban people are not all the people. More than half the people of our country are rural dwellers. What then is the status of Negro History Week in the rural sections of the country? Up to this point in the history of the Association the opinion has been that Negro History Week is confined to the cities and colleges, some of which are in very small places. I wish to make the assertion on this occasion that Negro History

Week has now gone beyond the cities into the vast rural areas of our country. In so doing it is reaching even a larger number of people than those aroused in the cities. This extension of the celebration into rural territory marks the greatest achievement of the Association among the masses, perhaps the most popular thing the organization has done.

In using the term "the people" we can not mean all the people. No organization, except the civil state, ever reaches such an end. In like manner, by no means, has any effort of the Association reached the great rural masses of Negroes in the far South. Yet, on the other hand, a strong beginning has been made in that direction. Negro History Week has made heavy inroads in the rural section of the states of the upper South; it is destined to grow in the rural territory of the lower South.

Some light on this subject may be obtained from Virginia and Georgia. The best authorities on events of an educational nature in the rural South are the Jeanes Supervisors of Negro schools in the various counties. These administrators have recently furnished the speaker with data on their respective counties. In Virginia, seventeen of these persons have reported on the activities of nineteen counties; in Georgia, five have reported by written correspondence and two verbally. In addition to these administrators, a large number of the seven hundred teachers of Virginia in attendance at the Virginia State College summer school this year, have testified with respect to what is taking place in staging this celebration in their counties.

For lack of space details on each of these reports can not be given. We shall content ourselves with a few counties only, which in turn indicate the activities of the majority of all the counties in the state. From Surry County, Virginia, comes this report, "Five years ago the schools of the county were not so well informed as to the necessity of acquainting the pupils with the great men, women, and deeds of the Negro race. But now every school in the county (and there are twenty-two of them) observes Negro History Week . . . . This year we gave a county-wide program at the largest church in our county to which all school communities were invited . . . . Negro History Week is growing in popularity in Surry county, and each year it is looked forward to with greater interest and growing enthusiasm.''

From Campbell county, Virginia, comes this report. ''Practically every school in Campbell county observes Negro History Week . . . . The idea of observing (this week) has grown in Campbell county from what it was five years ago. Our pupils have found out many things that they never knew (before) that Negroes had any part in such (things) as exploration, invention, literature, music, and art. They are learning to appreciate the part that the Negro has contributed to the development of this country.'' The supervisor of King William county reports that the observance of the week in her county has been more marked and better organized than heretofore. She reports that last year the exercises for the week were held in every one of the nineteen schools. She says further, ''We in King William are trying to impress the young people with the idea that the Negro has made a contribution to something other than crime.''

One of the most far reaching celebrations in Virginia apparently is held in Mecklenburg, a county in the cotton belt of the state with a large Negro population. This county has two supervisors; and, judging from all appearances, one can say that these two women get things done with respect to Negro history. One of these workers reports, ''For the last ten years we have observed Negro History Week. Our people look forward to the program with a deal of pleasure and pride. Each year we see a marked improvement in the programs . . . . Each of our fifty-six schools conducts (exercises) each morning at their devotional period giving the life of some noted Negro . . . .

Through us the teachers, pupils, patrons, ministers, and Sunday School teachers are notified to do their bit to acquaint the Negroes and some whites who attend our programs with the accomplishments of the members of our race.'' Southampton county, the county of Nat Turner, by irony is in like manner a beehive for Negro history activity. There are fifty-eight schools in this county with ninety-eight teachers, and all of them observe the annual celebration. In this county, and perhaps in many of the others, the supervisor says that she instructs her ninety-eight teachers to make every week in the school year a Negro history week.

I have dwelt somewhat at length on Virginia. All that has been said here for this one state may likewise be said for the rural sections of Maryland, Delaware, North Carolina, West Virginia, Missouri, Kentucky and perhaps Tennessee. Dr. Savage of Lincoln University, Missouri, estimates that three-fourths of all the schools in Missouri observe Negro History Week. This estimate for Missouri may be applied to the states of the upper South as a whole. In Virginia, out of seventeen reports only two of them indicate a partial observance. The one great characteristic of the Virginia reports as just read is that Negro History Week is a growing thing in all of the counties.

So much for Virginia; now what of Georgia? Here the observance is not so extensive as in Virginia. It is the opinion of one prominent worker of Savannah, Georgia, that the schools of his state (rural schools) are not familiar with Negro life and history. Negro History Week likewise lacks attention throughout the state generally. The cities of Georgia and some rural high schools, we must note, are as active as in other parts of the country. Rural Georgia shows up best where there is a county supervisor, but since there are only thirty-five such administrators in a state of 140 counties, large areas of Georgia are in darkness respecting any thing the Negro has ever done. This appraisal of Georgia may likewise be applied to the states of South Carolina, Alabama, Mississippi, and Louisiana. Rural Florida and Texas report a little more progress in this direction.

We need not go into the details of why Negro History Week is given less attention in Georgia than in Virginia except to say that although conditions are bad enough in both states Virginia surpasses Georgia in salaries paid teachers and in the academic preparation of the teachers. In Georgia and some of the other states of the lower South a majority of the rural school teachers have less than high school training. Since these instructors have neither attended a normal school nor a college they have had no contacts by which to do anything beyond that which is given in text books. The colleges of the South, we should note in passing, are great centers for Negro achievement. The presidents of the colleges, particularly the state colleges where most of the teachers at present are trained, are thoroughly in accord with the Association, and they lend valuable assistance in promoting the study of the Negro.

We have laid great emphasis on Negro History Week in this address for the reason that it is the feeder for every other activity of the Association. By reason of Negro History Week the study of Negro History has found its way into the school curriculum here and there in twenty-one states or more. This creates a demand for books, literature, and pictures on the Negro. THE JOURNAL OF NEGRO HISTORY grows by reason of this expansion while public addresses by college professors and others well informed are becoming more and more in demand.

Negro History Week has brought the Association to the people and the people to the Association. P. B. Young, editor of the *Norfolk Journal and Guide,* lays great emphasis on this observance. In 1928 at the close of the third year of the celebration he declared that in this one year more was said, "written and otherwise demonstrated concerning the ancestry, historical past, and buried deeds of the Negro in the past four or five years than at any time during the modern era of civilization.''

The people of this country have reacted to the Association for the Study of Negro Life and History. They are doing it not only with respect to a study of the Negro, but also with respect to making financial contributions to support the work. Whereas up until a few years ago the bulk of the support for the Association came from the big foundations of the country at present the load has shifted from these sources to the people, the Negro element. Virginia at this time is putting forward every effort to support adequately the Association. At the time of this writing, 1,700 school teachers in Virginia of all grades have made contributions of fifteen, twenty-five, and fifty cents. The total amount they have given is $341.00. We are headed for one thousand dollars by the first of November. Our aim is to have all the 3,900 Negro teachers in Virginia contribute to this worthy cause. At present nearly half of them have already done so.

Throughout this paper we have made some passing reference to white people. We have noted here and there that they participate on Negro programs, serve as officers, and in various ways have encouraged the movement. In this connection we should say that the majority of the state superintendents in the South, as well as many local city and county superintendents, support and promote the celebration of Negro History Week and the other offerings of the Association. The program here today also shows that white scholars have praised this work and have given it valuable assistance.

These helpful signs, however, should not lead us into a false generalization of the whole. Up to the present the study of the Negro in the white teachers colleges of the land is either not attempted at all or in a very meager way. The white teachers of elementary schools in the land are thus in no position to make a contribution to the problems growing out of our biracial situation. Indeed in Virginia as elsewhere in the country, efforts to make the Negro a subject matter of instruction in white schools are firmly resisted. To the great masses of the American white people the Negro is entertained only as an inferior and not as a person who has capabilities in common with mankind in general. The larger task of the Association, then, is to educate the great American public in general as it has made a strong beginning with Negroes.

Some one has said that after all an institution is but the lengthened shadow of a man. The Association for the Study of Negro Life and History is Carter G. Woodson. His efforts have reached the people. On this occasion a tribute is due this man. Gordon B. Hancock of Richmond, Virginia, has already expressed it in these words: "Carter G. Woodson has done more to instill pride of race into the Negro than any man living or dead." For this contribution the people of this country are very grateful.

Luther P. Jackson

Virginia State College,
Petersburg, Va.

AN EVALUATION OF THE FIRST TWENTY VOLUMES OF *THE JOURNAL OF NEGRO HISTORY*[1]

The founding and continued publication during twenty years of THE JOURNAL OF NEGRO HISTORY constitute a significant landmark in American historiography, a monument to Negro creative ability and historical scholarship, and the most indispensable contribution to this field of research. Its founding was significant because although the *American Historical Review* was not established until nearly one hundred twenty years after the United States declared its independence, THE JOURNAL OF NEGRO HISTORY began publication fifty years after Negroes won their freedom. Moreover, THE JOURNAL OF NEGRO HISTORY made its appearance thirteen years before the *Journal of Modern History,* the review of American scholars interestd in European history, and two years before the *Hispanic American Historical Review.*

That there is need for scholarly journals devoted to specialized fields is evident from the existence of the *New England Quarterly,* the *Mississippi Valley Historical Review,* the *Iowa Journal of History and Politics,* and a host of other sectional and special quarterlies. This opinion, moreover, is the mature conclusion of one of the grand old men of American historical scholarship, Dr. J. Franklin Jameson, one of the founders in 1884 of the American Historical Association, one of its former presidents, one of the former editors of the *American Historical Review,* the present chief of the Manuscripts Division of the Library of Congress and a distinguished scholar who is not ashamed to manifest interest in the strivings of a despised race. Surely, if any man in America is qualified to evaluate the need for a historical review, Dr. Jameson is that

[1] A paper read at the Annual Meeting and the Celebration of the Twentieth Anniversary of the Association for the Study of Negro Life and History in Chicago, Illinois, September 9-11, 1935.

man. When the *Hispanic American Historical Review* first appeared, he showed the role that journal should play. In the early days of the *American Historical Review,* he was frequently obliged, he pointed out,

"to conclude, concerning some book on a quite special subject, that no one in America had qualified himself to review with authority a book in that particular field. Where perhaps some thirty different subjects for doctoral dissertations were being worked upon in 1895, four hundred were being investigated in the present academic year [i. e., 1917-1918]"[2]

He further showed this need from another point of view.

"The healthiest and most well-rounded development of historical science in the United States," he wrote, "would require, first, the existence of one or more general historical journals of high quality; secondly, a multitude of local historical journals, cultivating restricted fields, but not provincial in quality; and thirdly, a considerable number of ably-conducted special journals, whose fields are restricted not by geographical boundaries but by concentration on particular portions or aspects of history."[3]

With special reference to this latter group, he continued:

"In January, 1916, appeared the first number of two other historical quarterlies representing two widely different specialties, the *Military Historian and Economist* and THE JOURNAL OF NEGRO HISTORY, both of which have since led prosperous careers and have greatly increased the interest of students in two important fields of historical inquiry."[4]

If a judgment based upon only two volumes of THE JOURNAL OF NEGRO HISTORY may seem premature, it will be profitable to examine the opinion of another distinguished American scholar. Dr. Evarts B. Greene of Columbia University, a member of the Executive Council of the Association for the Study of Negro Life and History,

---

[2] J. Franklin Jameson, "A New Historical Journal," *Hispanic American Historical Review,* vol. i (February, 1918), p. 2.

[3] *Ibid.*, p. 4.

[4] *Ibid.*, p. 5.

after surveying the first sixteen volumes of THE JOURNAL OF NEGRO HISTORY, wrote in 1930, that he was not "indulging in any idle compliment" when he said that these volumes made "an impressive record of honest, substantial scholarship."[5] In these days when superlatives are commonly employed this may seem like faint praise. But if it is remembered that the historian is given to understatement rather than to exaggeration, this conclusion is indeed no idle compliment.

Only those who have studied THE JOURNAL OF NEGRO HISTORY since its inception have any idea of the universal, encyclopedic scope of its contents. Up to the present time, there have appeared some 350 articles and series of documents. Of these, 241 articles and series of documents have been devoted wholly or largely to Negroes in the United States. Thus, nearly one-third of the total contents has dealt with the Negro outside the United States. Of these 109 articles and series of documents the distribution has been as follows: Africa, 35; Great Britain and Europe, 24; Latin America, 18; Canada, 17; West Indies, other than Haiti and Cuba, 10; the Pacific Area, 4; and the Near East, 1. This distribution justifies, one may believe, the title THE JOURNAL OF NEGRO HISTORY.

In point of time, these articles and documents cover events from the most remote antiquity to present politics as soon as they have become history. The topics treated have included not only political, constitutional, and military history but also social, economic, diplomatic, church, and cultural history. Not only the great figures of history, but the lowly washerwomen have received the attention of scholars. Nor have the auxiliaries of history been neglected: anthropology, ethnology, ethnography, have been studied to reveal additional light.

From the qualitative point of view, a high standard has

[5] Evarts B. Greene, "Perspectives in History," *The Journal of Negro History*, vol. xvii (January, 1932), p. 10.

been maintained, both with respect to the value of the information and the manner of presentation. Some of the articles have been excellent, a few mediocre, but the general average has been entirely creditable. A large number of these articles utilized primary sources not only in English, but in French, German, and Spanish. It is gratifying to find a growing number of Negro scholars able to read easily French. All too small a number, however, have mastered German. Some have used the rich store of Spanish sources. But the great mine of Brazilian sources in the Portuguese language has been left almost totally unexplored.

A comparison may be made here with the first oil mine of the late Edward Doheny. The *Chicago Tribune* reported that "Seeing a colored man hauling a cart of black, tarry stuff, Doheny learned on inquiry that it was used as fuel. He recognized it as an oil exude and hastened to purchase the lot from which the man had shoveled it."[6] Unless Negro scholars explore the rich mine of Brazilian sources, it is perfectly possible that other students will prostitute them to prove their distorted interpretations just as Doheny exploited his oil fields for undesirable purposes. The present crisis in Ethiopia suggests the prime necessity for Negro scholars to acquaint themselves with Italian and Amharic. It is to be hoped also that we shall eventually have scholars familiar with some of the principal *linguae francae* of Africa, such as Hausa and Swahili. There are probably works in Arabic that still deserve careful analysis in the original. These are requirements of the highest degree, but Negro scholars may be relied upon to master these tools as they have others.

In this connection I wish also to express the hope that funds may be obtained for photostating documents in certain foreign countries so that a considerable number of scholars in this country may have access to them. If the

[6] *Chicago Tribune*, September 9, 1935, p. 1.

Journal is to maintain in the future the high place in American historiography that it has maintained during the past twenty years, our historians must have constantly available new material.

Improvement might also be occasionally noted in the mechanics of presentation. Professor Arthur M. Schlesinger, one of America's most distinguished scholars and a member of the Executive Council of the Association for the Study of Negro Life and History, has well said that the writing of history is a craft. There is some evidence that our scholars have acquired greater skill in gathering material than in molding it into shape. This is especially true in such matters as the use of quotations and footnotes. But the encouraging aspect is the constant improvement in these skills. When one remembers the relatively small number of Negroes who have done graduate work in history, the even smaller number who have made a special study of Negro history, and the very limited number who have sufficient time from their heavy teaching loads to do any research, the marvel is that the high degree of excellence has been maintained. One should also recall that *The American Historical Review* is able to pay for its articles whereas contributors to the Journal do a work of love.

Let no one conclude from these suggestions that the attempt is being made to convey the idea in an inoffensive way that the Journal has failed to meet the strict requirements of historical scholarship. They are submitted in the light of the editor's specific instructions that this evaluation was not to be a eulogy. The writer of this paper would be the first, moreover, to admit his own shortcomings. But an historical association is not a mutual admiration society. Inasmuch as writers in *The American Historical Review* are frequently subjected to criticism, it should not be wondered at that The Journal of Negro History has not yet achieved perfection.

If any additional testimony were needed of the important place that the JOURNAL holds in American historiography, the following facts may be noted: (1) *The American Historical Review* has frequently included in its lists of important articles published in other journals many that have appeared in THE JOURNAL OF NEGRO HISTORY. (2) Many libraries of the leading universities and colleges of this country have complete files of THE JOURNAL OF NEGRO HISTORY. In this respect, they are ahead of some of our own institutions of higher learning which have neither the past nor the current issues. Some of these schools can not invoke the excuse of lack of funds, for they do have complete files of certain periodicals which can be fittingly described by a word dear to the vocabulary of many American scholars, namely "tripe." (3) The subscription list of THE JOURNAL OF NEGRO HISTORY exceeds that of many local and special historical reviews. Some scholars and libraries in European countries subscribe for THE JOURNAL OF NEGRO HISTORY. (4) Authors of authoritative monographs have culled from its pages important information that they could not obtain elsewhere. (5) Although the *Readers' Guide to Periodical Literature* does not index articles appearing in THE JOURNAL OF NEGRO HISTORY, the *International Index to Periodicals* does. Moreover, during the all too short-lived existence of *Social Science Abstracts,* an indispensable tool to scholars, it contained many abstracts from articles in the JOURNAL. Finally, the *International Bibliography of Historical Sciences,* which is necessarily highly selective, lists articles from THE JOURNAL OF NEGRO HISTORY that are deemed worthy of being called to the attention of scholars all over the world.

The documents published have been of the greatest value. The first fourteen volumes contained 4,712 pages of articles and some 2,000 pages of documents. This recognition of the value of documents stamps the JOURNAL as a truly scientific review. The JOURNAL, in this respect, shows probably a higher proportion of documents than does the *American Historical Review.* It has attempted to do something of the sort of thing that is done, for example, by the *Archivo Historico Diplomatico Mexicano* or the *Colección de Historiadores y Documentos Relativos a la Independencia de Chile,* and the *Revista do Instituto Historico e Geographico Brazileiro.*

It is no mere coincidence few documents have been published since 1930. The gathering of documents is particularly expensive. Frequently extensive travel is necessary to locate them. Often they can be obtained only by outright purchase at a considerable sum. Funds for this all-important but expensive material have not been available since 1930 as they were before the stock market crash of October, 1929, brought to an abrupt end the so-called "Lotus Decade." Just as soon as additional funds are available, the publication of documents may be resumed.

The quotation from Dr. Jameson alluded to the necessity for competent critics of new books in specialized fields. Where, except in the pages of The Journal of Negro History, could a fairly adequate number of books dealing with this subject have been given critical reviews? Where, other than in the pages of the Journal, could Negro scholars have obtained the training necessary to the development of this skill? Only a few of our institutions give even an elementary course in the technique of book reviewing. Naturally, some of these reviews have left something to be desired. But that is true also of even the best of quarterlies published by other groups that have been able to pay their reviewers. This is not to suggest that the general level of reviews in The Journal of Negro History is as high as that in the best of the other quarterlies. This is not to be expected. But when the Journal has had an existence as long as has *The American Historical Review,* it is confidently expected that the Journal will not suffer by comparison with the best in the world.

Two constructive criticisms may be offered here. An insufficient distinction has sometimes been made between books that deserve long reviews and those that merit only a brief mention. It is suggested that the editor send to reviewers a form indicating the length of the review desired. This will permit the inclusion in each issue of a larger number of reviews. Second, some important publications have not been reviewed as promptly as they might. The failure to do so is not necessarily the fault of the editor. It results rather from the small number of scholars who are competent to review these books. This will probably be eradicated also as the JOURNAL continues to serve as a training ground for Negroes in the reviewing of books.

Two forms of "notes" have been particularly valuable. In the first place are those that give a resumé of the career of worthwhile Negroes. If ever a Dictionary of Negro Biography is compiled THE JOURNAL OF NEGRO HISTORY will be one of the most valuable sources available. The second group of "notes" is concerned with the listing of important articles that have appeared in scholarly journals not only in America but in foreign countries. It is particularly gratifying that the recent issues have given increasing space to these "notes." Much time will be saved for scholars if they can regularly rely upon these notes for a list of these important publications.

Not the least service that THE JOURNAL OF NEGRO HISTORY has rendered has been the constant reminder that the word Negro should always be capitalized. If Indian, Arabian, Jew, Irish, and other words indicating racial identities are capitalized, there is no reason why Negro should not be. If there has been a constantly growing tendency on the part of the publishers and editors to recognize this fact, the style of the JOURNAL has surely not been without effect.

The need for THE JOURNAL OF NEGRO HISTORY is probably greater today than when it was founded. During these twenty years the Neo-Confederates have redoubled their efforts to prove that slavery was an idyllic existence, that slave children were never sold away from their parents, that slavery had nothing to do with the Civil War, that the South would have freed its slaves if there had been no war, that reconstruction was an orgy of corruption, unrelieved by any contributions to the social and economic development of the South. The wide acclaim given in many historical quarterlies to such pleadings as Ulrich B. Phillips' *Life and Labor in the Old South,* Frank Owsley's *King Cotton Diplomacy,* George Fort Milton's *Stephen A. Douglas and The Needless War* and Claude Bowers' *The Tragic Era* indicates clearly both the general acceptance of these views and the necessity for offering proof of the opposite interpretations. If contributors to The Journal of Negro History will present their evidence with an even-tempered objectivity, they will not only reveal hidden facts of history but will gradually stem the tide of belittlement of the Negro indulged in by a militant, numerous group of special pleaders parading in the guise of historians.

Rayford W. Logan

Atlanta University.

THE ASSOCIATION FOR THE STUDY OF NEGRO LIFE AND HISTORY: ITS CONTRIBUTION TO OUR MODERN LIFE[1]

Mr. Chairman, ladies and gentlemen: I count myself greatly privileged to greet you personally on this your Twentieth Anniversary. I stand tonight in the presence of truth seekers, truth seekers not only, but interpreters of truth and disseminators of truth. This, I believe, is the supreme contribution of this Association to our day and generation—the discovery, the interpretation and the dissemination of truth in the field of Negro life—truth, scientifically arrived at, critically interpreted and universally disseminated. In the presence of this audience, I am filled with respect and intellectual humility.

In the time that is mine this evening, I wish to amplify and to make more specific this which I think is the contribution of the Association to our modern life. In the first place, I wish to observe, "that the search for truth is not for timid souls. When we set out upon the search for truth we should not assume that we already know for certain what truth is or what the best way of life is; otherwise, why bother about a further search for truth? The search for truth may very well change our notion of what is good or best. The search for truth is a search for what is really true, not for what may be comfortable to believe, and so we dare not limit our search for truth by insisting that what we find in the search shall be something we should have thought good before we found it. The great thing is to learn to be unafraid of knowledge."

The problem of our generation is the problem of finding ways and means of harnessing science in the service of humanity. I am made happy in the thought that the promoters and the investigators of this organization bring to

[1] An address delivered on the occasion of the celebration of the Twentieth Anniversary of the Association for the Study of Negro Life and History in Chicago, Illinois, September 9, 1935.

their task the scientific technique, that they are actuated by the scientific spirit, for truly do we live in the scientific age. The workers, the investigators, are pioneers, trail-blazers, adventurers in handling facts in this particular field. Theirs has been the task and the responsibility, to quote Father Fox, "of finding the facts, focussing the facts, of filtering the facts." They have separated the facts from the admixtures of prejudice, passion and selfish interest. They cannot afford to pre-judge, for they cannot fly in the face of the facts without courting ultimate disaster. Now, facts are not important for their own sake. They are important only as a basis for human action. The investigators, then, must focus upon the issues we face.

One outcome of scientific research and investigation in the field of Negro life and history is knowledge. A vast portion of social knowledge and information is shrouded in tradition, is not recorded in books and magazines; nevertheless it exists, and extends far back into the hoary past. As a result of the work of this Association we are securing knowledge and information that is characterized by its clarity—information that is objective and precise, information that is relevant in the field of Negro life and history. The life struggles of Negro men and women have been chronicled by the Association, and their achievements emphasized. The sweeping glance of these lives have helped us to see more clearly what is important and what is unimportant—what is essential and what is non-essential in our own lives. The struggles and victories of these men and women under adverse circumstances have stirred us to activity in a way that the exploits of fictitious characters could never have done.

The story is told that in the hey-day of the Roman Empire the highways of the Romans were literally studded with the statues of their illustrious men—their men of achievement. These statues were erected that the Roman youth, gazing upon their faces, might be stimulated to greater achievement and accomplishment. I like to think of the service of the Association for the Study of Negro Life and History in a similar vein. Who knows but that as Negro boys and girls have, through their study of accomplishments and achievements by Negro men and women, been pushed forward toward their destinies? This, then, it appears to me is one field in which the Association for the Study of Negro Life and History has made a distinct and constructive contribution to our modern Twentieth Century life—in the field of research and investigation, in the advancement of knowledge, in the accumulation of racial information and facts, in the discovery of truth as it relates primarily to the Negro and to Negro life.

But knowledge or information in and of itself is not power, is not progress. Progress in the knowledge of Negro life and history is in the hands of the interpreter as well as in the hands of the investigator or discoverer. Already we have an ample supply of investigators, but it appears to me that there is a shortage of readable and responsible interpreters, men and women who can effectively play the role of mediator between the trained investigator and the masses.

"We do not live by bread alone," by facts; our spirits must be fed by sustaining truths. Some truths are merely true; they inform our minds. Other truths are nourishing; they feed our spirits. The great adventure of life lies in finding the truths we can live by, the gleams that we can safely follow, the goals that are worth working toward. What are the meanings of the knowledge discovered? What are the implications of the facts brought to light? Whither do they lead? What is their significance? Of what value are they? What is their place in our very complex social and economic order? What use can be made of them in assisting initially, ill-adapted individuals to a harmonious and beneficial adjustment? These are questions that should challenge the action and thought of our leaders.

This is the work of the philosopher, the interpreter, the crusading critic. It is in this field of interpretation, I think, that the major work of this Association lies for the next few years. The task of interpreting Negro thought, Negro achievement, Negro accomplishment, Negro culture patterns to the great masses of Negroes themselves, first, and ultimately, to their white brethren.

We ourselves as laymen have fixed and definite responsibilities. The findings of our trained investigators must be faced. It is sometimes hard for us to look a fact in the face without blinking, but sooner or later we shall all learn that the energy spent in trying to get around, under or over the facts is wasted energy. Facts have a ruthless way of winning the day sooner or later.

Again, facts to be really useful for us must be followed. We must say of them as Job said of God: Though they slay us, yet we shall trust them. If the facts threaten to cherish our beliefs or plans it will pay us to re-examine them. This way lies realism, and realism is ultimate progress and good. This, then, is another contribution that the Association for the Study of Negro Life and History has made and can make; namely, that of sitting in judgment on the findings of the investigators in the field of Negro life, of evaluating these findings, of setting up useful goals, of indicating traits and attitudes, of establishing points of view; in short, of interpreting to the Negro himself primarily, and to the world, the significance and the meaning of Negro achievements and accomplishments.

The temptation of the scholar is to keep the new truth he finds stacked in the warehouse. It shocks his sense of scholarly dignity to see his discoveries hawked in the market place by the popularizer. But the social usefulness of scholarship and its findings depends upon its translation into the common tongue. A dozen fields of thought are today confused with knowledge that the physical and social sciences have unearthed, and the whole tenor and temper of American life can be lifted by putting this knowledge into general circulation. Similarly is this true in its application to the Association for the Study of Negro Life and History. We must have the popularizer to stand between the masses whose knowledge of things is indefinite and the research worker whose knowledge is authoritative. Persons who can do for Negro life and history what Will Durant has done for philosophy and Edwin Slosson for science.

I have attempted in this brief paper to say that the contribution of the Association for the Study of Negro Life and History to our modern day has been first that of investigation, investigation in a virgin field, investigation that has brought to light a wealth of material pertaining to Negro life and culture, past and present; second, that it has contributed in the way of interpreting the Negro to himself and to the white race, and that in this field for some years to come is its immediate task. In the third place, this Association has functioned as a channel of communication. It is making possible the dissemination of information and knowledge concerning Negro life and history in increasing proportions. In brief, the Association for the Study of Negro Life and History has pioneered in advancing knowledge in field of Negro history accumulating a fund of factual material, useful as a basis for thinking and action, useful as an integrating and synthesizing agency in promoting racial solidarity and cohesiveness, useful in helping to mould viewpoints, wholesome personal and social philosophies—national goodwill.

Mary McLeod Bethune

THE RECONSTRUCTION OF HISTORY

The conception of history, which we acknowledge to-day, includes the study of the development of men and things throughout the ages. This concept has not been an accepted one by the writers of history who have lived during these ages. It has been necessary for history to be changed and reconstructed before it could reach this stage of definition. Herodotus stated in his monumental work that it was "the publication of Herodotus of Halicarnassus, in order that the actions of men may not be effaced by time, nor the great and wondrous deeds displayed by Greeks and Barbarians deprived of renown; and among the rest, for which cause they waged war upon each other." In these words, this early historian asserts that it was his object to recount the great and wondrous happenings of his time. Distinctions were to be made by the writer between the Greeks and the Barbarians. Among other things, war was to be one of the principal subjects. Only incidentally did the author include geographical descriptions, religious rites, national and tribal manners and customs, personal anecdotes, conversations, speeches and dialogues. The major space was devoted to dynasties, kings, conquests, battles and individual heroic deeds. Herodotus is the professional storyteller, mixing fact and fable.

Thucydides, Xenophon, and the Roman historians Livy, Tacitus and Suetonius practised a higher art but with many similar imperfections. The deeds of their peoples and governments were given increasing prominence, and others were neglected.

Throughout the Middle Ages, the Church was the dominant institution and ideal. The historians of this period either accepted the Christian philosophy of history as did those primarily interested in the Church or they functioned merely as chroniclers and annalists. From Augustine to the Renaissance, religious ideas continued to dominate most writings of history. The Renaissance witnessed the development of the critical attitude and the correlation of history with literature. Lorenzo Valla attacked and proved the Donation of Constantine a forgery and cast doubt upon the Apostolic origin of the Apostles Creed. He was the first critical historian of his day. Froissart stimulated effort in this direction by writing of his travels and by recounting the story of many thrilling adventures. In the sixteenth and seventeenth centuries, history began to take on the aspect of specialized research. But scientific history needed working tools; and without maps, dictionaries, manuals and accessible manuscripts, the historical scholars of this period could not be removed far from the medieval chronicler.

In the latter part of the eighteenth and nineteenth centuries, history experienced vast changes. Research and the collection of materials became the chief work of this period. The rise of nationalism gave inspiration to the working up of materials dealing with the past. National historical collections and national historical associations were formed. The immense increase in sources made possible the rise of historical criticism. Ranke, Gibbon, Grote and Guizot made the application of the newer principles a feature of their works which remain as monuments along the pathway of historiography. The reform which they instituted consisted in the main in the elimination of literary ornaments and the insistence that historical statements carry definite proof of their validity.

In the modern presentation of history there are several significant tendencies which have led to a reconstruction of historical writing. Historical scholarship has not confined its activities to the narrow limits of ancient days. Within the past half-century two trends may be noted. These factors are seeking to give history almost a new direction. They are: (1) The extension of the field of history, and (2) the search for truth.

The Expansion of the Field

Professor E. A. Freeman, English historian of the nineteenth century, delineated historiography by the assertion that "history is past politics and politics present history." As by Herodotus and others history was narrowed by Freeman. Instead of being concerned with wars and things heroic, Freeman believed that history should be restricted to politics and government. This narrowing of the field was not destined to last very long, however, for, toward the close of the century, there arose a dissatisfaction with the treatment and subject-matter of history; and this has increased to such an extent that one writer may call Freeman "a superseded fossil." From the time of Voltaire, in fact, there has been a current of opposition to the view that history should concern itself with only national governments and their affairs. Voltaire stated in his *Essay on General History,* "One demands of modern historians—more attention to usuages, to laws, to manners, to commerce, to finance, to agriculture, to population." The German historians saw this need and created the "kulturgeschichte" to indicate a fuller content of history.

Two scholars, one in England and another in America, pointed out the narrowness of former points of view. Professor J. R. Green in stating his purpose in his interesting study *A Short History of the English People* said, "The aim of the following work is defined by its title: it is a history, not of English kings or English conquests but of the English People. At the risk of sacrificing much that was interesting and attractive in itself, and which the constant usage of our historians has made familiar to English readers, I have preferred to pass lightly and briefly over the details of foreign wars and diplomacies, the personal adventures of kings and nobles, the pomp of courts or the intrigues of favorites, and to dwell at length on the incidents of that constitutional, intellectual and social advance in which we read the history of the nation itself. It is with this purpose that I have devoted more space to Chaucer than to Cressy, to Caxton than to the petty strife of Yorkist and Lancastrian, to the Poor Law of Elizabeth than to the victory at Cadiz, to the Methodist Revival than to the escape of the Young Pretender.''

Professor John Bach McMaster in his study, *A History of the People of the United States,* has accomplished a similar task. The author stated that the subject of his narrative was ''the history of the people of the United States of America from the close of the War for Independence down to the opening of the war between the states. In the course of this narrative much, indeed, must be written of wars, conspiracies, and rebellions, of presidents, of congresses, of embassies, of treaties, of the ambition of political leaders in the senate house, and of the rise of great political parties in the nation. Yet the history of the people shall be the chief theme. At every stage of the splendid progress which separates the America of Washington and Adams from the America in which we live, it shall be my purpose to describe the dress, the occupations, the amusements, the literary canons of the times; to note the changes of manners and morals; to trace the growth of that humane spirit which abolished punishment for debt, which reformed the discipline of prisons and of jails, and which has, in our own time, destroyed slavery and lessened the miseries of dumb brutes.''

Slowly the field of history was expanded so that it would involve all happenings. Teachers of history would no longer hear lessons based merely upon the lives, the dates and chief events of kings, queens and rulers. They were not to regard battles, wars, court intrigues and usurpations as the most important historical events. A larger place began to be ascribed to the development of the people and to the changes which have affected them more directly. This variation in treatment could not be noted so plainly by the public because the thoughts of the New School of writers were expressed in the historical societies, in the publications with circulations limited to the scholarly and in privately printed works.

Lord Bryce, in his presidential address before the International Congress of Historical Studies in 1913, called attention to the "immense expansion which has taken place in historical studies." Continuing, he said, "We have now come to regard history as a record of every form of human effort and achievement concerned not any more definitely with political events and institutions than with all the other factors that have moulded man and all the other expressions his creative activity has found." As an illustration of this enlargement of view, he mentioned specifically the interest taken by historians in the study of primitive man, interest in the study of habits and customs of men, interest in the early religious ideas of men, interest in the rudimentary political institutions and in the general social life of backward races and tribes. The trends were in motion to break down the distinctions between the "Greeks and the Barbarians." Economic determinism began to be more generally used as an explanation for historical events than political forces or great men.

The term which has been used to include this expansion has received the designation, "the New History." Ultimately, its further purpose was not only to explain more of the past but also to present a basis, as one exponent phrases it, "for an adequate and intelligent control, direction and reorganization of the social order." This point of view is really not a new one. It was known in Europe long before it received recognition in the United States. It was referred to at that time in its embryonic stage as the philosophy of history. The idea was given general acclaim through the publication in 1912 by James Harvey Robinson of a volume entitled *The New History*. His thought in this respect was carried further with the publication of another volume, *The Mind in the Making*.

The expression of these views and their elaboration by others have led to the expansion of the field so that it includes all aspects of man's life. "The New History" would embrace the ways in which all of the people have lived through all of the ages, man's custom and manner of living, his working and striving for better things, his philosophy, his literature, his industry, his religion. "The New History" was not to be narrow, tribal or nationalistic. World history was to be as important as localized national history. Books and courses in international relations were introduced into the college and the university. Along with this conception, there developed a new internationalism, which made few distinctions between "the Greeks and the Barbarians." The historian was expected to be fair to all nations and to give each an equitable place in the history of the world. The field of history was in these ways rapidly expanded.

THE SEARCH FOR TRUTH

The second tendency in historical development has been the search for truth. Historians in all times have claimed that this has been their objective, but with all of their efforts the old question "What is Truth?" goes unanswered. The experience of the human race has been that what is accepted as truth in one generation is frequently branded as falsehood in a subsequent generation. It is a commonplace that new truth is stubbornly resisted. This resistance is revealed most strikingly in the progress of science. It is also true concerning our historical beliefs and cherished memories. Historians have insisted that their purposes have been to disclose the truth and to reconstruct the past as it has actually happened. This insistence has been manifested in documentary support and footnoted studies. But under the best circumstances, there has been a measure of uncertainty concerning the truth of history, because historians have had to deal with the actions of men and their report of these actions as well as the actions of those whose relations to the events may not be altogether without bias.

The search for truth has expressed itself recently in two fields, in a new treatment of nationalism and a new treatment of biography. Nationalism has been one of the factors which assisted the development of the writing and teaching of history. The love of country has demanded a group of cherished memories and also a desire to perpetuate the ideals of the past. Even in the days of the ancient world, historians took pride in the splendor of Greece and the glories of Rome. Temporarily, during the Middle Ages nationality was lost, by being subordinated to feudalism and to the church, but with the rise of strong monarchies under Henry VII in England, Louis XI in France, Ferdinand and Isabella in Spain, the foundations for the revival of the national spirit were laid. With the rise of the struggle for colonial empires, there came the clash of national ambitions in a long series of wars which culminated in the World War. As a reaction from the war, there has come sober thinking concerning the nationalistic conception of history. Historians have constructed their country's history so as to encourage patriotism, and out of this there has developed the national idea of conscious superiority. Racial superiority is a child of the same parent, and also thrives upon a narrowed conception of history.

Since the World War, a reaction has set in especially since the disdain and neglect of other nations have been noticeable in numerous text books. In this respect history has had to be reconstructed, and it is doubtful whether the history of Greece, Rome or other countries would be recognized as descriptions of these states if they could be seen by the writers of the sixteenth and seventeenth centuries. Many writers of text books in American History have come to the conclusion that truth is of far more value than the encouragement of patriotism. According to the new view, history is to teach the truth about the national life and its development. Classes in civics, citizenship, the state and the government may well consider local welfare and encourage whatever national mythology which may be necessary for the masses. But classes in history are to study the past as it is. In the face of modern scholarship, the American Revolution cannot continue to be regarded as the "uprising of a united people against a dark and bloody despot." It was an internal revolution, which divided a people against itself. The names now glorified as "patriots" were the "radicals" of revolutionary days. They were regarded as unsafe leaders by the loyalists who made up the most numerous, the most prosperous and the most conservative class. Truth as to the conduct of all wars from the Revolution to the present may not lead to the development of selfish patriotism, but it will lead Americans to a larger appreciation for the nations against whom we fought and will diminish much our national conceit. But how stubborn is the opposition in this matter! The opponents of truth would organize and memorialize school boards and teaching bodies in order to perpetuate the recital of the teaching of patriotic myths, which must finally make the teaching of history in America about as effective as it was in Prussian and Austrian schools prior to the war, and symbolic of Nazi and Fascist history today.

The recent treatment of biography shows also a break with the writings of the past. During the past twenty years new evaluations are being made of great men and women in history. Victoria of England, Catherine of Russia, Catherine de Medici, Napoleon, the rulers and statesmen of the nineteenth century are better known as a result of recent biographical efforts. New approaches to George Washington, Thomas Jefferson, Alexander Hamilton and Abraham Lincoln have demonstrated that they were not demi-gods but men, even as you and I. The new type of writing reveals what the old type suppressed. When Jared

Sparks edited the writings of George Washington, it is said that he omitted phrases and corrected the language of the originals, because it did not seem fitting that the Father of the Country should be made so much of a human as his fellows. Myth-makers of the Parson Weems type, who pose as scholarly writers, are responsible for the saints of plaster who have arisen in the places of the human beings whom we might have known. It is also evident that most grown-ups have obtained their knowledge of history from the older text books produced before the newer school of historians began their work. The history which is reconstructed in the light of the new investigations is manifestly different from the old type, and it is extremely difficult for these older persons to readjust their points of view to the new thought. Literary historians and dramatists have been in some measure responsible for the distorted pictures of the past. They have nurtured and conserved historical myths, and the public has been only too willing to have its traditional views confirmed.

The opposition to the New History has been determined. Individual journals and organizations have joined in the cry that the new treatment of American History is resulting in a foreign and European point of view. Many of us are familiar with the storm which has centered around the so-called pro-British text books. The Sons of the American Revolution, the Daughters of the American Revolution, the Veterans of Foreign Wars and numerous other organizations have raised objections to the New History and have bombarded school boards and textbook committees with their protests. In spite of this opposition, the reconstruction of history continues, and truth is rapidly winning its way.

While history has expanded to include the impartial treatment of nations and individuals, minority groups in the United States have asserted that they have not been treated fairly by American historians. They have seen the field of history expand so as to include nationalities, but they have also seen smaller nationalities and minorities within national boundaries given inadequate treatment. This neglect has been due both to a conscious and an unconscious racial bias. In order to correct this error of omission and to establish the truth, historical societies on the racial basis have arisen. With the support of these societies, scholars have reconstructed the past so that the presentations have been more complete. Manifestly, it is possible to overstate the case for a particular group and to overemphasize the unimportant, but when these result in a renewed stimulation for the suppressed and neglected group, it is far better than the neglect common to the past. Into the field there have come the Irish Historical Society, known as the American-Irish Historical Society, the German-American Historical Society, the American-Jewish Historical Society, the Huguenot Society of America, the Scotch-Irish Society of America, the Holland Society of New York, and the Association for the Study of Negro Life and History. This last mentioned organization was founded through the vision of Dr. Carter G. Woodson in Chicago in 1915 and was incorporated under the laws of the District of Columbia the same year. We are under deep obligation to this distinguished man who has unselfishly maintained this Association through the years, and as we come in this meeting to this Twentieth Anniversary he should receive a deserved acclaim. I am happy to express my own personal obligation to him for the stimulation which comes from the contact of mind with mind and for the encouragement obtained through his pioneering leadership.

In a citizenship which is composed of various racial groups, it is inevitable that there would be writers who consciously and unconsciously neglect and ignore racial contributions to American life. Michael J. O'Brien, chief historiographer for the American-Irish Historical Society, in a volume entitled, *A Hidden Phase of American History*, sets forth the contributions of the Irish to Amer-

ican History. *The Irish World* in reviewing this book
states, "All the Anglo-Saxon writers from Bancroft on
suppressed, ridiculed where they could not suppress, mu-
tilated where they could neither suppress nor ridicule,
everything Irish in American History." No Irish-Ameri-
can could read this book without a sense of pride. As for
this comment on this book, with the substitution of the
word "Negro" for the word "Irish," this sentence would
be equally true, if not more so in relation to the Negro.

Albert B. Faust has written a volume under the title,
The German Element in the United States. He states that
many historians have made "a blanket indictment"
against the Germans in the United States. He writes,
"That race comprises upward of twenty-five per cent of
the American people and has been a stalwart factor in
American life since the middle of the seventeenth century." It was the expressed purpose of the author to
present this book to the Germans of the United States so
as to insure to them "a proper pride of ancestry." The
Jews have experienced a similar neglect. Numerous books
have endeavored to supply the historical data to give the
Jews their place in American life. All of these societies
have been engaged in the reconstruction of history. Our
Association for the Study of Negro Life and History also
has expanded the field of history so as to include the Negro. This organization has pursued the truth concerning
this race and has lifted it into view so that all who read
may learn.

History is not the story of men and women of one race
or color and the neglect and omission of the men and
women of another race or color. It is neither the glorification of white people nor black people, but it is the story
of the people irrespective of race or color. It should deal
with people in all times and places and should present the
contribution of all the people to civilization. When a part
of the people has been neglected or given subordinate

places, history in order to be truthful must be reconstructed.

In this connection, there are several axioms which I
want to lay down for our guidance and thinking: *History
should be reconstructed so that Africa—the home of the
darker races—shall have its proper place.* Africa was
once known as a continent without a history or a civilization. Its study was left to anthropology and ethnology.
Traditions concerning this land developed and were kept
alive by travelers and missionaries. The eleventh edition
of the *Encyclopedia Brittanica* could then say almost
without contradiction that, "Africa with the exception of
the lower Nile Valley and what is known as Roman Africa,
so far as its native inhabitants are concerned, is a continent practically without a history and possessing no
records from which such a history might be constructed."
Subsequent editions of this work have had to change this
view, due largely to the work of our Association for the
Study of Negro Life and History and other circles of
scholars thus interested. We know now that there were
kingdoms in Africa as brilliant as those of the Goths, the
Vandals, the Huns, the Angles, the Saxons, the Jutes and
other European tribes of the North prior to their taking
over the civilizations of Greece and Rome. Africa had no
opportunity of profiting by such contacts, but without
them, there was an indigenous civilization which compared
favorably with any civilization in Europe. There were organized governments, laws, roads, buildings, artistic manifestations which challenge the admiration of students of
our time.

Civilizations flourished in west and central Africa,
from which a majority of the American slaves came.
Benin, Yoruba, Nupe, Melle, Songhay, Mossi and other
kingdoms had civilizations worthy of commendation.
Europe is not alone in being able to point to a glorious
past. Europe had its Charlemagne, its Charles the Great.
Africa had its Askia Mohammed, its Askia the Great.

When the European tribal life was primitive in large areas, Africa had organized kingdoms, spread over the west and central parts of that continent. These civilizations declined through the Mohammedan conquests and the rise of the slave trade. Some few smaller kingdoms were stimulated to greater temporary activity by the Mohammedan influences, but the slave trade proved to be a blight upon civilizing developments. Whole villages were depopulated, and kings turned to the easier ways of living provided by the trade in men rather than to the slower processes of permanent state building. With the facts which are coming to light concerning African History, the traditions of its past must be changed. Africa, then, must take its place in history as have recently done Japan, China, and India. It will be found that America has not only a European background but also an African background, which should receive attention because a large part of its population has a direct connection with the African continent.

2. *History should be reconstructed so that Negroes shall be known on a higher level than that of jokes and minstrels.* The appearance of a Negro face in many public places is an occasion for a smile, however serious the event may be. Many persons are accustomed to think of the Negro as stereotype, a smiling Uncle Tom, and have never known that there is also another type of Negro. This type is not necessarily the so-called New Negro, a phrase which gives the impression that there is a sharp break with past types.

From the earliest periods Negroes have been connected with the best trends in American life. This is evident not only after 1865, but long before that time, even prior to the establishment of the national government. For instance, a Hessian officer wrote in October, 1774, "No regiment is seen in which there are not Negroes in abundance and among them are able-bodied strong fellows. Here, too, there are many families of free Negroes who live in good homes, have property and live just like the rest of the inhabitants." The eighteenth century as well as the period after the Civil War witnessed Negroes relating themselves to American life. They had freed themselves and had become American citizens and voters. At the time of the first census in 1790, there were 59,000 free Negroes in the first American states. Some, among whom were Phillis Wheatley and Jupiter Hammon, were contributing to American literature. While they made no innovations in this field, they nevertheless manifested talent which was far above the average. Absalom Jones and Richard Allen led in the organization of the Free African Society and of churches in Pennsylvania. They also organized schools. Andrew Bryan and George Leile were engaged in the same work in Georgia. Prince Hall developed the same program in Boston, and out of his Free African Society there came the first Masonic lodge for Negroes. Benjamin Bannaker drew up a plan for World Peace during the first administration of George Washington, and shortly after our first President made the appointment of a Secretary of War there came Bannaker's suggestion for the appointment of a Secretary of Peace, a proposal which antedates by a century the plans for peace familiar to our generation. As the years advanced, these Negroes grew in number. They were not jokes and minstrels supplying occasions for laughter from other Americans. They were not members of a child race, who had to be nurtured and led slowly along the way from barbarism to civilization.

3. *History should be reconstructed so that Negroes shall appear not only as the recipients of liberty but as the winners of it, not only for themselves but also for others.* It is common for Americans to think of Negroes as a docile, cowardly race. The tradition is that freedom was given to them, almost against their will. Many instances are played up, to the effect that Negro slaves preferred to remain in slavery and declined to go free when the opportunity was offered. These traditions and isolated instances are not supported by facts. Negroes after toiling

during the day for their masters so highly prized freedom as to work at night or holidays to earn money to purchase themselves and their families. During the colonial era they revolted and ran away, taking refuge among the Indians. Negroes fostered insurrections in the United States throughout the period of slavery. Many thousands of them made the dash for liberty as fugitives to free soil.

Equally zealous, too, were the Negroes in fighting for this country. More than three thousand black men served in the American Revolution. Their individual deeds stand out on the pages of history, and their brilliant record cannot be effaced. The first martyr of the American Revolution, who fell in the Boston Massacre, was Crispus Attucks, a Negro. He with three others shed the first blood for freedom. It can be said almost with a sense of reality that Thomas Jefferson, thinking on this scene, dipped his pen in the blood of this first martyr to liberty and wrote the immortal Declaration of Independence. Peter Salem and Salem Poor added new luster to these pages of history. In the War of 1812, brave black men of this type stood with Perry on water and with Jackson on land.

Negroes also fought for their own freedom. Under the leadership of Denmark Vesey and Nat Turner, they struck for freedom. They heard David Walker's Appeal and joined the forces fighting the institution of slavery. Negroes entered the ranks of the abolitionists from the first years of their efforts and marched shoulder to shoulder with these servants of the truth. Garrison's largest number of subscribers to his *Liberator* came from free Negroes. When he desired to go to England to join hands with the emancipationists there, the Negroes assisted in financing this voyage. When in England Garrison did not have the funds with which to come back to the United States, he sought the Rev. Nathaniel Paul, a Negro, from whom he borrowed money with which to return home. Three Negroes were on the Executive Committee of the

American Anti-Slavery Society. They were speakers, agents and workers for the cause of freedom. The names of William C. Nell, Samuel R. Ward, James W. C. Pennington, William Wells Brown, Charles L. Reason, Henry Highland Garnett and Frederick Douglass should take their places with those of Phillips, Garrison, and Weld in the movement for freedom. Any other type of history is a misrepresentation.

4. *History should be reconstructed so that Negroes shall be regarded as Americans and not simply as slaves or as an alien part of the population.* Set off from the rest of the American population by a segregated life, Negroes are prone to regard themselves as a thing apart as well as to accept such a classification in history. Birth within the allegiance has been the test of citizenship and nationality in past history. The Fourteenth Amendment to our Constitution wrote into law the theory of previous years. From the earliest periods Negroes have been associated with American life along with other citizens. On the contrary, it has been asserted that this is a "White Man's Country." This land, however, is the country of all who were born here and subject to its jurisdiction. Bancroft, Wiener, Winsor and other historians attest to striking evidences of African connections with early America. Negroes were found here nearly a century prior to the coming of the English to Jamestown. They were with De Ayllon when he established a settlement in Virginia in 1526. They built ships there, revolted and many sailed away to the West Indies. They were with Balboa, De Soto, Cortez, Melendez, Coronado and others as companions, guides and explorers. One of their number, Estevanico, was an explorer in his own right. Therefore, if length of residence has anything to do with the Negro's claim to America, the Negro is an American among Americans.

Negroes passed during succeeding years from slaves to free men, from chattels to citizens, from poverty to comfort and lived just as other Americans have done. Our black heroes, then, deserve a place with other Americans in history. These facts are neglected in the teaching and writing of history, and accordingly there is room for reconstruction.

Robert Browning writes that

"God has conceded two sights to a man,
One, Time's completed plan,
The other, Man's first step towards the plan's completeness."

In a sense, we are working along these lines. In the completed plan, one may envision the America, in which the Irish-Americans, the Jewish-Americans, the German-Americans and all other Americans shall join hands in the making of the New America. It has been seen by one who wrote,

"O beautiful for spacious skies, for amber waves of grain,
For purple mountain majesties above the fruited plain,
America! America! God shed His grace on thee
And crown thy good with brotherhood
From sea to shining sea."

That is the completed plan. The first step is to cause these Americans to be proud of themselves, so that as the Irish look to Ireland with pride in spite of its tribal life and native superstitions and as the other minorities look to their native lands, so may Negroes lift their eyes and shoulders and feel that they too are Americans. Ours is then the first step, to write, to publish, to read and to believe in ourselves and our capacities. To this first task, may we devote ourselves confident of success, for pride in self has been the touchstone of destiny for nations and races in all the past. History's reconstruction will make the way clearer for the advancement of the Negro in American life; and to be certain, this task is largely that of the Negro himself.

CHARLES H. WESLEY.

NEGRO MUSICIANS AND THEIR MUSIC[1]

The unusual contribution of our American forefathers in demonstrating the power and beauty of music is a marvel of the age. Certainly this God-given talent enabled the burden bearers of America for two hundred and fifty years to march from darkness to light with an unprecedented faith. Notwithstanding the fact that the masses of slaves could neither read nor write, they left an indelible stamp upon the cultural and religious life of the South. Through documents we are enabled to know something of their aspirations and struggles, but there is no stronger medium to tell us of their affliction, doubt, despair, sorrow, hope, joy and faith than is evidenced through the transplanted African rhythm, southern melody and harmony of these spirituals and labor songs.

Inquiry into the origin of American Negro music discloses the fact that it was often created spontaneously on river barges, in fields, in box-cars, at camp meetings, in prisons, on construction crews, on the levees, anywhere and at any time that their emotional outburst saw fit to reveal itself. Was there a better way to express their despair than is evidenced in the words of "Sometimes I Feel Like a Motherless Child a Long Way from Home?" Or their dislike of social and economic conditions told in the words of "Many Thousands Go?" Prohibited by law and custom from learning any other means of expression, the Negro found in music the only medium with which he could unfold his soul to the world.

> No more peck of corn for me,
> No more drivers lash for me,
> No more pint of salt for me,
> No more hundred lash for me,
> No more mistress call for me.

[1] An address delivered in connection with the musical opening the celebration of the Twentieth Anniversary of the Association for the Study of Negro Life and History in Chicago, Illinois.

Can one find a better expression of sorrow than is shown in the Negro's "Nobody Knows the Trouble I See, Nobody Knows but Jesus?" Can a stronger doubt of Christianity of those about him be better set forth than in: "Everybody Talkin' 'bout Heav'n Aint Goin' There?" Love for home is seen in "Carry Me Back to Old Virginny; There's Where the Cotton and the Corn and Taters Grow." Gratitude is expressed in "I Thank God I'm Free At Last." And supplication in "Lord, I Want to be a Christian in My Heart." Only a Christian's faith enabled them to sing "Walk Together, Children; Don't You Get Weary; There's a Great Camp Meeting in the Promised Land." And finally the triumphant end of a terrible struggle is pictured in "Swing Low, Sweet Chariot, Coming for to Carry Me Home."

Does not this language of the emotions, bequeathed to us by our foreparents, create within us a burning desire to know something of our historical background, and hurl to us, through the years, a challenge to build on that background and take our rightful places by the side of other benefactors of mankind? Certainly this is not impossible, as proved when we review the lives of achievement led by those of Negro blood in earlier years in European environment. We might name the Chevalier de St. Georges, who was one of the first French musicians to write string quartette music; Samuel Coleridge-Taylor of London, whose most distinctive work is probably that reflecting his interest in Negro folk song; George Augustus Bridgetower of Poland, who became the friend and associate of Beethoven.

Among American composers we find Edmund Dede of New Orleans; the musical Lambert family of seven members of Louisiana; Harry T. Burleigh, one of the foremost composers of the world, who assisted D'vorak, the great Hungarian musician, in his "New World Symphony" based on the Negro folk song "Going Home;" James

Weldon Johnson and J. Rosamond Johnson, brothers, who, among other compositions, have given us the anthem, "Lift Every Voice and Sing;" R. Nathaniel Dett, a composer, who enjoys a place among world artists; William Still, a new creator, who is doing startling things in the same field; Clarence Williams, native of Louisiana, who has produced and published over one thousand compositions.

Among singers we find Elizabeth Taylor Greenfield, a Mississippian whose voice embraced twenty-seven notes reaching from a sonorous bass to a few notes above even Jenny Lind's highest; Anna and Emma Hyers, noted musical sisters of California; Madam Selika, world-famous singer; Roland Hayes, the great tenor of our time; Marian Anderson, the famous contralto; and Eva Taylor, the first Negro soloist over a national and international hook-up.

As pianists we find among the first Thomas Bethune or "Blind Tom," our race prodigy. Then there is Helen Hagan, who a few years ago was awarded the Sandford Scholarship from Yale, and since her return from France has delighted American audiences. Others of equal fame are Raymond Augustus Lawson, Hazel Harrison and Ethel Richardson.

Since Africans were the first to use stringed instruments, it is not surprising to find among outstanding Americans such violinists as Clarence Cameron White, Joseph Douglass, Louia Vaughn Jones, and Kemper Harreld. The four Mills Brothers, with a guitar, are making their contribution along with others.

These are a few who have achieved and are achieving, but what are we doing for the masses? We grant that music enabled our forefathers to withstand physical slavery. Do we, as their descendants, need its power and beauty? Are we economically free? Are we politically free? Will not the demonstration of these achievements convince others that we are entitled to more than we receive?

It was my pleasure a short while ago, with the assistance of principals and teachers of Lexington, Kentucky, City Schools to make a survey among one thousand, eight hundred and sixty-seven pupils, ranging from six to seventeen years of age. It was found that all were students of music appreciation classes, but only two hundred and sixty-four were students of or could play any instrumental music, while nine hundred and twelve expressed a desire to learn how to perform on some instrument.

Does not this forty-nine per cent of anxious pupils, or thirty-seven per cent of disinterested pupils concern us? We have been placed in a world of music evidenced through singing birds, whistling breezes, roaring winds, mighty woods, desert sands, rippling brooks and breaking waves. Shall we not accept our background of music as a challenge to help our children appreciate and reproduce the music surrounding them, which in turn will assist them to

"Hum, sing and play their way,
Through prejudice to a better day?"

The story is told that on the first appearance of our great tenor, Roland Hayes, before a white audience in Louisville, Kentucky, he was forced, because of prejudice, to sing from behind a curtain. His wonderful spiritual talent, and time, have removed that curtain, and Mr. Hayes is now gladly received by audiences everywhere. The phonograph and radio are curtains used today between Negro musicians, their music, and the world. Negro artists and their art are unconsciously being received, and appreciated, in hitherto unopened homes. Shall we not labor that, when television has progressed to the point where black faces can be seen through the radio as Negroes sing, bonds of sympathy and understanding shall have eliminated prejudice so that artists, regardless of color, may have an equal chance to make their contribution to the progress of the world? Then, and not until then, shall a great world symphony be broadcast to that Eternal City, through a grand cosmopolitan organ, by the two major branches and their kindred, of the "One Human Race." The white branch, as one has imagined, representing the white keys to this great organ, shall be assisted by the black branch representing its black keys, and completing its rhythm, melody and harmony, declaring and attesting to God in the Highest that, there is "Peace on Earth and Good Will to Men."

LUCY HARTH SMITH

THE NEGRO AND THE PUBLIC MIND TODAY[1]

There are two words of great significance in this subject, "Negro" and "Public." The inquiry is what is the attitude of the public mind toward the Negro today, after efforts such as these which we are rehearsing in this conference, looking back even beyond twenty years? "Today" suggests that one expects to find something different from what it was yesterday.

The Negro in America is different today from what he was yesterday. His ignorance due to illiteracy has largely disappeared. The percentage figures on this subject prove at a glance the powerful charm education has exercised over the Negro. His moral condition has greatly improved. In the days of slavery so cruelly was the Negro crushed that he became "unmoral." His financial condition has improved; the census figures will tell us how far from zero the Negro has climbed in home and farm ownings and in the establishment of business enterprises, small though they may appear to be. His spiritual condition has risen to a higher level—the Negro thinks better of himself today and of his own than he did in the years gone by.

The laws of the U. S. have changed. Slavery in 1860 was a legal institution; then came war and the Thirteenth, Fourteenth and Fifteenth Amendments. The Negro was at high tide in the public mind; then came the ebb of reconstruction, the ascendancy of hatred and prejudice and the success of bigotry. America was unwilling to incorporate the Negro into its body politic; and so, while tolerating his presence, set him aside by segregation and discrimination.

This attitude towards the Negro was fostered and built up from the foundation of *Uncle Tom*, by joke, cartoon

[1] An address delivered on the occasion of the celebration of the Twentieth Anniversary of the Association for the Study of Negro Life and History in Chicago, Illinois, September 9, 1935.

and minstrelsy, and finally by theatrical performances by the Negro himself. These all tended to set him apart and to deal with him in a special manner. America was unfair, not to say unkind, to those of its citizens born free and equal, and endowed by their Creator with certain unalienable rights—but who happened to be colored. However, the march was definitely started toward that goal of Americanism which should see justice and freedom for all without regard to race, color or religion.

The Negro has had his part to play in this drama of progress. He had to rid himself of his ignorance; he had to regain his spirit and his morals; he had to gather experience, and he had to work toward establishing himself on an economic basis. I think he has done well at that task and that today the Negro shows a good measure of gold in the assay of his worth. There is still too much dross, but the gold is none the less gold.

There have been developed against the Negro in America many instruments to impede him in his progress, to deny him opportunity, to crush his aspirations, to thwart him in his efforts. They may all be embraced under the heading ''segregation'' which means separation and therefore a deadline across which the Negro may not go. It has manifested itself in the very small matters of life in many parts of the country, and it still shows itself in high public places. Our Civil Service laws, for instance, require a photograph of the applicant in order that no mistake may be made because of superior intelligence.

Against these mounting difficulties, the Negro has persistently waged his war. He has demonstrated his abilities in a thousand cases. No longer does he cry with Frederick Douglas, ''Judge us not by the heights we have reached but by the depths from which we have come,'' Now he cries with full confidence in himself ''Be American in spirit and in fact; give us freedom and opportunity, and we shall take our place by your side as Americans, and you will not be ashamed of us nor will you be harmed.''

But today the Negro finds the public mind much inclined to feel that he should stay apart and be a Negro among Negroes and make his contribution in America from his segregated life. In the matter of his home, he is not wanted in so-called white neighborhoods. The cry is that he depreciates property values; but as a matter of fact his coming discloses a new property value. The Negro is not wanted in public places and when received is placed in the rear or separated by a curtain. But the Negro in his separate coach or behind the curtain demonstrates his good qualities and often puts to unacknowledged shame those who enforce the segregation.

The Negro is not even welcome in the churches. I verily believe the white Christian, if he could think so far ahead, would be unable to understand Heaven, if the Negroes were accorded equal privileges with him. In fact, I even think the Negro Christian himself expects to have some sort of a jim-crow section, which he secretly thinks will be the nicest part of Heaven.

It is not, however, all a song of despair and hopelessness. In the spirit of the cry that "Ethiopia shall yet stretch forth her hand unto God" the Negro in America today believes that he will yet enjoy in full and equal measure all the rights and privileges of American citizenship. Already he has broken through in many places along the line. In music his artists and composers are accorded recognition and given praise for their worth. In poetry Paul Laurence Dunbar has become a world figure. In painting H. O. Tanner has achieved international standing. In the field of education Booker Washington's fame has become secure. Many of our teachers and scholars find welcome in collegiate circles.

In the world of business, in finance, we are doing a big thing in what seems to be a small way; but mark my words. Every Negro who starts a business, becomes a customer of a wholesale house and patron of some bank, has put in a wedge that by and by will make an opening for our boys and girls to pass on into the business life of our country and enter the long road to economic independence.

The world looks on today to see what the Negro is accomplishing in his own field. It has but scant welcome for him into its field. The Negro hopes to achieve and accomplish so much that it will be larger than his own field can contain and must necessarily go over into the larger field of Americanism.

There is no unanimity among Negroes as to just what they do want. There is too much of jealousy and envy and selfishness. There is too little of encouragement and applause for those who are striving to carry the group upward and onward. There is a great lack of sound leadership and of intelligent following. The Negro is so divided along many lines that cohesion is impossible. It is only in the common suffering of segregation and discrimination that the Negro realizes that they are all in one boat and that all will be affected in the public mind by the acts of one. Hence, it behooves us to give great care to the matter of homes and home training and to religion and morals as well as to secular education, that our own may learn to avoid the doing of things which bring suffering and punishment and denial of opportunity to us all.

Today the white man is uncertain as to the Negro; he is much inclined to leave him alone. He is fearful of the consequences of receiving him into the full fellowship of citizenship. He is looking at the achievements and accomplishments of Negroes and finding much which commands his respect; but he also sees much of which he cannot approve.

I do not believe the Negro in America need despair. Seventy years ago he was almost at zero—empty. Today he can give a good account of himself. He had friends then, and he has friends now. I believe the public mind in America today has reached a state of balance on the Negro, and it is the duty of the Negro to choose and to do and to go the way that will bring this balance down in his favor. The words of the Declaration of Independence and of the Constitution and our Fourth of July speeches seem mockery at times in the presence of lynchings, jim-crow-isms and other discriminations; but these pronouncements are the sentiments upon which American institutions are built; they are its heart-beats; they are its fundamental sense of justice to all men; they are too broad and too deep and too firm to be over-ridden by prejudice and eventually will cause America to

"Crown thy good with Brotherhood,
From sea to shining sea."

ALBERT B. GEORGE

ITALO-ETHIOPIAN RELATIONS[1]

Mussolini's boastful determination to add Ethiopia to Italy's colonial possessions is no new and sudden inspiration. Ever since Leopold II of Belgium took over the Congo and made it pay, European nations have vied with each other in an unholy rush to appropriate to themselves the continent of Africa. By 1885 the rivalries among them had become so intense and so bitter that Jules Ferry of France and Bismarck of Germany saw the necessity of calling the Conference of Berlin to set up rules of the game for the future grab acts. Directly from this conference at Berlin the representatives of all the colonial-minded states of Europe hastened into Africa with rifles in one hand and gin in the other, having their pockets filled with blank treaties upon which the African chiefs under the influence of the gin and at sight of the rifles were induced to make their marks, thus giving away all their lands to some European power for less than a mess of pottage. Upon thus securing the mark of a chief, the European representatives ran up their country's flag and sang or repeated if unable to sing, "God save the" majesty in whose name they acted, but nobody added "and have mercy upon the black man" whose possessions they were taking from him. The case of Ethiopia is not different from that which has happened to the rest of Africa except that in the Ethiopian, Europe has found a man who refuses to put his mark upon the dotted line and one who will not accept a mistranslation of the Treaty of Uccialli.

By the Anglo-German treaty of 1890, Germany was eliminated from the race for the territory north of Lake Victoria. From that date on the race for Ethiopia was narrowed down to three European states, namely, England, France and Italy. Each of these three powers was

[1] An address delivered on the occasion of the celebration of the Twentieth Anniversary of the Association for the Study of Negro Life and History in Chicago, Illinois, September 10, 1935.

dreaming of a great African Empire. France sought to make of her scattered coastal possessions of French Congo, Algeria, and Jibuti one vast North African Empire extending right across the continent and including all the territory north of Belgian Congo and Lake Victoria with the exception of small bits of land about the coast already in the possession of some other European power. England, under the influence of such empire builders as Cecil Rhodes in South Africa and Joseph Chamberlain in London, wished to connect her possessions in South Africa with Egypt in a great Cape-to-Cairo strip of pink extending clear across the continent from north to south. Italy, arriving late, undertook to extend her little possession of Assab on the Red Sea so as to connect her with her recently acquired Somaliland on the Indian Ocean.

It will be seen at once that the wishes of England and Italy somewhat paralleled each other while the dream of France ran directly counter to both of the two other states. Thus it was to the advantage of both Italy and England that they cooperate in their African policy while France felt it to her interests to oppose their efforts. Accordingly by a series of protocols—March 24, April 15, 1891, and May 5, 1894—England and Italy divided northern Africa between them. In general the line of division was to follow the 35th meridian east of Greenwich. In all territory west of this line England was to have a free hand so far as Italy was concerned, while to the east of it Italy was given a free hand so far as England was concerned. Thus Ethiopia to the west of Lake Tsana was assigned to England while that to the east was handed over to the tender mercies of Italy.

In the meantime, Italy, in anticipation of taking possession of Ethiopia, had concluded a treaty of *friendship* and commerce with Menelik II, *Negus Negasti* of Ethiopia, whom she, for a purpose, had aided in securing the throne. This is the famous treaty of Uccialli, concluded May 2, 1889, about Article XVII of which there centered a long controversy culminating in war in 1896 and which Mussolini now brings back into the picture. To understand this treaty and to be able to form any judgment in regard to its meaning one must read carefully the discussion presented with documentary evidences contained in the author's book *Ethiopia, A PAWN in European Diplomacy* just off the press. Suffice it to say here that the Ethiopian text of this Article XVII, which was the only one actually signed, read, "His Majesty, Menelik II, King of Kings of Ethiopia, may if he wishes to do so, make use of the government of His Majesty the King of Italy for all transactions he may have with other Powers or Governments." Whereas the Italian translation of this Article read, "His Majesty, Menelik II, King of Kings of Ethiopia, *consents* to make use of the government of His Majesty the King of Italy, for all transactions he may have with other Powers or Governments." By the Amharic version Menelik had a choice. By the Italian he was *obliged*. By the Amharic text Ethiopia remained a free and independent state. By the Italian Ethiopia became a protectorate of Italy.

According to Article XXXIV of the Conference of Berlin (1885) Crispi, then Prime Minister of Italy, notified the other Powers that Ethiopia had now become a protectorate of Italy. When Menelik discovered this claim of Italy he repudiated, first Article XVII and later the whole treaty of Uccialli and promptly notified all the European Powers that Ethiopia would take care of herself. She had need of no European state to protect her. "She stretches forth her hands unto God."

There followed numerous, long and heated diplomatic efforts of Italy to have Menelik accept the Italian translation with Menelik stoutly refusing to do so. Finally, Crispi felt that he must either force Menelik to become a vassal of Italy or lose control of the government at home. Accordingly on March 1, 1896, there was fought the battle of Adowa in which Menelik's highland warriors annihi-

lated the Italian Army. The results were wholly disastrous
to Italian prestige in Africa. Crispi's government fell and
the Rudini government which succeeded sought peace with
Menelik upon the best terms obtainable. Nothing but
complete and immediate recognition of Ethiopian independence was acceptable to Menelik. As a result, on
October 26, 1896, Italy concluded a treaty of peace with
Menelik whereby Italy recognized the complete independence of Ethiopia forever, and for the time being Italy
dropped out of the contest.

Following Italy's utter defeat at Adowa, France became
active in an effort to realize her dream of a great African
empire. She dispatched Marchand up the Congo toward
the Nile and at the same time, through Menelik, whose
good graces she had gained by aiding him against Italian
aggression, she sent several expeditions across Ethiopia
from Jibuti toward the Nile. These French efforts culminated in the "Fashoda Incident" in which France, because
of English interference, failed to "clasp hands across the
Nile" and into which we need not go here except to find a
basis for the European diplomatic rivalries over "peaceful penetration" at Menelik's Court which, with general
Ethiopian conditions at the time, furnished the opportunity for Italy to return to the Ethiopian theater.

Beaten at Fashoda, France transferred her activities to
Addis Ababa where she had, for the time being, dominant
influence. Through a concession she had previously secured for building a railway across Ethiopia from Jibuti
to the Nile by way of Addis Ababa, she hoped to win
through economic penetration that which she had lost in
political control through English interference. In the
course of the Anglo-French controversy over the nature
of the proposed railway, Italy slipped back into the picture
as a champion of the English proposals. During the three-
cornered controversy that followed, the feeling among the
three European nations became so intense that it was
likely to disturb the delicate general situation which ex-

isted before the World War. To save this general European situation the three nations came to the Anglo-Franco-Italian agreement of 1906.

By this tripartite agreement, the three European nations guaranteed to each other the *status quo* of Ethiopia so far as these nations were concerned. They divided Ethiopia up into three spheres of influence assigning to England dominant influence in the west and control of the water supply of the Nile valley. To France they accorded the railway and the territory adjacent to Jibuti and along the railway, while to Italy was assigned the right to connect Eritrea and Italian Somaliland by a railway to the west of Addis Ababa so as not to interfere with the French railway. But while they guaranteed the *status quo* of Ethiopia they also agreed that *should it ever become necessary* to disturb that status they would consult among themselves and decide what should become of Ethiopia. They reserved to themselves the right to decide whether or not the *status quo* of Ethiopia shall be disturbed and they alone are to be the sole judges as to what shall be done when they decide to disturb Ethiopia. This treaty still stands. Evidently the time has come when these three European Powers have decided that Ethiopia's status should be disturbed. Evidently Ethiopia's independence is to be sacrificed in an effort to maintain the peace of Europe. If so the sacrifice is too great. Such unrighteous action will not long maintain the peace of Europe, and Ethiopia may easily prove to be the rock of offense upon which Europe herself shall be broken.

This tripartite treaty of 1906 is often referred to as the European guarantee of Ethiopian independence, but to one who makes any sort of a careful examination of the treaty it is very evident that the three European Powers concerned, while they have guaranteed certain things connected with Ethiopia to each other, have guaranteed nothing to Ethiopia. The very existence of the treaty of 1906 constitutes a threat to the independence of Ethiopia rather than a guarantee of that independence. Three nations do not get together unasked to guarantee the independence of a fourth nation unless that independence is in danger from one of them and perhaps from all of them. That Ethiopia is and has long been in constant danger of losing her independence to these very guarantors is clearly evident from the history of the situation since 1906.

In 1915 when England and France were trying to woo Italy from her unnatural infatuation with Germany and Austria, they made Italy tempting offers of colonial aggrandizement. Among these allurements they promised that, should England and France annex the German colonies in Africa after the World War, they would recognize Italy's right to expand from Eritrea and Italian Somaliland. It is now, of course, a well known fact that England and France did annex the German colonies at the close of the World War. Italy, however, has not yet expanded from Eritrea and Somaliland. That Ethiopia is the only place for such expansion is so evident that one needs to know only the most elementary geography of Africa to be convinced that the Powers in 1915 meant that Italy should have Ethiopia. This Italy still claims as her right. That she did not get Ethiopia in the Versailles peace arrangements is no doubt due largely to the fact that Ethiopia did not take the position in the World War thought likely for her in 1915. At that time Lij Yassu was acting *Negus Negasti* of Ethiopia, and he was making an effort to lead Ethiopia into the camp of the Central Powers and the Mohammedan religion. It is no doubt to this period that Mussolini refers when he now complains that the hostility of Ethiopia toward Italy was such as to demand part of Italy's forces during the World War to be placed along the Ethiopian border that her African colonies might be protected. The Ethiopians themselves, however, rose in rebellion against their young emperor, overthrew him and proclaimed his aunt, Zauditu, empress with Ras Tafari, the present Haile Selassie I, as regent. Thus at the close of the war Ethiopia was found ranged on the side of the allies rather than against them. Therefore, Italy could not be permitted to take over Ethiopia as she had hoped to do by the treaty of London, 1915.

Now, however, Mussolini is determined to make a great effort to force Ethiopia to become a protectorate of Italy. He has repeatedly demanded that other European nations must recognize Italy's right to expand in Africa. For years he has been preparing his people for war. That Italy's population might be greatly increased he has been urging larger families and now he claims there must be some place where the surplus population may live. He has created a great military machine and proclaimed the glorious destiny of Italy. He has sought to isolate Ethiopia and to find a time when the influence of the League of Nations is at its lowest ebb.

That France will not oppose Italy's aggression in Ethiopia was, without doubt, settled last January when Premier Laval was in conference with Mussolini in Rome. Not all that transpired between Mussolini and Laval at that time is yet known, but enough has become public to assure us that they have reached an accord over Ethiopian matters. Clearly France has been silenced. Evidently for some *quid pro quo* within the European field—most likely a guarantee that Italy will stand with France in European questions, especially those affecting Germany and Austria —France has assigned to Italy a one-fifth interest in the Franco-Ethiopian railway and ceded to her that part of French Somaliland facing the Straits of Bab-el-Mandeb. Surrounded as Ethiopia is on all sides by territory already in possession of England, France and Italy, these three countries can control all exports and imports, including those of munitions of war. Now with Italy part owner in the only railway within the country and with France, her partner, in control of the balance, these countries can so shut off Ethiopia from the rest of the world as to isolate her completely. There can be no reason why

Italy should want from France that utterly barren waste of land facing the Straits of Bab-el-Mandeb other than for strategic military purposes. Doubtless Mussolini wishes to be in position to close the southern end of the Red Sea to battleships should Japan, for instance, decide to come to Ethiopia's aid. That Italy may land troops and munitions of war in Eritrea she needs a protected harbor. She would not care to meet the Japanese fleet there—nor anywhere else most likely—hence the desire to close the Red Sea.

Spokesmen for England still talk and I feel that the sympathies of the English are with the Ethiopians, but that the British Government will do anything to stop Mussolini is to be seriously doubted. Back in 1925 the British Government agreed with Mussolini to a division of Ethiopia into British and Italian spheres of influence with a mutual guarantee that the one would support the other diplomatically in gaining economic concessions within their respective spheres. When they had matters all settled between themselves they presented their demands simultaneously to Ras Tafari, then regent, now Emperor Haile Selassie I. His Majesty at once appealed to the League of Nations, of which Ethiopia had become a member in 1923, stating that within the League all nations had entered on equal terms—that each member was an independent sovereign state and that here were two members agreeing together to support each other in questions referring to a third member. This action seemed to him an encroachment upon Ethiopia's sovereignty. He wrote, "The people of Abyssinia are anxious to do right . . . . but throughout their history they have seldom met with foreigners who did not desire to possess themselves of Abyssinian territory and to destroy their independence. With God's help, and thanks to the courage of our soldiers, we have always, come what might, stood proud and free upon our native mountains." At that time the League of Nations still had some influence. Then, too, France

joined in protest to the Anglo-Italian proposition—not
that she loved Ethiopia but that she had not been consulted as she should have been by the terms of the tripartite treaty of 1906. Whereupon England and Italy
hastened to explain that they had meant no attack upon
Ethiopia's sovereignty, and the matter was dropped. The
Anglo-Italian agreement, however, was not cancelled. Under these circumstances England will, most likely, continue
to seek some way to settle the present difficulty short of
war, but Mussolini knows that that is largely for English
home consumption and when he proceeds to take over
Ethiopia, England, like Maria Theresa of Austria, who
wept over the partition of Poland but continued to take
her share, will say to Mussolini, it is too bad but we will
not oppose you provided you give us a share of the booty
in the form of control of Lake Tsana and the Nile water
supply.

With Ethiopia thus isolated and the stage all set, all
that was lacking was an occasion for action. Opportunely
border incidents began to occur. Among these perhaps
the one at Ualual (Walwal) has attracted the most attention. This incident is now so well known and our space
so limited that we need not recite the details. The most
important point at issue in the matter is to determine who
was the aggressor. If Ualual is within Ethiopia then
clearly Italy was the aggressor, but if Ualual is a part of
Italian Somaliland, then Ethiopia is at fault. This boundary line between Ethiopia and Italian Somaliland has
never been established "on the spot," as the treaty of
1908 provides, but all maps of that part of Africa, including those made by Italy, show Ualual well within Ethiopia.
Certainly Italy has become the aggressor.

That His Majesty, Haile Selassie, is willing to have the
matter settled by arbitration as the Italo-Ethiopian treaty
of 1928 provides is evident. At every turn he has appealed
to the League of Nations to have the matter settled im-

partially, stating that Ethiopia will abide by the decision thus reached. But that Mussolini has no intention to permit any peaceful settlement short of Ethiopia's becoming an Italian protectorate is just as evident. Clearly then, Mussolini intends to make of the matter another Manchukuo affair. He will find this decided difference, however—Ethiopia's highlanders are a brave and warlike people, and they will defend their independence with their lives. Italy will find that the invasion of Ethiopia will be no easy matter.

Space does not permit us to discuss the matter further, but cannot some way be devised by which this utterly unrighteous, most immoral attack upon Ethiopia can be stopped? I am for peace and wish nobody disaster, but should Italy proceed in this as clearly Mussolini intends to do, I should have no particular regrets should the Red Sea repeat her Pharaoh act. Failing that, let Ethiopia repeat her Adowa! It becomes us to heed the plea of Ethiopia's Emperor to pray that peace may prevail and that justice may be done. Should Mussolini succeed in forcing an Italian protectorate upon this last independent bit of Africa the black man's culture will disappear from the earth under a veneer of European imposition.

In general the world accords a place of very high honor and respect to the patriotism of a ruler and his people, who have endured great sacrifices to maintain the integrity and independence of their country against the aggressions of more powerful neighbors. Menelik and his highland warriors defended their independence at Adowa against the Italians in the same way that the Greeks defended theirs at Thermopylae and Marathon. They were as courageous as the Belgians in the face of the German army in 1914. But while the world sings the praises of the exploits of these, it leaves the no less courageous Ethiopians to their fate in the face of the more powerful Europeans.

F. ERNEST WORK

WILLIAM SYPHAX, A PIONEER IN NEGRO EDUCATION IN THE DISTRICT OF COLUMBIA

It is a matter of the utmost difficulty to portray satisfactorily the life of such an interesting character as William Syphax. Only detached, incoherent and inconclusive reports have been preserved while passing years have dimmed the memories of his descendants, and those who lived and associated with him have passed away. Syphax was born shortly after the troublous days of the Missouri Compromise; he witnessed the growing hatred and sectional discords that resulted in the Compromise of 1850; he saw the devastating effects of the Kansas-Nebraska Bill, the Dred Scott Decision, the John Brown Raid, and lived through the hectic days of disunion, civil war and subsequent reconstruction. Through it all he had an abiding faith in his people, and at every possible opportunity he evinced a manliness and a fortitude in his efforts to champion their cause. He was honest, courageous, thrifty in all his dealings and never descended from his lofty pedestal.

William Syphax was the offspring of a distinguished line. His grandfather, William Syphax, was a free Negro, who lived on Fairfax Street, in Alexandria, Virginia. The house in which he lived had at one time been the office of William Herbert, a leading citizen of Alexandria and a descendant of Carlyle. He lived near the old bank of Alexandria and was constantly on the ground of the Carlyle House, over which the Braddock House was afterward built. The elder Syphax was well versed in the prophetical portions of the Scriptures, and ever and anon he was wont to stand on the street corners and preach his doctrines to passersby. He was quite a character in Alexandria and was "very industrious and much respected."[1]

Charles Syphax, the only son of William, was a slave and he belonged to George Washington Parke Custis, who owned Arlington, Virginia, and its environs. When about ten years of age he accompanied George Washington Parke Custis to Arlington, where he grew up with Custis' daughter, Mary, who later married General R. E. Lee.[2] Syphax became enamored of one Maria Carter while working as one of the "White House" servants whose duties were confined to the serving of meals in the Arlington Mansion, and they were married at Arlington by an Episcopal minister, about 1821.[3] By this marriage Elinor was born 1823, and William 1825.[4] Charles, it seems, had considerable liberty, for although he was not freed until after the death of Custis, he was a member, in good standing, of a Baptist Church in Alexandria, of which the Rev. Wm. Madden was pastor. Inasmuch as he belonged to the Custis family at Arlington, he was full of recollections of the early presidents and statesmen, and his memory was stored with anecdotes of those he met there, and who were in the habit of conversing with him. He was acquainted with George Washington and gave vivid accounts of Jefferson, Monroe and others. It is said that during the Civil War, soldiers camped around his residence, took great delight in listening to his vivid descriptions of the past. He was well liked by all regardless of color and was considered a good Christian. He died in 1869 at the ripe old age of seventy-eight.[5]

[1] *Alexandria, Va., Gazette*, February 1917, date defaced.

[2] *Morning (Washington, D. C.) News*, October 9, 1869.

[3] As related to the writer by Mrs. Mary Gibson Brewer, great granddaughter of Charles and Maria.

[4] "Sketch of the Life of Wm. Syphax," a paper written by his daughter, Maria Browne Syphax, for the dedication of Wm. Syphax School, October 31, 1902. She gives his birth as April 4, 1825, in Alexandria County, Virginia. This date is on his tombstone at Harmony Cemetery, Washington, D. C.

[5] *Morning (Washington, D. C.) News*, October 9, 11, 1869.

On his mother's side William Syphax descended not only from a distinguished line but his ancestry savored very definitely of the plantation aristocracy of the South. Maria Syphax was the daughter of George Washington Parke Custis and a maid of Martha Washington.[6] George Washington Parke Custis was the last male line of a family of Custis, and he was lord of the Arlington estate of 1,110 acres.[7] In the treatment of his slaves Custis is said to have been as considerate as he was regarding any other class of human beings, and the glaring evils of iniquitous slavery were never apparent on his property. Each slave had a house apportioned him and a bit of ground, the produce of which he owned as "securely as if his title to the land he occupied was duly recorded in the records of the county courts."[8] From time to time, Custis freed some of his slaves. Particularly was this true as regarded his female servants for whom he seemed to show an interest out of all proportion to those motives actuated by humanitarian impulses. He freed Louisa, the daughter of his servant Judith, on the 5th of April,

[6] From a newspaper clipping of June 1866 entitled "Colonel Custis' Daughter." Unfortunately neither the paper nor the exact date was preserved. The writer made efforts to obtain a copy of the paper but eventually gave up the task. This clipping is in the possession of Mrs. Ennis Syphax, the widow of Ennis Syphax, a brother of William Syphax. She resides on the original Arlington plot, across the Potomac River opposite the Nation's capital, in Virginia. Hereafter this clipping will be referred to as *Newspaper*, ante.

[7] The present estate of Arlington, Va., was originally a part of 6,000 acres of land, made October 21, 1669, by Sir William Berkley, Governor of Virginia, to Robert Howsen as a reward for bringing settlers in the colony. He sold the property to John Alexander for six hogsheads of tobacco. On December 25, 1778, Gerard Alexander sold the Arlington portion (1,110 acres) to John Custis for 11,000 pounds. George Washington Parke Custis was born April 30, 1781. His grandmother was married a second time, to George Washington, who adopted George Washington Parke Custis.

See—*Story of Arlington* by John Ball Osborne; Century, April 1889 and "Arlington House" in *Harper's*, September 1853.

[8] Decker, Karl, and McSween, Angus: *Historic Arlington*, p. 37.

1803;[9] John, the son of Judith; Charles, the son of Eloisa; and John, and Eliza, the children of Oney, in 1818.[10] In or about 1826 Custis manumitted Maria, who at the time had two children, Elinor, six years of age, and William, "a baby boy."[11] Her two children were freed along with her, though her husband, Charles, seems not to have received his freedom until after the death of Custis, who left a will manumitting all his slaves.[12] It is stated, however, that Custis recognized Maria as his child and gave her a piece of property on the Arlington

[9] "Know all men by these presents that I, George Washington Parke Custis, for *divers good causes* and considerations . . . do liberate, emancipate and manumit Louisa, a child about two years old, the daughter of Judith, one of my slaves, in the Dower of the late Martha Washington and lately resident of Mt. Vernon and I do by these presents discharge and release the said Louisa and any offspring she may have from all service to be rendered by her on them unto me, the said George Washington Parke Custis. For witness whereof I have hereunto set my hand and seal this first day of April 1803." G. W. P. CUSTIS. Sealed and delivered, in presence of James Kieth, Thomas Kieth. Proved by oath and recorded April 5, 1803. *Deed Liber* E, 1803, in the county courthouse at Alexandria, Va.

[10] "Know all men by these presents that I, George Washington Parke Custis . . . do manumit and set free the following slaves, viz: John, the son of my servant Judith, said John about 14 years of age; Charles, the son of my servant Eloisa, deceased, said Charles about 14 years of age; Edmund, son of my servant Oney, said Edmund about 11 years of age; and Eliza, daughter of my servant Oney, said Eliza about 8 years of age, and by these presents have manumitted and set free the aforesaid, John, Charles, Edmund and Eliza. As witness my hand and seal this 14th day of May 1818. G. W. P. CUSTIS. *Deed Liber* G, No. 2, 1818-19, in the county courthouse at Alexandria, Va.

[11] *Newspaper*, ante.

[12] "I give freedom to my slaves, the said slaves to be emancipated by my executors in such manner as to my executors may seem most expedient and proper, the said emancipation to be accomplished in not exceeding five years from time of my decease." March 26, 1855.

Osborne, John Ball: *Story of Arlington*, p. 81. Speaking of Charles Syphax the *Washington, D. C., News* verified the fact that he was a slave until after the death of Custis. *Washington, D. C., News*, October 8, 1869.

estate.[13] This piece of land constituted 15 acres off the northwest corner of the Arlington estate and "her white cottage was surrounded by tall trees and pleasant stretches of grassland and the place was beautiful as well as homelike."[14] It is also stated that "the family of Robert E. Lee inherited the respect for the blood of the former slave woman, and they (the wife of Robert E. Lee was the daughter of Custis and the half-sister of Maria Syphax) confirmed the legacy of Custis by saying that the bit of land was hers although there was no deed to show the fact."[15] William Syphax, therefore, came from a distinguished line.

Charles and Maria spent their entire lives on that plot of land and besides the two children previously mentioned eight others were born and reared there. They were Cornelius, Charles, Colbert, Shaulter, Austin, John, Ennis and Maria. All lived to maturity, and all except Shaulter and Austin had families.

The ever-increasing hatreds, party feuds and sectional discords over the slavery issue resulted in the Civil War, and the Arlington Estate was necessarily affected. Robert E. Lee took command of the Confederate forces while his family left the grounds. Federal troops occupied Arlington from the first days of the war and had many personal contacts with the Syphaxes.[16] On August 5, 1861, the Government had passed the Direct Tax Act.[17]

[13] The writer spent two full days ransacking the musty deed books in the courthouse at Alexandria, Virginia, in a vain endeavor to locate either the manumission of Maria Syphax or a statement regarding the Arlington property. He found no references to her whatsoever, though he came across other deeds of Custis.

[14] *Newspaper*, ante.

[15] *Ibid.*

[16] *Washington, D. C., News*, October 11, 1869.

[17] This Act provided for increased revenues from imports to pay the interest on the public debt and "for other purposes." It provided for the levying of a direct tax upon the United States annually of $22,000,000 apportioned among the several States. Virginia's share of the direct tax amounted to $937,550 2/3. *United States Statutes at Large*, vol. xii, chapter xxxxv.

Inasmuch as Virginia was in "open rebellion" against the United States, the Federal Government realized the impossibility of collecting the taxes. The government then decided that when the civil authority in any State was so obstructed, due to the insurrection, as to prostrate the peaceful collection of the direct tax, that the tax apportioned should be charged or apportioned in each insurrectionary district upon all lands and lots of ground according to the enumeration and valuation of the last assessment preceding the breaking out of the War.[18] The Act was amended in 1863, and from November 21, 1863, to January 10, 1864, the sale of the Arlington Estate was advertised in a Virginia newspaper.[19] On the 11th of January, 1864, the Arlington Estate of 1,110 acres was purchased by the Government for $26,100, and the cemetery began May 13, 1864, through the influence of General Meigs.

While all this was going on the Syphaxes were living on the little plot of land left Maria by Custis. There was no deed, record, will or document of any sort to show the right of possession and even had there been, the action of the Federal Government would have rendered such ownership null and void. Maria, with her family, had lived there for upwards of fifty years, and now that the vast estate had been reduced to a waste and a camping ground for the Government's troops, the family began to bestir itself to maintain possession of its property. William, who by this time had become prominent in

[18] The Act also provided for the sale of all such tracts or parcels of land in order to secure the payment of the tax and described at length the manner in which such sale should be conducted. Commissioners were appointed to apportion the assessments and conduct the sales lawfully. The Act provided further that "at such sales any tracts, parcels, or lots of land which may be selected under the direction of the President for Government use for war, military, naval, revenue, charitable, educational or police purposes may at said sale be bid in by high commissioners under the direction of the President for and struck off to the United States." *Ibid.*

[19] *Virginia State Journal*, November 21, 1863, to January 10, 1864.

Washington, came to his mother's rescue. Through his efforts the matter was brought to the attention of Congress, and with little delay and no debate the Bill for the Relief of Maria Syphax was passed.

On May 16, 1866, Senator Harris, from the Committee on Private Land Claims, to which was referred the "memorial of William Syphax, praying to be confirmed in his title of land in the Arlington estate (so called), Virginia, granted to his mother by the late George Washington Parke Custis" reported a bill (S. No. 321) for the relief of Maria Syphax.[20] The bill proposed to release and confirm to Maria Syphax, her heirs and assigns, the title to a piece of land, being a part of the Arlington estate, upon which she had resided since about the year 1826.[21]

The Bill for the Relief of Maria Syphax came up for a second hearing in the Senate May 18, 1866. Senator Morrill inquired of Senator Harris on what grounds the bill was placed. Senator Harris stated that the person named in the bill was a mulatto woman who was once the slave of Mr. Custis. He said:

---

[20] *Cong. Globe,* 39th Cong., 1st Session, p. 2612.

[21] The Bill reads: "Be it enacted by the Senate and House of Representatives of the United States of America in Congress assembled, That the title to a piece of land being part of the Arlington estate, in the county of Alexandria in the State of Virginia, upon which Maria Syphax has resided since about the year 1826 bounded and described as follows to wit: Beginning at the intersection of the South Line of said Arlington estate with the center line of a small run, said point of intersection being about 1/4 of a mile from the S. W. corner of said Arlington estate, running thence westerly along said south line seven chains and 40 links; thence in a N. E. direction, on a line making an angle of 35 degrees with the said south line, 22 chains and 38 links; thence at right angles, in a S. E. direction 15 chains and 67 links to the said south line of the Arlington estate; thence westerly along the said south line of the said Arlington estate 19 chains and 92 links, to the place of beginning, containing 17 acres and 5 3/100 of an acre of land, be the same, more or less be, and the same is hereby, released and confirmed unto the said Maria Syphax her heirs and assigns." *United States Statutes at Large,* vol. xiv, ch. cxxi, p. 589.

"Mr. Custis, at the time she married about forty years ago feeling an interest in the woman, something perhaps akin to a *paternal instinct,* manumitted her, and gave her this piece of land. It has been set apart to her, and it has been occupied by her and her family for forty years. Under the circumstances the Committee thought it no more than just, the government having acquired title to this property under a sale for taxes, that this title should be confirmed to her."[22]

Senator Harris explained that "the title runs to this woman and her heirs."[23] On June 8, 1866, the House advised the Senate that Bill S. No. 321 for the Relief of Maria Syphax had passed, without amendment.[24] It passed the Senate June 11, 1866,[25] and was signed by President Andrew Johnson, June 12, 1866.[26]

Very little information has been preserved about the early life of William Syphax. It is said that he came to Washington, D. C., at the age of eleven and attended private schools taught by an Englishman named Nutall, John T. Johnson and Enoch Ambush, also private schools in Alexandria.[27] Whether he made daily excursions from Arlington to Washington, or returned to Arlington from Alexandria and Washington at certain definite intervals, is not clear in the writer's mind. He made no effort to obtain his manumission certificate until he was quite a man, when, desiring to accompany Robert C. Winthrop to Boston as an attendant, he went to Alexandria "to get his papers." He found, in the archives of Alexandria, the document which Custis had signed giving his mother her freedom and that of her daughter, Bertha Elinor,

[22] *Cong. Globe,* 39th Cong., 1st Session, p. 2673-74. In the absence of any evidence from Custis himself, this statement of Senator Harris about confirms the relationship between Custis and Maria Syphax.

[23] *Ibid.*

[24] *Ibid,* p. 3026.

[25] *Ibid.,* p. 3075.

[26] *Ibid.,* p. 3126.

[27] *Sketch of Life of Wm. Syphax,* paper written by Maria Browne Syphax, October 31, 1902.

six years old, and one male infant. An octogenarian Quaker affirmed that the male child was the young Negro and he received his credentials.''[28]

As a man William Syphax was a remarkable type. He was six feet tall with broad shoulders, broad forehead, high cheekbones, straight nose, thin lips and light brown skin. In an article entitled the ''Boss Head of the Lot,'' the *Washington Post* of May 18, 1878, made the following observation:

''The head of William Syphax, for many years the colored chief messenger of the Interior Department, and the reputed half brother of a great general, is a magnificent one, indicating force, intensity and coolness of intellect. It is remarkably even and harmonious in its lines. It is the head of Caius Marius in meditation amid the ruins of Carthage, the busy brain within suggesting schemes of subverting Sylla while dreaming on the desolation before him. It is the largest in our collection and measures fully 24¼ inches for a 7¾ hat.''[29]

Syphax took a prominent part in all movements and assumed leadership in many enterprises for the advancement of Negroes in the city of Washington along social, educational and religious lines. He was one of the founders of the Civil and Statistical Association (1850), the aim of which was the educational, moral and financial advancement of the Negroes of the District of Columbia.[30] He sponsored and secured the incorporation of Columbian Harmony Cemetery in 1889.[31] Affiliating himself with the Nineteenth Street Baptist Church in 1857, he became a deacon there and thus functioned for a period of rela-

[28] *Newspaper*, ante. No member of the Syphax family seems to know anything about the manumission papers of Maria and William. It seems improbable that William would have lost them, yet they are not to be found. The impression seems to be that Custis gave Maria and her family a ''word of mouth'' freedom for obvious reasons, yet it seems to have been generally known that they were free.

[29] *Washington Post*, May 18, 1878.

[30] *Sketch of Life of William Syphax*, paper written by Maria Browne Syphax, October 31, 1902.

[31] *Senate Miscl. Doc.* No. 91, 50th Congress, 2nd Session, p. 1-2.

tively 20 years.[32] He was appointed copyist in the Interior Department in 1851 at $720 a year, promoted July 14, 1874, to $900 a year and appointed to a clerkship at $1,000 a year October 31, 1885.[33] He served under nine Secretaries of the Interior.[34]

Seriously interested in the advancement of his people, Syphax had his first great opportunity in the passing of the act "Relating to Schools for the Education of Colored children in the cities of Washington and Georgetown in the District of Columbia," July 11, 1862.[35] The act created a board of trustees of the schools for Negro children, specified their duties, term of office, etc., and empowered the Secretary of the Interior to fill vacancies and make appointments from residents "of the cities" at the expiration of the term of one of the trustees. William Syphax had long been thus interested.

Syphax became the first president of the Board of Trustees of the Colored Public Schools of Washington, D. C., serving from July 1, 1868, to June 30, 1871. It was in this capacity that he made his chief contribution, for he was a pioneer in the educational movement for the intellectual advancement of the Negroes of Washington, D. C., and did much to lay the foundation for the present school system now enjoyed by the Colored People in the District of Columbia.[36] He was not only the presiding officer of this body from 1868 to 1870, but also treasurer from 1870 to 1871. He and his coworkers discharged the functions

[32] William Syphax was dismissed, at his own request, from the First Baptist Church, white, while in Washington, D. C., June 12, 1857. The letter stated that William Syphax was a member ''in good standing with us, and having asked for a letter of dismission to you, we thereby grant his request, cordially recommending him to your fellowship and care, and shall consider him dismissed from us when advised that he is received by you.'' The letter was signed by John W. Clarke, Church Clerk. See also *Washington Post*, June 18, 1891, and *Washington Star*, June 19, 1891.

[33] *Ibid.* The writer has the original promotion copies before him.

[34] *Washington Post*, June 10, 1891.

[35] At this time Washington and Georgetown were separate municipalities, both being in the District of Columbia.

[36] *Washington Times*, October 31, 1902; *Washington Star*, June 19, 1891.

exercised formerly by white trustees with only one Negro member in the minority.

On March 2, 1869, the trustees[37] of Colored Schools sent their first report, along with recommendations, to Orville H. Browning, Secretary of the Interior,[38] who sent it to the Senate, of which B. F. Wade was president. The report stated that there were fifty schools under the control of the trustees and fifty teachers, five of whom had been furnished by friends in New England, through a committee of which Edward W. Howland, Esq., of New Bedford, Mass., was chairman; forty-five were paid by the trustees, who also paid the incidental expenses of all the schools. The trustees also reported that three additional teachers were in the city who would soon begin work. They were furnished by the Presbyterian Home Mission of New York, through the kind agency of the Rev. J. Stella Martin. The report stated further that more assistance could have been obtained from other parts had not the impression been circulated that the educational interests of the colored children were amply provided for. Of the fifty teachers employed twenty-five were white and twenty-five were colored. The trustees were of the opinion that qualified teachers, regardless of color, provided the best assurance of the progress of the colored schools.

Desiring to have good comfortable buildings for the schools, the trustees pointed out the generally poor conditions of both the frame and brick structures. The frame building in Georgetown occupied by seven schools was uncomfortable and unsuited to its purposes. It was necessary to have the sides (of the frame building at the corner of 17th and M streets, which contained eight

[37] There were to be three trustees holding office for 1, 2 or 3 years, which was to be determined by lot. Appointments were made July first. *Statutes at Large*, vol. xii, p. 537-38.

[38] The trustees of colored schools were: William Syphax, chairman, Albert G. Hall, and Alfred Jones.

schools) propped up in order to render it secure. The brick building on O street, commodious enough for eight schools, did not present a neat appearance due to lack of paint. The trustees stated that a new building had been completed and would soon be ready for occupancy. The building and grounds, which cost about $26,000, were 48 by 88 feet and four stories high. Its first story, fourteen feet high, was divided into a vestibule with a room 15 by 16 feet on each side and a hall 72 feet long and 45 wide. Each of the remaining stories had a hall through the center and on both sides two rooms, each 37 feet 5 inches long and 23 feet wide. The building had also arrangements for gas and water, and in its general outline presented quite a handsome appearance. The trustees sought to offer an humble tribute of grateful remembrance to the (deceased) Hon. Thaddeus Stevens, of Pennsylvania, the earnest champion of free and equal school privileges for all classes and conditions of the children of men. They therefore called it "The Stevens School House."[39]

The treasurer's report showed that the total annual receipts for operation of the schools were $45,495.03 and the expenditures $43,866.75, leaving a balance in the treasury of $1,608.28. The trustees claimed that they had done their utmost to discharge their various duties, but to meet outstanding liability and to make needed repairs and improvement upon the property confided to their care and management, means were needed, which would readily be at their command if the mayor of Washington, the Hon. Sayles J. Bowen, "were not so backward in his compliance with the laws with reference to the support of the Colored Schools."[40] Concerning his Honor the Mayor, the report added:

[39] *Senate Ex. Doc.* No. 56, 40th Cong. 3rd Session, p. 1-2.

[40] *Ibid.*, p. 3.

"This reticence upon his part is a matter of surprise to the trustees, in view of his zeal in behalf of our schools as manifested in his correspondence when a member of this board with his immediate predecessor in the Mayoralty; especially is this a matter of surprise to them, when, as they have been credibly informed, checks for the payment of the teachers in the public white schools during the month of February 1869 were signed by that officer, while teachers in the public colored schools were compelled to go unpaid by his refusal to sign a check in favor of the latter schools."[41]

The report cited three communications sent the Mayor concerning this matter and ended with the recommendation that the treasurer of the board of trustees be required by law to give bond and security, in such manner as approved by the Secretary of the Interior and that the trustees be required to make quarterly reports to the same officer.

The letter referred to in the report was written to the Mayor and signed by the trustees, January 18, 1869. It called the attention of the Mayor to the several acts of Congress providing for the support for colored schools in the District of Columbia. The act of Congress, June 25, 1864, was mentioned.[42] Section 19 of the same act referred to monies received from fines, penalties and forfeitures and provided that the funds thus obtained for educational purposes should be applied to the education of both white and colored children in the proportion of the numbers of each between the ages of six and seventeen years, as determined by the latest census report that shall

---

[a] Ibid.

[42] That from the whole fund received from all sources by such authorities . . . to purposes of public education such a proportionate part thereof as the number of colored children between the ages of 6 and 17 years in the respective cities bear to the whole number thereof, for the purpose of establishing and maintaining public schools in said cities for the education of colored children; that the proportion shall be ascertained by the last reported census of the population of said cities made prior to said apportionment and at all times be regulated thereby. *United States Statutes at Large,* vol. xiii, secs. 17 and 18, p. 191-92.

have been made prior to said apportionment; and the mayors of the cities of Washington and Georgetown were authorized to pay such parts thereof as were applicable under that section.[43] The act of July 23, 1866, provided:

"That the moneys shall be considered due and payable to said trustees on the first day of October of each year and if not then paid over to them interest at the rate of 10 per cent on the amount unpaid may be demanded and collected from the authorities of the delinquent city by said trustees."[44]

Congress, by resolution, approved March 29, 1867, provided that the Commissioner of Education be directed to ascertain the number of children resident in the District of Columbia over the age of six years and under the age of 18 years, etc., and report whether legislation was necessary to secure the advantages of said system to all of said children.[45] The corporation of the city of Washington appropriated $1,000 to aid in defraying the expenses of taking the census, and on January 20, 1868, Appleton Clark introduced a resolution in the board of common council requesting the Commissioner of the Board of Education to inform the council, the number of children between the ages of six and seventeen in Washington.

The Commissioner of Education returned, through the Mayor, to the board of common council that the number of children entitled to school privileges on the eleventh of November, 1867, was 27,624, as follows: whites, 19,-223; colored, 8,401, or a little more than 30.41 per cent colored. The trustees maintained that the majority of Washingtonians were desirous that the proportion of school money applicable to the support of schools for colored children, according to the several acts of Congress, *should be paid to the trustees of schools for colored chil-*

[43] *Ibid.*, p. 19. 45. *Sen. Ex. Doc.* No. 56, 40th Cong. 3rd Session, p. 4.

[44] *Senate Ex. Doc.* No. 56, 3rd Session, p. 4.

[45] *Ibid.*, p. 5.

dren; that no one could question that the laws made it the Mayor's duty to pay the amount due to the trustees of schools for colored children on the first of October of each year. The trustees stated that there could be no discrimination allowed between the different classes of children respecting the apportionment of school money. The acts of Congress were very explicit and in precise terms, so that there could be no question as to the intention of the general government to enact that the school money should be apportioned to the support of schools for the white children and for the colored children in exact accordance with the last known numbering of them. The trustees stated further, that at least two-thirds of the Negro children had not been provided with any opportunity to attend school, and they deemed it their duty to request and justly and reasonably demand that the Mayor pay them the amount due, namely, 30.41 per cent of the school money for the then current fiscal year. Two additional letters were written by William Syphax, requesting the Mayor to give the trustees the proportionate sums due, to compensate the teachers and otherwise meet their financial obligations. The letters were written February 20, and 25, 1869, respectively.[46]

Such was the aggressive policy of William Syphax. A man of dauntless courage and unwavering integrity, he dared to demand what was due his race, fearing no man regardless of position or color. In this respect he was far superior to many of the self-appointed pseudo leaders of today, who squirm and tremble at the oppressor's voice and dare do anything for personal glorification even to the detriment of the race to which they belong. Not so with William Syphax, for personal desires and ambitions were relegated to the background, and his people were first and all with him. He took issue with the greatest minds of his day, did not hesitate to

[46] *Ibid.*, p. 5-6.

expose publicly those whose intentions were dishonorable and was always on the alert to demand that his people receive what was justly and rightly due them.

Nor was Syphax blind to the shortcomings of his own people. In a circular to the Negroes of Washington and Georgetown September 10, 1868, he urged them to cooperate with the trustees in their efforts to render the schools as efficient as possible to "the great end for which they were established."[47] In his zeal for parental cooperation he evinced a vision and an interpretation of school values that placed him well ahead of his time. He could well be living in the twentieth century. He asked the ministers (1) to hold before their congregations the necessity of education, to fit their children for the new duties of freedom and civil equality in order to fill worthily positions of honor and responsibility. This could not be done in ignorance. (2) Parents should send their children to school promptly on the first day of the year, in order that the school be organized quickly and to prevent certain pupils from getting the start on the late comers. (3) Parents were urged to send their children regularly and punctually to school. Many parents, not fully appreciating the importance of regular school attendance, had frequently kept their children at home for trivial reasons to the great injury of their children and the whole school. There were 82,000 absences of a half a day each during the preceding years, 50 per cent of which were unnecessary. Tardiness, too, was a great vice. There were 23,681 cases the preceding year. The habit of rising early and getting to school on time would cultivate the habit of early rising and punctuality that would be of value to children and parents through life. (4) Parents should be advised always to sustain the regulations and the good

[47] *Circular*, September 10, 1868. This circular was sent to the ministers and prominent Negroes in Washington and Georgetown by William Syphax. The writer made use of the original copy.

discipline of the schools. They should never be disre-spectful to a teacher in the presence of their children; nor take sides with pupils against a teacher until after a visit and a calm inquiry into the matter of complaint has been made and the teacher found to be clearly in the wrong. Even in such instances the parent should speak to the teacher privately or to the superintendent or to the trustees, rather than blame the teacher in front of the pupils. (5) Parents should visit the schools, make the acquaintance of the teachers and see how the schools were conducted. This would indicate an interest in their children's progress and would stimulate the teachers to a greater interest in their work. (6) The ministers would set a good example by visiting the schools also; the children would then feel that harmony existed between the church and the school. (7) All should sustain the trustees in their determination to elevate the character of the schools, by insisting on a high standard of qualifi-cations for teachers regardless of color. Preference would be given colored teachers, their qualifications being equal, for we ''deem it a violation of our official oath to employ inferior teachers when superior teachers can be had for the same money.''[48] Negro teachers would be employed as rapidly as they became competent after they had enjoyed ''equal advantages for a sufficient length of time.''[49] Such were the exhortations and admonitions of William Syphax to his people.

One can readily see by these vigorous efforts on the part of William Syphax and his associates, to solicit funds, to obtain the proper monies that had been appro-priated for Negro schools, to break down discrimination and to check administrative inefficiency, that the schools in general and the Negro schools in particular were in need of much improvement. There were those who felt that the school situation in the District of Columbia

[48] Ibid.
[49] Ibid.

was a disgrace, not only to Washington, but to the nation. They argued that since popular education was confessedly the only sure basis of a republican government, and since Washington was the nation's capital, the question of public instruction was more than a matter of local concern; the whole nation should have an interest in it and should have a guardian care over the schools.

A group of representative citizens, therefore, petitioned Congress, January 24, 1870, and after having described at length the varied deficiencies in the present system offered certain remedial suggestions. The Negro population had increased by 1867 over 1860 nearly 200 per cent in Washington, 70 per cent in Georgetown and 52 per cent "in the county."[50] The injustice of requiring the property holders to bear the whole pecuniary burden of educating the children of non-taxpayers was apparent without argument. The number of children attending school was as follows: white, 7,132; colored, 4,095, with 7,445 children of both races in private schools. In short, there were 18,672 children attending school. Since the census of 1867 revealed 33,115 children of school age in Washington, Georgetown and the county, it can readily be seen that 14,443 children had not attended school. In other words, about 35 per cent of the children of school age were enjoying the benefits of public instruction, and "yet the funds raised by the several municipal authorities within the District for school purposes, under what the people deem onerous rates of taxation, are quite inadequate for the needs of even this small proportion."[51]

The petitioners pointed out that at the beginning of the school term $62,000 of the appropriations of preceding years remained unexpended, yet the school fund property was largely overdrawn; and although the city coun-

---

[50] There were 20,984 Negroes in Washington, 1,849 in Georgetown, and 2,044 in the county. Most of these were freedmen or refugees and paid no taxes at all. *Senate Misc. Doc.* No. 24, 41st Cong., 2nd Session, p. 2.

[51] *Ibid.*, p. 3.

cils had appropriated $263,234.50 for both white and colored schools, the financial officers of the corporation had advised the trustees that the revenues for school purposes would be far short of that amount. Attention was called to the wretchedly dilapidated school buildings, many of which should be condemned. It was stated also that the proportion of the colored school fund, even if promptly paid, would be but a fraction of the amount necessary for school operation. The educational needs of Negroes had been supplemented considerably by private benevolence, but this had practically ceased.

The committee suggested that Congress make an appropriation of 1,000,000 acres of public lands, the proceeds thereof to constitute a fund for the use of the public schools in the District of Columbia, to be apportioned to the several municipalities in the ratio of their school population; that an appropriation be made in money from the national amount equal to one-third of all sums raised or appropriated for school purposes by the several municipal authorities of the District, for four successive years, commencing July 1, 1869.[52] The report of the trustees of colored schools of the District of Columbia for the year ending June 20, 1870, cited the defects of the school system, urged the removal of the superintendent, and advocated legislative reforms. In the midst of the efforts to build up these Negro schools the trustees called to the position of superintendent, O. V. Catto, of Philadelphia, who during his brief tenure of office prepared an improved system of classification and course of instructions for the Negro schools. Plans for organizing a high school were in progress. After the sudden death

[52] The committee members were: A. Hyde, chairman of Convention and of Georgetown Board of Guardians; A. E. Newton, Secretary and Member of Board of Trustees, Washington, D. C.; G. F. McLellan, Board of Trustees, Washington, D. C.; Z. Richards, Superintendent of Schools, Washington, D. C.; W. T. Dunlop, Joseph Libbey, Board of Guardians, Georgetown; J. A. Rowland, A. Garden, Committee on Schools of Levy Court; W. B. Lary, A. B. Johnson, Commissioners of Schools of county; William Syphax, chairman, Board of Trustees Colored Schools. Petition dated Jan. 28, 1870.

of Catto, the position of superintendent was offered to a A. E. Newton, a former superintendent, who had participated in the organization of the colored schools. Newton assumed office October 20, 1870, after an interval of two years.[53]

With regard to the receipts and expenditures for the year ending June 30, 1870, the trustees felt that the transactions and accounts for that year were marked by some irregularities and inaccuracies which they could not sanction. In one instance a sale was made of bonds of the city of Washington by which the sum of $3,055.50 of the people's money was sacrificed. The bonds were held by the board merely as collateral security, subject to redemptions by the city, and their sale was made without the authority of any action of the board and "in our judgment was entirely unnecessary."[54] The trustees being desirous of more information relative to the manner in which business had been transacted during the preceding year than was afforded by the records of the office, caused an examination to be made of the accounts and vouchers as filed in the Interior Department. The results showed such grave discrepancies and other serious defects that a copy of the audit was submitted to the Secretary of the Interior along with their report.[55]

[53] *Report of the Board of Trustees of Colored Schools*, Dec. 8, 1870; p. 4, 42, 18. Also *Senate Ex. Doc.* No. 20, 41st Congress, 3rd Session, p. 2, 10.

[54] *Senate Ex. Doc.* No. 20, 41st Congress, 3rd Session, p. 4, 5.

[55] The Superintendent's report dated October 20, 1870, pointed out discrepancies as follows: (1) Expenditures as per statement $69,030.29; per voucher $67,170.52, amount in excess in vouchers $1,859.77. (2) A discrepancy between amount of balance in treasury at end of year as given by treasurer's statement and that shown by deducting the total expenditures from the total receipts, showed an unexpended balance $2,826.08. A payment had been made to one person (A. Pannell) on 62 different vouchers amounting to $10,253.21 for "work done." The vouchers contained no definite items, or the quality of work done, or the kind of material used. Many were not signed by the trustees. A portion of a letter written by A. E. Newton, Superintendent of Schools, in the District of Columbia (dated) October 20, 1870, to Messrs. William Syphax and William H. A. Wormley, Trustees of Colored Schools in Washington and Georgetown. *Senate Ex. Doc.* No. 20, 41st Cong., 2nd Session, p. 20, 21.

The schools had increased to sixty-six with sixty-four teachers. The New England Friends' Association had furnished five additional teachers, who would be compelled to withdraw before the end of the school term for want of funds. The buildings owned by the trustees seated but 2,944 pupils of the 9,300 children, while another 6 per cent were poorly accommodated in rented buildings which were unfit for teaching purposes. According to the report upwards of 63 per cent of the Negro children were unprovided with public school accommodations of any kind, while few enjoyed the advantages of private schools worthy of the name. The trustees reported, however, that they had contracted for the erection of a large and commodious school building which would seat 550 pupils at a cost of $25,000. It would be located at 2nd and C Streets, S. E. (Lincoln School).

It is interesting (to some extent amazing) to read the protests of these trustees of the colored schools of Washington and Georgetown and to compare their philosophy with the opinion of leading Negroes of today. The report of the trustees of colored schools of Washington and Georgetown to the Hon. C. Delano, Secretary of the Interior, dated Dec. 31, 1870, and signed by Messrs. William Syphax and William H. A. Wormley, vigorously denounced segregated education and called for additional legislation abolishing the present order and creating a new system of mixed schools.[56] They said that the best interests of Negroes required the abrogation of all laws, and institutions creating or tending to perpetuate distinctions based on color and the substituting of enactments providing for the equal privileges to all classes of citizens. The laws that created the double school system had been enacted as a temporary expedient to meet a condition of things which had disappeared. Separate schools recognized and perpetuated a cruel, unreasonable

[56] *Senate Ex. Doc.* No. 20, 41st Cong., 3rd Session, p. 6.

and unchristian prejudice which is exceedingly harmful to the Negro.

"And custom is now fully reconciled at this capital to the seating side by side of white and colored people, in the railway car, the jury box, the municipal and government offices, in the city councils and even in the halls of the two houses of Congress, yet while the fathers may sit together in those high places of honor and trust, the children are required by law to be educated apart. We see neither reason nor justice in this discrimination. If the fathers are fit to associate, why are the children not equally so?"[57] The trustees endorsed the Sumner Bill.[58]

The trustees recommended further a larger board and the power of the board to employ the superintendent of schools for a term of three years, a treasurer and a secretary (exclusive of their number). The report stated that a high school had been started and that there was urgent need for a school for the special training of teachers. Thus were sown the seeds for the erection of a normal school for the training of teachers at public expense.[59]

[57] *Ibid.*

[58] Bill S. No. 361. "To secure equal rights in the public schools of Washington and Georgetown, reported in Senate January 10, 1870. *Cong. Globe*, 41st Congress, 2nd Session, p. 323. Reported again with amendment May 6, 1870. *Ibid.*, p. 3273. The bill, presented by the Hon. Charles Sumner, provided for the abolition of the Board of Trustees of the colored schools of Washington and Georgetown and the creation of a board of Trustees of "such persons as have official control of the public schools" in the District of Columbia. There should be no distinction "on account of race, color or previous condition of servitude" in the admission of pupils to any of the public schools, or in the mode of education or treatment of the pupils, and instead of separate funds, there would be a common fund set apart and devoted to educational purposes. There should be shown no prejudice to an applicant for the service of teachers "on account of race, color or previous condition of servitude" nor any difference "on this account" in the grade or compensation of teachers. If any trustee, commission or other persons having control of the public schools violated any provisions of the act, his official powers in the premises would "ipso facto cease and be vacated." The vacancy should be filled without delay and in such appointment there must be no distinction "on account of race, color or previous condition of servitude." Any person excluded "from the equal rights herein secured" was entitled to recover damages, etc. *Senate Bills*, 41st Cong., 2nd Session, p. 1869-70. Bill S. 361.

[59] *Senate Ex. Doc.* No. 20, 41st Cong., 3rd Session, p. 8.

The trustees argued that the great majority of the colored children were suffering the hereditary effects of the deprivations and wrongs of centuries and that the poverty of their parents afforded them, at best, only a brief period in which they could enjoy the advantages of schools. It was imperative, therefore, to provide for these teachers so trained and skilled in their work that they could impart the greatest practicable amount of instruction in the shortest time. They also suggested that provisions be made to apprehend any member of the board of trustees whose action appeared directly or indirectly to subserve the private interest of any member to the detriment of the public good. They requested that Congress make no changes in the administrative set up until after June 30, 1871, because of their deep-seated esteem for the ability and integrity of Superintendent A. E. Newton; a change before that time would disturb the organization of things, prostrate the plans of the administration and retard the progress of the pupils. Several additional buildings and a high school soon followed.

The present magnificent Dunbar High School is the descendant of the Preparatory High School for colored youth, established in November, 1870, in the basement of the Fifteenth Street Presbyterian Church, when A. E. Newton was superintendent of schools and William Syphax and William H. A. Wormley (as has been stated above) were trustees of the colored schools of Washington and Georgetown. The first teacher was Miss Emma J. Hutchins, and her class consisted of four pupils as follows: Rosetta Coakley, John Nalle, Mary Nalle, and Caroline Parke. The course of study included (1) higher arithmetic, algebra, mensuration, geometry, trigonometry and astronomy; (2) language, grammar, composition, elocution, rhetoric and English literature; (3) history — United States, English and general; (4) science—natural philosophy, chemistry, botany, moral and mental philosophy, physical geography; and other branches, drawing, penmanship and book-keeping, with "such instruction in the ancient or modern languages as the trustees may direct."[60]

A word should be said about Superintendent A. E. Newton. In his detailed report to the Commissioners, December 27, 1870, he called attention to the paucity of official records and the careless recording of material in such records as he did find. He criticised the discipline of the schools, calling attention to the numerous cases of tardiness, absence, corporal punishment and expulsion. Warning against severe corporal punishment, he advised that, as the number of corporal punishments was 1,741 plus several "fews," the excellence of discipline was usually in inverse proportion to the prevalence of punishments, since it showed a want of governing power on the part of the teacher. He advised moderation. Citing the number of children out of school, the inadequacy of private schools, need for Negro schools, and parental cooperation, he dwelt upon the quality of instruction. He advocated a normal school as necessary to complete the high school training that had recently started. He criticised the Stevens School, erected in 1868, stating that its location was unfit; it lacked the means of proper ventilation and of heating, and as a result hundreds of pupils were exposed to disease and discomfort. The building showed malconstruction in the extreme, and he sharply denounced "so flagrant a misuse of funds which should have been sacredly devoted to providing the best possible facilities for the education of youth."[61] Advocating mixed schools and blaming the educational set-up for the poor showing of the schools, rather than any particular agency, he recommended a larger board of trustees.

[60] *Senate Ex. Doc.* No. 2, 41st Cong., 3rd Session. For official proof see p. 8, 9, 10, 16. The establishment of the high school is on p. 16, in a letter written by Newton to Syphax and Wormley, dated December 27, 1870. Also p. 24. High School Course on p. 29.

[61] *Ibid.*, p. 18.

By 1871 the Sumner School was in process of erection at the corner of 17th and M Streets, N. W., Washington, D. C., at a cost of $50,728.38, and the Lincoln School, at the corner of Second and C Streets, S. E., had been completed at a cost of $31,944.12.[62] Thus during this formative period of the system the Stevens, the Lincoln and the Sumner School had been built and named, a high school for Negro youth had been created, and a normal school had been advocated.[63]

Syphax was so active and prominent in the political, social and educational affairs of his time that his domestic side may be considered of minor significance, though such is not necessarily the case. William Syphax married Mary M. Browne, an octoroon of Scotch, Cherokee Indian and free Negro blood, who was born in Fredericksburg, Virginia. Her first cousin was Charles H. Middleton, who taught a private school for Negroes in the District of Columbia before the Civil War. Her nephew, Hugh M. Browne, son of John and Elizabeth Wormley Browne, was the educator for whom Browne Junior High School, Washington, D. C., was named. There were born to this couple Maria B. Syphax, William B. Syphax and Mary M. Syphax (all deceased). The latter was a teacher in the District of Columbia Public Schools 1886-1895 and, as Mrs. Gibson, principal of the Children's House at Tuskegee Institute, 1903-05. The only living direct descendant of William Syphax is Mary Gibson Brewer, his granddaughter, a teacher of French in the Dunbar High School, Washington, D. C.

William Syphax showed that same altruism, and self-denial toward his family that had characterized his policies for the advancement of his race while a member of

---

[62] A letter of William Syphax to the Hon. Henry D. Cook, governor of the District of Columbia, dated July 17, 1876. *Senate Doc.* No. 27. House of Delegates Leg. Assembly, 1st Session, p. 2.

[63] *Washington (D. C.) Post*, June 18, 1891.

the board of trustees. He endeavored to bring up his children in the fear of God, to give them the best possible education and to teach them to support themselves and in all things to prepare them for a life of usefulness. Exhorting his children to love and respect their mother always as well as to love each other, he patriarchally admonished the son to look after and care for his mother and sisters; the daughters to keep a tender and watchful eye over their brother and all to live in love and peace and to divide and share with each other through life. Ever mindful of the vicissitudes and irregularities of life, he made his will December 4, 1873, about eighteen years prior to his death. By this testament he provided for his family and commended his dear mother, Maria Syphax, to the affectionate care and consideration of his wife and children, with the request that they look after and care for her and not let her want in her declining years, but assist her even to the extent of depriving themselves.[64]

It is reasonable to assume that the saddest moment in the life of William Syphax was the death of his mother in 1886. Her funeral from the Mt. Zion Baptist Church, at Arlington, Virginia, was largely attended. Maria Syphax was a Christian woman "with whom faith and works went hand in hand;" and at the time of her death, at the age of eighty-three, she had been a member of the First Baptist Church, of Alexandria, for sixty-one years. The Rev. Joseph Matthews preached her funeral, and six of her grandsons acted as pallbearers.[65] She left a will

[64] This bit of family traditions was told me by *Mrs. Mary Gibson Brewer*, granddaughter of William Syphax. I have before me a facsimile of the *will* of William Syphax, dated December 4, 1873. His ability to manage and put his money to use is seen in the fact that he had purchased a house "in the country" on corner of 17th and P Streets, N. W., Washington, D. C., Square 180, and real estate which at his death was valued at $30,000.

[65] From a *newspaper clipping*, both name and date of which were missing.

naming William as her executor.[66] When one enters the Lee Mansion at Arlington Cemetery, and turns to the right and walks a few paces, he sees directly in front of him on the wall a map of the original plot, entitled, "Plan of Arlington Estate on Potomack River," bearing a diagram of the Syphax Estate labelled "Maria Syphax"; the seventeen acres, the trees, cabin and chapel are clearly indicated.[67] This property was involved in this will.

William Syphax, after a residence in Washington, D. C., of about fifty-five years, died June 15, 1891, leaving a wife, two daughters and one son. Funeral services were held at his late residence.[68] Rev. Walter H. Brooks officiated. Numerous friends and admirers followed his remains to the place of their last repose.

The descendants of Charles and Maria Syphax living on the original Arlington plot at this writing are as follows: Of the children of Colbert are Charles S. and Colbert S. Syphax; of the family of Ennis are Mrs. Ennis Syphax, sister-in-law of William, her children, Selina, Parke Custis and William S. Syphax; and the daughter of Maria, Mrs. Maria Frost Ritchie. There are many Syphaxes and an enumeration of their activities would constitute a volume. Elinor Syphax Reeves, sister of William, directed sewing for the contrabands in Freedman's Village, Arlington, Virginia, shortly after the Civil War; John Syphax, a brother, was a member of the Vir-

---

[66] William was to have the land surveyed and apportioned to Maria's children as he saw fit. None of the children should be permitted to *mortgage* the property or otherwise make it *liable* for debt. William was given two acres in the northwest corner or any other two he desired; he was to hold the rest in trust or to convey the rest to the children "in parcels and his act shall be valid as if done by me." Will of Maria Syphax, Sept. 29, 1885.

[67] The Plot is triangular in shape.

[68] *Washington Star*, June 17, 1891; *Washington Post*, June 18, 1891.

ginia State Legislature.[69] Of the children of Charles
Syphax, Carrie Syphax Watson was the first Negro di-
rectress of domestic art in the Public Schools of the District of Columbia; Mary E. Syphax (deceased), Julia
Syphax Willis, teachers in the public schools, Washington, D. C., and two grandchildren, M. Louise Syphax,
teacher, and Mary A. Brodie, former teacher, in the public schools of the District of Columbia. Of the children
of Colbert Syphax are, Prof. Charles S. Syphax, in the
department of mathematics at Howard University (now
improving his summer home on Syphax Place, where
he and his family usually spend their vacations); John
E. Syphax, administrative principal of public schools,
Washington, D. C.; Cordelia S. (deceased) and Edward
M. Syphax, teachers in the District of Columbia; Fred
B. Syphax, a teacher at Tuskegee Institute, and the
grandchildren, Elizabeth Syphax Johnson and Edna Boyd
Gary, teachers in Washington, D. C., and Dr. C. Sumner
Syphax, physician in Detroit, Michigan. Emma Green Al-
len, Washington, D. C., granddaughter of Elinor, and
Bessie Lawson Blackman, Los Angeles, Cal., grand-
daughter of Cornelius, are graduate nurses.

The grandsons of Ennis Syphax are Francis E. (deceased), a young artist who sponsored the first exhibit
of the work of Negro artists in Denver, Colorado, March,
1930, and Robert E. Syphax, a teacher in the Washington,
D. C., schools. Douglas Syphax, a first cousin of William
Syphax, served in the Civil War, was a member of the
O. P. Morton Grand Army Post and was buried in Arlington National Cemetery. His son, Ernest Syphax
(deceased), was a pharmacist in Pittsburgh, Pennsylvania,
and his grandson, Rev. Elmer Wright, is an Episcopal

[69] This bit of family achievements has been ''picked up'' by the writer
after conversing with many of the Syphax families. Since this article is
written primarily on William Syphax, no effort has been made to verify the
family history given. The words of the members of the Syphax family are
taken as *original sources*.

minister in Memphis, Tennessee. Peter Joseph, a second cousin of William Syphax, was captain of the U. S. Customs Inspectors (1881-1892) at New Orleans. His daughters, Martha, Ellender and Odile, were former teachers there, and three other daughters, Mosella, Zipporah and Carrie, were teachers in Kansas City, Missouri. His grandson, Dr. Valaurez B. Spratlin, is acting head of the Department of Romance Languages of Howard University, and his granddaughter, Estrelda Spratlin Burrell, is teacher of physical education in the Armstrong High School, Washington, D. C.

William Syphax's achievements were not forgotten, for in 1902 a school dedicated on Half Street, between N and O Streets, S. W., Washington, D. C., was named in his honor. At the exercises W. H. A. Wormley formally presented the school with the picture of William Syphax, which was accepted in behalf of the school by Dr. W. S. Montgomery, at that time assistant superintendent of schools.[70]

E. DELORUS PRESTON, JR.

Washington, D. C.

[70] *Washington Evening Times*, October 31, 1902.

BOOK REVIEWS

The Musical Instruments of the Native Races of South Africa. By Percival R. Kirby. (Oxford University Press. London: Humphrey Milford, 1934. Pp. 285. 73 plates.)

This study of the musical instruments of the native races of South Africa aims to supply specific and very detailed information on the subject. The author, a professor of music at the University of Witwatersrand at Johannesburg, has attempted to correlate somewhat the earlier and often rather vague generalizations on this subject which have appeared in the work of travelers. This study was made possible by a grant from the Carnegie Corporation of New York, through the Research Grant Board of the Union of South Africa. This enabled the author to make nine special expeditions to distant native areas in search of material.

Mr. Kirby has traced where possible the history of the musical instruments found in South Africa, using as his basis the wealth of historical materials which the country is fortunate in possessing, together with the evidence of native tradition and ritual. He has tried to indicate the geographical and tribal distribution of the instruments with their nomenclature. By personally studying most of the instruments under the guidance of native experts he has been able to reveal their true nature as well as the material from and the manner in which they are made.

Because of the many musical instruments treated in the book one realizes how full and varied is the musical life of the African to whom "music is life." The instruments described are divided by types some of which include rattlers and clappers, the former being used as an adjunct to the dance, the drums which vary in form and function, xylophones, which are commonly called Marimbas and the most elaborate instruments found in South Africa, bull-roarers and spinning disks which are not used in any ritual, but are now children's toys. Then there are horns and trumpets, often used to accompany drums, reed-flute ensemble, the first musical instrument to be described by travelers and which is played by a band of performers each of whom was responsible for a single note, the Gora, a stringwind instrument, and stringed instruments of which eleven types are given.

The author was particularly well-fitted to make this study because of his position and his acquisition of over three hundred specimens of South African native musical instruments. In addition he has observed all of the instruments in public collections in England and Europe. The volume contains over two hundred excellent photographic plates. Throughout the book there are helpful musical notations. Finally, there is a very full index of musical instruments compiled to assist students who may wish to identify specimens whether in the field, in museums, or those described in other books.

DOROTHY B. PORTER

Howard University Library.

Arts of West Africa (excluding music). By Michael E. Sadler with an introduction by Sir William Rothenstein. (Published for the International Institute of African Languages and Cultures by the Oxford University Press. London: Humphrey Milford, 1935. Pp. 101. 32 plates.)

This introductory book was written to call attention to the significance and utility of the art of West Africa and serves as a guide especially for the Englishman and, of course, for others interested in the life and welfare of West Africa. The publication of the volume was made possible by a fund given by the International Institute of African Languages and Culture. The book is divided into four major sections of which three are essays and one a descriptive catalogue of the thirty plates in the book.

"The Significance and Vitality of African Art," by Sir Michael Sadler, stresses the importance of recording, calling attention to and preserving the indigenous art of the African. "The shadow is falling fast on what is best in African art" and there the writer suggests that capable and sympathetic artists be sent to Africa in order to review all the indigenous arts of the country, to excite as much interest in the study of African art, to recommend and criticize the work of the school in this field of education, and then to make it possible for these artists to exhibit that which is best in West African art.

The author indicates that in addition to this it is necessary to arouse and challenge public opinion. The indigenous arts have primary value for the communal life of Africa. None are more necessary and fundamental in early education and none have a wider social value among adults. It is through them that Africa has already influenced the mind and habit of Europe and the west. These arts are "the artistic language through which Africa will most effectively speak to the world and through which Europe will speak to Africa."

"The Educational Significance of Indigenous African Art," by G. A. Stevens, and "Teaching Wood Carving at Achimota," by Gabriel Pippet, are short sketches verifying the fact that artistic expression created by the African today is most similar and more clearly related to the true African art when stimulated by examples of the indigenous art produced several generations ago. Mr. Stevens, an instructor for three years in the Government Training College for Teachers, relates in his essay his experiences in attempting to draw indigenous art expression from his class of West Africans. Mr. Pippet states that the African students quite effectively produced carved stools, animals, household implements and other objects when they had as their teacher a native African from the interior who had no trace or very little if any of European influence upon his work.

The major and most significant part of the book is the section "Arts of West Africa," with thirty-two plates and descriptive notes by Richard Caroline. The plates cover a wide range of subjects—sculptured figures in wood, earthenware, beaten brass implements, musical instruments, masks in wood and the like. These objects have been drawn from several sections, including Nigeria, Belgian Congo, Ivory Coast, Gabun, Gold Coast, Sierra Leone, Dahomey, Angola, Gambia and Cameroon. Mr. Caroline quite thoroughly describes each plate giving the subject which the specimen represents, materials employed, the provenance given, if any, if not, the probable provenance in the opinion of the writer, the name of the collection, where the specimen belonged at the time of writing, the date when it was acquired and the name of the explorer or other means by which it was obtained in Africa. These descriptive notes are documented with footnotes.

The volume contains an annotated bibliography of twenty-three titles on the indigenous art in tropical Africa and is one of the several that has appeared during this year which attempts to keep before and emphasize to the layman, as well as to scholars and others interested, the importance of recognizing the artistic value of the arts of the peoples of Africa, particularly those of West Africa.

DOROTHY B. PORTER

Howard University Library.

The Negro Professional Man and the Community. By Carter G. Woodson. (Association for the Study of Negro Life and History, Inc., Washington, D. C., 1934. Pp. 365. Price $3.00.)

This book is well described by the title. It not only gives a scientific statement of the education, services, contacts and achievements of the personnel in the leading professions in the Negro race but gives a careful and unbiased estimate of the social significance and service or lack of service of these groups. Thus many erroneous, popular ideas are exposed, and proof is given to substantiate claims heretofore made dogmatically. In connection with teachers, ministers, physicians, dentists, pharmacists, lawyers, actors, musicians, social and religious workers, authors, editors, and several other smaller professions, there are given ample statistics, tables and diagrams to support the convincing and clear statements of the author. The work, however, is restricted mainly to those engaged in the legal and medical professions.

Along with these data the author has included a liberal number of well thought out criticisms of his own and of other competent observers in the effort to interpret the facts collected. The reader will find these interesting but should not consider them as the last word on the subject, for some of these must be proved by time. These comments, however, reflect very well what the Negro professional man is in his community or what he and his friends consider him to be. This picture in itself is as much a fact as the existence of the professional man himself.

Another valuable feature of the book is a comprehensive appendix containing the various questionnaires and the like used in collecting the information compiled and interpreted. There is also an adequate index. The reader is in position, then, not only to make use of the facts thus compiled but to evaluate the facts on the basis of the methods by which they were obtained. The book is valuable, therefore, not only because it is the only scientific treatment of the Negro professional but because it is one of the few treatments on the Negro set forth in this definitive form.

Except the charts, figures, etc., mentioned above, there is absence of illustrative matter in the book. The reviewer feels that a few judiciously selected pictures and other illustrations would have made the book more informing and interesting to the general readers, especially those outside the racial group under treatment. For the professional worker the volume in its present form meets the requirements of modern historiography. As such the work has met with extensive circulation, and the demand does not seem to diminish. Scholarly circles abroad have found the data thus assembled very useful in the study of the Negro in the United States.

In view of the fact that the author has included a chapter on ''Various Observations,'' the main text would not have suffered with fewer expressions of opinions. The book has so many merits, however, that any person or group interested in the life and history of Negroes in America will find it a valuable contribution to the literature on the subject.

A. H. Gordon

Georgia State Industrial College,
Savannah, Ga.

Porfirio Diaz, Dictator of Mexico. By Carleton Beal. (Philadelphia. J. P. Lippincott Company, 1932. Illus. Pp. 463.)

Diaz is described as son of the Oaxaca valley region inwardly torn by the blood of two races and brought up in days after the collapse of Iturbide's Empire when the political stage was dominated by such leaders as: Guadelupe Victoria, Santa Anna, Juan Alvarez and Benito Pablo Juarez. In the paths of these men the author follows the hero of the volume and shows how during the last days of the second Empire "bayonets crossed and blood flowed in torrents" (p. 105) while Maximilian sought in vain to secure European aid to bolster up the imperial wreck which the United States aided in destroying immediately after freeing her hands from internal strife. These were the days when Diaz was a man of statesmanlike qualities, says the author.

Then the statesman gradually changes to a crafty politician filled with ambitious designs which, according to Mr. Beal, led him to break with his old comrade Juarez and open the struggle which ultimately brought him to power as Dictator of Mexico. After his first term he kept his promise and did not run for re-election. His successor ruled well for one term and, according to agreement, gave the reins of government back to Diaz who kept them until he was forced to resign in 1911.

Both sides of Diaz' regime are depicted. On one hand, the author describes buildings constructed, roads built, irrigation developments carried out and the like; and, on the other hand, he shows that many of the political, social and economic problems were neglected by the administration. Speaking of the level to which the poorer folk on plantations had sunk, he says, "everywhere the hacendado had first right to women. Frequently the hacendado or foreman, after enjoying a girl just entering puberty, would call in some young peon, with the remark 'this is your wife;' such was the marriage ceremony" (p. 307). Moreover, in financial and political matters the Dictator's policy, according to the author, was of a questionable brand. In 1893 "another costly loan had bridged the economic crisis. At sixty cents on the dollar and 6 per cent, a German banking house had advanced three million pounds sterling" (p. 332). "His group had only one basic idea, to steal, much, often and scientifically" (p. 334). In the end this mestizo leader who certainly, according to the author, had a capacity for demonstrating the policy of divide and rule, met his *nemesis* in Francisco I. Madero, and Diaz's weak advisers and friends deserted the sinking ship like the proverbial rats.

A number of points in the volume seem to be open to question.

One doubts that there are places in Mexico ''... where the Indians cultivate the very crags to eke out a miserable existence'' (pp. 134-135). While one can readily agree with Mr. Beal that there is more to history than what Marx (434) dubbed the ''class struggle,'' and that there is more to Mexico's history than a series of dominating personalities like Diaz, one wonders why more of theories of causation were not used. Was not the church in part responsible for the order of things? Is it fair to heap the whole mess of disorder at the feet of the man who was unwise enough to marry a woman above his class and then allow the class to win him over against his better judgment and the lesser folk who made his rise to power possible?

Often one suspects that Mr. Beal is too much concerned with dramatizing and less concerned with the real facts, and one's suspicions grow deeper when he realizes that only Mr. Beal's long years in Mexico and his word rather than documentation support the main part of what he says. However, for 166 pages of exciting history containing 126 illustrations and replete with vivid quotations and for the most part accurate, this volume is a worthwhile contribution to the literature on Mexico.

JAMES B. BROWNING

Howard University.

Impressions of South America. By André Siegfried. Translated by H. H. Hemming and Doris Hemming. (London: Jonathan Cape, 1933. Pp. 128.)

The author of this little volume has been for many years a distinguished Professor at l'Ecole des Sciences Politiques in Paris and is reputed to be one of the keenest observers of historical trends. He is commonly referred to as the greatest interpreter of America to France. In this work he sustains that reputation.

This book is divided into six short chapters which discuss the following topics: ''From France to Panama,'' ''Peru,'' ''Chile,'' ''Argentina,'' ''Brazil,'' and ''General Impressions.'' The reader is carried to the Antilles, and then, after a brief pause, to Venezuela. The story next goes southward along the Pacific coast to Peru and Chile where in the author's opinion "the regime is presidential. The president, who is elected by a plebiscite, is really the only important figure in the constitution" (pp. 42-43).

In Argentina Buenos Aires ". . . seems to be a New York set on top of Barcelona" (p. 66), and like most of the other countries the political power is held by ". . . aristocrats and the social circles which gravitated around them" (p. 77). However, unlike most of the other countries, "As for the Negroes there are none . . . or rather there are none any longer. Argentina is in no sense a black man's country" (p. 73). In Brazil, on the other hand, the situation is quite different and, "There has always been a mingling of the Portuguese blood with the Negroes, and freeing the slaves has not checked it in any way. . ." (p. 97).

The final chapter explains some of the causes of the existing social and political order in South America and points out that Anglo-Saxon civilization will not in all probability diminish the cultural influences of the Iberian Peninsula and France.

The book is in readable English, and the author's keen analysis of the problems of the important South American countries enables the reader to see that the backwardness of Haiti is due to a large extent to the fact that, like her neighbors, she had borrowed without counting the costs, focused too much attention on public works, allowed absenteeism to develop to a burdensome extent, and has allowed personalities rather than issues, to decide elections. Nevertheless, these are characteristics of Haiti's sister republic and not peculiar to the "Black Republic."

James B. Browning

Howard University.

The United States and the Caribbean Area. By Dana G. Munro. (Boston, World Peace Foundation, 1934. 322 pages.)

This volume of six chapters and an appendix presents a picture of the ensemble of Caribbean Republics. The first chapter describes the emergence of Cuba from a delayed colonial status to independence under the watchful eyes of the supporters of the Platt Amendment. The author endeavors to show that the sugar interest of American business men has been a less potent factor than is commonly supposed, (p. 17) that Negroes revolted because Americans checked their demands for political spoils, (p. 34) that "unlike previous political conflicts in Cuba, the revolution of 1933 seems to be something more than a contest for power and office" (p. 57).

The reader is next shown how repeated negotiations through such treaties as the Clayton-Bulwer and the Hay-Bunau the United States of America secured "the right" to build the Panama Canal. However, the pictures of American attempts and final payment of $25,000,000 to Colombia in 1921 demonstrate that while American intentions might have been honest our policy was a violation of international law.

American "Relations with the Dominican Republic" are next depicted. Here Professor Munro states that "the establishment of a customs receivership thus appeared to be a remedy not only for financial ills but also for internal political disorder," (p. 112) and in speaking of future possibilities in this region he says, "a satisfactory final adjustment of the Republic's financial problems, however, can hardly be hoped for until conditions in the sugar industry improve or until other products are developed to give renewed life to agriculture and industry" (p. 142).

A longer account is given of the American intervention in the smaller and racially darker section of Haiti. Here the author contends that in addition to protecting American investments our government intervened "in Haiti as in other Caribbean countries because the United States feared that a continuance of disorder would lead to complications with other European States" (p. 151). The author does not give his readers merely the bright side of the American occupation of Haiti, but descriptions of sanitation and public improvements, the construction of public buildings, the beautification of cities, the operation of modern hospitals and clinics, the training of military officers and the construction of roads he rounds out by telling of the trial of Haitians by military courts, illegal executions, the working at cross purposes by American officials, the lack of tact of "a few American constabulary officers who directed road construction in exacting labor from the inhabitants, and the abuses which aroused deep resentments among the peasant population" (p. 166).

The fifth chapter deals with the "Efforts to Promote Stable Government in Central America." Here, in Costa Rica, the whitest section of the region, broke out the first instance of a revolution after 1911 (p. 206) and here repeated attempts at union have failed. To the credit of the region, however, the author says "Central America suffered, it is true, from the wave of revolt which swept over Latin America during the depression, but the disorder which occurred there was less serious and less prolonged than in many of the more advanced South American countries."

The last chapter of this work deals with "American Intervention in Nicaragua." The author believes that "as in most of the other South American countries, intimidation and fraud too often made elections a mere form, and revolution had always been the only effective method of changing governments."

In the Appendix are several treaties which serve to illuminate the text, but in vain does one search for maps to designate regions referred to in the volume; and now and then one feels that a simple statistical chart would have saved the writer many words in his discussion of financial matters. Professor Munro, however, has published a well written, documented account of our relations with the Caribbean area and deserves much praise for his scholarly achievement.

JAMES B. BROWNING

Howard University.

Negroes in the United States, 1920-1932. Compiled by Charles E. Hall, specialist in Negro Statistics, assisted by Charles W. White of the United States Bureau of the Census in the Department of Commerce. (Washington, D. C., United States Government Printing Office, 1935. Pp. 845. Price $2.25.)

This work supplements the volume, *Negro Population in the United States, 1790-1915.* The volume covers the period implied in the title. It is based on data published in the United States Bureau of Census reports of 1920-32, the data published in the report of religious bodies in 1926, certain other statistics on Negro births, and special reports which have been made by the

United States Bureau of the Census since the publication of the last general report. Valuable facts are brought together, therefore, in a single volume and in handy form.

The work deals with the proportion of Negroes in the total population, nativity, urbanization, the black belt, sex distribution, age distribution, marital conditions, the ratio of children to women of childbearing age, school attendance, illiteracy, family classification, occupations, vital statistics, churches, and prisons. Of special value are the data on the Negro in the professions, home ownership and business establishments. The volume is worked out in the usual order of the reports of the United States Bureau of Census. It goes into such details as to time and place, indicating the status of rural and urban areas and the progress made from decade to decade or from century to century.

It is unfortunate that race distinctions are so marked in the United States as to require the compilation of data with respect to race; but since these obtain it is fortunate that we have these data bearing upon the Negro that the race may be given credit for what it actually accomplished and may know wherein it has not advanced as rapidly as it must to equal the pace of the more highly favored competitors.

This race is especially indebted to the untiring efforts of Charles E. Hall who has made the publication of this volume possible. He deserves unstinted praise not only for this particular task but for other services which he has daily rendered investigators who have sought from the Bureau of Census various statistics bearing upon the Negro. Many an author who has attained fame and position of influence could not have been able thus to impress the public had he not been assisted by Charles E. Hall and his staff of co-workers.

C. G. Woodson

European Civilization, Its Origin and Development. By various contributors, under the direction of Edward Eyre. Volumes I, II, and III. (Oxford University Press, London, 1934-1935.)

This is a monumental work under the direction of a distinguished man who visions world history as it has been influenced by Europe or the Europeanization of the universe. Some of the greatest scholars of England are cooperating with him to produce the seven volumes of which the work will consist. The first volume deals with such topics as primitive man, early culture in the East, especially in Ancient Egypt, Judea, and Greece. The second volume takes up the Roman Republic, the prehistoric era in the West, the Roman Empire and Christianity, and the Later Empire and the barbarians. The third volume, carrying forward the work of the others, goes into the struggles of the church as treated under such captions as "The Contrast and the Tradition, The Tradition at Work," "The Second Attack," "The Centre Returns to Rome," "The Third Attack," and "The Great Revival." The Volume then deals with "The Renaissance of Monarchy," "The Crusades," "Medieval Institutions," "Medieval Culture," and "The Beginnings of Transformation."

With respect to the Negro himself little about him in particular has been said. He is mentioned casually among the others in the treatment of world problems. In the first volume the influence of Christianity in Africa, the early culture of that continent, the relation of the natives to the Greeks, the languages of the people, and the Egyptian and Carthaginian elements played conspicuous parts. In the second volume attention is directed to African art, the extension of the influence of the church to that quarter, and the influence of the Romans in the Northern part of the continent. In the third volume the same efforts are noted especially with respect to Gregory the Great and Justinian. The penetration of Arabs in North Africa is also treated.

It is expected that the remaining four volumes of this work coming nearer to affairs of our day will have more to say about the Africans and their descendants in other parts of the world. Numbers of Africans were carried to Europe, especially after the Crusades, and when the Europeans entered upon the great commercial expansion by which America was accidentally discovered the Negroes already in Europe came with the explorers to this side of the Atlantic, and the slave trade of later years brought them from Africa to the Western Hemisphere in larger numbers.

C. G. WOODSON

Ethiopia, a Pawn in European Diplomacy. By F. Ernest Work. (Published by the author and sold by the Associated Publishers, Washington, D. C., 1935. Pp. 354. Price $3.15.)

The publication of this book is timely, and it is fortunate that the author, who served as educational adviser to the Negus of Abyssinia, had the opportunity to obtain his information by his own observation and independent research. He claims to have had access to documents which the public hitherto had not been able to reach and can, therefore, speak with more authority than those who are now writing freely but not intelligently upon Abyssinia. A book of this type, then, should fill a long felt want especially in this country where practically nothing is known concerning this so-called ancient Ethiopia. Even in European circles there is no historian who has been able to trace definitively the connection between the present Empire and the Ancient Ethiopia. These people have their own annals and chronicles in the Amharic, their native tongue, but these archives have not as yet been exploited by scholars. For this reason our knowledge about Ethiopia is limited to what we can learn about it in approaching that past through the better known contemporary accounts of ancient Judea, Arabia, Egypt, Greece, and Rome. These sources, of course, are meager.

Dr. Work, however, has not dealt with this early history. He is concerned with that phase of it implied in the title of the volume itself. The book mentions briefly only the background of the people and proceeds almost abruptly to the task of showing how European nations in deceiving the native kings and grabbing their land finally met in Ethiopia a ruler who would not drink their gin and sign the proposed treaties while under intoxication.

The work deals mainly with the situation of 1885 when the partition of Africa had been generally agreed upon by the conquering nations of Europe. It accounts for the elimination of Germany from Northeast Africa by the treaty of 1890 which provided that she should not advance farther North than Lake Victoria. This, of course, left Italy, France and England as the competitors for Abyssinia. The ambitious schemes of Italy resulting in the signing of the treaty of Uccialli which she tried to interpret as making Ethiopia her colony led to the annihilation of the Italian army in the battle of Adowa in 1896 and consequently the recognition of Abyssinia as an independent nation.

Italy was not through with the game, however, and in her weak condition threw her influence toward England contending at that time for a sphere of influence to control the waters of Lake Tsana in opposition to France endeavoring at the same time to establish a sphere of economic influence from Jibuti into the heart of the country. This effort has later been crowned with the success of building a railroad from that point to the capital. These three nations finally reached an agreement in the treaty of 1906 which they now refer to as "guaranteeing the integrity and independence of Abyssinia." This, however, was not their intention, and the treaty does not carry any such provision. It merely provides that no one of these three powers will take any part of this territory without consulting the other. It is implied that the three may agree upon an equal partition of this area.

After that time, however, the World War came. Menelik died and was succeeded by an emperor whom the people dethroned for going over to the Mohammedan religion, and probably because he supported the central powers during the World War. Menelik's daughter was placed on the throne and she turned the support of the country to the allies. These powers, however, in order to procure the support of Italy in the World War had actually promised her Abyssinia if at the close of the World War the German colonies should fall into the hands of the allies and be disposed of to France and England as it actually happened. Not having the heart, however, to turn Abyssinia over to another country when she had supported the allies during this international conflict, Italy came out of the war without very much territorial expansion. Yet when the League of Nations was formed the Italian representatives were among the first to insist that Abyssinia be admitted on equal footing with the other nations, while England, which today is opposing any aggression in Abyssinia, objected to its admission to the League of Nations because of undesirable conditions obtaining there at that time. With the rise of Mussolini, however, things assumed a new aspect. All of this is set forth in this interesting work on Abyssinia by Dr. F. E. Work.

C. G. WOODSON

The Adventures of the Black Girl in Her Search for God. By
George Bernard Shaw. (New York, Dodd, Mead and Company, 1933.)

Picture if you can a Negro woman, heroine of a religious
work, sans Mumbo-Jumbo, sans Jesus, sans tom-tom, sans spirituals, sans nose rings, sans tribal superstition, sans animal skins;
in fact, divested of all those peculiar racial and religious worship impedimenta, and you have the unusual personality around
which Shaw builds an African religious fable.

This work is an odyssey in symbolism delightfully illustrated by the famous woodcutter, John Farleigh. Converted to
Christianity by an English missionary, a native girl sets out
through the dense African forest in a quest for God, taking with
her her knobkerry and a Bible, the latter a birthday gift from
the missionary. With the knobkerry she rejects all inadequate
deities. Her Bible she carries for spiritual guidance, but with
each opening an impertinent wind blows its crumbling pages beyond her grasp.

The black girl's meeting with the diverse gods is patterned
in detail in chronological sequence corresponding to Biblical and
historical precedence. In this great parliament of divine law-
givers she finds representing the old testament nations the gods
of Genesis, Job, Ecclesiastes and Micah; for Christendom, Jesus;
for the followers of Allah, Mohamet; and for the moderns Voltaire and Shaw.

After he has rehearsed the myth of Jupiter and Semele,
Voltaire advises the Black Girl to give up the elusive search and
to cultivate a garden to the glory of God. Voltaire, because of
his advanced years, later advises her to marry a Young Irish
socialist. She marries George Bernard Shaw against his will,
but finds solace in his companionship and in their children.

Beside the various gods in this journal of the African forest
she encounters other individuals whose manner and dress be-
speak their function of their post and nationality. Among these
persons is a myop whose chief aim in life centers upon spec-
tacular additions to the world's body of scientifically ascertained knowledge. Then there is a Greek youth, a Roman soldier
on guard at the foot of the cross. Later she meets a colorful
caravan of churches, cathedrals and mosques borne on the

shoulders of overburdened men on parade, each bearer claiming
vicegerency to the only truth, and chief marshalled by St. Peter.
Her meeting with the Caravan of the curious outstrips easily in
interest all other adventures with other than gods in this narrative. This expeditionary group evades her god-seeking queries
and begins to argue terracentrically on all the sciences, finally con-
cluding that higher mathematics is the root of all truth. The
Black Girl expresses anger for their treatment of her com-
patriots until one of the women declares that she is upsetting
the men and threatens to kill the god-seeker with her own re-
volver if no one else will volunteer. With this threat the Black
Girl brandishes her knobkerry and flees, always measuring her
distance with a backward glance in fear of pursuit. After this
she meets an image maker with whom her chief quarrel is the
coldness of his images and the mock modesty of his images who
cover their persons.

The daring symbolism of the fable is couched in frequently
recurring subtleties. In detailed progress the gods become less
and less harsh, younger and younger in physical appearance developing from a savage idolatry and bloodlusty divinity into a
metaphysical comprehension. The first god is a white-haired,
fair of mien aristocrat, seeking blood sacrifice. The second who
craves verbal controversy however irrelevant has hair of silver.
The third god's hair is of black. The cleverest exercise in the use
of symbols consists in the channels through which the Black Girl
is attracted to the various gods. The first two she meets through
the reptile family, but the symbolism is so finely shaded that the
first snake portrayed is of a poisonous specie; the second snake
is likewise venomous but the second, however, will not attack
before warning.

The God of Genesis ungratefully kills the first snake; the
second, the God of Job, awards that snake an egg in reparation
for his prospective conversationalist. Having been led to a god
twice by the reptile kingdom, her third channel is through a
maneless lion, made maneless in order that he might see more
clearly. The next god she meets through the physical senses,
hearing him before she sees him, for he frightens her and the
lion away by the ferocity of her boisterous gospel. The Black
Girl hears of gods number Four, Five and Six by the Caravan's

cursory mention. The seventh god offers her a drink of water in his name and in this manner alleviates her suffering. The next god she meets through his proxy who explains and vindicates his methods of translating Allah's canon to reward the righteous and frighten the wicked simultaneously. Her intellect leads her to Voltaire, Jupiter and Shaw.

Despite its nomenclature, Shaw's fable is practically devoid of an interest peculiar to the Negro. Only once does the race issue loom vital, and that singularity occurs as the Black Girl looks backward during her flight from the Caravan of the Curious. Her fear is the expressed result of recognition of her pigmentary disadvantage should legal action be brought against her by the Caravan. Otherwise the adventures of the Black Girl are barren of interest except for the forementioned triviality and for the exuberantly adjectived paragraphs contrasting the Black Girl with the sallow missionary, her satin skin against the ashen Caravan of the Curious, her coffee colored children against her black breasts—children of her white husband.

The Black Girl was knighted by the author to crusade for his Grail because of her facile adaption to his purpose. A recent convert is uninhibited in her credulencies and skepticisms and respects by traditional discretion. Even in her debate with the Caravan of the Curious, the Black Girl's expression of resentment is the flaming protest of a long smouldering anger of a majority proletariat becoming necessarily hardened by intense servitude against a decadent eventually self destructive capitalist imperialism doomed by its canon of inequal distribution.

For his usual preface George Bernard Shaw substitutes a complex postlude which argues politically, economically and religiously for and against Communism, the St. James version of the Holy Bible, scientific atheism, missionaries sponsored by not wholly credulent themselves congregations, Russia, liberalism, fetichism, official Christianity, subsequent delineations of the teachings of religious leaders, Voltaire and George Bernard Shaw.

Just when the reading public of church goers will become sufficiently inured to shock to welcome this book is a question very dependent upon immediate international economic policy; but its finely chromatic, delicate symbolism merits high ranking for lovers of fable and ear-filling rhetoric.

JESSIE CARTER

NOTES

Books of American History

Benjamin Rush, Physician and Citizen, by Nathan G. Goodman, has come from the press of the University of Pennsylvania. Besides noting his achievements in medicine the author mentions his interest in such reforms as had to do with education and improving the lot of the Negro. In *Lafayette in America Day by Day,* by J. Bennett Nolan, from the Johns Hopkins Press in Baltimore, one expects to find some mention of the improvement of the condition of the Negro, a matter in which the Marquis was much interested when in America and at home in France. *Zachary Macaulay: His Part in the Movement for the Abolition of the Slave Trade and Slavery,* by Charles Booth, is made more illuminating by Macaulay's diary than other treatments of this career, although the author shows too much enthusiasm for the man whose biography he writes.

Interesting Cuban-American History has been recently treated. In the *Columbia University Studies in History, Economics and Public Law* has appeared *The Cuban Crisis as Reflected in the New York Press (1895-1898),* by Joseph E. Wisan. The work is more of a source-book than a new point of view. With the twofold purpose of giving pleasure and conveying historical information Hudson Strode has published through Harrison Smith and Robert Haas, of New York, *The Pageant of Cuba.* This work differs from that of Wisan in being an effort to write "an emotional and spiritual history of Cuba as well as a factual." Strode tried to make colorful the career of the European and African inhabitants of that island. *Chasing Villa; The Story Behind the Story of Pershing's Expedition into Mexico,* by Frank Tomkins, is a fine tribute to the American cavalry which "has never, in all American history, shown to better advantage," says the author. It should be noted that Negro cavalrymen were the heroes of this expedition.

The workers in Southern history are still active and productive. *The Secession Movement in Virginia, 1847-1861,* by Henry T. Shanks, published in 1934 at Richmond, is beginning to receive attention. *The Secession Movement in Alabama,* by Clarence

Phillips Denman, published at Montgomery, Alabama, in 1933, is also finding its way to historical circles. Some historians may not agree with the interpretation given in these works, but what these authors think about that drama is just as much history as the drama itself.

Looking at a subsequent period from a slightly different point of view, Professor W. B. Hesseltine, of the University of Wisconsin, has published through Dodd, Mead and Company in New York City *Ulysses S. Grant: Politician and Statesman.* The rise of the Negro in Politics in Chicago has been treated in Harold F. Gosnell's *Negro Politician* published by the University of Chicago Press. This work will be reviewed shortly in THE JOURNAL OF NEGRO HISTORY.

Other works of varying value have also appeared. From the University of Virginia have come two Phelps-Stokes Fellowship Papers: *Red Hill—Neighborhood Life and Race Relations in a Rural Section,* by W. L. Leap, and *Charlottesville—A Study of Negro Life and Personality,* by Helen De Corse. From the Friendship Press in New York City has come Winfred Elizabeth Hulbert's *Latin American Backgrounds* which all but ignores the Negro who figured conspicuously in that area. The A. M. E. Book Concern in Philadelphia has published Joseph Roosevelt Coan's *Daniel Alexander Payne, Christian Educator,* a book inadequate from the point of view of exposition but containing valuable source material.

ARTICLES IN AMERICAN MAGAZINES

Questions bearing particularly upon the Negro in the United States still occupy considerable space in the magazines of the country. In the May issue of the *Journal of Southern History* appeared "British Consuls and the Negro Seamen Acts," by Jarvis M. Morse; and "Thirty Years of a Mississippi Plantation: Charles Whitmore of 'Montpelier'," by Mack Swearingen. In the June number of the *Mississippi Valley Historical Review* appeared "Sources of Southern Migration into the Old Northwest," by John D. Barnhart. In the September issue of the same magazine appeared "Economic Factors in the Abandonment of Reconstruction," by William B. Hasseltine; and "Zachariah Chandler's Part in the Reelection of Abraham Lincoln," by Winfred A.

Harbison. Professor W. A. Russ has continued the publication of various chapters from his thesis with an article on "Disfranchisement in Virginia under Radical Reconstruction" in *Tyler's Quarterly Historical and Genealogical Magazine,* July, 1935. William A. Mabry contributed an article along practically the same line in the discussion of "Negro Suffrage and Fusion Rule in North Carolina" in *North Carolina Historical Review,* April, 1935.

BOOKS ON AFRICA

The problem of Indirect Rule in Africa is taken up in *Anthropology in Action* by G. Gordon Brown with the Oxford University Press as the publishers. An important study has been given the public as *The Ovimbundu of Angola,* by Dr. W. D. Hambly, a publication of the Field Museum of Natural History of Chicago, 1934. L. Bittremieux's *Mayombsche Namen* from the press of S. S. Coeurs of Louvain comes within the same field; and so does R. R. Markett's *Sacraments of Simple Folks* from the Clarendon Press in 1933. Attention has been directed to Von Wilhelm Immenroth's Inaugural dissertation at Göttingen in 1933 entitled *Kultur und Umwelt der Kleinwüchsigen in Afrika.* It is noted that the historical traditions of the Hausa people have been continued in publishing in 1933 from the C. M. S. Bookshop in Lagos *Labarun Hausawa da Makwabtansu, Littafi na biyu.*

Interesting is W. P. Kennedy's *Law and Custom of the South African Constitution,* published by the Oxford University Press in 1935. The work takes up such questions as "Coloured and Native Franchise," "Native Courts," and "Native Commissioners," which show the exclusion of the natives from the national government. Of still greater interest to the Africans themselves probably is the work of the Rev. W. J. Platt entitled *The African Prophet,* an account of an unusual success of a Negro evangelist, brought out by the Student Christian Movement Press in 1934. Of this same type are such works as *Angola, the Land of the Blacksmith Prince,* by John T. Tucker, from the World Dominion Press in 1933, *Die Geschichte der Schweizer Mission in Südafrika von ihren Anfängen bis zur Gegenwart,* by Valentin Nüesch, Zurich, 1933; and *Das Buch der Deutschen Weltmission,* by Von D. Julius Richter, Gotha, 1935.

Through the Oxford University Press H. A. Wyndham has brought out a work of a rather pretentious title, *Native Education: Ceylon, Java, Formosa, the Philippine Islands, French Indo-China, and British Malaya.* In covering such a large area the author had to depend upon the observations and opinions of others. He raises, however, that important question, "Why does one race take upon itself the education of another race, is not education something belonging to, and sacred to, a people for preparing their own children in their own way for their own lives?"

Other works of importance on Africa have recently been published in France. One notes among these *La Conquête du Cameroun,* by General de Division Aymérich (Paris, 1933); *Plan de Monographie Régionale,* by Henri Labouret (Paris, 1933); *Les Manding et Leur Langue,* by the same author (Paris, 1934); *La Colonisation Italienne en Libye, Problemes et Methodes,* by M. Augustin Bernard (Paris, 1935); *Les Pêcheurs de Guet N'Dar,* by N. Leca (Paris, 1935); *Le Sénégal,* by G. G. Beslier (Paris, 1935); *L'Afrique Noire,* by Jacques Weulersse (Paris, 1935); *Tableau de l'Expansion Européenne a travers le Monde de la Fin du XIIe au Début du XIXe Siècle,* by Alfred Martineau and Ph. May (Paris, 1935).

One sees displayed today in the bookstores of Paris *L'Empire des Négus de la Reine de Saba a la Société des Nations,* by Pierre-Alype (Paris, 1925); *A Travers l'Empire de Menelik,* by Jean d'Esme (Paris, 1928); *La Voie sans Disque,* by André Armandy (Paris, 1931); *Vers les Terres Hostiles de l'Éthiopie,* by Henry de Monfreid; *Éthiopie XXe Siècle,* by Henriette Celarié (Paris, 1934); *Les Flambeurs d'Hommes,* by Marcel Griaule (Paris, 1934); *Éthiopie Moderne,* by La Comtesse de Jumilhac (Paris, 1933); *Chez le Roi des Rois d'Éthiopie,* by Henri Rebeaud (Paris, 1934); *Éthiopie, Empire des Nègres Blancs,* by Alexandre Liano (Paris, 1935).

ARTICLES ON AFRICA

Articles bearing upon the natives in various parts of Africa have been informing. Among these are "Black and White in Rhodesia," by B. W. Lloyd (*Empire Review,* July, 1935); "Kamba Riddles, Proverbs and Songs" (*Archives d'Etudes Orientales,*

Vol. XX, No. 3, Upsala 1931); and "Zur Biologie und Anthropologie der Kenja," by L. Balner and V. Lebzelter (*Anthropos*, Nos. 1-2, 1935).

In the July issue of *Africa* appeared the following: "Nupe State and Community," by S. F. Nadel, "An Experiment in Applied Anthropology," by G. C. Baker; "Field Methods in the Study of Modern Culture Contacts," by I. Schapera; "Essentials of African Culture," by Agnes C. L. Donohugh; "Notes sur le Mariage chez des Paiens Du Nord-Cameroun," by Ad. Leger; "The Divine Umundri King," by M. D. W. Jeffreys; "Von Der Gottesvorstellung Der Bakwiri," by J. Ittmann.

In the July issue of the *Journal of the Royal African Society* appeared the following: "The Royal African Society," by the Earl of Athlone; "Some Notes on the History of the African Society," by Captain Frederick Shelford; "Education under Indirect Rule," by A. Victor Murray; "Secret Letters from the Khedive Ismail," by E. A. Stanton; "The Meaning of 'Indirect Rule'," by W. Ormsby-Gore; "The Recruiting of Native Labour;" "Land Apportionment in Southern Rhodesia," by A. C. Jennings; "Native Education in South Africa," by Dr. Jean Van Der Poel; "The African Conception of Law," by J. H. Driberg.

In the *Journal de la Société des Africanistes,* tome v, fasciule i, 1935, appeared "Les Tatouages chez les Indigènes de Madagascar," by Raymond Decary; "Le Tibesti et les Téda: Une Circoncision," by Charles Le Coeur; "Sur La Sébiba," by Captain Guy; "Le Néolithique au Cameroun," by Jacques Fourneau; "Notice sur la 'Ville Inconnue'," by Captain Carroque; "Les Peintures Rupestres de l'Ennedi," by E. Passemard and H. De Saint-Floris.

In the delayed numbers of *Outre-Mer* for 1934 other interesting articles may be found. Among these are "Les Gourounsi du groupe Voltaique. De L'individu jusqu'a l'âge adulte," by G. L. Ponton; "L'Esprit de la colonisation portugaise, le Statut indigène," by Gastao Sousa Dias; "L'propagande de la Deutsche Kolonialgesellschaft," by R. Guignard; "Lyon et la propagande coloniale," by M. Chabert; "Le Statut des Indigènes convertis ou evolués en Afrique Occidentale Française, by R. Randau; "La nouvelle Charte organique de l'Empire colonial portugais," by

M. Bataillon; "Matam, Cercle du Senegal," by Christian Laigret; "La réforme de l'administration indigène au Congo Belge," by Louis Geismar; "L'action gouvernementale et les coutumes indigènes en Afrique Orientale Française," by the same author; "L'Évolution de nos colonies de peuplement," by M. Latron; "Colonisation," by Governour General J. Brévié; "Recherche des Fondements d'une administration indigène associée à l'effort d'organisation français," by F. Rougier; "Recherche sur une économie paysanne africaine," by A. Rinkenbach; "Fondements naturels politiques et moraux des travaux nigériens, by E. Bélime; Rôle social de l'enseignement en Afrique Occidentale Française, by Colonel Conil; "L'outillage économique et le developpement social en Afrique Occidentale Française," by J. Mahé.

In the *Bulletin du Comite d'Études Historiques et Scientifiques de l'Afrique Occidentale Française,* tome xvii, No. 3, 1934, appeared among other articles "Note sur les parlers touaregs du Soudan," by A. Basset, and "L'organisation coutumière de la Collectivité Leboue de Dakar," by C. Michel.

In the May-June number of the *Revue de l'Aucam* for 1935, giving an account of the second congress of the Academica Unio Catholicas Adjuvans Missiones, at Louvain, Belgium, an interesting program is reported. Among the persons who spoke on the topic "Chez les Noirs d'Afrique" were M. Pinto, M. Duboccage, and Mademoiselle Hanquet. Louis T. Achille, instructor at Howard University, spoke on the Negroes in America.

The various articles on Abyssinia now appearing in the magazines and newspapers are too numerous to mention. Most of them are misinforming for the reason that they are written by persons who have never seen the country or have merely visited that land. They cannot speak with authority. Abyssinia is one of those parts of the world which have gone along for centuries without noticing what was going on without and attracting the attention of few persons desirous of knowing what was being transacted within its limits. Persons who are interested in understanding the present controversy will find it profitable to read Dr. F. Ernest Work's ETHIOPIA, OR ABYSSINIA, A PAWN IN EUROPEAN DIPLOMACY, now being sold by the Associated Publishers.

The following articles which have recently appeared in magazines may be also helpful: "Mussolini's 'Masterwork' in Africa," by Ignatius Phayre (*The Quarterly Review*, July, 1935); "Abyssinia, the League on Trial," by the Editor (*Reviews of Reviews*, London, August, 1935); "Le Destin de l'Abyssinie," by André Armandy (*Lectures Pour Tous*, September, 1935); "La Question Éthiopienne," by Roland de Marès (*Revue de Paris*, September, 1935); "Éthiopie, 1935," by the Editor (*La Revue Belge*, September, 1935); "Italy's Gamble for Ethiopia," by Allan Nevins and "The Risks of the Game," by Ignatius Phayre (*Current History*, September, 1935); "Le Conflit Italo-Abyssin vu d'Extreme Orient," by Leon Archimbaud (*Revue du Pacifique*, July-August, 1935); "The League and Abyssinia," by Sir Edward Grigg (*The Fortnightly*, August, 1935); "Conditions of Warfare in Abyssinia," by J. H. Driberg (*The New Statesman and Nation*, August 31, 1935); "Italy and Ethiopia," by H. Scaetta, Robert G. Woolbert, W. E. B. Du Bois, and Halford L. Hoskins, also a short bibliography of the Ethiopian dispute (*Foreign Affairs*, October, 1935); "Mussolini, the Foreign Office and Abyssinia," by the Rt. Hon. Sir Herbert Samuel (*The Contemporary Review*, September, 1935); "A Realist Looks at Ethiopia," by Carleton S. Coon (*Atlantic*, September, 1935); and "Die Stammsäge der Athiopish-Abessinischen Dynastie" (legends on the origin of the Abyssinian dynasty), by H. V. Mzik (*Mitteilungen der Anthropologischen Gesellschaft in Wien*, XLV, 1935).

GENERAL

With the scientific approach certain contributors to the current magazines have written articles which deserve attention. Among these are "Religious Sectarianism and Race Prejudice," by Lyford P. Edwards; and "Race Prejudice in the Administration of Justice," by Thorsten Sellin (*The American Journal of Sociology*, September, 1932); "Scientific Pitfalls of Racialism," by Julian Huxley (*The Yale Review*, Summer, 1935); "Il problema della tubercolosi nelle razze di colore," by F. Frassetto (*Giornale di Medicina Militare*, No. 6, 1934). Professor Melville J. Herskovits, of Northwestern University, has made available in off-printed form the interesting Chapter VII of *A Handbook of Social Psychology* entitled "Social History of the Negro."

Mixing science somewhat with nationalism, the first number of the *Zeitschrift fur Rassenkunde* for 1934 carried an article on "The Influence of Economic Conditions on the Admixture of Races," by C. Davenport. In the same magazine appeared "Der heutige Stand der farbigen Gefahr," by E. Schultz-Ewerth. In the second issue of this magazine of this year appeared "Gedanken zu einer Pathologie der menschlichen Rassen Gruppen," by V. Suk, consisting of reflections on the pathology of racial groups; and there appeared several installments of "Die Rassenforschung in Poland" (racial research in Poland), by I. Schwidetzky.

Personal

Recently there passed from life Dr. Alice Werner, the woman who established throughout the world an excellent reputation for her knowledge of African natives and their languages. The various works which she produced are too numerous to be mentioned in this brief notice. Probably no other woman following Miss Kingsley did so much to enlighten the world on Africa and to inculcate an appreciation of the civilizations of that continent. In her passing science has lost a great worker and humanity a dear friend.

The following comment by the Rev. E. W. Smith appeared in the July issue of the *Journal of the Royal African Society:*

Perhaps it may be permitted to one who twelve years ago took over from Dr. Alice Werner her share in the responsibility for the editorial pages of the JOURNAL to write of his personal knowledge of her. The writer has enjoyed her friendship, was at one time her pupil, and has been closely associated with her in more than one enterprise on behalf of the Africa whom they both loved. She was an extraordinarily gifted woman who bore her weight of learning with a charming modesty. In this country she stood almost alone, for many years, as an authority on Bantu languages; in her chosen field of scholarship she was sound and accurate; eminently sane where many indulge in vain speculation. She was always ready to place her vast stores of knowledge at the disposal of students. Her interest in the African people was genuine, profound and informed; in her passing they lost a real friend. Her memory will be cherished by all who knew her, not only for her learning, but still more for her kindly nature and goodness of heart.

Another great worker for humanity passed away March 29, 1935. This was Archdeacon James S. Russell, founder and principal of the St. Paul Normal and Industrial School, Lawrenceville, Virginia. In the Richmond *Times* of that day appeared as an editorial the following well-deserved tribute:

It is no exaggeration to say that Archdeacon James S. Russell, whose death occurred yesterday, was one of the greatest of contemporary Virginians. His work as the founder and principal of St. Paul's Normal and Industrial School for Negroes at Lawrenceville was monumental. Not only as an educator, but as a religious leader, he was one of the towering figures of his day. Twice he declined a bishopric in the Episcopal Church. The Virginia Theological Seminary conferred upon him the degree of doctor of divinity. His school was the largest institution of its kind in the United States fostered by the Episcopal Church.

Archdeacon Russell was born in Mecklenburg County, of slave parents. By persistent effort, he became finely trained, a man of scholarly attainments. Then he set out on his great mission to aid in educating his race. In St. Paul's first graduating class were two Negroes. Now the school has an enrollment of more than 1,200 and draws its students from virtually every State in the Union.

Archdeacon Russell exercised an extraordinary influence over his pupils. A man of irreproachable conduct himself, he enjoyed the faculty of leading others into the path of rectitude. During the campaign last summer to make up a deficiency in the school budget, the statement was made that, during the 46 years of its existence, no student at St. Paul's had ever been arrested in Brunswick County on a criminal charge.

Many thousands of students, learning such trades and occupations as carpentry, brick masonry, printing, plumbing, tailoring, agriculture, dressmaking and domestic science, have passed through the Lawrenceville school since Archdeacon Russell founded it 47 years ago. Today these useful citizens in all parts of the United States rise up to call him blessed.

INDEX TO VOLUME XX

A

Abbot, R. S., Remarks by, 373

Abrams, Ray D., "Copperhead Newspapers and the Negro," by, 131-152

Abyssinia, the discussion of the status of, 438-447; 489-490

Achievements of the Negro related, 435-437

Adams, John Quincy, reference to, 356

Adventures of the Black Girl in Her Search for God, The, 84-85; reviewed, 491-493

Adventures of Gabriel in His Search for Mr. Shaw, The, a story, 84-85

Africa, Moors in, 29-31; books on, 103-110; history of, referred to, 125; war on, 237; discussion of, 376, 438-447; ignored by historians, 422-423

African Background Outlined or Handbook for the Study of the Negro, 365-366

African Heroes and Heroines, project for, 366-367

African influences in Spain and Portugal, 190-243

Alabama, penal system of, 159, 160, 161, 162, 169, 173, 175; slavery in, 298, 302

Alarcon, Pedro, attitude of, 236, 237

Alford, Ella, 317, 324; report of, on slavery, 302, 328, 329, 330.

Allen, Grant, work of, 66-69

Allen, Richard, mention of, 424

"Alpha Lodge, No. 116, New Jersey," by Harry E. Davis, 180-189

Alta Californian, quotation from, 142

Amantes de Teruel, Los, reference to, 235

Ambush, Enoch, a teacher, 455

American books on the Negro, 256-258

American Historical Review, The, mention of, 397, 401, 402, 403

American Revolution, the, reference to, 425

"An Evaluation of the First Twenty Volumes of THE JOURNAL OF NEGRO HISTORY," 397-405

Anderson, Marian, a contralto, 430

Andrews, Charles M., work of, referred to, 357

Anglo-Franco-Italian agreement of 1906, 442

Annals of the Poor, The, reference to, 61

Annual Meeting of 1934, proceedings of, 1-12

Annual Meeting of the Association for the Study of Negro Life and History and Celebration of its Twentieth Anniversary in 1935, 373-378

"Annual Report of the Director," 363-372

Anslie's Ju Ju, reference to, 72

Anthony, Susan B., reference to, 288

Antislavery Impulse, The, reviewed, 94-96

Arabic influences in Spain and Portugal, 190-243

Archie, Chock, experience of, in slavery, 311

Archivo Historico Diplomatico Mexicano, mention of, 403

Argyll, the Duke of, reference to, 292

Arkansas, prison system of, 158

Arlington, the estate of, 448-476

Arnold, Matthew, reference to, 32

Art, the Negro in, in Spain, 240-242; art and handicraft in Africa, discussed, 376

Arthur, George R., introduction of, 373; help for the Association, sought by, 378

Arthurian romances, attitudes in, 31-35, 212

Articles on Africa in magazines, 103-110, 260-266, 361-362, 497-501

Articles on the Negro in American magazines, 101-103, 258-259, 359, 495-496

Arts of West Africa, reviewed, 478-480

Assab, settlement of, by Italians, 439

Association for the Study of Negro Life and History, its contribution analyzed, 406-410

Atkins, Mrs. J. A., assistance of, 6

Atkins, Simon G., sketch of, 112-114

"Attitudes in English literature," 27-84

"Attitudes of the Iberian Peninsula," 190-243

Attucks, Crispus, the martyrdom of, 425

Auburn prison traditions, 166, 171, 172

Azikiwe, Nnamdi, review written by, 96-99; *Liberia in World Politics* by, reviewed, 351-353

Azurara, lamentation of, quoted, 201-204

B

Beal, Carlton, review of book written by, 481-483

Bacote, C. A., address by, 7

Bailey, J. A., paper read by, 6, 19-26

Balboa, Negroes with, 426

Ballantyne, R. M., picture of slavery by, 66

Bancroft, Frederic, work of, referred to, 356

Bancroft, George H., reference to, 426

Bankhead, J. H., a warden in Alabama, 160, 173

Banks, W. R., arrangements by, for visit to Prairie View, 4

Bannaker, Benjamin, work of, 424

Baranco, Oralee, address by, 3

Barbould, Deborah, reference to, 60, 63

Barkley, Mamie M., report of, on slavery, 299, 300, 321, 325, 327, 328, 330

Barnes, Gilbert H., book by, reviewed, 94-96; work compiled and edited by, reviewed, 344-347

Barnes, Roan, report of, on slavery, 299-334

Bate, Henry, opera by, 42

Baxter, James M., efforts of, 188

Beauregard, General, reference to, 276

Behn, Aphra, the black element in the work of, 41-42

Bell, Sir H. Hesketh, story by, 75-76

Beneath Her Station, a novel, 72

Bentley, Richard, letter to, 58

Bernadino, Fray, attitude of, 205

Berry, Mary, letter to, 60

Bethune, Mary McLeod, address by, 375, 406-410

Bethune, Thomas, mention of, 430

Bickerstaffe, Isaac, opera by, 42

Bigham, J. A., a member of the Executive Council of the Association, 379

Bindless, Harold, novels by, 72-73

Birney, James G., mention of, 344

Bishop, Morris, *The Odyssey of Cabeza de Vaca*, by, reviewed, 245-247

Bismarck of Germany, reference to, 438

"Black Belt," penal slavery in, 153-179

Black Ivory, reference to, 66

Black Knight, mention of, 31-35

Black Mary, reference to, 70-72

"Black Moor," "Blackamoor," use of, 31

Blackamoor Wash'd White, an opera, 42

Blaine, James G., biography of, referred to, 358

"Blind Tom," mention of, 430

Bollo, Luis Cincinato, *Los Negros en Africa y America* by, reviewed, 247-249

Bond, Horace Mann, book by, reviewed, 353-355

Bonham, Governor of South Carolina, 278

Bonds, Margaret, selections by, 373

Booker, E. M., remarks by, 374

Books on Africa, 103-110, 259-260, 359-361, 496-597

Books of American History bearing on the Negro, 100-101, 256-258, 356-359, 494-495

Bornu, reference to, 125

Boulton, Mrs. Laura, lecture of, on African music, 376

Bowen, Sayles J., mayor of Washington, 459-460

Bowers, Claude, work of, referred to, 405

Boykin, Sam, experiences of, in slavery, 313

Bradford, Lue, experiences of, in slavery, 312-321

Branches of the Association, 370-371; the work of, 386-387

Brasher, Helen, remarks by, 373

Brawley, Benjamin, reference to, 22

Brazeal, R. R., remarks by, 374

Brazil, Negroes in, 208, 209

Breckinridge, S. P., a member of the Executive Council of the Association, 379

Breeding, Mrs. Elsie, selections by choir conducted by, 373

Breton, Manuel, mention of, 234

Brewer, J. Mason, address by, 8

Brewer, Mary Gibson, reference to, 472

Briggs, Martha Bailey, sketch of, 270-272

British slavery, 28-31

Brougham, Lord Henry, attitude of, toward Sara Parker Remond, 290

Brown, M. M., report of, on slavery, 314, 323, 325, 330, 333

Brown, William Wells, mention of, 426

Browne, Mary M., of Fredericksburg, 472

Browning, Elizabeth Barrett, thoughts of, on the Negro, 53

Browning, James B., reviews written by, 94-96; 244, 247, 481-486

Browning, Orville H., mention of, 458

Browning, Robert, thoughts of, on the Negro, 53-57; quotation from, 427

Bryan, Andrew, a pioneer preacher, 424

Bryce, James, ideas of, as to history, 415

Buchan, John, work of, 69

Bullock, Rufus, policy of, 156

Bunche, Ralph J., address by, 376

Burdens of slaves, 335-337

Burleigh, Harry T., mention of, 429

Burns, Henry, adverse criticism of, 134-135

Burrell, Estrelda Spratlin, a Syphax descendant, 476

Butler, Benjamin F., prison policy of, 157; troops raised by, 273-274, 279, 281, 282, 284, 285

Buxton, Thomas F., antislavery reformer, 28, 292

Byron, Lord, on freedom, 49-51

C

Caballero, Fernan, reference to, 234

Cabin, Lucinda, report of, on slavery, 321

Cable, George Washington, suggestion of, on prisons, 170-171

Cade, John B., mention of, 7; "Out of the Mouth of Ex-Slaves" by, 294-337

Calderon, attitude of, toward Negro in writings, 230-232

Caldwell, Joe, experiences of, in slavery, 320

Calloway, N. O., remarks by, 374

Cameroun, Le, reviewed, 347-350

Captive of the Castle of Sennaar, The, reference to, 60

Carlson, H. E., reference to, 356

Carolinas, penal system in, 162, 163, 164, 169

Carlyle, Thomas, thoughts of, on slavery, 64-66

Carter, Bishop R. A., a presiding officer, 374

Carter, J. H., report of, on slavery, 304, 310, 318, 333

Carter, Jessie, review written by, 491-493

Casterman, A. W., report of, on slavery, 328, 332, 334, 335, 337

Catterall, H. T., work of, referred to, 356-357

Catto, O. V., superintendent of schools, 466

Cervantes, Miguel, attitude of, in his writings, 216-220

Chace, Elizabeth Buffum, mention of, 293

Chain, Lucinda, report of, on slavery, 311

Chamberlain, D. H., policy of, 165

Chamberlain, Joseph, mention of, 439

Channell, L. M., report of, on slavery, 305, 326, 334

Charles V, attitude of, 211

Chatham, Lord, attitude of, 28

Chicago Times, quotations from, 136, 139, 145, 151

Chidsey, D. B., work of, referred to, 358

Christensen, T. P., *The Discovery and Re-Discovery of America* by, reviewed, 253-255

Christian Recorder, The, quotation from, 137-138

Cid, the story of, 212

Civil War, treatment of colored troops during, 273-286

Clark, Bennet Champ, work of, referred to, 356

Clark, J. S., address by, 3; mention of, 4

Clarkson, Thomas, work of, 28

Clawson, William M., mention of, 188

Clement, George C., sketch of, 117-118

Clubs, the work of, 386-387

Coakley, Rosetta, a student, 470

Coleción de Historiadores y Documentos Relativos a la Independencia de Chile, mention of, 403

Coleridge-Taylor Choral Club of Houston, 6

Colored Troops, treatment of, by the Confederates, 273-283

Committee on Findings, 10-12

Concession Hunters, referred to, 72

Confederates, treatment of Negro troops by, 273-286

Conference of Berlin, 438

Conferences held by the Association for the Study of Negro Life and History, 387

Congo, reference to, 125

Conkling, Roscoe, biography of, referred to, 358

Convict Life in the South, 170-179

Convicts, Negro, 170-179

Cook, W. Mercer, *Le Noir* by, reviewed, 86-89

Cooke, Abram T., mention of, 188

"Copperhead Newspapers and the Negro," 131-152

Coronado, Negroes with, 426

Corps d'Afrique of Louisiana, 173, 274

Cortez, Negroes with, 426

Couvent, Bernard, mention of, 9

Cowper, William, on liberty, 46-48

Craft, Ellen, mention of, 293

Craft, William, reference to, 293

Crespo, Antonio C. G., poet mentioned, 216

Crusader and Feminist, Letters of Jane Grey Swisshelm, 1858-1865, reviewed, 350-351

"Cuevo Negro," the tradition of, 234

Cumberland, George, work of, 60

Cumberland, Richard, a comedy by, 43

Currie, James, on freedom, 49

Cushite Lodge, 181

Custis, George Washington Parke, interest of, in the Syphax Family, 449-476

D

Dama Boba, La, a play referred to, 221

Dark Beauty, mentioned by Vicente Medina, 237

"Dark Lady," the, in Shakespeare, 36-38

Davis, Burton, report of, on slavery, 315

Davis, Harry E., article on Alpha Lodge, No. 116, New Jersey, by, 180-189; efforts of, in Cleveland, 371

Davis, Jefferson, attitude of, 273-286

Davis, John W., *Land-Grant Colleges for Negroes* by, reviewed, 250-252

Davis, W. L., presiding officer, 3; activities of, 4; efforts of, 371

De Avillaneda, Gertrudis Gomez, antagonism of, toward slavery, 238

De Claramonte, Andrés, drama by, 228-229

Declaration of Independence, the, 425

Dede, Edmund, mention of, 9; a musician, 429

Defoe, Daniel, references of, to plight of Negro, 57

De la Concepción Valdes, Gabriel, "Placido," Poet, 238-240; martyrdom of, 239-240

Delafosse, Maurice, works of, 383

Delano, C., Secretary of the Interior, 468

De las Casas, Bishop of Chiapas in Guatemala, suggestion of, as to slavery, 204-206

De Pareja, Juan, artist, friend of Velasquez, 240

De Soto, Negroes with, 426

Detroit Free Press, quotation from, 144

Diario de un testigo de la guerra de Africa, 236-237

Dias, Enriques, record of, 209

Diaz, Bartholomew, explorations of, 196

Dilliard, Irving, winner of history prize, 11

Dillon, H. A., report of, on slavery, 333

Discovery and Re-Discovery of America, The, review of, 253-255

Disloyalty in the Confederacy, review of, 252-253

District of Columbia, early education in, 448-476

Dogan, M. W., presiding officer, 6

Doheny, Edward, reference to, 400

Don Juan of Austria, friend of Juan Latino, 221, 222, 223, 224, 225

Don Quixote, the Negro in, 220; poem referred to, 221

Donnan, Elizabeth, work of, on the slave trade, 356-357

Douglass, Frederick, mention of, 124, 436-434

Douglass, Joseph, reference to, 430

Drama, the black element in, 36-44

Dreer, Herman, efforts of, mentioned, 5, 371, 387; discussion by, 374

Dryden, John, on liberty, 45

Du Bois, W. E. B., mention of, 294

Duke of Rivas, attitude of, 233

Dummond, Dwight L., joint compiler of book reviewed, 344-347

Dunbar, Paul Laurence, mention of, 124, reference to, 435

Durant, Will, mention of, 410

Dyer, Brainerd, "The Treatment of Colored Union Troops by the Confederates, 1861-65," by, 273-286

E

Easton Argus, quotations from, 142, 143

Economic History of the South, review of, 249-250

Eden, Richard, translator, 29-30

Education of the Negro in the American Social Order, The, reviewed, 353-355

Educational work of the Association for the Study of Negro Life and History, 367-369

Egypt, reference to, 125; dramatization of, 230, 231

El Greco, mention of, 240

El Valiente Negro en Flandes, referred to, 227-228

Ellsworth, Clayton S., review of book by, 344-347

Embree, E. R., quotation from, 21-22; book by, 256

England and Abyssinia, 438-447

Englestein, Harry M., introduction of, 373

English literature, attitudes in, 27-84

Eritrea, reference to, 443

Estevanico, story of, in footnote, 208

Ethiopia, reference to, 30, 125; dramatization of, 230-231, discussion of, 438-447, 489-490

Ethiopia or Abyssinia, a Pawn in European Diplomacy, reviewed, 489-490

European Civilization, Its Origin and Development, reviewed, 487-488

Evans, Jeremiah, mention of, 181-188

Evans, L. J., report of, on slavery, 300, 311, 318, 322, 323, 326

Evenings at Home, treatment of, 63

Evolution of the Negro College, The, a review of, 89-94

Ewell, S. M. E., report of, on slavery, 305

Ex-Slave Family, address on, 11

Ex-Slaves, testimony of, 293-337

Eyre, Edward, work by, reviewed, 487-488

F

Falls, Dr. A. G., introduction of, 373

Familia de Alvareda, La, reference to, 234

Family life of slaves, 302-308

Farrison, W. Edward, review written by, 342-344

Faust, A. B., the work of, referred to, 421

Ferry, Jules, reference to, 438

Fletcher, Ralph and Mildred, "Some Data on Occupations of Negroes in St. Louis from 1866 to 1897" by, 338-341

Final de Norma, El, reference to, 236

Financial Statement, 1934-1935, 363

Financial Statement of the Association for twenty years, 1915 to 1935, 383

Findings, Committee on, 10-12

First Baptist Church of Alexandria, 473

Fisher, Ruth A., research of, 381

Fletcher, T. F. H., article by, 381

Florida, penal system in, 159

Fort Pillow affair, 284

Foster, P. D., assistance of, 6

Fox, Father, quotation from, 407

France and Abyssinia, 438-447

Franks, D. A., report of, on slavery, 304-335

Free African Society, 424

Free Negroes, armed, taken as captives, treatment of, during Civil War, 273-286

Freeman, Douglass Southall, work of referred to, 357

Freeman, E. A., ideas of, 413

G

Gandy, John M., a presiding officer, 375

Garden of Resurrection, The, a story, 76-78

Gardner, Rhiner, story of slavery given by, 297; report of, on slavery, 327

Garnett, Henry Highland, mention of, 426

Garrison, William Lloyd, reference to, 290, 292, 344-347, 425, 426

Gaspar, King of Tarshish, mention of, 30

Gentleman from Verona, The, black element in, 36

George, Judge Albert B., address by, 374, 433-437

George, Maude Roberts, direction of musical by, 373

Georgia, penal developments in, 156; slavery in, 315

German Element in the United States, The, mention of, 421

Germany, attitude of after 1870, 190

Ghana (Kumbi-Kumbi), reference to, 125

Gil y Zarate, Don Antonio, attitude of, in writings, 233-234

Glass, D. R., mention of, 4

God's Step-Children, a story, 78-84

Gomez, Sebastian, protégé of Murillo, 241-242

Gonçalvez, importation of Negroes by, 197

Gordon, A. H., review by, 480-481

Goya, the Negro in the art of, 241

Grahame, work of, on slave trade, 49

Grant, U. S., biography of, referred to, 357-358

Gray, Emma, experiences of, in slavery, 315

Gray, J. E., report of, on slavery, 297, 325, 326, 327

Green, Gertrude, discussion by, 2

Green, John R., ideas of, as to history, 413-414

Greene, Evarts B., opinion of, 398-399

Greene, Lorenzo J., addresses by, 5, 128, 375

Greenfield, Elizabeth Taylor, mention of, 430

Griffin, G. L., reference to, 324

Griffin, G. T., report of, on slavery, 302, 320, 334

Griffin, S. C., report of, on slavery, 299

Grigsby, Snow F., efforts of, 370-371; response by, 373

Grisham, G. N., election of, as a member of the Executive Council, 379

Guzman el Bueno, reference to, 233-234

H

Hagan, Helen, selections by, 6; reference to, 430

Haile Selassie, Ras Tafari, 443, 444-447

Hall, Charles E., review of work compiled by, 486-487

Hall, George C., a participant in founding the Association for the Study of Negro Life and History, 379

Hall, Prince, an organizer, 424

Hambly, W. D., address by, on African art and handicraft, 376

Hamilton, Lucy, report of, on slavery, 336

Hammon, Jupiter, referred to, 424

Hampton, Wade, policy of, 165

Hancock, Gordon B., remark by, 396

Hare, Maude Cuney, book written by, 366

Harreld, Kemper, mention of, 430

Harris, Louisa, report of, on slavery, 318

Harris, Senator, an explanation by, 454, 455

Harrison, G. B., comment by, 36-38

Harrison, Hazel, mention of, 430

Harsh, Vivian, introduction of, 373

Hartgrove, W. B., a participant in founding the Association for the Study of Negro Life and History, 379

Hartzenbusch, Juan Engenio, attitude of, 235-236

Harvey, Callie F., report of, on slavery, 320, 323, 325, 329, 335, 336

Hawk, Emory O., *Economic History of the South* by, reviewed, 249-250

Hawkins, Sir John R., trading of, 28

Healey, George, fraternal interest of, 188

Heard, cruel slaveholder, 321

Henderson, Lee, testimony of, with respect to slavery, 297; report of, on slavery, 301, 310, 316, 325

Herbert, William, ancestor, 448

Herodotus, ideas of, as to history, 411

Herskovits, Melville J., an address by, 375-376

Herson, Ella, report of, on slavery, 332

Hesseltine, W. B., address by, 375, 495, 496

Heyward, Dubose, mention of, 294

"Hidden Phase of American History, A," reference to, 420-421

Hispanic American Historical Review, reference to, 398

Historians of Spain, attitudes of, 215

History of Oroonoko, The, or The Royal Slave, reference to, 41-42

Holden, William, mention of, 163

Holmes, D. O. W., review of book by, 89-94

Holy Grail, the black knight and, 32, 33, 34, 212

Hood, Thomas, on humanity, 51

Hour and the Man, The, story of, 62

Houston Glee Club, 6

Howard, Juanita, remarks by, 374

Howitt, William, mention of, 293

Howland, Edward W., interest of, in securing teachers, 458

Hughes, Langston, mention of, 294

Hunt, James H., review of a book by, 247-249

Hutchins, Emma J., a teacher, 470

Hutchinson, Clara E., paper by, 373

Huxley, T. H., mention of, 253

Hyers, Anna, reference to, 430

Hyers, Emma, mention of, 430

I

"Idylls of the King," reference to, 32

Illinois, slavery in, 314

Impressions of South America, reviewed, 483-484

In the Shadow, reference to, 69, 73

Inedependica, La, reference to, 234

Insuá, a play by, 242

Interbreeding in Latin America, 207

International Bibliography of Historical Sciences, reference to, 402

International House, dinner at, 373

International Index to Periodicals, reference to, 402

Iowa Journal of History and Politics, reference to, 397

Italy and Ethiopia or Abyssinia, 438-447

J

Jackson, Alexander L., chairman of committee on celebration, 377-378;

a participant in founding the Association for the Study of Negro Life and History, 379

Jackson, D. J., address by, 8-9

Jackson, L. P., winner of history prize, 11; work of, in Virginia, 371; addresses by, 128, 374, 385-396

Jamaica, Maroons in, 208

Jameson, J. Franklin, opinion of, 397, 398

Jealous Husband, The, by Cervantes, 42

Jeanes Supervisors, interest of, 391

Jefferson, Thomas, penal system suggested by, 166; mention of, 449

Jernegan, M. W., reference to, 356

Jeromine Fathers, mention of, 205

Jews in Spain, attitudes toward, 214, 215, 216, 228

Johnson, Alexander, experiences of, in slavery, 315-316

Johnson, Henry, quotation from, 23

Johnson, James Weldon, mention of, 294, 430

Johnson, John, testimony of, on slavery, 299

Johnson, John T., a teacher, 455

Johnson, L. M., discussion by, 2

Johnson, Rosa B., report of, on slavery, 297, 305-306, 333, 335

Johnson, Rosamond, mention of, 430

Johnson, Virginia, experiences of, in slavery, 311

Johnston, Sir H. H., quotation from, 194

Jones, Absalom, referred to, 424

Jones, J. W., assistance of, 6

Jones, Laurence C., remarks by, 373

Jones, Louia Vaughn, mention of, 430

Jones, M. J., report of, on slavery, 329, 332

Jones, Richard L., remarks by, 373

Jourdain, E. B., address by, 377

Journal of Negro History, The, report on, 372; an evaluation of the first twenty volumes of, 397-405

Journal of the Royal African Society, quotation from, 502

Juan de Valladolid, ''Mayoral'' of Seville, 198-199

K

Kelly, John E., *Pedro de Alvarado, Conquistador*, by, reviewed, 244-245

Kentucky, prison system of, 158, 163, 169; slavery in, 302, 311, 312

Ketring, Ruth A., review by, 252-253

Kimball, H. I., policy of, 156

King Cotton Diplomacy, mention of, 405

''King Horn,'' reference to, 33

''King Mark of Cornwall,'' reference to, 32

''*King of Tars*,'' reference to, 33

Kirby, Percival R., review of book by, 477-478

Knights, Arthurian, attitudes of, 31-35

Knights of the Round Table, 212

Kumbi-Kumbi (Ghana), mention of, 200

L

Labor of slaves, 308-316

Lafon, Tomy, mention of, 9

Lamb, Charles, a thought of, on the Negro, 52

Land-Grant Colleges for Negroes, review of, 250-252

Lanier, R. O., address by, 7

Larkin, Patsy, testimony of, on slavery, 302

Larsen, Arthur J., book compiled by, reviewed, 350-351

Latin America, attitude of toward race admixture, 207, 208

Latino, Juan, career of, 220, 221-227

Latins, attitude of, toward slavery, 204-207

Lawson, Raymond Augustus, an instrumentalist, 430

Le Noir, a review of, 86-89

League of Nations and Abyssinia, 443-447

Leary, Mable L., report of, on slavery, 304, 308, 316, 336

Lecesne, Victoria, mention of, 9

Lee, J. R. E., as a presiding officer, 376

Lee, Robert E., biography of, referred to, 357; the family of, 452; marriage of, 449

Legends, attitudes in, 31-35

Leile, George, a pioneer minister, 424

Lemon, Mark, in *Uncle Tom's Cabin* in England, 43

Leopold II, mention of, 438

Letters of Theodore Dwight Weld, Angelina Grimké Weld and Sarah Grimké reviewed, 344-347

''Levantar Ferro,'' reference to, 216

Lewis, H. G., report of, on slavery, 312, 320, 336

Lewis, Lloyd O., as a presiding officer, 374; as secretary pro tempore, 377

Lewis, Morris, introduction of, 373; secretary of committee on celebration of Twentieth Anniversary, 377-378

Liberationist, The, a novel, 72

Liberator, The, supported by Negroes, 425

Liberia in World Politics, reviewed, 351, 353

Life and Adventures and Piracies of the Famous Captain Singleton, reference to, 57

Life and Labor in the Old South, mention of, 405

Lij Yassu, ascension of, to throne of Ethiopia, 443

Lincoln, Abraham, interpretation of the Declaration of Independence by, 133; books on, 258; attitude of, toward Negro troops, 274

Lindsay, A. G., response by, 373

Linson, Jorgé Dougan, a lawyer in Spain, 242-243

Linwoods, The, refused in America, 63

Lipscomb, T. J., reference to, 166

Liverpool, writers of, 49

Locke, Alain, quotations from, 22, 26

Logan, Rayford W., mention of, 4; addresses by, 4-5, 18, 128, 374, 397-405; discussion by, 9; reviews by, 249-250, 347-350

London Review, quotation from, 133

Lope de Vega, attitude of, 221, 225, 228, 229

Louisiana, penal system in, 174; testimonies of slaves in, 294-337

Love, Mrs. L. L., music rendered by, 6

Love in Black, a story, 75-76

Lushington, antislavery reformer, 28

M

MacAulay, Allan, work of, 70-72

Macaulay, Zachary, efforts of, 28

Madden, William, a pastor, 449

Magazine articles on the Negro in Africa, 103-109, 261-266, 361-362, 497-501; on the Negro in America, 101-103, 258-259, 359, 495-496

Manding empire, mention of, 200

Mann, letter to, 57, 58, 59

Mansfield, Lord, discussion of, 28

Mansfield, Luetha, report of, on slavery, 307, 311, 328, 334

Marital relations of slaves, 302-308

Martin, Crawford, report of, on slavery, 332

Martin, J. Sella, mention of, 293, 458

Martineau, Harriet, reference to, 62-63

Masefield, John, work of, 74-75

Mason, William, letter to, 59

Masonic lodge of importance, No. 116, in Newark, 180-189

Masse, Fernand, research of, 381

Matthews, Reverend Joseph, 473

McBride, Mary, charge against, 134-135

McClellan, George B., biography of, referred to, 357

McCormick, Robert R., biography of U. S. Grant by, mentioned, 357-358

McDonald, Mr., of Galveston, presiding officer, 2

McDowell, Mary E., remarks by, 373

McKelvey, Blake, article by, on penal slavery, 153-179

McLaughlin, A. C., work of, referred to, 357

McMaster, John B., ideas of, as to history, 414

Mediaeval romances, the black element in, 31-35

Medina, Vicente, poem by, 237

Mehlinger, Louis R., report of, as secretary-treasurer, 363; as a presiding officer, 376-377

Melchior, King of Nubia, mention of, 30

Melendez, Negroes with, 426

Melle (Manding), reference to, 125

Menelik II, reference to, 439, 440, 441

Mercer, General, reference to, 276

Merry Wives of Windsor, the black element in, 36

Middleton, Charles H., a teacher, 472

Miles, W. S., report of, on slavery, 298

Military Historian and Economist, The, reference to, 398

Mill, John Stuart, reference to, 292

Millin, Gertrude, story by, 78-84

Mills Brothers, reference to, 430

Milton, George Fort, work of, mentioned, 405

Milton, John, on liberty, 44-45

Miner Teachers' College, Founders Day at, 270-272

Miracle mystery plays, discussion of, 30-31

Miscegenation in Latin America, 207

Mississippi, prison system in, 156-157; slavery in, 298, 299, 301, 325, 333

Mississippi Valley Historical Review, reference to, 397

Missouri, prison system of, 158, 163; Negro history in, 393

Mohammedans in Africa, 29, 30

Monroe, James, mention of, 449

Monson, Lettie, report of, on slavery, 308, 336

Montgomery, James, on the slave trade, 49

Montgomery, W. S., assistant superintendent of schools, 474

Moore, E. W., discussion led by, 374

Moore, Mae D., report of, on slavery, 300, 302, 310, 324, 326; experiences of, 317

Moorland, Jesse E., services of, as secretary-treasurer, 379

Moors, advance of, 29; attitudes toward, in Spain, 214, 215, 216, 228

More, Hannah, letter to, 59, 60

Moro Exposito, El, mention of, 233

Morrill, Senator, inquiry of, 454

Moslem influence in the Iberian Peninsula, 190-243

Multitude and Solitude, a story, 74-75

Munro, Dana G., review of book written by, 484-486

Murillo, art of, 240-241; friend of Sebastian Gomez, 240-241

Musical Instruments of Native Races of South Africa, The, reviewed, 447-478

Mussolini and Abyssinia, 444-447

Muzzey, David S., work of, referred to, 358

Myers, William Starr, work of, referred to, 357

N

Naish, W., reference to, 61-62

Nalle, John C., a student, 470

Nalle, Mary, a student, 470

Napoleon, the betrayal of, 62

Needless War, The, mention of, 405

"Negra estrella," reference to, 234

Negro, the development of the meaning of the word, 214-215

Negro blood, 194, 195

Negro Boy, mention of, 63

Negro cavalrymen praised, 494

Negro Citizen of West Virginia, review of, 342-344; reference to, 366

Negro count in Spain, 198-199

"Negro History in Texas High Schools," 13-18

"Negro History Week," the celebration of, 123-130, 369-370; results from, 386; a popularizing force, 390-396

"Negro Musicians and Their Music," an address by Lucy Harth Smith, 428-432

"Negro in the Public Mind Today, The," 433-437

Negro prisoners in the South, 153-179

Negro Professional Man and the Community, The, reviewed, 480-481

Negro Servant, The, mention of, 61

Negro Slave, The, reference to, 61-62

Negro Slaves urged for America, 204-206

Negroes, attitudes toward, 424-427

Negroes in the United States, 1920-1932, reviewed, 486-487

Negros en Africa y America, Los, reviewed, 247-249

Nell, William C., mention of, 426

Nelson, Lord, attitude of, 28

New England Quarterly, reference to, 397

New History, 416-420

New Jersey, Alpha Lodge No. 116, in, 180-189

New Orleans Era, quotation from, 139

New York Tribune, quotation from, 139-140

New York World, quotation from, 140-141

Newark, Alpha Lodge No. 116 in, 180-189

Newport News, efforts at, 371

Newton, A. E., superintendent of schools in Washington, D. C., 467, 471

Nichols, Shelby, selections by, 373

Nineteenth Street Baptist Church, mention of, 456-457

No Other Way, reference to, 72

Norfolk Journal and Guide, The, remark in, 394-395

North Carolina, penal system in, 162, 163, 164

Northwestern University, session at, 377

Noy, William, work of, 63

Nutall, a teacher in Washington, D. C., 455

O

O'Brien, Michael J., statement by, 420-421

Occupations of Negroes in St. Louis from 1866 to 1897, 338-341

Odum, Howard, mention of, 294

Odyssey of Cabeza de Vaca, The, reviewed, 245-247

O'Fake, Porter P., fraternal interest of, 188

Officers of the Association, reelection of, 9-10

Ohio Statesman, The, quotation from, 134

Oroonoko, the story of, 41-42

O'Neal, E. A., policy of, 160

Osbin, A. L., report of, on slavery, 336

Othello, the black element in, 36-37, 39

"Out of the Mouths of Ex-Slaves," 294-337

Owens, Priscilla, experiences of, in slavery, 316, 328, 335

Owsley, Frank, work of, referred to, 405

P

Pack, Louise H., remarks by, 374

Padlock, The, mention of, 42

Paintings in Spain, attitudes in, 213

"Palamides," "Palomides," references to, 31, 32

Palmares, record of, 208, 209

Palmer, L. F., efforts of, 371, 387

Parke, Caroline, a student, 470

Parker, Theodore M., fraternal interest of, 188

Parmele, Theodore, reference to, 165

Parsifal, reference to, 32

Patterson, Adam E., remarks by, 375

Patton, J. Leslie, address by, 1

Paul, Nathaniel, help given William Lloyd Garrison by, 425

Payne, Daniel A., mention of, 293

Pedro de Alvarado, Conquistador, reviewed, 244-245

"Penal Slavery and Southern Reconstruction," 153-179

Pennington, J. W. C., mention of, 426

"Perspectives in the Teaching of Negro History," 19-26

Peterkin, Julia, mention of, 294

Philadelphia, copperhead newspapers in, 131-152

Philadelphia Age, The, quotations from, 131-152

Philip II, attitude of, 211

Phillips, U. B., reference to, 405

Phillips, Wendell, mention of, 427

"Placido," poetry by, 238-240; martyrdom of, 238-240

"Plegaria a Dios," a poem by "Placido," 239

Poor, Salem, a hero of the American Revolution, 425

Pope, Alexander, on liberty, 45

Porfirio Diaz, Dictator of Mexico, reviewed, 481-483

Porter, Dorothy B., "Sara Parker Remond, Abolitionist and Physician" by, 287-293; review by, 447-480

Portugal, attitude of, toward the Negro, 190-243; help of, sought by African kings, 201

Posey, Thomas E., *The Negro Citizen of West Virginia* by, reviewed, 342-344

Powell, J. C., opinion of, on prisons, 173

Prairie View State College, visit to, 4

Prester, John, reference to, 69

Price, Florence B., selections by, 373

Prince Hall Grand Lodge, 187

Prince Henry of Portugal, interest of, in exploration and trade, 195-196

Prison systems in the South after the Civil War, 153-179

"Proceedings of the Annual Meeting of the Association for the Study of Negro Life and History held in Houston, Texas, from November 10 to 14, 1934," 1-12

"Proceedings of the Annual Meeting and the Celebration of the Twentieth Anniversary of the Association for the Study of Negro Life and History in Chicago, September 9-11, 1935," 373-378

Preston, E. D., the work of, 366; article by, 448-476

Punishments of slaves, 316-327

Q

Queen of Sheba, reference to, in play, 230, 231

R

Race Relations, courses in, 380-381

Racial Myth, The, review of, 96-99

Radin, Paul, work by, reviewed, 96-99

Readers' Guide to Periodical Literature, The, narrowness of, shown in attitude, 402

Reason, Charles L., mention of, 426

"Reconstruction of History, The," 411-427

Recreation for slaves, 327-337

Reddick, L. D., discussion by, 7; winner of history prize, 11

Regional history, address on, 8

Religion of the slave, 327-337

Remond, Charles Lennox, references to, 287-293

Remond, John, father of Sara Parker and Charles Lennox Remond, 287

Remond, Nancy, mother of Sara Parker and Charles Lennox Remond, 287

Remond, Sara Parker, career of, sketched, 287-293

"Report, Annual, of the Director," 363-372

Research, directed by the Association for the Study of Negro Life and History, 365-367

Reuter, E. B., quotation from, 20-21

Reverend John Creedy, The, reference to, 66-69

Revista do Instituto Historico e Geographico Brazileiro, mention of, 403

Rhoads, J. J., mention of, 4; address by, 11

Rhodes, Cecil, a builder, 439

Rice, John W., address by, 5; presiding officer, 8

Richmond Enquirer, The, quotation from, 136

Richmond, Legh, work of, referred to, 61

Richard Coeur de Lion, the geste, 32

Richardson, C. F., address by, 6

Richardson, Ethel, mention of, 430

Rillieux, Norbert, mention of, 9

Rio Bravo, reference to, 63

Rivers, W. Napoleon, work of, 382

Roberson, Frank, experiences of, 313

Robinson, testimony of, with respect to slavery, 299; quotation from, 328; report of, on slavery, 331

Roman, Charles Victor, sketch of, 116-117

Roman Republic, reference to, 27

Romanceros, attitudes in, 213, 214

Romances, the black element in, 31-35

Rorem, C. R., remarks by, 373

Roscoe, William, on freedom, 49

Rowan, Levi J., sketch of, 114-116

Rowland, Henry Cottrell, work of, 73-74

Rosenwald, Julius, interest of in the Association recalled, 378

Ross, A. C., reference to, 356
Roudanez, I., mention of, 9
Rousseve, F. L., address by, 5
Ruger, T. H., reference to, 156
Rushton, Edward, attitude of, toward freedom, 49
Russell, James S., sketch of, 503
Ryan, James D., toastmaster at dinner, 5

S

Sab, an antislavery story, 238
Sabin, Edwin L., work of, 63
Sadler, Michael E., book by, reviewed, 478-480
Saint Louis, occupations of Negroes in, from 1866 to 1897, 338-341
Salem, Peter, heroism of, 425
"Sara Parker Remond, Abolitionist and Physician," 287-293
Saracens, advance of, 29
Savage, Mrs. Roena Muckleroy, selections by, 373
Savage, W. Sherman, address by, 374, 379-384; work of, 393
Schevill, Rudolph, quotation from, 227
Schlesinger, A. M., statement made by, 401
Scott, Dr. A. L., remarks by, 373, 375
Scott, Linzy, experiences of, in slavery, 313
Scott, R. K., policy of, 165
Scott, Walter Dill, as a presiding officer, 377
Secretary-Treasurer, report of, 363
Seddon, Secretary of War, 275, 276
Selika, Madame, a singer, 430
Selwyn, Edwin, work of, 63
Seville, Negroes in, 198, 199, 200
Shakespeare, the black element in, 36-40
Sharp, Granville, efforts of, 28
Shaw, George Bernard, story by, 84-85; book by, reviewed, 491-493
Shelley, Percy B., on freedom, 48

Shelton, Lizzie, experiences of, in slavery, 320
Shingler, Colonel W. P., report of, on soldiers, 284
Siegfried, André, review of book written by, 483-484
Simpson, L. B., opinion of, 204
Singer, Alexander, mention of, 188
Skinner, Sara, testimony of, with respect to slavery, 299, 304; report of, on slavery, 331, 332
Slaton, Johnnie B., report of, on slavery, 302, 312, 321, 322, 324
Slave Son, The, mention of, 63
Slave trade, English, 49; Spanish, 197, 198, 199, 201-203; in the South, 316-327
Slavery among ancients, 27-28; in British Isles, 27-31; portrayed by slaves, 294-337; in New England, 375
Slaves, in arms, treatment of, during Civil War, 273-286; testimonies of, regarding slavery, 294-337
Slosson, Edwin, mention of, 410
Smith, E. O., address by, 1-2
Smith, Ezra Ezekiel, sketch of, 111-112
Smith, Gertrude, report of, on slavery, 327, 334
Smith, J. M., mention of, 156
Smith, James, testimony of, 297; report of, on slavery, 302, 309, 327, 330
Smith, Kirby, reference to, 283, 284
Smith, Lucy Harth, mention of, 4; addresses by, 6, 373, 428-432; presiding officer, 11; the work of, 387
Smith, Mrs. P. O., assistance of, 6
Social Science Abstracts, reference to, 402
Social Science Research Council, aid given by, 382
Society in America, reference to, 62-63
Solomon, reference to, in play, 230, 231

Somaliland, reference to, 439, 443

"Some Attitudes in English Litera-ture," 27-84

"Some Data on Occupations among Negroes in St. Louis from 1866 to 1897," 338-341

Song of Roland, 212

Songhay, reference to, 125, 200

Sorolla, mention of, 141-242

South Carolina, penal system in, 162, 163, 164, 165; slavery in, 309

Southern States, treatment of colored troops by, during the Civil War, 273-286

Southerne, Thomas, work of, referred to, 42

Spain, attitude of, toward the Ne-gro, 190-243

Spanish Art, the Negro in, 240-242

Spanish Explorers, Negroes with, 207-208

Speke, Captain, quotation from, 133-134

Spencer, Herbert, mention of, 293

Spratlin, V. B., winner of history prize, 11; review by, 86-89; ref-erence to article by, 381-382; a Syphax descendant, 476

Stamps, J. E., a participant in founding the Association for the Study of Negro Life and History, 379

Stephen A. Douglas, mention of, 405

Stowe, Harriet Beecher, work of, in England, 42, 43-44

Stribling, T. S., mention of, 294

Stuart, Charles, mention of, 344

Swearingen, Mary L., report of, on slavery, 306, 318, 331, 335

Sweres, F. H., mention of, 181, 188

Swinburne, A. C., reference to, 32

Swisshelm, Jane Grey, letters of, 350-351

Syphax, Charles, mention of, 449, manumission of, 451

Syphax, Charles Sumner, a physician, 475

Syphax, Eliza, the freedom of, 451

Syphax, Eloisa, the manumission of, 451

Syphax Family, the record of, 448-476

Syphax, John, the freedom of, 451

Syphax, Judith, the manumission of, 451

Syphax, Louise, freedom of, 450-451

Syphax, Maria, bill for the relief of, 453-454; a Christian woman, 473

Syphax, Oney, the manumission of, 451

Syphax, Robert E., a teacher, 475

Syphax, William, record of, 448-476

T

Tales from the Woods and Fields, refused in America, 63

Tanner, H. O., the painter, 435

Tappan, Lewis, mention of, 344

Tatum, Georgia Lee, Disloyalty in the Confederacy by, reviewed, 252-253

Tatum, H. Theo., discussion by, 374

Taylor, A. A., works by, 380

Taylor, Eva, a singer, 430

Taylor, Lue, statement made by, 298

Taylor, Thomas, in Uncle Tom's Cabin in England, 43

"Teaching Negro Life and History in Texas High Schools," 13-18

Tennessee, prison system of, 158

Tennyson, Alfred, reference to, 32

Terry, Annie, testimony of, with re-spect to slavery, 310

Texas, penal system of, 159, 169; slavery in, 300, 307, 312, 317, 327

Texas High Schools, teaching the Negro in, 13-18

Thackery, W. M., reference to, 63-64

Thome, James, mention of, 344

Thomson, James, on liberty, 45

"Three Kings of Cologne," mention of, 30

Thurston, E. Temple, story by, 76-78

Ticknor, George, Quotation from, 227-228

Times, The Richmond, quotation from, 502

Tims, M. J., report of, on slavery, 311, 318, 321, 322, 324, 328, 330, 336

Titus Andronicus, the black element in, 36

Tomkins, Frank, tribute by, 494

Tours in the interest of Negro history, 388

Toussaint Louverture, dramatization of, 62

Tragic Era, The, reference to, 405

Tragical Battle of Alcazar in Barbary, The, 34

"Treatment of Colored Union Troops by the Confederates, 1861-65, The," 273-286

"Triangle," The, a liberal play, 242

Truth, the search for, 416-420

Turner, Nat, insurrection planned by, 425

Turner, W. L., address by, 6

"Twenty Years of the Association for the Study of Negro Life and History," 379-384

U

Uccialli, treaty of, 438

Umbrian Glee Club, selections by, 373

Uncle Tom's Cabin, in England, 42, 43-44; reference to, 356

United States and the Caribbean, The, reviewed, 484-486

V

Van Deusen, John G., article by, 257

Van Dyke, Reverend, Henry J., mention of, 132

Vance, Governor of North Carolina, 278

Vanity Fair, mention of, 63-64

Velasquez, the art of, 240; a friend of Juan de Pareja, 240

Vesey, Denmark, rising planned by, 425

Vibert, Faith, research of, 381

Vicente, Gil, poetry of, 216

Virginia, penal system in, 162, 163, 166, 167; slavery in, 305-306, 311; Negro history in, 392, 393, 394, 395, 396

Voltaire, ideas of, as to history, 413

W

Wade, Benjamin F., mention of, 458

Wagner, Richard, reference to, 32

Wagney, Booker T., report of, on slavery, 336

Walker, David, the appeal of, 425

Walker, Maggie Lena, sketch of, 121, 122

Walker, Maude Roberts, selections by, 373

Walpole, Horace, letters of, 57-60

War in Africa, 237

Warbourg, Eugene, mention of, 9

Ward, Samuel R., reference to, 426

Waring, Dr. Mary F., remraks by, 373

Warren, L. A., quoted, 191-193, 194-195

Washington, Booker T., mention of, 124; work of, 353, 435

Washington, D. C., early education in, 448-476

Washington, George, reference to, 449

Washington, Martha, experiences of, in slavery, 315; report of, on slavery, 335

Washington, Thomas F., fraternal connection of, 188

Watson, Carrie Syphax, a teacher, 475

Watson, John B., mention of, 4; discussion by, 7

Watson, Mrs. J. B., mention of, 4

Wayland, John W., quotation from, 26

Weld, Theodore D., mention of, 426

Werner, Alice, sketch of, 502

Wesley, Charles H., review written by, 89-94; addresses by, 128, 377, 411-427

West Africa, a field for research, 376

West African trade, 28

West Indian, The, a comedy, 43

West Indies, trade to, 28

Wharton, Ulysses Samuel, sketch of, 119-121

Wheatley, Phillis, referred to, 424

Whishaw, Bernard, statement by, 198, 199, 200

Whishaw, Ellen M., report of, 198, 199

White, Clarence Cameron, mention of, 430

White, Fannie, report of, on slavery, 300, 303-304

White, Walter, mention of, 294

Wiener, Leo, reference to work of, 426

Wilbois, J., *Le Cameroun,* book by reviewed, 347-350

Wilcher, Mrs. Julian, experiences of, in slavery, 306

Wilkinson, G. C., a member of the Executive Council of the Association, 379

"William Syphax, a Pioneer in Negro Education in the District of Columbia," 448-476

Williams, L. V., presiding officer, 1, address by, 5-6, 13-18

Wilson, A. S., address by, 4

Winn, Rosetta, experiences of, in slavery, 305-306

Winsor, Justin, mention of, 426

Winthrop, Robert C., mention of, 455

Woods, Kalvin, experiences of, in slavery, 331

Woodson, Anne Eliza, mother of Carter G. Woodson, 306

Woodson, Carter G., addresses by, 3-4, 5, 375; paper by, 27-28; slave mother of, 306; report of, on slavery, 319-320; reviews of books by, 351-353, 353-355, 486-489; report of, 372; works of, referred to, 380-381; references to, 294, 385, 386, 387, 388, 389, 396, 420, 480, 481

Woodson, George, uncle of Carter G. Woodson, 319-320

Woodson, James Henry, father of Carter G. Woodson, 319-320

Wordsworth, William, poem by, 28; on the Negro, 52-53

Work, F. Ernest, address by, on Ethiopia, 376, 438-447; book written by reviewed, 489-490

"Work of the Association and the People, The," 385-396

World peace advocated by Benjamin Bannaker, 424

Wormley, Charles Sumner, sketch of, 267-269

Wormley, Wm. H. A., work of, 468, presentation of portrait by, 474

Wright, Elmer, a minister, 476

Wright, R. R., remarks by, 376

Y

Young, Huey, cruelty of, 315

Young, Joseph, report of, on slavery, 300; experiences of, in slavery, 333

Young, Nancy, experiences of, 314; report of, on slavery, 333

Young, P. B., remark by, 394-395

Z

Zauditu, as empress, 443

Zuloaga, reference to, 241-242